A Life on the Edge

Experiences in "Black and White" in North America

Memoirs of

Wilson Head

A Life on the Edge
Experiences in "Black and White" in North America

Copyright © 1995 A.R. Sandy Head

All rights reserved. No part of this book may be reproduced, stored in a retrieval system, or transmitted, in any form or by any means, electronic, mechanical, photocopying, recording, or otherwise, without prior written permission of the copyright holders, except for the inclusion of brief quotations in a review. Correspondence can be sent to:

>Dr. Wilson Head Institute
>675 King Street West
>Suite 202
>Toronto, ON
>M5V 1M9

Telephone: (416) 703–6607 ext. 26   Fax: (416) 703–4415

Internet: http://www.uarr.org   e-Mail: wilsonhead@uarr.org

Canadian Cataloguing in Publication Data

Head, Wilson A.

   A life on the edge: experiences in "black and white" in North America

ISBN   0-9680066-0-4

1. Head, Wilson A.
2. North America — Race relations.
3. Civil rights workers — Canada — Biography.
4. Blacks — Canada — Biography.
5. College teachers — Ontario — Toronto — Biography.
I. Title

FC106.B6H4 1995   323'.092   C95-932543-3
F1035.N3H4 1995

Printed in Canada by University of Toronto Press
0 9 8 7 6 5 4 3 2 1

This is the remarkable life of a black man relentlessly pursuing social justice and equality in the face of tremendous odds.

Whether in the Deep South, Central and South America, Europe and Canada, no one nor anything could deter his quest.

This is a gripping revelation of one man's courage, strength, confidence and hope which will inspire many, leaving them with a feeling of gratitude and pride and others with guilt and shame.

— Lincoln Alexander

Table of Contents

Preface vii

PART ONE: Growing Up in the Deep South 1
    Chapter 1: Growing Up: Family, Farm, and Suburbia 3
    Chapter 2: New Experiences and Developments 28
    Chapter 3: Aspects of Survival in a Hostile Land 47
    Chapter 4: Tuskegee Institute: An Educational Philosophy, Authority and Resistance 77
    Chapter 5: Inter-racial Experiences 95
    Chapter 6: Militarism and Non-violence: Making a Choice 114

PART TWO: North to the Promised Land 127
    Chapter 7: World War II: A Personal Journey 129
    Chapter 8: CPS: A Final Assignment and a New Adventure 157
    Chapter 9: Community Development and Civil Rights: A North/South Experience and Perspective (Indianapolis) 178
    Chapter 10: Struggle Against Poverty, Alienation and Racism: Chicago 202
    Chapter 11: Conservatism and Breaking Barriers (Columbus) 227

Table of Contents

PART THREE: Canada, The True North Strong and Free? 249
    Chapter 12: Crossing the River and
                     a New Challenge (Windsor) 251
    Chapter 13: Toronto: The First Decade, 1965–1975 267
    Chapter 14: Toronto: Polite Racism and
                     Marshmallow Politics (The Second Decade),
                     1975–1985 295
    Chapter 15: Toronto: Changes and Challenges, 1985–1993 329

EPILOGUE by Madame Rosalie Silberman Abella 355

Preface

Writing these memoirs has not been an easy task. I have often thought of a former Canadian senator who wrote that he would rather go to jail than write his autobiography. I sympathize with that view. Over the years numerous friends and associates have suggested that, in view of my long and active career, I should write that story for the benefit of future generations and, more specifically, for the present generation of young blacks who, aside from sports heroes have few role models.

Perhaps it was my natural modesty and shyness, but I found it difficult to write about myself and my previous writings, limited to essays, short chapters in books edited by others, articles in magazines and research reports, were focused on external matters, and certainly not on the life and experiences of Wilson Adonijah Head!

I finally decided that with the availability of a tape recorder, a gift of six tapes from my son Norman along with the fact that I was getting older, I might as well get on with the task. A Canada Council grant gave added stimulus to the project. Suddenly I realized that I was attempting to remember materials covering more than 70 years, a nearly impossible task since I had never kept a diary or any other record of the many events in my life.

I make no claim for total and exact recall and others who were present in my life may, if given the opportunity, express different views and interpretations of events as outlined here. Our perceptions are coloured by previous events in a wide variety of human experiences. Discussions with old friends and relatives were extremely useful in clearing up some events in which I had forgotten details and in other instances the actual event itself! I am often amazed at what appears to be the total recall of some writers when describing incidents in the past. I have some doubts of the accuracy of those who quote "word for word" details of these events. But perhaps these writers posses powers which makes this recall possible. For example, it will be noted that my descriptions of conversations with my co-worker, whom I will call Charlie and my boss at Eastern Airlines are not the precise descriptions of what was actually said, but my best recall of those specific events.

Fortunately I had included a travel budget in my application to the Canada Council and with the exception of Chicago I visited, during the course of the research and writing, every community in which I had lived and worked. Talking with old friends and acquaintances helped to revive long forgotten memories of events and reactions to them. It became increasingly apparent that the project was becoming more than merely writing accounts of past history, but in addition, a reliving of many family, community, educational and other growth experiences. I am now pleased that, whatever the quality of the final product, it was worthwhile renewing the old friendships of Bob and Marian Judkins at Tuskegee, Asa Yancey and Charles Barlow in Atlanta, Mike Ransom and Alexander and Francis Moore in Indianapolis, and the Stows, Robinsons and Van Wormers in Columbus, all of whom provided information and a renewed friendship which, because of distance, had lost some of the old freshness and vitality. I am grateful for their support and renewed friendship.

However, it is impossible for anyone to measure or to extend proper appreciation to the many individuals and groups who influenced one's life. Unfortunately the early death of my father limited his influence on my life and I remember him best for his shyness and reticence under some circumstances (basically around whites), and his exuberance and gaiety under others. it is to my mother that I owe much of my social development during my formative years. Several teachers, including my high school principal were major influences during my adolescence, on my physical and cognitive development. There were others, much too numerous to mention, whose interest and friendship I still treasure. I was fortunate to be the recipient of the support of my uncle and aunt, the Rev. and Aunt Maria Head (usually known as "Aunt Sister"), Mrs. Gertrude Barlow and others.

But I also had another set of friends, namely books. As an avid reader in high school I was extremely curious regarding the nature and values of the society in which I lived, and particularly with regard to the obvious contradictions between the economic, social and political writings of the great European philosophers and the realities of my everyday life. The prime example of these contradictions was the noble statement of Thomas Jefferson, "All men are created free and equal and endowed with certain inalienable rights..." It did not require great insight of intelligence to perceive the unreality of those words, or those of Jean Jacques Rousseau and other writers and thinkers. They were far beyond the possibilities of realization in our daily lives in the U.S. environment.

Nevertheless, I found these and other writings, including those of Frederick Douglass, Charles Dickens, Adam Smith, Karl Marx, Dostoevski, John Stuart Mill, Leo Tolstoy and de Tocqueville of intense interest. Among my favourite twentieth century writers were Max Weber, Richard Wright, C. Wright Mills, Albert Schweitzer, Aldous Huxley, George Orwell, Ralph Ellison, W.E.B. Dubois, John Kenneth Galbraith, Malcolm X, Martin Luther King and James Baldwin.

These individuals have had considerable influence on the development of my thinking, but there are many others. In one sense, my general outlook and philosophy of life is an amalgam or blend of these influences, but with my own interpretation based on my background and concerns. I have benefitted from all, but am a committed disciple to none.

I have been fortunate in my struggle to move from the black ghettos of the rural south and from northern U.S. cities. Many others have failed to achieve that goal and have become victims of past and present racism. I claim no great credit for my success but I managed to seize opportunities as they came.

The completion of these memoirs was greatly facilitated by the cooperation and support of editor/typist Bonnie Slade, the careful editing of Bill Linge and his daughter Ailsa and my wife Sandy who read the entire manuscript and made valuable suggestions for change. Special thanks are due for the reading and comments of Shirley Farlinger. Several other friends expressed an interest in reading the manuscript and many valuable comments were made and incorporated in the final draft. These individuals felt that I had an important story to tell and wanted to help me present it as well as possible.

As the final responsibility always rests with the author, any errors present are my responsibility and not those of my volunteer editors and readers. I am also indebted to the publisher, their editors and staffs for preparing this manuscript for publication. The Canada Council grant was essential to the completion of this work and is greatly appreciated.

Wilson A. Head
1993

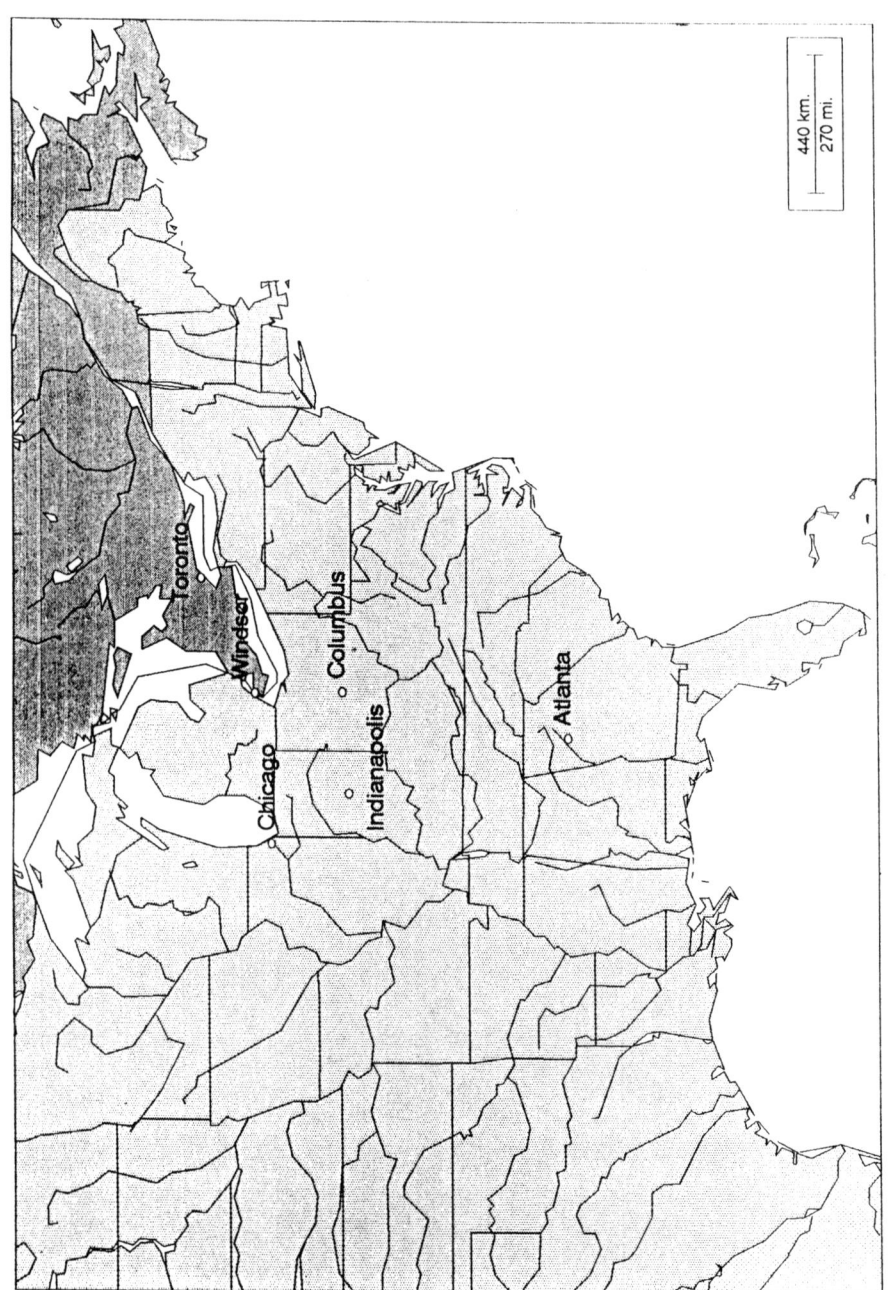

Wilson Head's story took place mainly in these six locations.

PART ONE

Growing Up in the Deep South

CHAPTER 1 *Growing Up: Family, Farm and Suburbia*

I was born on September 30, 1914, a bright sunny day shortly after the beginning of World War I. I grew up on a farm located in north central Georgia, not very far from the capital city of Atlanta. My father was a tenant farmer, or a "share cropper" — a farmer who toiled on land owned by another individual. Since very few blacks owned land at that time the general practice was that land was owned by a white person and the farmer worked the land. The arrangement was labelled as "halves", a term which referred to the fact that, in theory, the produce of the labour and of the soil was divided equally between the two parties. The tenant farmer, having worked the land, brought the cash crop to the owner who made a decision as to the value of it. The owner kept the books which included whatever debts the farmer owed, such as the value of seed for planting, rent of the house in which the farmer and his family lived and other items related to the production of the crop.

This arrangement was usually worked out by the destitute and landless ex-slaves following the U.S. Civil War and was not an arrangement between men of equal economic, social or political power. It enabled the former slave master to continue the exploitation of slave labour. Quite often the unscrupulous land owner told his tenant that the value of his work only managed to pay for items purchased from either himself or from the local store which was also often owned by the landlord. The result was that the tenant farmer usually found himself in a position in which he could not possibly get out of debt. This resulted in "peonage", a status only slightly elevated from slavery.

My father and his friends enjoyed their humorous interchanges which, from the perspective of today, were methods of breaking the grimness of their daily lives. Poignant stories of their experiences were often told helping to generate a sense of some power in dealing with the realities of their condition. Among these stories was that of the tenant farmer Sam Jones and his landlord. At the end of his harvest, Sam usually delivered six or seven bales of cotton, the customary crop, to the landowner for weighing and pricing. On this occasion

Sam told the landlord that he was bringing his usual number of bales of cotton. The landlord went through his usual practice of weighing the cotton and deciding on its worth. After deducting the expenses of buying supplies from the landlord's store, Sam was informed that he barely made enough money to cover his expenses. This meant that he was not, as usual, in debt to the landlord, but he also had no money for feeding and clothing his family.

Sam expressed his satisfaction that he was not in debt and then informed the landlord that he had held back three bales of cotton which would give him a tidy profit. The landlord emphatically stated that Sam should not have done that, now it would be necessary to calculate the transaction again so that it would come out balanced and even! Similar stories, too numerous to mention here, were a part of the general atmosphere when friends met at our house for an evening of laughter and general merriment.

Both my father, Evander Head, and my mother whose maiden name was Evelyn Whittle were born on farms, my father in 1892 and my mother in 1898. Their births occurred only a generation following the U.S. Civil War which, in 1865, had officially freed the slaves and, at least in theory, provided the rights of citizenship including the right to vote, to own property, to receive an education and other ordinary civil rights presumably enjoyed by all American citizens. For the ex-slave however, these rights were more fully realized in theory than in practice. Various barriers were placed in the way to their enjoyment of full U.S. citizenship. One barrier of course was the difficulty of buying land. Having been slaves and having toiled on the land of their masters, most ex-slaves were desperately poor but nevertheless wanted to buy and own land. This goal was generally an impossible dream. Although the victorious federal government had promised that freed slaves would be given "40 acres and a mule" in order to establish themselves as free citizens, this promise was rarely fulfilled.

My parents had five children, of which I was the eldest. Following me were Frank, my sister Minnie, Glenn and Marvin. The first four of us were born on the farm while Marvin was born in the small suburban community of East Point. Our farm, like many others, was characterized by its rich, red soil, so typical of north central Georgia. Our farm included 100 acres of fertile land, suitable for growing a wide variety of crops, fruit trees and vegetables. Under normal circumstances, it should have been large enough to supply adequate amounts of food, cash crops and feed for the animals. The land, however, while originally rich and fertile was undergoing rapid depletion. "Crop rotation", a method of leaving the land unused for two or three years and giving it an opportunity to regenerate, was largely unknown in the early 1900s and it was necessary for my father to buy increasing amounts of fertilizer to supplement the nutrients of the soil. Although this was increasingly costly, my impression was that my father could have overcome that problem had it not been for the destructive effects of the boll weevil, an insect which destroyed cotton plants, the major cash crop of the rural South.

As children we were not concerned with these adult problems. Our lives centred around our house and the various activities involved in daily living. We were happy and carefree. The house was a large, unpainted, one-storey wooden building with an attic which was used as bedrooms for the children. Our furniture was generally primitive and mostly handmade by my father and my grandfather. Everything was unpainted, well-constructed and served its purpose quite adequately.

Although my mother and father were hard workers, there was never enough money to buy the bare necessities of life. The result was that they, like hundreds of thousands of other descendants of slaves, lived in abject poverty for most of their lives. So had my grandfather and grandmother. Occasionally, a few blacks, through luck and very hard work and sometimes the sympathy and support of ex-masters, managed to gain sufficient wealth to buy a farm and a house. These individuals, however, were often subjected to harassment and persecution by envious whites.

Widespread intimidation and fear were characteristics of the rural black communities. Several states including Georgia, Alabama, Mississippi, South Carolina, Louisiana, and Texas were particularly noted for this type of intimidation. My paternal grandfather, having been born shortly after the termination of the Civil War, was a victim of this kind of terrorism. Although he refused to discuss this matter, certainly not with me as a grandchild, it was very clear from some conversations I overheard that his way of life and view of the world were affected by this terrorism and intimidation. Although a very religious man, a strong and consistent church goer, there were times when my father indicated very clearly his abhorrence of black people being forced to remain in positions of subjugation and inferiority.

For the most part, revolts against masters have been violently suppressed. For the slave, the most effective way of avoiding the lash of the master was to escape. Studies of that period have reported that thousands of U.S. slaves escaped, many to Canada through the "Underground Railroad". My great-grandfather may have been among those who managed to escape from his master as it was reported that he escaped to an Indian reservation. This method of escape did not always lead to safety as Native people in the United States were often forced at gunpoint to leave their lands and to live on reservations. My grandmother was the result of a liaison between my great-grandfather and an Indian woman. Although I only met her on two or three occasions, I have a distinct memory of her native features, including high cheek bones and long straight black hair. The Cherokee nation was one of several similar Native groups inhabiting the present territory of the southern part of what is now the United States. The Cherokees inhabited the land lying between the Gulf of Mexico and the present state of North Carolina.

The ancestry of my mother was quite different. While we do not know the exact circumstances, it is almost certain that my great-grandfather was a white male because under conditions of slavery, the white master had total access to slave women. It did not matter whether or not the women were married. If the master wanted a slave woman for sexual purposes, he simply took her. The male slave lacked the ability to protect his wife or daughters from the sexual desires of masters. The result is that there were thousands and perhaps hundreds of thousands of blacks in the United States of "mixed blood", including many children of the founding fathers of the United States. My grandmother could have been the result of a similar relationship.

Because of her almost white skin, my grandmother usually visited us at night. Our parents and the children often met her at the front door and jokingly asked if she was "white" or "coloured" today? From that perspective one could argue that my mother was one quarter white and three-quarters black. This absurdity reminds me of a story told about members of the Virginia legislature. They were about to pass an act declaring that anyone with one-sixteenth "black blood" would be officially considered as black or coloured (coloured or negro were the usual racial designations of that time). Obviously the fact that a person possessing only one sixteenth "black blood" would be classified as black suggests that "black blood" is extremely powerful! The bill would also make it illegal for whites and blacks to co-habit. Even after slavery was officially abolished the master/slave mentality was still alive and well. The legislators did not care how many white men had children by black women; they simply did not want these children to be considered as "white" and to inherit property when their fathers died. There was an economic factor in these attitudes. As this act was about to be passed a member of the legislature stood up and said, "Gentlemen, if we pass this bill, there won't be a single white man left in the whole state of Virginia."

My mother, unlike my grandmother, was not blue-eyed, light skinned and brown haired. However, she was considerably fairer in complexion than my father who was fairly dark skinned, tall, slender, and considered by many people to be a handsome man.

The current emphasis on seeking out and establishing a genealogical portrait of family history was not a matter of great importance in our society. Only rarely were records of births and deaths kept by slave masters. Records of buying and selling slaves were basically financial transactions and the limited records available in our family were usually written in pencil in the family Bible, perhaps the most valuable and carefully protected item in the family. I have no idea how the family managed to come into possession of that huge four-inch thick document. With its leather cover and gold binding, this must have been very expensive and it reflected the great value placed on religion by my family. The names, dates of birth, and in some instances, deaths of relatives were carefully recorded in that Bible. Recent dates, i.e. those of my mother, father and the children were recorded as we were born and the Bible was the source of all knowledge of the family until we left the farm and moved into the city. Unfortunately it was the only historical record we had ever possessed and its disappearance during our several moves was a great loss.

Family life was remarkably serene and reasonably happy, particularly given the situation in which we lived. It was clear that my family, although generally content, nevertheless suffered from the fear of attack and persecution by marauding whites, particularly members of the Ku Klux Klan which at that time was active in all of the southern states. This instrument, organized and supported by thousands of white southerners, was devised for the express purpose of keeping the black population in a condition of actual if not legal slavery. Unrelenting terrorism was the major weapon of the Klan. Membership often included some of the highest ranking individuals in the community such as lawyers, doctors, mayors, police chiefs, sheriffs of counties and even on occasion judges and high-ranking politicians. KKK intimidation was for many years successful in keeping blacks subordinate and "in their place". The record of its activity indicates clearly that racist harassment, persecution and killings resulted in the deaths of hundreds of black men throughout the southern states. At one point during the 1920s and 1930s between 30 and 50 blacks were lynched annually. This referred to the forcible seizing of a black man, dragging him from his house, place of work or his farm, and taking him to an isolated area. The victim would be beaten, tortured and hung from the branches of a tree. The guilt or innocence of the victim of the lynch mob was insignificant but it was important that black people observe and learn from this experience that if they did not behave in the accustomed manner, they might suffer a similar fate. Many of them learned.

Lynching often reflected strong sexual symbolism. Quite often the lynch mobs cut off the genitals of their victims to serve as an object lesson which was not lost on the black population: its meaning was clearly understood. The importance of this symbolism was clarified for me by a book written by Lillian Smith, a young white English woman who had come to Georgia and organized a "finishing school" for daughters of the landed aristocracy of the old South. *Strange Fruit* referred to the phenomenon of lynchers mutilating and hanging the bodies of their victims. Smith understood and wrote of the guilt felt by many white men for the crimes they had committed against helpless black women. Their need to castrate black men was, in all likelihood, related to their fear that black men would seek revenge by raping their own wives, sisters and other female relatives. Cutting off the genitals of victims appeared to relieve these men of their guilt and fear. The rape of a black woman by a white man was not considered as important by white authorities. Not surprisingly, however, rape or sexual assault was a crime punishable by death when committed by a black man against a white woman.

In spite of our daily lives in which segregation and exploitation were never absent, the actual meaning of the phenomena did not penetrate deeply into my mind and spirit at the time. We were too young to understand the meaning and causes of the hatred and deprivation, yet it was impossible to be totally immune from the impact of those attitudes. Since almost everyone we knew was in a similar position, we simply took poverty and deprivation as "facts of life". For example, our house was only approximately 150 to 200 yards, or metres, from a major highway and occasionally we saw black men dressed in black and white striped clothes, working on that highway. The men, with their white guards armed with shot guns, came over to our farm to have their lunch while sitting under one of our apple trees. We were not aware of the reason why the blacks were wearing iron balls and metal chains on their legs, but I suspected that they had done something "bad".

We were witnessing another feature of southern "justice": the "chain gangs" in their black and white striped shirts and pants were a significant aspect of the subjugation of blacks in the southern states. There was no place in the southern criminal justice system for blacks to secure "justice"; the purpose of the law was not to protect blacks, but rather to maintain their subordination. Usually twenty to twenty-five blacks worked in the hot sun guarded by two white men with shot guns and tracking dogs used if a prisoner made an attempt to escape. It was not punishment enough for black prisoners to work on highway construction and other public works, they were often assigned to work in the fields of a white farmer, always under the supervision of the guards and dogs. Although it would be difficult to argue that white men did not commit crimes, I never saw a single white prisoner in the Georgia chain gangs. I could not understand the meaning of this until I reached high school but I grew to dislike black and white striped clothing. Even today when I see an individual dressed in black and white striped clothes, I remember with distaste those images of black prisoners. They will never be forgotten.

My father and mother, although poor, obviously wanted to provide the best they could for their children. We were too poor to wear the latest fashions, in fact fashion was of no importance to us at that time. Although we had very little money, my father and mother made every effort to keep us well fed and clean. Cleanliness was obviously next to godliness in my family's sense of values. Godliness was exemplified by regular church attendance and participation. A strong religious sentiment was a central aspect of their lives. Even after these many years, I still have a very fond memory of my father singing religious songs as he performed his chores in the yard and on the farm. My mother, though less expressive in her religious feelings, was nevertheless a very committed Christian. In fact, my mother believed in every single word in the Bible. I recall many times when I asked, "Mother aren't there some contradictions in the Bible?" or "How can both of these things be true?" These questions were in reference to the idea of a vengeful God and, at the same time, a God of love and forgiveness. My mother would get upset and say "You ask too many questions, boy. Just read the Bible and believe what you read!"

Aside from his religious expression, my father was a very quiet person. In fact I have very few memories of him discussing issues during the time the family was at home and together. Usually when he expressed himself freely it was in a religious setting or when friends came over to visit since, in those days, farm families often entertained visitors from far and wide. People regularly stopped at our house and asked for food during the difficulties of the 1920s. Cousins, uncles and others dropped in from time to time and spent the evening, sometimes staying overnight with us. Those were joyous periods as we sat on the stairways to the attic listening to the stories told by the adults in our living room.

Our parents went to great lengths to provide a very happy Christmas for their children. My mother would bake cakes and pies, as well as buying candies and other goodies. Large stockings were bought so that "Santa Claus" could fill them with fruits, nuts, and sticks of peppermint candy which were favourites. They usually told stories to us before Christmas and it was at that time that I first heard of Santa Claus and Christmas carols. For some reason, which I still don't fully understand, I was much more troublesome to my parents than the other children. I wanted to know, for example, how could Santa Claus come down the chimney when Christmas arrived? All the pictures I had seen of Santa Claus showed him as a big jolly fat man with rosy red cheeks. After all, we had a very small chimney and it was obvious that no large, fat individual could come down that chimney. Neither could I understand how there could be reindeers pulling sleds in the snow, when we had no snow. We very rarely had snow in Georgia and certainly not at Christmas time.

Nevertheless, we in our early youth, gladly and enthusiastically, bought the Santa Claus story and were quite happy to find one or two toys, perhaps an item of clothing and a stocking with an orange, apple, nuts, and perhaps a few pieces of peppermint candy. My mother usually prepared a big meal on Christmas day with lots of vegetables, meats, cakes, pies, drinks and other goodies. It was a very happy time for both parents and children.

My brothers and I were quite happy with simple things in those days. For example we often made our own toys. Frank and I would take the remaining parts of old toys that had been broken and were no longer functional. From these parts we made workable wagons, old cars, boats and airplanes. We made good use of the usable items available to us, a tremendous contrast to the proliferation of expensive toys available to children today. I am sure that we had more fun when we made our own! My favourite toy was a little car with a coiled spring serving as its motor. One could turn the key, wind up the spring inside the car and it would run for a distance of probably twenty-five or thirty feet. I would then wind the spring in the car again and again and watch it zip across the floor. That little toy car moving rapidly across the floor was always a source of great joy to me.

Easter was a time of buying and showing off new clothes and enjoying informal parades. Parents and children went to church on Sunday morning to celebrate the story of the resurrection of Jesus Christ and in the afternoon, after a big dinner, everyone would go out and parade up and down the neighbourhood streets. The Easter parade occurred not only in the towns, but also in the rural areas. It was a time to "show off" new clothes bought for the occasion. My siblings and I looked forward to that parade since we enjoyed walking up and down the streets talking to our friends, visiting their homes and otherwise having a very enjoyable time. We seem to have outgrown those simple pleasures but those were happy times in the midst of poverty and hardship.

Relationships

We enjoyed the usual childhood games of those times. Our relationships and play activities with the Whatleys, the Deeds and the children of other relatives and neighbours were highlights. Although we enjoyed playing with our own siblings, playing with children in the outside world was a special treat, and particularly when we played near the railroad tracks or highway. Phelmon and Charles Whatley and I would often go down to play on the tracks and try to balance ourselves on the tracks, a very difficult thing to do. My parents would not have appreciated these antics had they known! Our house was only a short distance from the railroad track and one could watch and wonder at the many passing trains, cars and trucks. Often I imagined that we were driving those vehicles. I wanted to be the engineer and driver of those magical trains as they went roaring toward the distant horizon!

I was probably only five or six years of age when I had my first little childhood romance. A little girl, the daughter of one of the families living near our farm was visiting us for a children's party. One of the little Deed girls caught my youthful fancy and I ran over to her, gave her a big hug and kiss on the cheek and then offered her my only penny. She accepted the gift. That was a big day in my life, my first romance. It lasted only a few days, but although I quickly forgot her name, the memory still remains strong. I never saw her again.

Relationships with the white community were generally cool and distant. My parents very rarely talked of the fact that white people lived not very far from our farm. The nearest farm was actually owned by a white family. In rural areas we did not have the rigid residential segregation so characteristic of life in the cities. It was not unusual that farms owned or worked by blacks and whites were located in the same area and often adjacent to each other. We could observe the white families some distance away as they worked outside in their fields. I often wondered what life was like in their homes, with their friends and in their communities. Even though we lived in close proximity to white families there was virtually no personal contact between us and them. We went our way and they went theirs!

We often saw white women wearing big hats to keep off the sun. That behaviour struck me as very strange. It was even a bit humorous, particularly in view of the fact that some black women bought beauty cream in a futile attempt to whiten their skins while other white women went to the beach or lay in the sun to "tan" (darken) their skin!

Other contact with white people came when my father took his fruit and vegetables to town to sell. I particularly remember one occasion when he took me with him on a trip to the town of Griffin to sell watermelons and fruits. He parked his horse and wagon on a main street and waited for potential customers. Many people stopped, looked at his produce, selected and paid for the fruit or watermelon they wanted. I sat beside him and watched these transactions. My father always dealt with white customers in a very quiet manner. One might feel that he almost resented having to sell to whites, but that attitude was never very obvious. He demonstrated neither superiority nor inferiority. It was simply a matter of conducting a business transaction. His manner was quite different when a black individual approached. That occasion was a time for teasing, joking and simply enjoying a pleasant relationship.

On one occasion my father became involved in an accident on his return home from a trip to town. A car driven by one of four young white boys struck his wagon and damaged the rear wheel and axle. My father came home and reported the accident to my mother and the children. He was indignant that the boys had been unwilling to give any indication that they were sorry for what they had done. On the other hand, a white man had driven past, stopped, got out of his car, and castigated the boys for their rudeness and lack of concern for the damage they had caused. My father reported the behaviour of the man with great satisfaction. He indicated that, at least on some occasions, white people would take the side of a black person when it was obvious that the black person had been injured or wronged. This was one of the few times I saw him react to a white person with any degree of satisfaction.

Frank and I had some limited contact with white people because there were apple trees growing near the highway on our farm. With a little help from our parents, we set up a little table near the highway and collected apples from our trees to sell. Quite frequently white people stopped their cars and came over to the table to buy apples. We thought that was a great experience because we were having fun, and at the same time making some money. Perhaps it was because we were small children but these whites were always friendly to us. This money, however, often ended up in the hands of our parents who needed it to buy such items as household supplies, clothing and kerosene for lamps. (We didn't have electricity at that time.)

Other experiences with whites came when my father was harvesting cotton and other farm products. He did not own a tractor, so when it was necessary to have heavy work done he arranged to have a white person who owned a tractor come to our farm. This experience only occurred on a few occasions but it gave me an opportunity to view and to speak to a friendly white man.

Frank and I were not fully aware of the tension that existed between white and black farmers in the local community. As far as we were concerned, the tractor owner was simply another man whose skin colour was different from ours. However, that difference was not that unusual since the number of people of mixed racial backgrounds in our neighbourhood was fairly large. We were accustomed to seeing people of varying skin colours. Therefore we did not see him as an enemy or an oppressor. Knowledge of the general white community only came to us several years later.

The slaughter of animals was a significant phenomenon in the lives of farm families, an activity that attracted a considerable number of local farmers and their families to our home. The killing of an animal, and particularly a hog, was commonplace in the countryside. When a farmer was about to kill a hog, calf or other animal, he informed his nearby neighbours who often came to lend a helping hand. The children would come along and witness the slaughter. Minnie was quite upset when a calf was killed and it was usually only several days later that she completely recovered from the shock of seeing the killing of her favourite animal. Following the slaughter, the owner of the animal would cut off pieces to be given to those who had helped with the operation. My father, of course, followed this custom and the result was that probably one-fifth to one-quarter of the animal was given to the various people who helped. Those who remained until the evening usually joined us for dinner, which included a part of the animal they had helped to slaughter.

We were never hungry because my father and mother planted and cultivated several types of vegetables including cabbage, turnips, lettuce, beans, green peas, tomatoes, peppers and others. We also raised large amounts of sweet and white potatoes which my mother called "Irish potatoes". Fruit trees included apple, pear, cherry and peach. My mother often canned large quantities of vegetables and fruit. I remember her spending considerable time in the kitchen heating water and canning these vegetables and fruit in glass jars.

I have very warm memories of my mother cooking large meals and inviting many of her relatives and friends to our house for dinners. Often on Sunday, she invited the minister of our local Baptist church for dinner. Having the preacher to dinner was a very important event for my mother and she went to great lengths to prepare the very best of food and to make certain that the preacher and his guests enjoyed a memorable meal. On these occasions, my mother served her guests first, leaving the children to sit outside on the back porch and wait for our turn. I remember my mother asking the ministers if they would like to have another serving of fried chicken. Almost invariably, they would say, "Yes, thank you very much. That is excellent chicken and we would love to have another piece!" We children sat and listened to this conversation and wondered when our turn would come. We wondered if there would be any food left, particularly the fried chicken, which all of us loved. My mother denied having said this up to her death but I am convinced that on one occasion when we asked her if there would be any food left, she said, "Wait your turn, children, here take a 'tater' and wait." (A "tater" was the southern vernacular for potato). We often teased her when a meal was late by saying, "Mom, do you want us to take a tater and wait?"

From this exposition one could easily get the impression that our life was idyllic and happy at all times. For the most part it was, but there were other occasions in which our parents spoke of their experiences and relationships with the local white population. My father was always somewhat reticent to talk about this relationship but there were moments when negative attitudes broke through. He made statements which led us to understand that there were some problems which he could not discuss fully in the presence of children. However, by the words and tone of their speech, it became fairly clear that tension and varying degrees of hostility were an aspect of daily life in our environment. My mother always referred to whites as "them old white folks", as "rednecks" or as "white trash".

Basically, my father's attitude toward the white population came through in business and personal relationships. He was responsible to the owner of the land for the upkeep of the house and its farming equipment and he felt that it was necessary to avoid creating any situation which might be seen as controversial, confrontational and "out of place".

Remaining in one's "place" was a very vital issue for blacks in southern society. It was always strange to me that a southern white could be very friendly toward a black if that person remained in a submissive or subordinate role. I experienced, first as a child and later as an adult growing up in the South, friendly personal relationships with whites. However, these relationships were always structured in a manner in which there was no doubt that the black person remained in the traditional role assigned to him or her by the "superior" white society. This traditional relationship was true whether or not the discussion focused on relationships between the farmer and the tenant, or on relationships between the domestic servant and her mistress. The white woman in her house occupied the same position of superiority as the white male occupied in dealing with blacks employed by him as his tenant farmers. We children, of course, gradually became aware of this central fact, but only in indirect ways. My father or his friends and other associates never spoke directly of their resentment of whites. However, that hostility was a central source of conversation whenever blacks got together. The intensity of these concerns was such that adults were not always aware that the children listened with great interest, even though not aware of the implications of what was said.

Exploitation of any type demeans the victim but these feelings must be kept well hidden from those who impose servitude upon the individual or group. It was too dangerous if the "superior" or dominant group were to become aware of the actual attitudes of their "inferiors". Success in concealing feelings was essential to survival.

Blacks in this interaction almost invariably presented themselves as smiling, happy-go-lucky, and content in their position. The impression was given to whites that blacks actually enjoyed the situation in which they found themselves. Therefore it was difficult for a white individual to really understand the depth of resentment felt by blacks. The white person was much more ignorant of the attitudes of blacks than blacks were of how whites felt. In general, blacks were keenly aware that most white people enjoyed their superior status in society and secondly, blacks knew intuitively that whites had no intention of allowing them to interact or to associate on a basis of equality. The white individual simply assumed this inequality was the way things should be. It is from this interaction that whites received the impression that blacks did not desire change in their condition and this in turn was used to support the stereotypings of blacks as lazy, inefficient, smiling, good natured, sexually promiscuous, and, of course, unable to handle responsibility without strict supervision by whites.

These attitudes, held by the general population, might have slowly disappeared had it not been for the impact of other significant factors, movies, newspapers, magazines, and such social institutions as churches, universities, public schools, and governments supportive of a negative view of blacks. They were constantly being enforced by all segments of society. Unfortunately, much of this negative attitude, maintained and perpetuated by the media and other social institutions, still exists in present day society.

The Negro spiritual was one avenue in which blacks could freely and openly express feelings. Church services were usually highly emotional and although unintelligible, these outpourings were recognized as a reflection of deep religious experience. Religion provided an opportunity for oppressed people to express themselves without facing the possibility of additional repression and punishment by hostile whites.

My siblings and I were growing up and assimilating through our skins as well as through our brains the attitudes and opinions of our parents, our relatives, friends and other significant figures in our lives. A part of our difficulty was that these attitudes and feelings were not clearly and directly expressed in any meaningful way. They were indirect and even contradictory, but nevertheless powerful and pervasive.

Another of our difficulties was our awareness that our country was supposedly based on the idea of freedom, democracy and equality but we could not escape awareness that this ideal was not the reality of our existence. Although unable to articulate feelings in a concrete way, my friends and I sensed that the ideal of freedom and justice did not apply to us. This awareness is one of the major difficulties of growing up as a child in a racist North American society, and more specifically the southern variety of that society. The messages our parents projected were often ambiguous and it appeared that my father appreciated the fact that Jewish storekeepers often provided credit to farmers who could not afford to pay cash when in need of the daily necessities of life. Although clearly appreciative, he often expressed contempt towards the Jewish merchants. One discussion regarding "Jewing" someone down, meaning that he had gotten the best of someone in a deal still remains in my mind. I had no idea what that expression meant, but I had the distinct impression that it was a derogatory reference to Jewish people. I thought that perhaps living in black neighbourhoods, Jews were not accepted in their own. This fact alone gave me a sense of appreciation that they were not anti-black. I never learned whether my father's remarks merely reflected the attitudes of his community or were motivated by deeply ingrained bigotry. I prefer to believe the former.

School and Community

Entering school was for me a very significant aspect of life. I recall my first day at school very well indeed. I was six years old and my mother took me by the hand and we walked perhaps a quarter of a mile to the school building.

We walked alone, so my siblings, Minnie and Frank, then two and four years of age, were left at home, probably with my father. When we arrived we were met by the teacher and a group of children who had arrived earlier. Several children were playing in the front yard of the school with the teacher providing some cursory supervision. I recall feeling a bit of apprehension while at the same time curiosity. The teacher was friendly, outgoing and actually playing with the children. This was reassuring. My mother introduced me to the teacher and left. I felt even more apprehension. However, we went into the school and sat down. The teacher tried to make us feel at ease by asking our names. She wrote them down, and finally began to assign us to our seats in the room. I no longer remember the name of this teacher but I have a vivid picture in my mind of the bright green dress she was wearing and her friendly smile.

Since there were only two rooms in the school, and two teachers, the first three grades were assigned to one room. Grades four, five and six were assigned to the other. That meant that those of us who were in first grade sat in the same classroom as grades two and three. Interestingly enough, while not ideal according to present standards, this arrangement did not appear as negative as one would expect. The children interacted very well with each other and after we finished our own lessons, we listened to the grades two and three children go through theirs. This made it possible for us not only to learn our own lessons, but also to hear and learn from the lessons of the other children in the same classroom.

The teacher, while not as highly educated as one finds today, nevertheless had the interest and ability to interact positively with the children in the three classes. My mother and father were very pleased with the relationship I had established with this teacher and often commented on their satisfaction with this arrangement and its influence upon my progress in my classes.

My father was less involved with my progress in school than my mother. I was quite aware that in the fall my father was very busy completing the harvest as well as in helping neighbours complete theirs. November was the month in Georgia by which most of the harvest had to be in. All family members, including children, were expected to help and the result was that many schools, particularly those in rural areas, did not start till early November.

I still have fond memories of the "spelling bees" in which students were required to participate. My happy memories are probably because I was one of the best spellers and usually won the competitions. In the spelling "bee" we lined up on one side of the room. The teacher called out words to be spelled. Each child was expected to spell the word correctly but if a child could not spell the word correctly he or she went to the foot of the line, and another child moved up and so on. I usually started around the middle of the line but, with one or two exceptions, always ended up at the top. There was only one occasion during my three years in that school when I missed a word and had to move down the line. My spelling ability was probably enhanced by my extensive reading and an excellent memory.

Sports were another activity in which I excelled. While not very competitive, I was a very fast sprinter and won most of the races. My parents were very proud of this success. Although the teachers often challenged us with their idea of cooperation to show the importance of working together, it became very clear to students that the teachers valued competition and winning. My ability to win, particularly in sports and in the classroom, was highly regarded by my teacher with the result that I became what might be called "a teacher's pet": a distinction which was not entirely welcomed!

One result of these and other successes was that I was given considerable recognition at sports and academic events. On one occasion I had a major role in a small dramatic production which was presented at the end of my first year in school. I was given a prize in an envelope which included two dimes. I was obviously very pleased and so were my parents. When we arrived at our home, however, the pleasure underwent a stunning change. We found that we did not have enough kerosene for the lamps. My father then sorrowfully took my envelope and told me that it was necessary to spend the money to buy a gallon of kerosene so that we could have light in our house for that evening. I would have much preferred to have spent that evening in the dark and to have kept my twenty cents for myself. That was the first prize I had ever won, and then quickly lost.

Those happy days were not to last for very much longer. It had become increasingly clear that we would no longer be able to remain on the farm. My father, in spite of his best efforts, hard work, and dedication to providing for his family, was simply unable to make a go of it and regretfully informed us that we would have to move. All of us initially rejected that idea. We were very upset when we heard my mother and father discussing the question of moving to the city. My sister Minnie broke into uncontrollable tears. I was only eight years old, my brother Frank was six and Minnie was only four years of age.

In spite of our unhappiness my mother and father made it very clear that they had no other alternative since they could not earn enough to feed the family and to keep the place. They would have to move to the city where my father had two brothers and several friends with whom we could stay until a place for the family could be found.

The boll weevil had effectively attacked and destroyed the cotton crop, the important cash crop which provided our finances for items other than the food we grew on the farm. Only subsistence farming remained when the cotton crop was destroyed. While we always had adequate supplies of food, we needed money for clothes, heating supplies, fertilizers, transportation costs, etc. It was good to be able to raise most of one's food, but that was not enough. The increasing cost of fertilizers was driving thousands of farmers from their farms. Later, of course, increasing mechanization added to the pressure on southern farmers, again driving thousands from farms to the cities of the North and the South. We were simply one family in a mass exodus from the farms.

Our father began to make the necessary arrangements for the move. It was not necessary to sell the house since it was considered a part of the land rented from the landlord. My parents immediately began to make plans to sell the animals, some furniture and tools they felt would not be needed in the city. The sale again caused a great deal of difficulty, pain and turmoil among the children. I am sure that my parents also strongly regretted the necessity to leave the farm. In spite of the difficulties, the hard work, my parents had enjoyed the farm experience and also regretted leaving their friends, relatives and other people with whom over many years they had developed strong and valued friendships. I felt badly over the prospects of leaving my classmates and friends but I also felt that facing a new challenge was exciting. We were leaving the only home I had ever known and that created both fear and anticipation. But I particularly hated to leave Phelmon and other members of the Whatley family who were our closest friends and neighbours.

Death and Life in Atlanta

Finally all preparations were completed and my father rented a truck on which with the help of friends, he loaded the furniture and other belongings and prepared to drive several miles to East Point in suburban Atlanta. The necessary arrangements for our new home had been made by one of our relatives.

It was often said by teachers, my parents and others that the road to success was through hard work but my father did not find this axiom to be true. He was a victim of what Gunnar Myrdal, a Swedish economist, called the "American Dilemma", referring to the contradictions between the promise and reality of the dream of wealth and happiness said to be available to all who strive for success. For many, including my father, that dream was a myth. The large northern cities, for example, Chicago, Detroit, Cleveland, Cincinnati, St. Louis and as far west as Los Angeles, served as magnets for farmers who were desperately seeking opportunities to build a new life. Most ex-farmers, however, did not possess the necessary skills for success in the big cities. Consequently many, after leaving their farms, found it necessary to live in poverty-stricken slum areas. Our new home, in East Point, was totally inadequate. We had only three rooms for a family of six in one of the poorest areas of town. Many farm families suffered almost as many hardships as they had on farms. In some respects the newcomers might have been better off on the farm because at least they could grow the fruits, vegetables and meats for their own consumption.

My father was successful in finding a job through the help of his friends and relatives who lived and worked in the city. His new job was driving a truck with the Georgia State Highway Department, a skill he had to learn since he had never owned a car. This job paid a "magnificent" sum of fifteen dollars per week! Of course, this amount was much more valuable than today. For example, a hamburger was only five to ten cents, a Coca-Cola could be bought for five cents, telephone calls were five cents, a streetcar ride from East Point to the centre of Atlanta was only six cents, and licence plates for a car were only three dollars annually. A family could live relatively cheaply as far as groceries were concerned.

It was unfortunate that I was living in a crowded home in which there was only a limited number of books and other educational materials. My father had however bought several volumes of histories of World War I. He had been called to serve in that war, but the conflict ended before he became actively involved. It was only on rare occasions that I saw him sitting and reading those volumes. In the meantime, I became quite interested in them myself and on occasion I would read historical records of that event. I became extremely interested in these stories of the courageous exploits of the men who fought in the "Great War". I learned, however, to critically view some of the works of historians. For example, it seemed to me that according to most historians, the Germans lost all of the battles in that terrible war. The British, Americans and French were always the winners of every conflict. The story of the battles at sea were also intriguing. I read the history of the battle of Jutland, in which the British navy lost far more ships than the Germans, but the Germans were reported to have been defeated. It occurred to me that it was a British or American historian who had written that account. Even at that time I wondered how that story would have been recorded had it been written by a German historian!

Writing more than forty years after the end of World War II reminds me of the story of the ladies from Boston on a bus tour of the battlefields of Tennessee where a number of Civil War battles were fought. The bus driver, a southerner, stated that on one occasion a few hundred Confederate soldiers had defeated a larger Union Army in a bloody battle. "Ladies", he noted, "on another occasion less than 5000 Confederate soldiers destroyed more than 10,000 Yanks in a great battle on that hill 'over yonder'". Finally the Boston tourists could no longer stand to hear these stories. After all, they were Bostonians, and from the North. In other words, they were "Yankees" and the Yankees had won the war. Finally one of the women called out, "Bus driver, didn't the North win any battles in the Civil War?" The driver quickly replied, "Not while I'm driving this bus lady, they didn't!"

I had already become an avid reader in those early years, reading almost anything I could get my hands on. The result was I learned a great deal about life in general; not all learning takes place in school and through the use of textbooks. I discovered there was a lot of interesting material which could be useful in learning about life and education. The school library was very small but I read practically everything I found there. In addition I borrowed as many books as I could from friends, neighbours and even teachers and became known among my fellow students, jokingly, as an "egghead", a term we used but did not fully understand.

We were required in school to listen to a Bible reading by our teacher and to recite a Bible verse each morning as a part of our morning exercises. We also had to salute the American flag and to recite the "Pledge of Allegiance" to the flag. I always considered these two exercises as totally useless and ridiculous. Most students viewed them as a waste of time and performed them in a disinterested manner. It became a standing routine that the first student called on to recite a Bible verse would always choose the shortest verse in the Bible, namely "Jesus Wept". I cannot say that repeating the Pledge of Allegiance to the flag made me more patriotic. Our recitation of the Pledge often received an unauthorized ending in both public and high schools. The Pledge ends, "With Liberty and Justice for All" but we often added, "If your skin is white"! Obviously the teachers were aware of our additions but made no comment.

Nevertheless there were other purposes and values to the school experiences. I received my first romantic letter from a fourteen-year-old girl when we were in the eighth grade. I cannot remember the exact words of the letter, but one phrase comes to mind. She wrote, "inter alia", that she "admired my hospitality". I was not certain what she meant by "hospitality", but assumed that this was her way of stating that she liked my friendly manners. The letter was delivered by a friend who told me that she wanted it to be kept a secret. However, the news somehow "got out" and eventually led to considerable embarrassment. The result was that I never responded to the letter. My admirer was not amused that the secret was exposed or by my lack of response. In any event we never spoke of the incident. Like most young teenage romances, the incident was quickly forgotten.

The Fulton County school programs for black students in East Point terminated at grade eight. After graduation students who wanted to continue had to travel by bus and streetcar to Atlanta to attend one of two of the Atlanta secondary schools. I look back with some satisfaction at the county public school system. Although the schools were not up to par academically, at least we learned a great deal from dedicated and committed teachers.

The next year I entered the ninth grade at a junior high school in the city of Atlanta. This step with its many difficulties was not required of white students in East Point who had access to the Russell Junior and Senior High schools located less than half a mile from where our family lived. My friends and I had to walk past this school to the bus which took us to downtown Atlanta, and then to transfer to a streetcar to the outskirts of the city. The Washington High School was, as expected, located in a relatively deprived all black community. Many of our graduates from the Fulton County system dropped out of school after the eighth grade. We keenly resented the segregated school system which we were forced to attend but about which nothing could be done, at least at that time. It required an additional thirty years for the civil rights movement to change an unequal and unjust educational system.

Family and Community

In the meantime my family had become settled into East Point, had made a number of friends and were involved in many local activities. Perhaps I should restrict this comment to my mother since my father was more reticent about involvement in East Point community activities but was very much involved in activities in our home. He was not as involved in the church, or in lodges, clubs and other social gatherings as he had been in the country. On the other hand, at home he was a very lively person and very much interested in his family. In part this change may have occurred because he now enjoyed regular working hours and did not have to work from "sunrise to sundown".

In the city as on the farm, mother continued her usual household chores. There was no need for her to go out to work in the fields as she often did on the farm. She had very little opportunity to be useful except in the home. By that time, my youngest brother Marvin had been born and having five children to care for was a full-time job in itself. My strongest memories of my mother involve her commitment to keeping the house clean and tidy. She was always busy, washing clothing, bathing the children, scrubbing the floors and other similar activities. In addition she was often busy sewing, patching our clothing, or making new clothes for herself or for the family. We had to wear patched clothing to school because we simply did not have enough money to buy new clothing. My mother did not worry about whether or not our clothes were patched. She only wanted to be sure that they were always clean.

I have never understood why Mondays were always "washdays" for many families in East Point. (Perhaps it was a holdover from life on the farm). The family laundry and the laundry for white families (for whom the women often worked) was almost always done on Mondays. The lengthy process involved lighting a fire under a huge outdoor pot, heating the water to the boiling point, adding homemade soap and inserting the dirty clothes. The "scrubboard" was then utilized and the clothes were washed clean, rinsed and ready to be hung on a clothes line for drying. All of our friends and neighbours engaged in the same process at the same time. That process had become an automatic ritual when we moved to suburban East Point.

Our lives in East Point were not always happy and productive. Unfortunately there were times when the shortages of funds made it very difficult for us to engage in the normal activities of life outside of our house. Whether we had decent clothing or shoes was not nearly so important to my parents as adequate food which we always had in plentiful supply. However, it was not always the most nutritious food. There were times when we only had biscuits and butter for breakfast with a bit of syrup poured on top. Because southern style grits were a very inexpensive food, they were often the main source of our breakfast. Living in the city was different from living in the country because we could not grow our own food; however, my mother did cultivate a small garden in our back yard.

While my father on the farm and as a truck driver in the city earned the family income, it was my mother who ran the household. After moving to the city and earning his small wage, my father brought his paycheck home and gave it to my mother. They would then sit down and agree on how the money was to be spent, including how much money should be given to him for expenses. I remember one occasion on which my father indicated that his old suit was wearing out and he needed a new one. That was a matter of considerable importance largely because of the cost. Both parents discussed this question for several days before a decision was made. The suit was bought when my mother felt that the necessary funds were available. This was not an isolated incident; rather, it was a common pattern of behaviour while we lived on the farm and in the town. Many of our neighbours and friends followed a similar pattern in the expenditure of the family income. From all indications it appeared that my father had no objection to this practice; he seemed to have welcomed it.

In addition to our poverty, we also faced the problem of racism. My father would come home from work and relate stories regarding racist occurrences on the job. He often encountered racist remarks, teasing, jokes and name calling. Like other black workers, he could not react negatively to these remarks and had to take what was "dished out" if he wanted to keep his job! But when he came home, he told us stories of how he had felt, but about which he could do nothing.

In many respects, the racism in East Point and in Atlanta was worse than in the rural areas of the South because the white population in the rural South was scattered and it was only occasionally that we had to come into direct contact with them. In the city, it was impossible to avoid contact on the job, in the streets, on buses and street cars, in stores and in all other aspects of life. Segregated churches, social and other clubs or recreational activities were the only exceptions.

The constant contact with racist attitudes resulted in anger and bitterness on both sides of the racial line, some of which resulted in violence against other blacks possibly as a means of relieving the violence blacks felt against whites. One example was the fist fights between two brothers upon our arrival in East Point. Those two sons of a prominent deacon in the Baptist church, were obviously frustrated with their impoverished lives. On more than one occasion, they took out their frustration on each other. I personally observed many similar violent incidents among black boys and men in the black communities of Atlanta and East Point but was never comfortable as an observer of these situations and avoided them as much as possible.

The constant poverty and racism led my father to consider leaving the South. His brother, my uncle Glenn, lived in Cleveland, Ohio and my father felt that it would be very fortunate if he could find a job in that northern city. His plan was to live with his brother until he could earn and save some money and then send for his family. After some weeks or months of discussion, my parents agreed that moving to Cleveland was the best step for him to take.

They began to save two or three dollars per week until he had enough money to buy a train ticket to Cleveland. He then left and we didn't see him again for several months. Occasionally he wrote letters home and included a few dollars to help with the support of the family.

In the meantime, my mother for the first time began to take part-time jobs outside of the home. Initially these consisted of washing and ironing clothing for local white families. She often took Frank and me with her so that we knew where to return the clothing. She washed and ironed them, and Frank and I returned them to the family and collected two or three dollars as payment for her work.

While living conditions were poor and we had very few material possessions, life was not unduly difficult. The reason for this was that almost everyone around us was also living in some degree of poverty. The only occasions when we saw people who were not living in poverty were when my friends and I went downtown and came into contact with the white population. On those occasions we learned that there were at least two kinds of white people: the poor white workers who did much the same kind of work as my father and other blacks and the wealthy white people who actually controlled the city. They owned and operated the various business establishments, banks, stores, manufacturing plants and other businesses. We occasionally walked past many large and well appointed homes located in the white residential districts. These homes, in our view, were mansions and fantasy castles! There is no question that these homes were far more costly than our parents could ever have afforded. I would guess that some of those homes, built in the old southern colonial style, must have had at least ten or twelve rooms. My friends, Charlie and Forrest Green, and I simply could not imagine what the inside looked like. Unfortunately, the opportunity to see for ourselves never occurred so we could only wonder and dream. It is interesting that we were never questioned or challenged when walking by the large homes, probably because we were thought to be simply servants or "yardboys" for one of the rich families.

Incidents

My first direct contact with racism and racial hostility occurred during a trip to the white community. Frank and I had delivered clothing to one of my mother's customers in a white neighbourhood. On our return trip, Frank, my cousin Sylvester, other boys and I were attacked by a group of local white boys. Sylvester was a very strong young man and a few years older than the rest of us. One of the white boys violently attacked him and my cousin retaliated. In the course of the fight my cousin unexpectedly knocked the boy down. The boy quickly jumped up and again attacked my cousin who immediately knocked him down again. The white boys looked on, not knowing what to do. We were also not quite certain what to do in this situation. After the third knockdown, the gang fled. We also left in a hurry because we were not sure whether they were going to return with reinforcements or whether their parents would come after us. We went to our respective homes with some apprehension as the fight had occurred in an all-white neighbourhood and our homes were some distance away. It was possible their parents might come to our neighbourhood to attack us or our parents. It was not inconceivable that bricks would be thrown through the windows of our homes, a common experience for blacks who dared to retaliate when attacked by whites in the Deep South. Fortunately, this did not happen and we breathed a sigh of relief.

A second incident occurred a few weeks later in another part of the city. On this occasion, my brother and I again were delivering clothing. On our way back home, we walked past a group of six or seven white boys who were sitting on a hill on the side of the road and chatting. Shortly after we had passed the group, a brick or a stone sailed by our heads. One of the boys had thrown the object at us but fortunately had missed his target. Frank and I quickly glanced at each other and then simply walked away as quick as possible. No words were spoken and no further incident occurred on that occasion. We were left wondering what was the reason for the attempted attack. The reason, of course, was these boys had been taught hostility towards us because of the colour of our skins. We were, in their view, merely a couple of "niggers" whom they could attack with absolute impunity.

These attacks simply reflected a more general problem and it is obvious that these young boys were not born with hostility and hate towards blacks. These were learned attitudes and behaviours and they were learned from their parents, relatives, friends, schools and their communities. Their parents and these boys had learned that an attack on black boys or adults could be done without guilt or fear of reprisal. It was, from their perspective, always "open season" for attacks on blacks. I was angry and frustrated by these and other similar attacks by whites on other blacks. Apparently, they were merely a part of life in the southern states. But that awareness was of little solace to me. I wanted to be free to walk the streets in peace, another fruitless dream in the Deep South.

At that time it was impossible for a black person to take a white person to court on any charge, including assault. Black individuals had no standing in a southern court. They were not permitted to testify against a white individual. In other words, blacks had no rights, as a United States Supreme Court had ruled in the Dred Scott decision in the 1850s, "that blacks had no rights that a white man had to respect"!

That attitude was a part of the "southern way of life" but it is difficult to believe that the victims did not experience a desire to strike back. However under the circumstances, retaliation was not a realistic possibility. There would have been nothing that Frank and I could do had that brick or stone struck and injured one of us. The results of an attempt to retaliate might well have been a devastating attack on the vulnerable black community by the KKK and other racist groups. I did not feel unusually apprehensive and therefore afraid to go about the daily business of living, yet one could say that the situation was somewhat analogous to the soldier on the battle field. Even though he is without weapons to defend himself and vulnerable, he is still hopeful that he will survive. I survived both physically and psychologically with only minor damage. But many other young blacks did not and will carry emotional scars the rest of their lives as a result of their experiences of growing up in a racist society.

In the meantime my mother did not neglect her religious and social activities even when busily engaged in raising a family and part-time work. I often wondered how she managed to carry on so well given the situation in which we lived. My youngest brother, Marvin, was born just before the departure of my father for Ohio. Nevertheless our mother, in spite of increasing demands, continued her many social activities, including membership and participation in several religious and social groups. She was a member of the senior choir of our local Baptist Church, and was also involved in the many fundraising activities sponsored by the church.

Her major social activity was her participation in the Hyacinth Art Social Club which met monthly at the homes of one of its members. This club was something special and there was a waiting list of potential members. It was routine that the chairperson always announced the closing of the meeting with a little prayer and the singing of a religious song, usually "God Be With You Till We Meet Again". Following the song, the hostess invited the ladies to have a seat for a "little refreshment". My mother and others always put on what was called a "good spread". Apparently it had become the pattern for each subsequent hostess to attempt to "outdo" the refreshments of the previous one. Finally it reached the stage where the ladies could no longer afford to prepare such elaborate meals and a decision was made to return to the more simple refreshments originally intended. My brothers and I often sat outside and waited until the departure of club members and I wondered what would happen if the hostess did not speak the "magic words" following the closing of the meeting. In any event we were happy when the club met at our house, and hopeful that some of the goodies would be left for us. A significant aspect of these events was that, although few members could afford the expense, they went to great lengths to impress fellow members. This was one of the few occasions on which a poor family could win recognition, however briefly.

It was also at this time that Frank and I began our regular participation in Sunday School classes. While my mother never attended Sunday School, she was determined that the two of us should attend every Sunday. Glenn and Minnie were too young at that time. One of the memorable aspects of those classes was that the teacher provided cards with Biblical pictures on one side and Bible verses printed on the other side. We were expected to memorize and recite one of the verses and present our interpretation. The teacher encouraged us to express our opinions without fear of being told that we were ignorant or mistaken.

Our family had also become closely attached as friends of the Barlow family. The mother, Gertrude, and father, Judge, had lived in East Point for some time prior to our arrival. As with the Whatley family, our close friends while living on the farm, the children of the Barlow family appeared to have been planned to arrive in concert with ours. The oldest daughter, Coleen, was roughly the same age as I. The second daughter, Helen was also approximately the same age as Frank. The same pattern occurred in relation to the births of their third and fourth children. These occurrences, of course, were a mere coincidence, but we were often teased regarding the almost uncanny similarities in the dates of births of our friends and ourselves!

The relationship between Mrs. Barlow and my mother was so close that many people assumed they were sisters. They appeared to always be together and often participated in the same organizations and social events. The result was that we were often at each others' homes. This close friendship continued for many years and until my mother left the city following the death of my father. Unfortunately Coleen, the Barlow's oldest daughter died at a very young age, but our family and the other Barlow children continued our contacts for many years.

This was a time when Frank and I, as the two eldest children, were expanding our interests beyond the family and establishing friendships and relationships in the general community. Attending the local school made it possible for us to meet and become acquainted with many other children from a variety of family backgrounds. Although we were close in age, Frank and I did not become close friends with the same boys or girls, probably because of my strong interest in sports, an interest which he did not share. Frank rarely joined us in the numerous baseball games which were so great a part of my recreational activities. There is no question however that he was totally committed, even at a young age, to supporting our mother in her efforts to maintain the necessary household activities. At this stage he was perhaps mother's strongest supporter.

Minnie, as the only girl in the family, received most attention from our mother. She and I also became fast friends and I have always held a special place in my affections for Minnie. My mother also felt very protective towards Minnie but there were some aspects of that relationship which I could not fully understand. On one occasion mother sent Minnie to live for a time with her brother, our uncle John, a discharged veteran of the First World War. It was obvious to all of us that Minnie did not want to leave her family, but my mother insisted. Minnie was only six or seven years of age at the time and it was years later that we learned how strongly Minnie felt regarding what she considered as rejection. Even today I am not certain why my mother took this step but I do know that it was a traumatic experience for Minnie. I suspect that Minnie was sent away from the family because of mother's feeling that as a girl, Minnie required more protection than she could provide while working full or part-time. Whatever the reason, the experience unfortunately damaged the relationship between the two.

Return of Father

My parents kept in fairly constant contact during my father's stay with my uncle in Cleveland. Periodically letters arrived from him and my mother would respond. Not many months after his arrival in Cleveland, however, we learned that he had fallen ill and a few weeks later we had a letter indicating that he was returning home to recuperate. He wanted to be with his family. Mother expressed some apprehension about this as she was not quite sure what that decision meant. The children were overjoyed that our father was returning home but he returned even earlier than was expected, travelling by train from Cleveland to Atlanta. Those were the days of steam engines and he was covered with black soot from the constant smoke from the steam engine. He was dirty, but we were happy!

We learned when he returned that he was seriously ill. Apparently he had received some medical attention in Cleveland, but this had not been effective. We never learned the exact nature of the diagnosis. The East Point community did not have regular medical care available for its black population. The doctor who treated black patients came only occasionally or on call from Atlanta. It was almost like a festival or celebration when Dr. Holmes came to visit patients in our neighbourhood. He always stopped at our house during father's illness. There was no medical insurance at that time and I am not sure how our mother managed to pay medical bills. Dr. Holmes, like many other doctors at that time, was probably never paid, at least not in full.

We children, of course, had little or no idea what was going on. Our questions were always answered in a vague manner and we were given very little information regarding the nature or implications of our father's illness. It appeared to me at least that everyone including our mother was unwilling or unable to provide us with the information we desired. With rare exceptions we were not permitted to enter his bedroom to even speak with him. There was almost an air of unreality in relationship to his illness. Friends and relatives often stopped by for a visit, then would depart without providing much information to the eagerly awaiting children. Marvin, then less than one year old, was close to the situation, but obviously too young to be able to keep us informed. The result was that the four of us lived in an atmosphere of uncertainty and confusion. We never knew whether our parents actually knew what was wrong or whether they simply did not want to tell us.

Father's condition grew steadily worse. I noticed that some people who visited would look at us with some degree of pity as if we were going to face a great catastrophe. As the oldest and perhaps the only one who had some indication of what those looks meant, my suspicion was that my father was dying. A few weeks later, in February 1925, I was playing in the back yard with my cousin Sylvester when the news came. I was only eleven years old. My impression from what I heard from various people was that my father died from internal bleeding or haemorrhages. However, we never learned why he had developed that particular condition. My premonition had regretfully been proven accurate but strangely, his death initially had little obvious effect on me. In retrospect it appeared that I had already prepared myself psychologically for the bad news.

Perhaps my lack of response was also related to the fact that there had been serious and prolonged arguments between my mother and father for some weeks before his death. I was upset by these arguments but they had not permitted the children to be privy to their differences so we had no idea what caused the hostile attitudes. I was the only member of the family who did not break down in tears upon my father's death but I clearly remember the confusion I felt. It was difficult and disheartening to lose a father. On the other hand, the end came as relief that the quarrels were over and perhaps peace would return to the family household.

The death of father was obviously a significant factor in the lives of our family. Its implications were to touch every aspect of our lives, but in very different ways. Mother was left to care for five children, varying from less than one to eleven years of age. Marvin was born in September of 1924, only five months previously. Mother was only twenty seven years of age when father died. He had belonged to a lodge, which provided for his burial expenses plus a small amount of money left over and mother was uncertain as to what to do with this small sum. She was sure, however, that she would have to go out to work on a full-time basis since there were no social welfare support programs in place at that time. A person in need either had to find work or depend on friends and relatives for support. Our mother chose to seek full-time employment and this was the beginning of a new life for her and for the family. However, she needed time to make this momentous step. It would be necessary to find a way to secure adequate housing for the family and at the same time to find work.

Following discussions with our grandmother, she made the decision for us to move to Atlanta and live with her mother and stepfather for a period of time. Although we had visited our grandmother from time to time during our stay in East Point, we had never thought of living there since my grandmother and her husband lived in a fairly small home with only three or four rooms. Obviously it would be difficult for the six of us to live comfortably in so small a house, located on Magnolia Street in the black ghetto of Atlanta. We moved from East Point shortly after my father died and began our lives in severely crowded conditions in Atlanta.

CHAPTER 2 *New Experiences and Developments*

Among the first things that mother did after the move was to enrol Frank and me in the local public school. While the Edmund Ware School was within walking distance from our house, unfortunately it was severely overcrowded and operated only on a half-day basis. Frank and I went to school from one o'clock to three thirty in the afternoon.

The teacher and class made every effort to make me feel at home. They apparently recognized that I would feel a bit shy and insecure, and they were right. I was told later, by a friend, that the teacher had warned students the day before my arrival that I would be coming and that I was a 'very nice boy'. In any event, I began my Atlanta public school educational experience on a very positive note. Asa Yancey, the boy who later became my special friend, sat in the front row of the classroom and he often turned around in his seat and took a quick glance at those of us in the back rows. From time to time I had the distinct impression that he was looking at me, although I was not sure. There was obvious curiosity but no discernible hostility by others during my first week in the new environment. My friendship with Asa lasted from February to June, when the school year ended. I did not see Asa again for several years until we met at the Booker T. Washington High School.

On our way to school we often met children returning home after having spent the half-day in morning classes. It was on one of these occasions that I saw my first serious fight between two school boys. A crowd of boys were standing around two kids who were fighting. One boy was lying on the ground and on his back. The other kid was kneeling over him and pummelling him in the face with his fists. That was a very shocking experience for me. Observing the fight and the kids standing around doing nothing was very emotionally draining. I didn't know whether to intervene or stay out of it. I was confused and uncertain and the result was that I, like the others, did nothing and continued our trip to the school. Frank and I never heard the results of that incident simply because the two boys in question were not in our classroom.

Fighting and other forms of violence proved to be frequent occurrences among school boys in that neighbourhood. One of our schoolmates was actually killed, accidentally, in a "cross fire" between two rival gangs who were fighting on the streets not far from where we lived. This was a very serious occurrence which caused a tremendous amount of concern in the neighbourhood. Many people tried to organize meetings to determine if some program could be worked out to reduce the amount of violence in that crime-ridden black ghetto. As is usual in these occurrences, a few meetings were held, people expressed their concern and nothing happened. The causes of violence and crime were deeply embedded in the total ghetto experience and residents were powerless, as most slum dwellers are today. As far as I was aware, no effort was ever made to identify and apprehend the guilty party or parties. Life went on as usual.

Frank and I had a very close relationship at that time, largely because of our attachment and sense of responsibility to our mother. The death of our father had resulted in the family drawing closer together. We had done very well in school and were pleased with the Atlanta school experience.

Interpersonal Relationships

My mother and grandmother did not always get along very well. There had often been a noticeable tension between them when our grandmother came to visit us in East Point. Now, in our new conditions in Atlanta, living together in a small crowded situation resulted in increased stress and negative relationships. Mr. McDay, my step-grandfather, did not help the situation. He was a very moody person who had little interest in the activities of children. It appeared to me that while he might have been able to live comfortably with one child, certainly the stress of living with five children was too much for him. The result was we stayed away from him as much as possible.

My grandmother had blue-grey eyes and light brown hair and because of her skin colour, she could "pass" for "white" when she was among white people and as "black" when among black people. Thus she was able to travel and to operate in both societies. While downtown, she was always "white" and could shop at places where blacks were not served. She could eat in "white" restaurants where black people were not permitted. Her only difficulty was that she had to be careful that she was not seen downtown in the "wrong" company at the "wrong" time!

The experience of my grandmother demonstrates the absurdity of hostility, prejudice and discrimination against an individual on the basis of colour. She was well accepted by whites when they thought she was "white". Being aware of her situation, blacks accepted and understood her position in a racist society. When she was "passing" among whites, blacks would pretend to not know her, or would act as if they were her maids or other servants! Blacks enjoyed this opportunity to engage in a little harmless deception since it was easy to deceive the white population. After all, it was inconceivable that a white individual would associate as an equal with a black.

By that time I was already beginning to understand, at least to some degree, the reality of the racial situation in the South. I was aware that black and white people were expected to be segregated and remain completely apart except under conditions of superiority and inferiority. Blacks and whites in Atlanta, and elsewhere, were expected to remain apart in public and high schools, colleges, work places, churches and all other aspects of life. Even burials of the dead in cemeteries were not exempted from this rigid requirement. Total separation of blacks and whites was the major purpose of the system of racial segregation.

I began to experience the realities of racial segregation at an early age when I obtained a temporary job working on a milk truck. This job required me to get up around five o'clock in the morning, go down to the plant where the milk was bottled and to help load the truck. My co-worker and I then drove the truck to our assigned route and went from house to house to deliver the bottled milk. I learned very quickly that I had to treat the whites quite differently from the blacks. The white people always welcomed me gladly as long as I appeared to be subservient. If I made any statement or action which seemed to suggest that I considered myself their equal, their whole attitude and behaviour immediately changed. I would then be considered "an uppity nigger" and not worthy of treatment as an ordinary human being. I was to encounter this attitude and behaviour many times throughout the period I lived in the South. That attitude changed only marginally after I became an adult.

Needless to say I resented this treatment by whites in Atlanta. I began to realize I was badly maladapted to the society in which I was living. The question at that young age was what else could I do? I was living in a family of a grandmother, step-grandfather, my widowed mother, four brothers and a sister who needed my help. So I saw my role at that point as becoming a sort of father surrogate to the other children. My mother encouraged that attitude and behaviour. She often told me, when she was going away, to "make sure the children got along alright." Even as young as eleven years of age since I was the oldest child in the family, it was necessary that I assumed some responsibility for my younger siblings.

My Uncle's Farm

During the summer of 1925, just after school ended, I suddenly became ill. The symptoms suggest that I had measles, but no one was certain. I was weak and lethargic and had little interest in my usual activities. I did not have access to a doctor because of the poor condition of our finances. My mother decided at the end of a week to send me down to visit and live for a time with my uncle Paul, my father's oldest brother. He and his wife lived on and operated a farm near Griffin, Georgia, a small town about thirty-five miles south of Atlanta. I was somewhat apprehensive about the prospect of going to visit Uncle Paul, whom I did not know very well. I had very little experience with him since we had left our farm a few years earlier and as a result, I felt that he was almost a total stranger. However, my mother decided I should go. One of my other uncles, the Reverend Pheneas Head, drove me to the farm in his car. My two uncles appeared to be on very friendly terms which was reassuring to me. My uncles and aunt were warm and friendly individuals who quickly made me feel at home.

Upon arrival I was given a very warm welcome and a big meal of meats, fruits, milk and other foods. The farm was the most prosperous I had ever seen, far more so than the farm on which my father had worked. Uncle Paul owned several horses, cows, hogs, sheep, and other livestock. In addition he also had a great number of pear, apple, peach and other fruit trees on his farm.

This visit was a very interesting experience for a young fellow with limited knowledge of life on a farm. I was given certain chores to perform including feeding the animals and I was also asked to help my aunt with some of the chores around the house. This work was not very difficult since my uncle and aunt were taking care that I never became overtired. For the most part I had a very enjoyable stay with my relatives. In some respects I think they treated me too well. They almost pushed food upon me to try to make certain that I recovered from what they considered as my "weakened state".

I was away from the turmoil and troubles of Atlanta and living a very sedate life. There were no incidents of prejudice or discrimination simply because I lived on a farm which had no interaction with white people. As my father had done, my uncle drove his truck into town from time to time to sell some of the products of his farm. His apples, pears and peaches were very popular and always sold well. Watermelons were also great favourites. Occasionally, he would refer to some negative treatment received in the town. There would be questions and comments about the prices he was charging and the suggestion that "this nigger is trying to get rich". Most often these comments were made in a jocular manner with smiles all around. Smiles however did not reflect the real feeling of my uncle. They represented a method of survival in which my uncle, a very bright man, knew exactly what was happening even though he could not react against this unwelcomed behaviour.

By the middle of August, it became obvious that my health had greatly improved and that I would be able to leave the farm. My mother had written a letter in which she suggested that Uncle Pheneas would pick me up on his trip home from one of his churches. He was the pastor of four rural churches each of which held services on a monthly basis. Thus he was able to serve a different church in each of the four weeks of the month.

I had enjoyed living on the farm and was not altogether happy when Uncle Pheneas came by to pick me up. My departure from the farm and my aunt and uncle was both sad and joyful. I could not have had better care from anyone, but at the same time, I wanted to return to my family. The return was the catalyst for great satisfaction on the part of my mother, brothers, sister and my grandparents.

There was, however, little time for celebration. The summer was almost over and the beginning of school was near. It was time for another move — this time back to the familiar surroundings of friends and relatives in East Point. We moved into our new house which had been built by my Uncle Pheneas and friends during the summer. It had only two rooms, each approximately 15 by 15 feet. There was the usual front porch, a characteristic of many homes in the

South. We appreciated the new home and the fact that it was available only through the active concern of our uncle.

I find it difficult to realize how the family could have lived in such small and cramped space. My mother, Marvin and Minnie slept in one bed. Frank and I slept in another bed while Glenn slept on a cot in the second room. We had to cook and heat the place from that one room. We did not find it too difficult and were able to live fairly comfortably, with only minor inconveniences.

Although we lived with only minor discomfort in that house, our attitudes changed as we grew up and friends wanted to visit us. Many years later, my sister reminded me that she was ashamed to invite friends to our house because she did not want them to observe the crowded conditions in which we lived. I felt the same way and often made excuses for not inviting friends over. Instead, we suggested that we visit them at their homes, or meet in some other place. On one occasion, when I was in high school, my friend Jimmy Holloway borrowed his aunt's car and drove out to East Point for a totally unexpected visit. I met him outside our house and suggested that we drive to a local restaurant and have a cold drink and a chat. I was relieved when he agreed!

Frank and I were successful in finding part time work after school and saved most of our earnings to help build a small additional room to serve as a kitchen. This new addition relieved, to some extent, the crowded conditions under which we had lived. One reason for our ability to cope with the cramped quarters was that few of us were ever at home at the same time. Neither were our living conditions unique; most of our friends and neighbours lived in similar conditions. I believe that this relative lack of stress and conflict in the home was also a result of the fact that Frank and I were determined to support our mother as much as possible in that situation. We realized that it was necessary for her to work outside the home and that it would be our responsibility to keep the household functioning in her absence. Consequently Frank and Glenn became expert cooks and housekeepers. I took responsibility for overall operation of the house including the care of my sister and Marvin. My mother obviously appreciated the way we were handling ourselves during her absence.

Mother's first full time job was working as a domestic in the home of a middle class white family. It was necessary for her to leave our house between 7:30 and 8 o'clock every morning, six days per week. She became quite friendly with her new employer. This lady used to tell mother stories about her imagination and fantasies, and particularly of her sexual fantasies. She asked my mother if she also enjoyed similar imagination and fantasies. My mother would often repeat these stories to her friends. We learned through overhearing conversations that she had no empathy whatsoever with the imaginative aspects of her employer's life. She emphasized that the lady was well off, had a good husband with a good job, and was living well. She could not understand why this woman had such strong sexual fantasies. This of course was totally anathema to my strongly religious mother. She also related that on one occasion when the woman of the house was not at home, the husband made sexual advances towards her.

We heard my mother explaining this matter to her friend, Mrs. Barlow. It was made very clear that she left the house immediately and would not return until the mistress returned from her shopping trip. The impression we received from these stories was that the woman and her husband were not very religious or ethical people. We had already learned that this kind of behaviour was simply unacceptable in our neighbourhood and home. It was expected that there would be total fidelity to the spouse at all times.

It was hard for us to realize the difficulty mother experienced working in that home. After some time, she resigned and took another position as a cook in a fraternity house on the campus of the Georgia Institute of Technology. Georgia "Tech" was the segregated all-white technical school supported by the state of Georgia. Mother was responsible for preparing meals for some 25 to 30 college boys. In many respects she found this job much more suitable since for the most part the students were away attending classes during the day and she was largely left to herself. During this time she did the cooking, cleaning, laundry and other household chores.

On occasion there would be a surplus of food when some of the young students were away from the house at mealtime, or attending other activities on campus including sports and social activities. Mother would often ask for permission to bring the surplus food home to her children. This request was usually granted and she would bring home pies, cakes and even steaks and other expensive foods which we could not possibly afford. These were times of great celebration!

I had the impression that mother really enjoyed work at the fraternity house. The hours were regular and she had some time for herself during the day. She made good use of those hours for sewing and knitting. This job lasted for perhaps two years after which she left the house for another job. Mother never explained to us why she left that situation.

It was through the efforts of Mrs. Barlow that she found a new position at the Atlanta International Airport. This position, like past positions, involved domestic work. Mrs. Barlow and my mother prepared food for the airport restaurant, did the cooking and served the meals for staff and airline passengers, then cleaned the tables after passengers had left the restaurant to board their planes for distant destinations. Mother appeared to like this job, largely because of her close association with Mrs. Barlow and also because she could be home to meet her children as we arrived from school. In addition, she could spend more time with the younger ones. She also resumed some of the various social and cultural activities in which she had been involved prior to our temporary move to Atlanta. She had little time, indeed, for social or recreational activities while living with our grandmother in Atlanta.

At this time mother decided that it would be necessary to move my sister Minnie from our home. She had made some inquiries and had come to the conclusion that a home and a school for young black girls would be the best place for my sister so that she could receive the proper attention, education and care. There was consternation in our home at that unwelcomed news. Minnie was very upset and so were the rest of us. But we found, on the basis of our discussion with our mother, that she felt there was no other alternative. The decision was therefore reluctantly accepted by the boys.

Mother was not greatly concerned regarding the welfare of her sons, but felt that the situation was different with girls. She always said that boys could get along, but girls needed more protection. She felt that under the circumstances, she could not adequately provide that protection. However, we were not really aware of how strongly Minnie felt about this move. There were of course some advantages for my sister and my mother. There was no way my mother could have afforded the care and attention which my sister could receive at the Chadwick Home and School in Atlanta. It was located adjacent to Spelman College and provided a variety of services, programs and opportunities which my mother could never have afforded. In many respects it was a stroke of luck that this opportunity arrived at a time of great need. I know for certain that my mother was very pleased and relieved for the opportunity for Minnie to be placed in the Chadwick School.

The result was that Minnie and other young black girls received the very best education available for blacks in the southern states including primary education at the Chadwick Home and School and high school at the Atlanta University School. Later Minnie was enroled in Spelman College, one of the best black colleges in the country, where she completed her BA degree in home economics. Spelman College, like many other colleges in the South, was completely segregated and only admitted young black female students. Its teaching staff, however, was composed of black and white teachers.

The Chadwick Home and School, by any measure, was an unusual institution. Miss Chadwick, a middle aged white woman, had arrived from England several years earlier and had established this school for young orphan black girls or those whose single parent was unable to pay for their education. In some cases, the children were only half orphans, as was Minnie. The school admitted children as young as five and up to 15 years of age who enjoyed a wide range of educational programs beginning at kindergarten and preparing them for college or university. She appeared to have strong connections with people of considerable wealth and had very little difficulty in raising the necessary funds for the operation of her boarding school. She was determined to provide the very best possible care for the children who lived at the home and attended the school.

Miss Chadwick was very warm and supportive of my situation. She realized that I was without a father and was under a great deal of pressure not only in school but also in having to work outside the home. She understood that I had to provide some support for my family. Often when I visited Minnie, Miss Chadwick came into the room to chat for several minutes. I got the impression that she rather liked me either because I was the brother of Minnie or because she thought I was a nice person. The result was that she often gave me a degree of support and encouragement. Several years later when I was attending Tuskegee Institute in Alabama, Miss Chadwick, on occasion, sent varying sums of money to me. I found this very unusual since I was not under her care.

My visits to the school were welcomed not only by Minnie but also by many of the other girls. It seemed to me that girls, living in isolation, had more than the usual curiosity about boys. I was often the centre of attention when I visited Minnie and could often look through the windows or the doors and see young girls observing me with great curiosity. I was told that many of these young girls had no brothers or any other male member of their family to whom they could relate. Personally I was flattered by their attention but had no great interest in girls at that time of my life. Nevertheless, I always enjoyed the visits when Minnie was attending high school, and still later, when she was enroled in Spelman College. By that time, the girls in the home were receiving more of my interest and admiration!

In the meantime the family was changing. We boys who had been left at home were developing physically, socially and educationally. We had much support from Uncle Pheneas and Aunt Maria. He, almost single handedly, had built the little house in East Point and Aunt Maria and their daughter Annie Mae often invited us to visit or have meals with them. These visits were always great occasions and we thoroughly enjoyed our relationship with our uncle, aunt and cousin Annie Mae. Of special interest to me were our occasional debates on religious issues. My uncle loved a debate, and I found myself being gradually drawn into these exciting events. It was during these conversations that I first developed my interest in discussions of a wide variety of public issues.

I obtained my first job in East Point shortly after returning from Atlanta. I was hired at a drug store as a part-time delivery boy. The other delivery boys were not attending school and could work full time. Riding a bike and delivering packages was not particularly hard work as there were varying periods of time between trips. The real difficulty was in having to get up early in the morning, go to school, work from 4:00 p.m. to 10:00 p.m., then go home with little time for study or doing homework.

It was at this time that I entered into debt for the first time. I had to buy a bicycle in order to obtain the job. My mother had to sign an agreement to make the necessary payments for me because I was only twelve years of age at that time. She signed and I bought a bright new shiny red Cherokee bicycle. "Cherokee" was the name of an Indian nation who had lived in Georgia but had been driven out across the plains into what is now the state of Oklahoma by the United States army in the early 19th century. The army embarked upon a systematic pattern of seizing native lands and driving the natives westward so the land would be available to European settlers. It is difficult to comprehend the brutality and cruelty of this seizure of the land of helpless people. Natives had lived on the land for thousands of years and to be forcibly driven out at the point of a gun was a massive denial of basic human rights. This action led to a blatant destruction of the civilization, culture, language and even the lives of thousands of native peoples who were forced into inadequate 'reservations' and have, since the early days, been consistently treated with contempt and hostility. Like the early black slave population, they are a part of my heritage and I identify with their pain and suffering.

I was not aware of those facts at that time. I was simply the proud owner of a beautiful red bicycle. I am not sure what I would have done had I known that part of U.S. history at that time, but the chances are, even though I was only twelve years of age, I would have rejected that bike and bought another. My hostility against racism was beginning to include sympathy for other oppressed people.

The work at the drugstore was fairly pleasant. The owner of the store, was a very nice, tall man who took some interest in me. He treated the three black delivery boys with a certain degree of paternalism, but also with kindness. I was to learn, however, that this kindness could not tolerate any misunderstanding or differences of opinion when expressed by a young black boy.

On one occasion we had a significant difference of opinion. He said that I had taken a package to a home but had not returned the money to him. I informed him that I did not take the package and that another of the delivery boys had taken it and had not yet returned. This response infuriated the doctor. In fact, he became so angry that he suggested that I was lying. I turned to walk away and without warning he approached and tried to kick me. Unfortunately for him when he raised his foot to kick me, I was alert enough to grab his foot before he could deliver the kick. He had to hang on to a table to prevent himself from falling. I dropped his foot and thought this was the end of the incident and turned to leave. Hearing a noise, I looked around and saw one of the clerks jumping over a counter and coming at me with a raised milk bottle. It seemed fairly obvious that he was coming at me with the intention of striking me on the head or body. I ran out of the store, jumped on my bicycle and rode home. My mother was still at work so I sat down and began to think about what happened. She arrived shortly afterwards and heard my account of the incident.

After I had explained the incident, my mother became quite upset and felt that something bad could happen because of my conflict with a white man. She insisted on taking me by the hand and we walked back down to the drug store to have a little chat with him. My mother approached him, told him that she was my mother and wanted to discuss the incident which had just occurred. He was still pretty angry. However he did sit down while my mother stood and tried to explain that she would make certain that such incidents would not happen in the future. Following that discussion, he "cooled down" and they both agreed that the situation had been cleared up and therefore considered closed. I was to return to work the next day as usual.

On our walk back home my mother made it clear that she was concerned about two major problems. The first difficulty was that I was trying to go to school while holding a job that began immediately after school and ended at ten o'clock at night. I also worked on some weekends. That job earned for me four and a half to five dollars per week. The amount varied because we were paid by the number of packages we delivered. We often delivered as many as five or six packages per trip. The result was that the more packages one could deliver, the more money one earned. I was at a disadvantage under this arrangement, simply because I was attending school full time and therefore could not work as long hours as my colleagues. Nevertheless, the money that I made in the late 1920s and early 1930s provided a considerable degree of financial support to the family.

Her second concern was the incident itself. She had already learned that I would not accept mistreatment from anyone and was afraid for my safety in contacts with southern whites. I could not assure her on that matter, but agreed to further talks.

On the morning following my incident with the drugstore owner, my mother went off to work assuring me that it was important for me to report for work. I looked at her and smiled as she went off to work. Shortly thereafter, I went off to school. At three thirty that afternoon I got on my bike and rode down to the drugstore. I hopped off my bike, went into the drug store, took off my bag and handed it to the owner who happened to be present. I said "I'm quitting" and walked out. Then I got back on my bike, rode home and waited for my mother to arrive.

I told her what I had done and sat back expecting her to give me a real "tongue lashing". Strangely enough, however, she did not and I remember her as looking at me and saying, "I guess you are simply one of those people who has a stubborn streak about you, and will not take any gab from anybody". I nodded and smiled at her and she smiled at me. That was the end of one incident of which I was to face more in a variety of situations during subsequent years.

Her concern about my school work was only a minor problem as I was doing quite well in school. I was still a voracious reader and read most of the time whether at home or sometimes when there was nothing to do at work. My reading on the job, however, was not very well appreciated. It was very obvious that some customers who came to the store did not appreciate seeing a black boy reading a book. It was not considered appropriate for blacks to get an education. Fortunately I did not suffer too much from this attitude because I was between grade six and seven at that time. My reading in my spare time was not considered a serious problem at least during my young adolescent years, but it was obvious that some people including some blacks felt that I should not be at school at all. In their view I should be working full time as were many other young blacks who had dropped out of school. My mother did not share these views. She always insisted that a good education was necessary and would often say, "people can rob you of money, but nobody can rob you of an education". I always felt strongly supported even when we needed every dollar of income we could earn.

There was little or no discussion of politics or other social issues in my home during my pre-adolescence and adolescent years. The major characteristic of southern politics at that time was its one party "lily white" nature. The term "lily white" referred to the fact that blacks were not permitted any role in the political processes of the South. (I cannot recall ever hearing any discussion of politics by my father or mother). The Democratic Party had lost the Civil War, but it was in virtually total control of political power in the southern states.

It was only after I took the position of delivery boy and worked in downtown East Point that I heard extensive discussion of party politics. My family, like many others, had heard with dismay, and even some amusement, the rhetoric of southern politicians running for office. We listened to candidates for governor of the state explaining how they could do more than their opponents to keep "nigras in their place". (They were a bit too polite to call us "niggers" on the radio). The beginning of my political education began during the 1928 campaign between Al Smith, the Catholic Democratic Party candidate, and Herbert Hoover, the Republican candidate. That was a difficult choice for southern democrats since they hated Catholics but found it equally difficult to support a republican. As a result Hoover was the first republican in more than sixty years to receive a substantial number of southern votes. I had previously paid little or no attention to these issues, but it was my first opportunity to hear political debate and I eagerly listened at every opportunity. Most of this debate, however, was insignificant to those of us in the black community. As far as we were concerned, it did not matter which candidate won. It would make absolutely no difference to our status as exploited blacks in the racist southern states. That was the first occasion I had opportunity to learn that many southern whites not only hated blacks but white Catholics as well!

Although an extensive reader, I encountered no stories of strong, brave and successful black men or women. The few stories of blacks which did appear focused on images of black inferiority. The picture of a shuffling black with downcast eyes, bowed head, saying "yessir boss" or "nosir boss" to everything said by a white person, was simply a story of black submission, popular with most southern whites. "Minstrel shows" usually focused on presentations of this distorted picture of blacks, but always portrayed by white men with blackened faces. One would never have gathered that there were men like Booker T. Washington, Marcus Garvey, W.E.B. DuBois, and Frederick Douglass or women like Harriet Tubman, Marian Anderson and others who had made a name for themselves as heroes of the black communities who had led the struggle against white oppression. Tubman was one of the great leaders of the "Underground Railroad", a secret method of helping slaves escape to freedom in Canada. She is reported to have made at least nineteen trips to the South and helped hundreds of slaves to escape. Had she been caught, in all probability, she would have been lynched. These stories, of course, were never told in school textbooks. It was very clear that the white community who controlled the schools preferred to see blacks in inferior positions so that their exploitation could be justified.

My next job also involved working after school. I worked at a restaurant owned by a white individual and with a staff of four or five white waitresses and waiters. My job was to wash dishes. Following the dinner hour, however, when the cook had left and when there were very few customers in the restaurant, I also served as a "short order" cook. My sandwiches were very popular and I had no problems as a dishwasher and as a cook. The low status of these jobs made them quite acceptable and appropriate for blacks, at least in the eyes of southern whites.

The accepted place of blacks was brought sharply to my attention by an incident during that period. I had been visiting downtown and on my way home saw a young white girl walking out of her home on a pair of crutches. As she walked down the steps to the sidewalk, she stumbled and fell. I was only about five or ten feet from her at that time so I stopped to help her get to her feet. Shortly after I looked around and noticed that a group of people were gathered around and staring at me. I wasn't sure what was the problem, but I walked away and continued on my way home. I went home and told my Uncle Pheneas about the incident and was very surprised when he looked at me with great horror. I can never forget the statement he made at that time. It was something like this "Don't you ever touch a white girl again. If she falls down let her stay there, but don't put your hands on her". That was particularly surprising because I had thought of myself as performing a humanitarian task. I was helping someone who was crippled, on crutches and had fallen and simply needed a helping hand to get back on her feet. It never occurred to me that this was considered a "no-no" situation. I learned later that it was definitely that. The reaction of my uncle made it appear as if I had committed a heinous crime. I was more angry at him than at the hostile crowd. From that point onward I vowed that I would never do anything to help a southern white person regardless of the situation, even if the individual was drowning or in some other great danger. That philosophy remained a part of my attitude for many years.

I was growing up and entering the final year at the Fulton County public school. The attention of my friends, and particularly Forrest Green, was becoming more and more focused on the girls in our classes. Forrest became known as a "ladies' man", a distinction which did not interest me in the slightest. One young girl had made an attempt to interest me in "going steady", but without success. My interest in girls developed more slowly. However, I could not escape the constant discussion of girls around me, and especially that of the older boys. Much of this discussion was of a sexual nature and focused on their "conquests". Many of us recognized that much, if not all of this, was simply boasting for the purpose of impressing us. The older boys were, in my view, merely "braggarts". Nevertheless, their constant talk of their exploits slowly began to turn my attention to girls in a different way. But I was too much involved in sports, reading, work and other activities to have time for girls. That focus would only change several years later, near the end of my high school career.

The older boys in my school, and in the community, were vitally concerned with their appearance. Clothes were a major focus of the usual interplay of groups of teenagers. It was extremely important to be "in style". Great emphasis was placed on wearing highly polished shoes, and the latest fashions in trousers and jackets. One had to buy trousers with 22-inch cuffs, and these had to be three inches in depth. It was also important for hair to be cut in precisely the fashionable manner. As a result of my mixed ancestry, I had what was labelled as "good hair", meaning that it was relatively straight, and somewhat similar to that of whites but I was always embarrassed at references to "good" and "bad" hair. Obviously most blacks had inherited their curly or "bad" hair but every effort was made by some young boys and even some men to straighten their hair so that it would look like mine. I sensed that this was a negative and self destructive attitude because it belittled and denigrated themselves and their own racial characteristics. I was always uncomfortable with this attitude and behaviour and usually departed from these discussions at the earliest possible moment.

It was also during this period that my friends, Charlie, Forrest and I returned to our former interest in sports. We organized and played "sandlot" baseball games, simply because there were no organized teams or regular fields on which to play in East Point. We made our own equipment, including our gloves and our bats. We went to great effort to trim a piece of two by four wood into the shape of a baseball bat. We often laid out some approximation of a baseball field for ourselves. We didn't even know the dimensions of a baseball field at that time but we built our baseball diamond on the available land, often on some vacant lot or uncultivated field.

A method of choosing teams was developed with each captain on a rotating basis, selecting whom he thought would be best for his team. The result was that often teams played games which ended with very close scores with no team being overwhelmingly superior to the other. There was one "no-no" however: baseball and other sports were not permitted on Sundays. In a very strongly religious neighbourhood dominated by both the Methodist and Baptist churches, it was simply impossible for anyone to get up the nerve to defy this religious restriction. We were expected to attend Sunday school every Sunday morning, church for the regular semi-monthly Sunday morning service and occasionally an afternoon young people's service.

There were other activities in the general community which we could not attend or participate in for different reasons. Among these were polo played on horseback. At the Fort McPherson military base, located between East Point and the city of Atlanta, we often watched the army officers playing. I had never seen polo before and I have rarely seen the game played since those adolescent years. But it was great fun to watch white army officers riding their horses and playing the exciting game. We never observed black officers playing polo because the U.S. military was segregated and at the time had no black officers. The one time a black person could get involved in polo was when the horses were ridden until exhausted and had to be walked until they cooled off, a task performed by a black man. He was the only black person I ever saw inside the confines of Fort McPherson.

Another of our recreational activities was to travel to Atlanta and watch football games played by Georgia "Tech", an institution which no black at that time could ever aspire to attend. The football games were played in a stadium, a part of whose fences were of wire. We could sit on the ground or stand outside the stadium, peer through the holes in the wire fence and watch football being played without ever having gone inside the stadium. It also did not cost any money! For us it was important that the white people had to pay to see the game while we saw it free of charge! We were pleased that we could get the "better of the deal" on at least a few occasions!

There were other strange relationships between blacks and whites in the U.S. South. Remaining in our commonly accepted place in society, we were often welcomed and could even engage in a certain amount of bantering with the white population. These activities had their limits and it was important that we knew exactly what those limits were. Perhaps one of the most negative aspects of that relationship was that blacks often behaved as models of the behaviour which they knew white people expected of them. There were activities in which we could participate and in which white people would express some degree of indulgence and amusement. Occasionally, a group of black boys were told to go and fight each other in what was called a "round robin". A group of eight or ten boys were put into a squared circle surrounded by cheering beer-drinking men anxious to see black boys "go in there and slaughter each other". These men wanted to see blood. After others had been eliminated, the two finalists would fight for a period of two or three rounds with the winner getting a very small prize of perhaps two to five dollars. The losers received nothing.

I attended one such event. Before entering the room I had decided that I would not participate in what I considered as a stupid and demeaning activity. My friends could not understand and I could not tell them but I was quite aware that I was not going to participate. I was not going to make a fool of myself for the enjoyment of a group of half-drunk white men. During the course of the fighting many of the whites made remarks which completely "turned me off". Shouts such as "Did you see that nigger slug that other nigger on the mouth?" or "That big nigger over there is going to be the winner. He's going to knock out all the little niggers." By this time the crowd was howling for action and it became apparent that the fight must go on. The usual rules of boxing were ignored: every one of the eight or nine boys was trying to win regardless of ordinary fairness and sportsmanship. Boys were struck from behind, below the "belts" and other violations were committed, much to the amusement of the rowdy crowd. Finally all except two of the boys had been eliminated and the two finalists then had to fight for the prize. By that time I had walked out of the room in total disgust. I later learned that the biggest boy in the ring had won, an entirely expected result. The crowd, however, was not satisfied; it had not seen an adequate flow of blood and wanted more. Better judgements prevailed, however, and the boys were permitted to leave unmolested. That encounter was a perfect example of brutality masquerading as sport and amusement. It was also an example of the exploitation of a vulnerable group by oppressors, again a not unusual phenomenon by those with power and control over the lives and behaviour of others.

There were very few role models in our lives. Aside from the leaders of the big bands, Duke Ellington, Cab Calloway, Benny Goodman and others, there were very few people we could aspire to emulate. Of the two important people whom we admired, one was the minister of the Baptist church, and the other was Mrs. Maxey, the principal of our school. In our younger days we had admired prize fighters such as Tiger Flowers, who at one time had been middleweight boxing champion of the world. Somewhat later, Joe Louis, a new hero emerged. He was beginning his career which was to lead eventually to becoming the heavyweight boxing champion. My friends and I eagerly listened on the radio to his fights since we did not have television at that time: radio was our medium of cheering for our heros. We were very anguished on one occasion when Joe Louis himself was knocked out by a German challenger who then became champion for the next year or so. The German leader, Adolf Hitler, a believer in the assumed superiority of whites, cheered the victory of his countryman over the black American.

Subsequently, another fight was arranged and Joe Louis knocked his opponent out in the second round and regained his title. This event was considered a great defeat for Adolf Hitler and his theory of white supremacy. A year or two later, the Olympic games were held in Berlin. Hitler was in the stands watching the events. Jesse Owens, the great black sprinter, won the unprecedented number of four gold medals. Hitler, finding it impossible to watch a black man win these events, rose and walked out of the stands to the booing of many of the athletes and spectators. It was great to see the defeat of Hitler's protégés by Jesse Owens. These victories were important to me simply because we had so few role models. Self-esteem required some tangible results and the victories of blacks provided that ingredient.

It was during that period of joyful and carefree existence that our family experienced what could have been a shocking disruption in our lives. We had survived the death of our father extremely well but we were not ready for the disappearance of my brother Glenn. My mother, Frank and I went to bed thinking that perhaps he was staying out late with friends but we discovered the next morning that he had not returned and apparently had run away from home. That possibility became a reality when we had heard nothing from him for several days. Our first news came when we received a letter from a well-known Baptist minister who lived in Savannah, Georgia, a distance of approximately 250 miles from Atlanta. The Rev. M. L. Glenn, the man whom my parents greatly admired and in whose honour they had named my brother, wrote to us that the runaway was temporarily staying at his home. He had planned that Glenn would be returned to us shortly. The minister then bought a train ticket and dispatched Glenn back to our home in East Point. We were extremely pleased to have him back home. Although sharply questioned by my mother, we could not obtain a credible answer to why he had run away. My mother in her anger and frustration struck him a few times but this did not change his refusal to respond to questions. The matter was finally dropped, although reluctantly.

By that time, my friends Forrest, Charlie and I had graduated from public school but none of us felt the graduation exercises were of great significance. It was eventful only in that for some of us it marked a transition in our lives. Many black youth would go no further in their formal educational attainment and would seek employment as unskilled workers in acceptable jobs such as labourers and restaurant workers. I hoped that phase of my life was now behind me. The higher educational phase was only beginning to open into new, broader and more exciting areas of exploration.

The pre-adolescent phase of my life was also rapidly drawing to a close. I was ready to become a high school student, a status attained by only a relatively few of my public school classmates. However, I entered that stage with a degree of trepidation. My friends and I were lucky to find jobs that summer since there was no way that my mother could have paid even the small cost of bus fares and lunches or of books and other school materials. Attending the nearby Russell High School could have saved us most of those expenses but that school was still restricted to whites only.

Our evaluations of the financial resources of the Green and Head families made it increasingly clear that it would be necessary for us to make a choice regarding full or part-time education in the next year. The dream of entering the Washington High School on a full-time basis was recognized by the Green's and by my family as unrealistic, leaving full-time work and part-time study as the only logical choice. The David T. Howard Junior High School was the only part-time program available to us. It was also the only evening program available to black students in Atlanta. We anticipated no problems in enroling in that program but the next task was to find full-time jobs and to save as much of our earnings as possible.

Our jobs were located in downtown Atlanta and, as in previous jobs, this one also involved work in a restaurant. Our jobs required selling cokes and other cold drinks to men working in crowded and noisy factories and office buildings. Charlie and I worked from 9 a.m. to 5 p.m. after which we picked up a quick snack, usually a sandwich or hamburger, and then were off to the Howard Junior High School. A streetcar carried us to the centre of the city and then we transferred to another streetcar which took us out to the junior high school, an evening school designed primarily for adult school dropouts.

That experience was not one of the more pleasant episodes of my life. The schoolwork was of a very low standard; the teachers were poorly trained, poorly motivated, classes were overcrowded, and the resources in classrooms were quite inadequate. In addition, students were generally tired from having worked all day. The result was that we were tired, bored and could not receive a satisfactory educational experience. Classes began at 6 p.m. and continued until 9 p.m. By

7:30 we found ourselves looking at the clock and wishing the class period would soon be over so we could go home.

After school we were often given rides home with Mr. Green avoiding the necessity of having to take streetcars and busses to get back home by 10:00 p.m. or later. In addition we avoided the humiliation of being forced to ride at the back of streetcars and buses.

All facilities, public or private, operated under strict segregation (Jim Crow) laws. Black passengers had to stand aside and wait until all white passengers entered the streetcar or bus. After all white passengers were on board, black passengers could enter at the front, push their way through the white passengers to the back of the bus where they could be seated, that is, provided there were still seats available. In many instances the white passengers would have taken all the seats from the front to the back. In those instances, blacks had no alternative except to remain standing. These patterns of racial segregation were enforced by state legislation in all southern states. It was extremely humiliating to all blacks, and certainly to those who were sensitive to the lack of elementary justice and fairness in the southern states. I was one of the sensitive ones and probably suffered more than most! This pattern of racial segregation continued until the Montgomery bus boycott occurred in the 1950s, an event which eventually led to the outlawing of segregation on buses and other forms of public transportation by the Supreme Court of the United States. The phenomenon of racial segregation was probably the most important and demeaning aspect of my life in the South. Travelling back and forth to school on segregated buses and streetcars evoked more anger and frustration than the inadequacy of the school system itself.

I can say without reservation that the experience at the Howard Junior High School was the least satisfactory I had ever experienced in my school career. Neither teachers nor students liked the school and the result was low morale and a very poor educational experience. Although I do not have access to the grades I earned during my year at the Howard Junior high school, I suspect they were only in the medium range. I particularly recall the poor instruction in algebra, a subject which was completely new to me. I had never had the experience of dealing with numbers and letters in the same equations and initially found it quite confusing. Like many other students, I tried to ignore the confusion and restlessness in the classrooms and it is understandable that our grades were not as high as we would have liked. The atmosphere of the school generally did not provide for the motivation I needed to engage myself in serious study. The result was that I was not particularly concerned and did not bother to examine my report card when it arrived in the mail for the perusal of my mother.

Charlie, Forrest, and I had already made arrangements to work full time during the summer months because we needed to earn as much money as possible so we could attend the senior high school on a full-time basis. I had accepted a job working in another restaurant. This job was obtained through the help of a friend of my mother and, as usual, my duties included washing dishes, serving customers and performing other tasks as required. Most blacks expected some racial incident to occur during the course of working with whites. I feared, almost daily, that some incident would occur and I would react strongly and quit the job. However, harmony prevailed and everything went well. The major reason for this exceptional situation was that all kitchen employees were black and did not have to associate with the white staff. Another reason was that all staff members at that level were young adolescents and dealt only indirectly with white adults. At no time did we ever have the opportunity to work with white youth and to learn of our common interests in sports, music and other activities. A major purpose of the pattern of segregation of the races was to ensure that this learning never had the opportunity to occur.

I resigned from that job in late August of the year and enroled in the Booker T. Washington high school in early September and thus began a new era of my educational and social life.

In retrospect my early childhood and pre-adolescent years were generally happy and contented. I did not have serious problems with my family although from time to time there were some minor problems as one would expect, particularly since I was the oldest of five children. School and community life were generally positive and pleasant as well. The few negative experiences in my life were minimal and occurred infrequently.

My relationship with the white community was quite different. It was irrational and unpredictable and one could never be sure of how one stood. The key to avoiding this unpredictability was the knowledge and acceptance of one's inferior social position in southern society. A black individual could get along very well with the white community if this position was accepted. It was clear that I did not always accept that status very well and therefore I often found myself in some difficulty with white people. It is obvious to me now that a game of mutual deception was played between members of the black and white groups. In general the blacks, occupying a subordinate position, usually gave the appearance of being happy, joyful, and glad to be in contact with white people. The white individual perceiving this apparent acceptance of subordination, felt that all was well and that the relationship between the two could continue.

I could not play this game very well and did not attempt to do so. I never had the experience of feeling subordinate to white people and made no attempt to conceal this attitude. I attribute the development of these attitudes largely to my mother since her constant refrain was that we had to be twice as good as whites if we were to succeed in life. While I never believed that I was twice as good, I most certainly believed that I was equally as good as anyone of any race or colour. My refusal to play that game became a characteristic of my life and experiences as I moved from adolescence to young adulthood and later phases of my life experiences.

The political scene was in turmoil as the emerging National Association for the Advancement of Colored People (NAACP) had begun its legal attack on specific instances of racial discrimination in the southern states. Whether by design or by coincidence, intimidation and harassment against blacks were becoming more frequent and widely publicized. While living in a suburban section of an urban area gave us some protection (I don't recall a single lynching in Atlanta at the time), we were keenly aware that as many as 30 to 50 blacks were lynched annually in the southern United States. While I have no recollection of discussions of these facts by my mother or my peers, there is no doubt that they had a chilling effect on our sense of psychological and physical security. After all, we had to live in this climate every day of our lives and we were aware that no redress was possible for an attack on us. We were vulnerable and our parents and community could offer us little or no protection.

CHAPTER 3 *Aspects of Survival in a Hostile Land*

Education
The Booker T. Washington high school was located in Atlanta in the foothills of the Piedmount mountains. The population of the city at that time was estimated at 250,000 to 300,000 with about 25 percent being black. The city was approximately 1000 feet above sea level which gave it a generally moderate climate and environment. The city prided itself as one of the most progressive southern cities and often called itself the "New York of the South". Many important businesses and commercial firms established headquarters in Atlanta when they moved from larger cities in the middle Atlantic and New England states. The city could boast that three outstanding white universities, the Georgia Institute of Technology, Emory University and Agnes Scott College (an all-white girls school), were located within or near its boundaries. All southern schools were totally segregated as a result of the notorious Jim Crow laws.

Atlanta also contained five post-secondary institutions serving the black community. Among these were Atlanta University, Morehouse, Morris Brown, Clark and Spelman Colleges. Spelman College, like many other schools established in the South after the American Civil War, was organized by white northerners who came south and lent their energies and skills to the improvement of the educational status of ex-slaves and their children. The fact that five all-black institutions of higher education were located in Atlanta was a unique phenomenon since most U.S. cities had none.

The black community of Atlanta was also unique in several respects. It had two thriving black business areas, one Auburn Ave., on the East side, and the other, Hunter St., on the west side of the city. The father of one of my best friends owned a jewellery store on one of these centres of black enterprise. At least two insurance companies, several restaurants, a variety of other businesses and a chain of drugstores were owned by blacks. A small professional class of doctors, dentists, college professors, a few lawyers and other professionals also existed. In addition, the first black daily newspaper, the *Atlanta Daily World* was established during the 1930s and remains in operation as of this writing.

These and others were a result of the ghettoization of the black population. As noted earlier the entire South as well as some parts of the northern United States were dominated by a pattern of racial prejudice and discrimination and many blacks took advantage of this phenomenon. Black business men and women, in the absence of competition from the dominant white community, were able to establish their own businesses, social and civic clubs, churches, schools and other organizations. This development gave employment to black professionals and some black workers. Few black businesses, however successful, employed any sizable number of blacks. For the most part blacks in Atlanta obtained their employment in the larger white society. Only on one occasion was I employed by a black business (the Atlanta Life Insurance Company). If "necessity is the mother of invention", many blacks clearly took advantage of this situation to create a more livable city than in most other parts of the American South or, for that matter, even in the North.

These success stories should not cloud the fact that most blacks in Atlanta lived in varying degrees of poverty. Most worked in unskilled and low-income jobs; very few moderate income jobs were available for individuals without some degree of college education. Overall hung the cloud of racial segregation and discrimination; a cloud which existed irrespective of status, education or ability of blacks in the U.S.

The school I was to attend in the fall was named after the famous black educator Booker T. Washington who was born a slave and was freed at the end of the Civil War. Later he graduated from the Hampton Institute in Virginia in the 1870s. The principal of Hampton Institute recommended Washington to go to Tuskegee, a small town in Alabama, and found a new school for young black people. Washington later made an outstanding reputation as an educator and leader on the national level. The Booker T. Washington High School was basically an academic high school for grades seven through twelve.

I overcame my initial shyness and immediately plunged into the various activities of the school. I joined the staff of the 10th grade newspaper and when the previous editor resigned during the year, I became editor. I was also involved in other grade 10 activities, including the biology and the history clubs. My achievement in the social sciences was not unusual as I had previously achieved success in these areas. What was unusual for me was that I found the physical sciences as attractive as the social sciences, excelling in biology, chemistry and physics. In fact, my most popular teachers at the end of the 10th and 11th grades were biology and chemistry teachers. In the 12th grade, it was the vice principal of the school who also taught physics.

Mr. Harper, the principal of the school, was a very unusual individual. Living in the Deep South and under the supervision of an all-white board of education and all-white school administrators, he had no hesitation to speak his mind on any subject relating to the education of black youth. Often when visitors came to the school, he would take the occasion to clearly indicate his very strong dislike of the segregated system. At graduation exercises when the superintendents and other top administrators were present, Mr. Harper usually addressed parents and students expressing his distaste for the segregated educational program and the lack of adequate funds and opportunities available to black youth.

I wondered how he managed to maintain his position given the fact that he was attacking the conventional southern system of racial segregation and discrimination. He was attacking a system which was strongly supported by his employers, the Atlanta Board of Education! I still have tremendous respect for the courage of that man.

One of the highlights of my high school experiences was my relationship to the teacher of civics (government) and history. This man was totally committed to the welfare of his students. He introduced us to many aspects of subjects that were not included in the curriculum. For example, he felt that the best way for students to learn politics was to engage in a simulated political election. Campaigns were structured for the whole school to elect a student council. Each class chose candidates for various offices who campaigned precisely as they would in a regular political election. I joined and worked for the candidate of the independent party. We campaigned for about three or four weeks with rallies, visits to classes, placards, and leaflets. On election day, we had a large outside rally in which the candidates spoke to the entire student body. The election was held shortly after the rally and students returned to their classes to cast their ballots. Results were announced at the end of the day. To my disappointment, our candidate had lost. The candidate who won was a very handsome and popular young senior student who made an impression based upon his ability to speak persuasively and in a very dramatic manner. It appeared that most of the girls voted for him! The election campaign was a tremendous learning opportunity and gave us much better insights into the dynamics of political behaviour than anything we could have learned from textbooks.

On the other side of the ledger was the geometry teacher. Mr. Davis, small in size, very quiet, unassuming and subdued in manner, was almost the laughing stock of his classes. He had a very strange habit of demonstrating a geometrical problem on the blackboard in front of the class and then emphatically saying "Q.E.D". Q.E.D. is the Latin term meaning "that which has been demonstrated". Mr. Davis was a man who demonstrated very little commitment or interest in students during the time we were in his classes. However, two or three years after I graduated from the school, Mr. Davies filed a complaint of racial discrimination against the board of education. Black teachers with the same level of experience and educational qualifications received less than two-thirds of the salary received by white teachers. There was no other explanation for this pattern other than discrimination based on race and colour.

By filing his complaint in the federal courts, Mr. Davis was challenging the system and as a result he was immediately fired. Filing a suit on the basis of discrimination was totally unprecedented in the South at that time and particularly in the Atlanta school system. Very few people expected Mr. Davis to win his case and none expected that he would be rehired even if he won. Much to our astonishment he did win his case and forced the board of education to give the same pay to blacks as they gave to white teachers with the same experience and educational qualifications. But as expected, he was not rehired. That was a magnificent victory and the first of its kind in the Deep South. Our former geometry teacher was one of the many unsung heros of the pre-civil right movements in the Deep South who made his move long before Rosa Park initiated the Montgomery bus boycott by her refusal to go to the back of a bus. Mr. Davis was a martyr to a noble cause.

My closest and most valuable friend among the faculty was Dr. Neal, my chemistry teacher and a part-time faculty member who also worked as a pharmacist at a local black-owned drug store. Asa, Jimmy and I used to stop by the drug store for chats with him during his free periods. Dr. Neal obviously enjoyed his interaction with students. I was one of his favourites and consequently he paid more attention to my progress in his classes than to some others. This situation had both positive and negative aspects. It was positive in the sense that I had the opportunity to talk to him outside of classes and occasionally get knowledge and insights which other students did not receive. The negative aspect was that this type of relationship sometimes gave the impression that I was the "teacher's pet" with all of the connotations involved in that situation.

As in my relationships in some other classes, particularly in history, I was often called upon by Dr. Neal to stand before the class and answer questions, especially when visitors, including the principal, were present. I remember very vividly one occasion when a visitor came into the room and Dr. Neal called on me to go to the blackboard and began to call out the names of chemicals and asked me to write the formulae for each. I was expected to write the proper formula and wait until he called out the next. I had expected him to call perhaps four or five chemicals and then permit me to return to my seat. However, he did not stop there and the process ended when I had written probably thirty to forty different formulae on the blackboard.

I did not know whether I had written some incorrect answers but I was satisfied that perhaps 80 to 90 percent were correct. Later I asked him if I had made any mistakes. He smiled and refused to answer. The smile, I thought, suggested that he was satisfied with what I had done even though perhaps I had made a few mistakes.

Relationships with Students

In general I had a very happy experience at the Washington High School. My relationship with fellow students and with faculty members was probably better than it had ever been in public school or at the junior high school. Asa, Jimmy and I were almost always together and we formed what was called the "big three". In many respects our activities were complementary because we had some different skills. Asa was extremely good in science and mathematics and often helped Jimmy and me with mathematical problems. Unfortunately we became perhaps a little too dependent on him and did not put as much effort in trying to understand algebraic problems as we might otherwise have done. Nevertheless our relationship was a matter of mutual interest and friendship. We could and did support and supplement the skills of each other.

Two significant events occurred in the 11th grade. Jimmy became deeply involved in a very intense relationship with a young ninth grade girl. They wrote letters every day, saw each other at recess, at lunchhour and at the end of the school day. Although this relationship did not break up our "threesome", it did, however, result in some minor changes. Both Asa and I felt that Jimmy's schoolwork might suffer because of this heavy involvement. Jimmy of course did not agree. On occasion he would speak to us about the relationship as he was not quite sure how he should behave and handle himself. On one occasion he related that he was driving his girlfriend in his aunt's car and he was stopped by two police who questioned him at great lengths as to what he was doing and why was he out in this car. Apparently the police thought he might have stolen the car. Jimmy, like many southern blacks, was of very light complexion and the police may have assumed he was a white man with a black girl. They would not have approved of that! He was finally permitted to leave but the incident left him angry and confused. They could have dragged him out of the car, savagely beaten him and nothing could have been done.

Jimmy's relationship, like most with high school students particularly as young as the ninth grade, did not last for very long. One could hypothesize that the "more intense the experience, the more likely the flames will burn out in a very short time". Jimmy was heartbroken when the affair ended but recovered very quickly.

The second significant event in the lives of the three of us occurred in relationship to a girl student and me. Jimmy, Asa and I had shared a locker in the school building for perhaps three or four months when I returned from class one day and found that a fourth person was also sharing the locker. Maxine, an attractive young woman, had approached Jimmy and Asa asking for permission to use our locker. That of course made the locker very crowded. I questioned them about this new situation only to learn that Maxine had shown an interest in me and thought that by putting her things in our locker, the two of us might be together more frequently and a romantic relationship would develop between us. I had known Maxine in other classes but had not considered her a particularly close friend. I had made no effort to develop any special relationship with her. Moreover, I did not welcome this move but was uncertain how it should be handled. In the meantime both Asa and Jimmy made no attempt to help solve the problem. Like many boys at that age I was teased unmercifully by my friends because of my attitude toward this young woman. There was no question that she was very attractive but many of us thought she wore too much makeup. Much of the teasing was based on this fact and my friends would often say that it would be nice to know what she really looked like. Of course this did not help my decision-making in the matter. Finally she must have decided that the attempt to develop a romantic relationship with me was not getting anywhere.

One afternoon when I returned to the locker her books and other articles had been moved. I felt somewhat sorry about this because she was a very nice person and I would have liked to have some kind of relationship with her but not at the level she apparently would have preferred. Under the pressure of incessant teasing by my friends I was simply not willing to develop that kind of relationship. The result was a complete termination of our tenuous relationship and although we were classmates, I cannot remember even a casual conversation with Maxine after she moved out of our locker.

In the 11th grade I met Eva, a young woman who greatly impressed me. I had seen her at bus stops as we waited downtown to transfer from a bus to a streetcar. She was always with her friend Ruth and the two seemed to be virtually inseparable. Charlie and Forrest, my friends from East Point, often waited with me for the buses or streetcars. I became strongly attracted to Eva but being somewhat shy and in the company of my friends, I did not make my feelings known to her. Although we became casual friends, I was sure that she never had any idea that I would have liked to have gone much further in developing a personal relationship with her. I also knew that if I had done so, my two friends, Asa and Jimmy, would have again teased me unmercifully. The three of us, with the exception of Jimmy, usually maintained a standoff relationship toward girls. We saw our classmates getting heavily involved but we always stood apart and were probably somewhat afraid to do anything else. That also was reflected in our behaviour during the few times we went to parties and dances sponsored by the school.

We, like many other young boys of our age, would have loved to participate in dances but always found some excuse to avoid the actual activity. I still look back with a great deal of amusement at the number of excuses we could make to avoid going out on the floor and asking a girl for a dance. Somehow we always managed to have a sprained ankle, a sore back, a toothache, or some other excuse which suggested that we were unable to participate!

Nevertheless, by the time we reached the 12th grade, we almost always attended social dances. But we were "wallflowers". Occasionally a teacher came and attempted to drag us out on the floor in spite of our objections. What could we do if a teacher asked us to dance? We could not plead illness. We reluctantly agreed and many of our teachers paid a heavy price for their insistence on taking us out on the dance floor. I must have stepped on the toes of at least a half dozen teachers during the 11th grade. The teachers did their job well. We learned to dance and by the time we reached the 12th grade we felt ready to ask any girl in our class for a dance.

Eva did not attend our senior prom. I missed my opportunity to show off my newfound confidence by asking her for a dance. After graduation she attended Spelman College, the college my sister would also later attend. I occasionally saw her when on the Spelman campus visiting my sister. We would meet and have a brief chat but it never went beyond that. My passion had cooled and I doubt that she ever knew how I felt when we were senior high school students.

Many of my extra-curricular activities in high school involved music. I had joined a very unusual harmonica band organized by Graham Jackson, the director of music. Graham was an exceptionally gifted musician. Had he been a white man, he would certainly have risen to the very top levels of musical theory and performance. Mr. Jackson also played at a number of large events sponsored by organizations in the white community including those in which he was the only black person present: no other black was permitted to attend. My friends and I deeply resented the fact that we could not attend concerts in which our teacher and friend was the featured performer. But that situation was not unusual in the South, or even in many northern cities. It was the typical pattern of overt racism.

Another of my special activities involved participation in the Washington high school choir. I had great respect for Mrs. Love, the choir director, who had trained us to sing in two operettas in our final year of high school. I thoroughly enjoyed participation in this choir, although by no means could I have been considered one of its stars. We had a number of good singers, one of whom was of special interest to me. Eloise Long had a very beautiful lyric soprano voice and could sing the very highest notes with great ease. Eloise was a member of my class and graduated with me in the class of 1933. Unfortunately within a year or two of her graduation, she became very ill and eventually died from a rare disease.

By the end of the 10th grade, I had decided that I was going to play an instrument. Prior to that time and even during my public school career, I had toyed with the idea of learning drums, trumpet, coronet or even the piano. However, I had given those ideas up primarily because of a lack of time. Then Graham Jackson asked me if I would be interested in learning to play the violin. I was pleased to be asked by this outstanding musician and, despite some qualms, I agreed to accept the invitation. After my first lesson with Graham Jackson, however, I was not so sure that I wanted to continue. He took me into a small room with one chair and one desk, gave me a violin and a bow and told me my first lesson was to practise bowing. He showed me how to hold the violin and the bow and instructed me on how to draw the bow across the strings. He then said that I should remain in the room for the next hour and practise. Then he left the room while I elicited some terrible noises from that violin.

Over and over again I practised pulling the bow across the strings. Most of the time I could not keep the bow on one string. Graham was not present for most of the time and did not hear the awful sounds I was making. He was lucky but returned to the room about the time I was making up my mind to drop the whole idea. He wanted to hear the sounds I was making. He listened for a few minutes and said, "That's okay for a start. Now come back tomorrow and get in more practice." I went back the next day and practised again. Graham Jackson then suggested that maybe the time would be coming soon that I should buy an instrument of my own so that I could take it home to practice after school and on weekends.

I made fairly rapid progress but I never played in the high school orchestra. By the time I was getting fairly good, I was at the point of graduation and had decided I was going to continue working on this instrument simply because it was a challenge. The violin, in my opinion, is one of the most difficult instruments to play well. Learning to play a guitar or some other stringed instrument would have been much easier than learning to play a violin. I persisted and continued my work on the violin after graduation from the school.

Our school, because of its relationship to the famous Booker T. Washington, attracted a considerable number of outstanding visitors and speakers including university presidents, famous clergymen and politicians. They spoke to either the school assembly or to one of the 12th grade classes. I met such outstanding people as Howard Thurman, dean of the chapel at Howard University in Washington D.C.; Benjamin Mays, then president of Morehouse College; A. Phillip Randolph, an outstanding socialist and president of the Brotherhood of Sleeping Car Porters, an all-black union formed because blacks were not acceptable in white unions; and other outstanding speakers.

From these men and one or two women I learned a great deal about the history of black people in Africa, the United States and the Caribbean. My history teacher made a special effort to ensure that we became acquainted with the literature about blacks and their accomplishments. As a result we read and studied the histories of Frederick Douglass, Langston Hughes, James Weldon Johnson, Marcus Garvey and other famous individuals, organizations and institutions in the various black communities across the country. This teacher went far beyond the bounds of the curriculum to help us learn and appreciate our history and heritage. He felt it was important that black people know their roots and was the first person I had ever met who recognized the importance of black people having some understanding of the legacy of oppression and racism to which they had been subjected during the last three hundred years.

Graduation

Our regular end-of-the-year graduation exercises were a huge event held at the Atlanta Civic Auditorium, which held four to five thousand people and was filled on the night of my graduation. I was pleased that Asa was chosen the valedictorian of the class because he was the top-ranking student in a class of more than 300 graduating students. Again our principal, Mr. Harper, delivered an impassioned speech on the role of black education in southern society. He pointed out that most black people lived in abject poverty in Atlanta and the surrounding areas. He also indicated that increasing numbers of black students were finishing high school and were entering the labour market with skills and abilities. However, because of discrimination and segregation, these skills and abilities were not being fully appreciated. He could not understand why society was willing to educate black youth through high school and often to the college level and, at the same time, was unwilling to make employment opportunities available to them once they had achieved their diplomas or degrees. I was very proud of Mr. Harper on that occasion.

For some reason my mother did not attend my high school graduation exercises and I was quite disappointed. Many of my relatives, friends and even casual acquaintances did make the trip to downtown Atlanta to greet and celebrate with me on this happy occasion. I went home loaded with gifts and best wishes from my friends and neighbours. It had been a great day since I was the first high school graduate in my immediate and extended family and one of the very few from the little town of East Point.

The Scottsboro Case

Scottsboro was a small southern town and the Scottsboro case was a perfect example of the interaction of the two worlds of blacks and whites. That incident involved the plight of seven young black boys who were riding on a freight train during the depression of the 1930s. The seven young black boys were later joined by two white girls. At the end of their trip and as they were leaving the freight car, the two white girls went to the police and said that they had been raped by the seven black boys. This accusation was of course a matter of tremendous concern in the black press. A rape of a white girl by a black man in the South almost automatically meant a death sentence for the black man. The young boys were arrested and taken to jail and the matter slowly came to public attention. After considerable controversy and disturbances in the black community they were tried, convicted and sentenced to death. None of these boys were more than 17 or 18 years of age. The youngest, as I recall, was about 14 years of age.

I read of this event during the last year of my attendance at the Washington High School. It became a matter of great concern and discussion among students and faculty members. We first heard the news of the alleged crime while on our way to a picnic sponsored by the class of 1933, the year of our graduation. Although we had only skimpy information, none of us believed that the boys were guilty — a reflection of our distrust of southern justice. Unfortunately for some reason we initially heard little about it in the Atlanta black community. However, several members of the academic and politically oriented community became very concerned and active in the case.

The black communities of Atlanta, of the South, and of the nation as a whole gradually became aware of the news of the sentences. Many demonstrations were held, marches were called and a strong attempt was made to organize sufficient pressure for the authorities to drop the charges. The National Association for the Advancement of Colored People (NAACP), became involved in the case. However, there was little they could do. Legally the boys had been given a trial, although it was doubtful that it was a fair trial, and convicted.

At that point a highly unconventional and unexpected event occurred. A group of white people from the Communist Party came down from several northern cities and began to organize the southern black communities to further protest what was considered a "legal lynching". They appeared to identify very closely with the aims, goals and conditions of the black communities, and used the Scottsboro case to impress the black community with their concern for its plight.

The same attention had been given by this group to many black communities in northern cities and as a result a considerable number of black intellectuals, artists, writers and labour leaders joined and became active members of the Communist Party. This was a time of emotional and intellectual turmoil in the United States. Neither President Franklin Roosevelt nor anyone else appeared to have any answers to the massive unemployment and poverty created by the free enterprise system under which we lived. The Communist Party promised an alternative to poverty, unemployment and racism. The result was that not only many intellectual leaders of the black community, but also a great number of labour, religious, civic and other leaders joined the party during the 1930s.

The trials, convictions, sentences and appeals of the Scottsboro boys dragged on for several years. After repeated trials and appeals, it appeared as if nothing further could be done. However, before the Scottsboro boys were actually hung or electrocuted, one of the girls confessed that the incident had been a frame-up and the alleged rape had never occurred. When the second girl was faced with the confession, she also confessed that the whole matter had been concocted. This of course brought about a huge sigh of relief among black communities across the country. The boys were eventually released to try to pick up whatever aspects of their lives were still possible after this traumatic experience. My deep sense of alienation from the values, goals and attitudes of white southerners plus my admiration of the effective role of the Communist Party caused considerable confusion in my mind.

Many of the black communities of the United States, in both North and South, also demonstrated a deep sense of confusion and uncertainty. They were thankful to the Communist Party for the work that group had done in obtaining a reversal of the conviction and the release of the boys. On the other hand, most blacks had also assumed the same negative attitudes towards the party that whites had preached. The Communist Party was considered as an alien, destructive and subversive group that should be rejected at all cost. My friends and I were confused and disillusioned. We were faced with the question of why we were rejecting people who had supported us while accepting the ideas and opinions of those who oppressed us. It was a difficult dilemma and one in which there was little guidance from our parents and teachers.

Fortunately for the black community, the Second World War changed that entire situation. I knew a few blacks who had joined the Communist Party but who had turned in their membership cards at the signing of the Molotov/Ribbentrop pact, a treaty which brought Communist Russia and Nazi Germany together and enabled Hitler to later attack Poland, thus leading to the Second World War. Many prominent black leaders left the party as a result of that event.

Efforts to forbid human contact between white and blacks were reflected in the following incident which occurred during the 1930s. Arthur Raper, a noted white sociologist on the faculty of Agnes Scott College, an exclusive school for the daughters of the white elites, was invited to address the students of another local college. A headline appeared in the local student newspaper informing the public that "Raper of Agnes Scott" was to visit the campus. The local bigots had a "field day" demanding that the invitation be cancelled as an insult to white womanhood, that the president of the inviting college be fired and the "rapist" be lynched. It was of course assumed that the "rapist" was black. There were many red faces when it was announced that the "rapist" was Arthur Raper, the noted white sociologist. He took the incident as an amusing reflection of southern bigotry and graciously accepted apologies. This was one of the rare occasions where the black community had a good laugh at the expense of its oppressors.

Employment

Approximately 20 percent of our class received scholarships to various institutions of higher education, mostly in the Atlanta area. I received a scholarship of 100 dollars from an insurance company but with a qualification. I and about ten other graduates were expected to work during the summer selling life insurance for the company. In return we were to be paid a commission. Initially I was satisfied with that arrangement. It seemed to me to be a good opportunity to earn some money during the summer and at the end have money to enrol in a college, perhaps Morehouse College. As it turned out, I was not a good salesperson. Knowing that most of these people were very poor and had little or no money, I found it very difficult to go to people's houses, knock on their doors and try to sell them life insurance. It seemed to me to be almost an absurdity. These attempts were made in the depths of the depression of the 1930s.

Obviously the insurance company was aware of the difficulties we would face. We were given a training program which included the various "tricks of the trade" in making the "right approach" to complete a sale. Even during those sessions, I was coming to the conclusion that this was not an occupation for me. I resigned from that program shortly thereafter. The motivation for going into that work was that the country was in the middle of the depression and was suffering from a very high level of unemployment. It was almost impossible for a black or even a white to get a decent job. Hundreds of thousands of people were on various kinds of welfare. I later learned that the company did not expect many of us to succeed in this highly competitive occupation. Only two or three of the original group managed to complete the training program. The manager indicated disappointment at my resignation but said that he understood my position. Some weeks later I learned that many of the men who had been assigned to train us were not happy about the possibility of students entering the field. They were not enthusiastic about the prospect of competitors in a very severely restricted field.

I began looking for other work shortly after leaving the life insurance company but it was very difficult to find jobs during that summer. In spite of my reluctance to depend on my mother for support, I refused to apply for the few jobs I might have obtained because I would not work under bosses or foremen who made a habit of insulting and humiliating blacks. Previous experiences had made it very clear that my attitude, and the possibility of being fired, would not deter me from responding to insults in a way that would not be considered appropriate for a black man in the South. I would not behave as a good "nigger" should.

My first temporary job was with a construction company doing some renovation work on a local theatre. It was understood that the job would be for only six weeks. The first day went well. I began the second day working on an outside project. The boss came around to me after I had been there for 15 minutes to give me instructions as to what I should be doing. Two or three hours later he came back to ask how I was getting along on the work. I showed him what I had been doing and he said that he had asked me to do something entirely different. It became very clear that there was going to be some conflict between the two of us. I said to him that I would like him to give me instructions again. He then became very angry and made it clear that unless I could do what I was told I would be fired. I decided at that point that there would be no point in staying. I walked off the job site, went to the basement of the building, took off my work clothes and prepared to go home. Apparently he had expected me to return to work the following day. One of my friends was asked if he had seen me, and if so, why was I not at work. I said to my friend that he could tell the boss that I would not return. That was my final day on that job. I never went back to collect my pay.

My next job was somewhat different. It too was a temporary job washing walls at Spelman College, the institution in which my sister would later enrol. My friend Jimmy had been instrumental in my getting this job because, as a student at Morehouse College, he had learned of the possibility of openings. I eagerly entered that residence building along with 20 other young men, almost all of whom were college or high school students. We examined the nature of the work to be done and decided to break up into teams of three or four men per room. This job turned out to be an informal educational experience for me. We stood on ladders and washed walls and ceilings.

Washing walls on that project was an experience involving working and talking. There was a great deal of discussion about the fact that we were working in an all girls' dormitory at the College. Many of the men were more than willing to relate their romantic experiences with women and their attitudes towards the possibility of romantic and sexual relations with students at this college. In some respects this kind of talk was shocking, but not altogether unexpected. I obviously had heard some of that kind of conversation on previous occasions. Young adolescent boys are likely to listen carefully to the sexual conversations of older boys and men. However, what I heard in this situation was more explicit. For example, one of the young men delighted in talking about getting married but not until he had "tried out" the girl to see to what extent they were sexually compatible. I thought that the term "tried out" was a very unusual term to use in relation to another human being.

Racism was the other focus of discussion. Again the focus on prejudice and discrimination was not new or unexpected. The intensity of those expressions of hatred against whites, however, was both unexpected and disturbing. In some respects, I was glad when the job was completed.

We completed the job in four or five weeks and just before the opening of school for the fall term. Jimmy, Asa and many of my other high school friends were again enroling in various colleges but it was impossible for me to go to college since I did not have the money for tuition. I had left the insurance company and lost the possibility for that $100 scholarship. It became obvious that for the 1933–34 college term, I would have to skip school to work with the hope that for the next year I would be able to begin my college studies. It was difficult to be left behind by my friends.

I finally found work following some months of unemployment, during which time I turned down the possibility of two or three traditional jobs for blacks only. Months later a friend who worked at the a theatre in East Point told me there would be an opening for a part-time worker to help him in his various duties. I agreed to accept the job because I thought that it was something that I would like, and it gave me an opportunity to work with an individual whom I knew and respected. I would also have the opportunity to see movies when I was not busy. I began to work near the end of that year. This job did not require a high degree of skill and was basically a janitorial job for the first half of the day and taking tickets from patrons in the evenings. The word "patron" should be qualified to mean "black patrons". As in other southern institutions, theatres were rigidly segregated and divided into "black" and "white" sections.

When the show had started my job was to observe and attempt to control potential disruptive behaviour in the balcony section. I was expected to warn patrons if they were too noisy or even to suggest that they would have to leave the theatre if they became unruly. Fortunately, that possibility did not occur very often but I was keenly aware that my role was that of a "watchdog", however well disguised.

I had ample opportunity to watch movies while I stood or sat in the black section. I must have seen well over 100 movies of various kinds during the time I was employed there. Watching movies, or at least being in a situation where it was almost impossible to avoid watching, resulted in some difficulty. Many white people did not like to see blacks in sedentary occupations. This, however, was not what got me into trouble. I was responsible for picking up the *Atlanta Constitution*, our daily newspaper, and taking it to the manager in the afternoons. After he had glanced over the paper, he would call me to take the paper and throw it out. On more than one occasion I took a quick glance at the paper before discarding it. On one occasion he caught me reading and upbraided me for wasting my time reading the newspaper. I didn't take this too seriously but a day later I received a notice that I had been fired. I was quite shocked at this action as I was not sure of the reason. My co-worker told me what had happened. The manager apparently did not like to see a black person reading the newspaper or any other reading material. Apparently he felt that it was a minor crime if black people were taught to read and write. He had recently learned that I was a high school graduate, another matter which gave him no pleasure, so I was again out of work.

I had already lost one year of schooling. Thus I had to make up my mind as to what I would do for the next year. I would have to find another job quickly or find a very important summer job where I could make enough money to carry me over for the next school year. I found a few temporary jobs, but it became obvious that I would have to work and stay out of school for a second year.

I was lucky on two levels. First, I succeeded in finding some part-time jobs which provided a minimal income and second, I chose to go back to school and take courses on a part-time basis. I was determined that my educational goals were not going to be defeated because these courses could be of great value if pursued with clear goals in mind. I had already become acquainted with the director of music at Morehouse College and at Atlanta University. Professor Harrell was a very committed individual who was anxious to support black people interested in music. He encouraged me to study with him on an informal basis. I would not enrol in the college and therefore would not have to pay tuition fees. I quickly agreed to this proposal since I had not had music lessons since I graduated from high school. I had, however, continued to practise on my violin. This had been difficult as I did not have the advantage of a teacher who could guide me in my studies.

He was very encouraging and felt that I had real potential as a violinist and that perhaps I would be able to obtain a job teaching music at a high school. I was even invited to play with the university string quartet, a task which I knew was above my capacity at that time. He agreed with this assessment and said that perhaps within a year or two I would have developed to the point where I could become a valuable member of the Morehouse String Quartet. I valued his encouragement, guidance and friendship.

I also met and developed a positive relationship with Professor Hale Woodruff, the director of art at Atlanta University. He was an outstanding artist who had received his training in Paris and in New York City. He suggested that I join his art classes at the university. As with Professor Harrell, I would be his informal non-registered student. Professor Woodruff, like Kemper Harrell, was a very unusual man. Teaching art was not simply a career for him. It was one aspect of his dedication to helping black students to excel and to become accepted and recognized in the wider community. Looking back I wonder how I was able to arrange for these informal contacts and opportunities. It may have been that I was known for my work and activity at Washington High School or it may have been my determined interest in these areas. At any rate the opportunities did occur and I took full advantage of them.

In addition I went back three days a week to my high school to take a course in typing since I had not studied commercial arts in my regular high school academic program. I was learning new skills while filling in time resulting from the lack of steady employment. The implications of the Great Depression were devastating to the lives and self-image of thousands of Americans of all races and backgrounds.

My brother Frank was quite different in personality and general orientation toward life. He had left school at the end of grade nine and had found a job which he thought would be permanent and which he seemed to like. It was agreed that he would continue to work at that job and perhaps return to school later. Unfortunately he never did return to school until he was much older and had served in the American army for three years. He could then return to school on the G.I. educational program, a program which made financial support available for ex-servicemen. He was a person of great stability and therefore in many ways a stronger support to our mother than I was.

Unlike me, it appeared that Frank had no real interest in returning to school and completing his high school diploma. He was quite happy to remain on a full-time job, help to support the family and to live his life in his own way. Frank bought the first automobile owned by anyone in our immediate family. We were quite surprised one day when he drove up in an old car obviously in very bad condition. Frank was very proud of it. We had no choice but to be proud of it even though I had some qualms regarding the possibilities of heavy repair bills in the future. As I suspected Frank spent a great deal of his time in an attempt to keep it in running condition. Working on that car became one of the most important aspects of his life.

My mother was still working at the Atlanta airport. Several months later I received a call from her asking me to come to the airport to apply for a job with Eastern Airlines. I met the local manager of the Eastern Airline operations. He looked me over, asked my age and how much schooling I had. I told him that I had finished high school. He seemed to be quite pleased with that and immediately offered me the job which entailed primarily janitorial work in the airport hangers. Other duties included work in the offices of the airline. The DC-3, the major flying equipment of the airline, did not have internal ramps for the passengers to enter or disembark and external ramps were used by passengers for this purpose. One of my jobs was to push the ramp up to the door of the plane and ensure that passengers could embark or disembark safely. Checking in the baggage was also an important aspect of my job.

The job at Eastern Airlines paid $65 per month plus a few tips if one were lucky enough to get them. This was a fairly decent salary, particularly for a young black man in the middle of the depression of the 1930s.

I met my co-workers, all of whom were black. One of whom I will call George was an older man who considered himself to be the unofficial head of the black staff at the airport. We worked on eight-hour shifts and a part of my job involved "filling in" when other workers were on vacation. I worked primarily the day shift but on occasion the night shift as well. This gave me the opportunity to meet, and to some extent, get to know all of the staff of the airport. In general, I found the staff, both black and white, very friendly and welcoming. I think the blacks were very happy to see me come on board because they had been short-staffed for some time and looked forward to a second person on each of the shifts to lighten their own workloads.

I was the victim of a little trick played by the staff on all newcomers. The second day I was on the job the head of the mechanics staff came to me with a big bucket. I was told to go around and check the other hangars to see if they had extra "propeller wash", to borrow a bucket full and bring it back to the Eastern Airline hangar. In all innocence, I took the bucket and went to the nearest hangar. Nobody had any propeller wash. Everybody was laughing and I was not sure what this meant. So I went to the second hangar and asked the same question. This group really broke out into laughter and I began to catch on. Propeller wash was the stream of air generated by the rapid motion of the propellers, exactly the same kind of phenomenon one finds from an electric fan. I realized that I had been the victim of someone's joke. I joined with them in the merriment because I realized that I had been initiated into the club!

In the Eastern Airline experience two people stand out in my mind. The first was a co-worker, whom I'll call Charlie. We worked the day shift together during most of the three months that I was in that position. Charlie liked me and we got along well but he could not understand why I wanted to go back to school. He kept telling me that I could make more money working for Eastern Airlines than I could make finishing college and becoming a teacher. He was probably right at the time as salaries for teachers were very low during the depression years. He simply could not understand why a black man would leave a steady job to return to school.

I had one unforgettable experience with Charlie. One of our responsibilities was to greet each plane as it arrived, take the baggage off the plane, place it on a cart and wheel it round to the front of the airport terminal. We took the baggage claim check from each passenger, picked the appropriate bag from the cart and handed it to the passenger. Quite frequently the passengers gave tips varying from 10 cents to as much as $1. Charlie was always more successful than I in getting tips and on one occasion Charlie spoke to me after the job had been finished and we had walked back to change to our usual clothes. As I remember the incident, Charlie said, "I can show you how to get better tips. Just watch me the next time a plane comes in and I will show you how to go about it."

I had already noticed some of the little things Charlie did which made him very popular with passengers. Among these were very friendly waving at them, perhaps dancing a little jig which he called the "buck step", and taking off his cap and waving it in a big circle at passengers. The next plane arrived and

Charlie repeated his little routine. Two laughing passengers handed him 50 cents each. Another man gave him a dollar and others gave him small amounts but everyone gave him a tip.

As usual, I met my passengers, took their claim checks, took the bags off the cart and handed it to them. They either gave me nothing or only 10 or 15 cents. After the passengers had entered the airport bus or their taxis and left, we returned to the change room. As I recall, the conversation went somewhat as follows: "Slim (I was usually called Slim by the staff), did you see how I got those tips?" I said, "Yes I did, Charlie." He said, "Now can you learn to do that?" I said, "No Charlie, I can't do that." He wanted to know, "Why can't you learn?" I said, "Because I don't want to." He laughingly said, "If you don't do what I did, you won't get the tips." And I said, "I guess you are right, Charlie, but I don't think that is what I would like to do. It seems to me that you are belittling yourself by the kind of act you are putting on and giving people the sense that you are simply another Uncle Tom." I remember saying, "Charlie, I will not play that game. If that is necessary to get larger tips, you go ahead and I will continue to get a few of the small ones."

It was totally impossible for Charlie to understand why anyone would not perform a few tricks as he was doing. We needed the money of course and he had a family to support and he needed the opportunity to show that he understood white people. Behind that facade of smiles and laughing, Charlie actually hated white people. But this was the kind of game that went on among many blacks in the southern United States during the 1930s and until the civil rights revolution of the 1950s and 1960s. Charlie was not alone. This behaviour was one of the survival methods used by blacks in a hostile land.

As one of the so-called "new Negros", I could not appreciate and accept the survival methods used by Charlie and his colleagues. However, I recognized the importance of his view of survival strategies. After all, his methods were at that time duplicated by hundreds of thousands of other blacks in the American South. I'm sure that many of them may have hated themselves for what they were doing but they saw no other alternative.

I had developed a warm and friendly relationship with my boss. He treated me almost as if I were his son, and was always very kind and helpful. If I wanted a day off he made sure that I got it. If I wanted a change in shifts, he would try to arrange that for me. This very warm relationship, however, was badly shattered on one sunny afternoon. As the hub of the Eastern Airline network, Atlanta was the place where all planes going north from Miami or Houston stopped so that passengers would get off for a rest in the airport lounge while the ground crew checked the gas, oil, etc. They made sure that everything was fine for the second half of the flight. The black ground crew, the porters and the baggage carriers, would enter the plane and tidy it up while the passengers were enjoying a rest in the waiting lounge. I was working in the plane on this occasion when one of the mechanics came and asked me to do some particular task. I dropped the work I was doing and immediately began the work he had asked me to do. A few minutes later my boss walked onto the plane and asked me why was I doing something which was not a regular part of my routine. I said that Mr. X had asked me to do so. He left. A few minutes later, he returned and angrily stated that he had checked with Mr. X. who said that he had not asked me to do that job. I said, "Well he did." I had never seen a man's face change so dramatically in so short a time. He turned bright red, obviously very angry and said, "Don't you ever contradict the word of a white man" and walked out. I sat stunned in a seat of that plane. I could hardly believe my ears or my eyes. However, after thirty or forty seconds I got up and walked out of the plane with the intention of taking off my uniform and going home. I have rarely been so angry. I would not accept what he had said and I was not going to remain on that job. I was determined that I was going to change into my street clothes and leave immediately.

Although I did not think about it, what I was doing was merely a replay of what I had done seven or eight years earlier when I walked out of the drugstore following the altercation with the owner. I had the opportunity on many occasions since that time to make decisions regarding my behaviour vis-à-vis white people. In every situation I had taken a very independent stance and not played the game as I was supposed to do. Before I could change clothes and leave, however, my boss walked into the room with a different mood and attitude. He came over to me and said something like this: "I got a bit upset about what happened on that plane, Slim, don't take it too seriously. Why don't you put your uniform back on and go out and continue your work on that plane. Everything is okay." Reluctantly I agreed to his request.

I found his behaviour almost inconceivable. I could not believe that he could change so rapidly. The thoughts that ran through my mind as I remember were, "Now I know how my white friends really are." They are "fairweather" friends. They accept me and think that I am great until I differ or contradict them in any way. They are my friends as long as I stay "in my place". I entertained these thoughts for several minutes and then slowly put my uniform back on and walked out toward the tarmac of the airport. He was obviously quite pleased that I had returned. However, I thought about that incident many times in subsequent weeks. I was never sure whether I should have gone back or not. But again, I needed the money so I accepted his apology and stayed on.

I saved some money during that summer and with the help of a scholarship, I enroled at Morris Brown College in September 1935. The college was a Methodist Church institution located on the west side of Atlanta not very far from Washington High School and occupied buildings which had initially been the home of Atlanta University. Although the buildings were old and in need of renovations, its location at the top of a hilly area, overlooking a wide landscape, gave the campus a certain charm and attractiveness. It would have been difficult to find a more suitable location. The school had a very strong religious orientation and students were required to attend chapel every morning. The president of the college was the son of Bishop William Fountain, the official leader of the

Methodist Church in the Atlanta area. My French teacher was the sister of the president, and the daughter of the bishop. At Morris Brown one was enroled in a college whose goal was to produce a tough academic program merged with a strong religious influence. I was surprised, however, at the impersonality of the college. It was not a large college and had a student body of perhaps 800 to 1000 students, but for some reason the teachers were not very friendly and seemed to have very little regard for the students. There seemed to be a master/servant rather than a "community of scholars" relationship. I recall my resentment at the behaviour of one of my teachers who taught a chemistry class three times a week at eight o'clock in the morning. The classroom was on the third floor of a building in which one had to walk up the stairs and this teacher would stand at the door of his classroom with his watch in his hand. At exactly eight o'clock, he slammed and locked the door so that students could no longer get into the room even though they might only have been one or two minutes late. This was the kind of authoritarianism to which I was not accustomed and although he was a very committed teacher, I found it very hard to warm up to him. I was always happy when my class with him was over.

I made a number of very good friends among students during that year at Morris Brown College. One of my best friends, a trombone player, had a girlfriend whom I admired a great deal. She was the first female student I had met who was extremely good in chemistry and other physical sciences. We had a sort of informal and friendly competition going on between us as to who would be the number one student in the chemistry class. When the year was over, she ranked number one in the class and I was number two.

I did well during the first semester of my stay at Morris Brown College. As a result I was summoned to the dean's office on one bright autumn morning. The dean was a very small, intelligent man but also somewhat autocratic. He was the man to whom students went with any problem relating to college experience. From my point of view, he was much more important than the president. When I arrived at his office, Dean Mitchell informed me that I had made the honour roll. I couldn't imagine why he wanted to have a little chat with me if I had made the college honour roll. As far as I was aware, he had not called other honour roll students to his office for a "chat". Dean Mitchell did not take very long to come to the real point. His first question to me was, "Have you ever thought of joining a fraternity?" Fraternities and sororities are "Greek letter" organizations operating on most college and university campuses throughout North America. Membership in fraternities is restricted to males, sororities to women.

One could look at fraternities and sororities in at least two ways. First they attempt to bring together students with common interests so that they could live and study together amid the isolation of a big institution in a big city. Many students at Morris Brown and other colleges at that time had come from the rural South and had little or no experience in city living. A fraternity or sorority house provided some guidance, companionship and even support in their studies.

The second and more negative aspect is somewhat different. Fraternities and sororities tended to be highly selective and elitist. It was that characteristic which even in high school had "turned me off" from fraternities or any other elitist organization. When the dean asked if I was interested in joining a fraternity those characteristics immediately came to mind. My answer to him was that I was not interested in joining a fraternity. He appeared to be quite surprised at that answer. He tried to sell me on the idea that living in a fraternity would make my college life much more fruitful, more enriching and that I would have lots of compatible friends. He particularly mentioned a specific fraternity. What Dean Mitchell did not know was that I was already beginning to develop a sense of independence, equality of people and a distaste for authoritarian or elitist organizations. I did not change my mind about fraternity membership.

I remained one year at Morris Brown College and completed the term on a positive note, with grades at the "B+" and "A" level. I did better than I expected having been away from formal study for two years.

Following the end of the school term at the end of May I was at home for a few days and was surprised to receive a telephone call from my former boss at Eastern Airlines, inviting me to return to my old job. I was very pleased to accept this offer since I was quite aware of the difficulty of finding a decent job in the middle of the devastating depression and high unemployment. I returned to work at Eastern Airlines around the middle of June of that year. I knew, however, that I would have to make the decision whether to return to school the following fall or to continue working at Eastern Airlines. The importance of my decision was intensified by the fact that we had a number of financial obligations to meet. There was a small mortgage on the house and I felt that it was important to get that mortgage paid off.

I was keenly aware that I had already been out of school for two years, and was reluctant to make the decision to not return to college. But in view of the current situation at home I felt that was the only thing that could be done. I discussed the matter with my mother and with Frank but they left the matter up to me. My boss had already indicated that he would be very pleased to have me extend my employment beyond the summer months. He was offering me a permanent job. I felt there was no alternative but to accept that opportunity. I finally agreed to do so and to postpone my return to college for an additional year.

Several of the mechanics who worked for Eastern Airlines also owned small planes. I began to take some informal flying lessons from a mechanic who took some interest in me. He was a very nice young blond fellow, about 25 years of age who really enjoyed flying in an old, open cockpit biplane. This mechanic occasionally took me up for a flight. After a few of these episodes, he asked me if I would like to learn to pilot the plane. I readily agreed to his idea. However, before this happened he decided to have some fun. He belted me in on one flight, took me up, and then began to do a series of "rolls" and swift turns. Obviously the intent was to frighten me out of my wits. To some extent he succeeded and I was beginning to feel a bit upset in the stomach.

However, when we landed I was not going to let him become aware of that condition. As we walked away from the plane, I said to him, "I still want to take those lessons, are you still willing to give them to me?" He agreed and a short time later he took me up on my first formal lesson. I enjoyed that experience and began to consider the possibility of joining with some of my friends and buying a small plane. At that time we could have bought a small Piper Cub for a very small amount. I thought that perhaps eight or ten of us would join together, pool our funds and buy a plane of that type. Obviously I was thinking a little too much in the rarefied air of unreality. There was no way that ten of my friends could have put together $250 each to buy a plane so that dream was short-lived. It was only later that I recognized the actual cost of owning, upkeep, storing and flying an airplane.

Another incident was somewhat different. Instead of an active incident it was more passive and indirect. Eastern Airlines like many others at that time operated a plan in which their employees could be given free passes for flights during their vacation. I applied for one of those passes. My black colleagues and friends were appalled. Charlie asked, "Slim, why would you do such a stupid thing? You know very well that no black individual has ever been given a pass from Eastern Airlines." I pointed out that company policy indicated that any employee after one year of work was entitled to a two-week pass to any destination to which the airline flew. They laughed because they knew very well that that policy was for white employees and white employees only. I persisted and applied for a pass to Chicago.

In spite of opposition, I refused to withdraw my application. I had serious doubts that the application would be successful but was not going to let the officials "off the hook". The next move was up to them. The date I had chosen for my flight to Chicago was drawing near. I decided to inquire regarding the status of my request. I wrote letters to the headquarters of Eastern Airlines and also attempted to talk to the station and the regional managers of the airline but never received a single reply. Finally the date arrived for me to check the status of my pass. I called the local office of the airline. I knew and was on good terms with the staff but they did not have a pass for me. Although I saw and spoke to them every work day, nothing was ever said or done by the white office staff of the airline. Nobody ever mentioned the matter. There was, in effect, a conspiracy of silence. To my surprise, the black employees were pleased that my attempt had failed. They had strongly opposed my application in the first place and now that I failed, they had been proved right. A black person should never have expected to break the tradition of the company regarding its policies on passes. Although I defended my actions and refused to withdraw the application, I did not really have any strong convictions that I would succeed in getting the pass. But I knew that whether I failed or succeeded my action would send a signal to the top brass of the organization. One reason many blacks were happy that I did not succeed was that they did not have to face the challenge of a similar struggle. They had no intention of challenging the status quo.

Otherwise, things continued as they had on a fairly routine basis. I still enjoyed the work, at least to some extent. The tension between my boss, other white employees and myself gradually subsided and in general I can say that it was a good year.

It was possible on the night shift to get in additional reading. Reading books and magazine articles also helped me to stay awake. I read some of the European philosophers, particularly those who lived during the "age of enlightenment". I became quite well-acquainted with the works of Voltaire, Anatole France, Spinoza, Jean-Jacques Rousseau, Immanuel Kant and several others. I was particularly interested in the ideas of Spinoza, Rousseau and Voltaire. Kant only left me puzzled. I remember one critic stating that Kant never wrote a simple sentence if the idea could be stated in more complicated language! This and other reading provided me with a solid background for the attitudes and philosophies which I had been developing over the last several years.

By the beginning of that summer I had already made the decision that I was going to return to college. There were more than twenty black colleges in the United States: however, I had narrowed down my choice to two colleges, Morehouse College, in Atlanta and Tuskegee Institute, in the adjoining state of Alabama. I had a number of chats with Miss Chadwick regarding my intention to resume my career as a college student. As usual, she helped me make the right choice. She was realistic and practical in her orientation and not particularly interested in ideas, academic activities or anything of the sort. What she wanted to know was what career was possible for me so that I could make an adequate living, and help to support the family.

Two or three of her girls were already in attendance at Tuskegee Institute. Finally we agreed that perhaps Tuskegee would be the best place for me to attend, largely because of its "work/study" program. Several programs at Tuskegee required students to work part-time which enabled the student to earn money and to pay part or all of his/her college expenses. That prospect appealed to me. I realized that although I had saved some funds, they would not be enough to cover the three years I would be away from home in residence at Tuskegee.

Before finally applying to Tuskegee I decided to travel down and observe the institution to get a feel of what it would be like to spend three years there. I left home early one morning by bus, rode down to Tuskegee, a distance of about 130 miles and stayed overnight. Satisfied with what I saw, I decided that Tuskegee was my best choice. I mailed off my application and within a few weeks I received a reply indicating that I had been accepted. This began another significant educational experience in my life.

Religion and Community

Religion in my family served a very strong supportive role for people who were under a great deal of stress in the struggle to survive. From their arrival in North America, blacks had a difficult time dealing with Christianity. Most slaves came from Western Africa in which a variety of religious practices was accepted. In North America, slaves found that they were under pressure to abandon their religions and accept the religion of their masters. That pressure of course created problems.

However, by the end of the 18th century, many blacks were slowly drifting into religious practices based upon the Christian faith, a result of the requirement to adopt the names, languages, cultures and the religions of their masters.

By the late 1700s it became obvious that the practice of segregation in churches no longer satisfied the aspirations of blacks. Neither was it desired by the whites. As a result, in 1792 a black minister, Richard Allen, formed the African Methodist Episcopal Church (AME), an all-black congregation which began to attract a considerable number of black worshippers, while slavery was still the dominant pattern of life in the southern part of the United States.

Conditions were only slightly different in northern cities. Black churches, particularly of the Baptist and Methodist faith, were founded in New York City, Philadelphia, and in Boston. In the southern states, blacks were permitted to establish their own churches, but under the watchful eye of the slave masters who were not concerned as long as they controlled the slaves and the preachers, who were also slaves. Slave masters often visited the church and listened to what blacks were saying. They were particularly impressed with the singing of religious songs by their black slaves.

By the 1850s, thousands of black churches had been established in all parts of the United States reflecting a variety of denominations. The churches, under slavery and shortly thereafter, became the major institutional influence in black communities in the United States, particularly in the southern states. Only after a considerable period did masters and later, landlords permit the establishment of lodges, social organizations and other social and civic structures.

But religion alone could not solve the many problems of black people. The result was many blacks turned to other methods of denial and concealing unresolved problems through the use of alcohol, drugs and violence.

Oppressed and exploited black people needed this opportunity for participation and emotional release to express their feelings in their own way without fear of retaliation by the slave master or boss. In this sense the church was their only institution in which there was no external control. There was no boss or slave master standing around and telling them what to do and threatening retaliation if they did not instantly obey. They were in their own milieu and felt a sense of release unavailable in any other situation. The "Negro spirituals" were a reflection of these feelings. I was amazed at the enthusiasm that black people exhibited in singing of the "Negro spirituals". These are songs of hope, liberation and freedom.

The vigorous singing of hymns and the highly charged words of the pastor created an atmosphere of excitement and hope. The manner in which the minister spoke was as important as the words themselves. These men knew how to appeal to the feelings and interests of their congregations. Our minister often spoke in analogies and metaphors. I used to listen in wonderment at the ability of these men to stir their congregations to high levels of spiritual awareness and unity. Listening to them during my childhood resulted in a wish to emulate them and to become a minister myself!

Even as a young boy I could understand that these songs had tremendous meaning for the people who sang them with such gusto. They made it possible for people to develop a sense of comradeship and unity. They helped develop a sense of community which made it possible for underprivileged and oppressed people to continue the struggle to survive.

The minister and the members of his deacon board were expected to be beyond reproach. They were not expected to "sin" which included drinking alcohol, playing cards, gambling, dancing and even playing baseball on Sundays! The pastor occupied the highest social status in black communities. There was, in my background, a great deal of respect for public school teachers and even more for high school teachers. However, the status of the pastor was unchallenged and his words were presumably inspired by God and therefore unassailable. There was no room for debate or doubt: the word of the preacher was the word of God.

One of the roles played by the black minister in small southern towns and rural areas was mediating between the black and white communities. While he was not held in as high esteem by whites as in his own community and church, the minister's role in mediation involved attempting to defuse a conflict situation with the hope that he could secure the release of an accused black or get some reduction in his/her punishment. If he succeeded his status in the black community rose. If he didn't succeed his status and authority were undermined. The real power in deciding, however, was firmly in the hands of the white power structure who controlled the police, courts and the mainstream economic and political institutions.

The increasing educational level of young black people was having some impact on the influence of religious institutions. Many young blacks were paying more attention to what they were learning in school and were beginning to challenge some doctrines of the church. Young people were listening to and increasingly influenced by theories and facts outside the realm of the church. We had become aware of Darwin and his theories of evolution. Most of our older church members still believed in creation doctrines and found our ideas totally unacceptable. For the most part my friends and I had to keep those ideas to ourselves but occasionally one of us would raise these doubts publicly and would immediately be challenged.

While in senior high school I occasionally accompanied my uncle Pheneas on his weekly trips to his churches. On one occasion, we stayed with a parishioner who also had a young teacher living with her as a boarder. This young teacher and my uncle became involved in a hot argument around issues in the Bible of which I was totally ignorant. It was, however, the first time I had heard any criticism of religious teaching. My uncle was furious, but could not convince the young man to change his views.

Later I realized that Uncle Pheneas was merely human and perhaps under a great deal of pressure. Nevertheless some of the moral authority which he held was diminished if it was not entirely lost. In spite of my doubts, I remained active in the local church while at the same time moving into more secular and scientific ways of thinking. I was elected assistant superintendent of my Sunday school which gave me a sense which I had never felt before — a sense that I was highly appreciated and much was expected of me. It was important that I was viewed as a role model for young children living in conditions of poverty and hopelessness. I had to show that I could stand up in front of the teachers and students and demonstrate that I could perform the actual duties of the superintendent. My success gave me considerable satisfaction.

My final activity of significance with the church involved the establishment of a boy scout troop. We needed a large space for meetings and the basement of our church seemed suitable. A boy scout troop was non-denominational and only partially religious. Basically the purpose of boy scouts was to develop "good citizens" and loyalty to God and country. I was in high school and later in college when I became interested in the possibility of organizing a troop in my city. At that time there were no black boy scouts in East Point and only a few in Atlanta. I raised this question with the elders of the church and I was quite surprised to find at best a lukewarm reaction to my proposal. I was grudgingly given approval in principle. Later, I took the matter to a meeting of the general membership of the church where I ran into a considerable amount of opposition because many people did not feel that non-religious organizations should meet in the basement of our church. As far as they were concerned, the church was the "House of God" and should only be available for worship. There was also some concern that boys from other churches could join the troop.

I was quite pleased to find that a number of people in the congregation supported my proposal. They mentioned that there were no other places in the community aside from the nearby Methodist church for a boy scout troop to meet. I had not spoken but simply listened to this point. Following about a half hour of discussion, however, I stood up and made my own pitch. I pointed out the importance of young people eight to 14 years of age, having some attachment to the church. A program for young black boys was essential in our neighbourhood. I also reiterated that our church basement was the only suitable place for meetings of this kind.

The minister then supported me, a move which I think made the difference. I again emphasized that a boy scout troop was not a religious organization per se and certainly not a denominational one. It was an organization designed to help boys to become better citizens, to become more conscious of their responsibilities to the community and to be helpful to all residents as best they could. The vote was called and my proposal was adopted.

Within a short time I had recruited a group of 14 boys varying in age from 12 to 15 years, most of whose parents were Methodist or Baptist. For the first time we had a situation in our church where children from another denomination were welcomed to make use of our facilities. That in itself was a breakthrough. I applied for and received the necessary training as a scout leader at the boy scout headquarters in Atlanta. I was given permission, after this training, by the headquarters to form my troop and to induct them into the larger boy scout movement. This was accomplished and a few months later I was ready to hold a formal induction ceremony in which all of our boys received their badges, repeated their pledges and were applauded by their parents and friends. I remained in this position as a boy scout leader for a period of two years.

My work in the church gave me a sense of contributing to the fullest possible development of underprivileged boys in the community as a whole. There is no doubt that I had achieved acceptance in the Baptist church. But even including my lingering doubts I am convinced that the church played a very significant role in the socialization of many black young people.

As a young boy growing up into adolescence and young adulthood, I lived in at least two different worlds. One was the world of my friends, neighbours and relatives who inhabited our ghettoized all-black community. The other world was a world in which we came into limited and restricted contact with the nearby white population. The latter world was one of some friendliness but also a great deal of anger and tension. Blacks were never quite sure when the friendliness would suddenly change into hostility. I was never sure of our acceptance, or of how long any acceptance would last. Outside of my work experience in which there was no alternative, as a young adult, I made every effort to minimize contact with the white world. I was moderately successful at achieving that goal. My experiences, both direct and indirect, clearly indicated the importance of that decision.

A memorable experience during my post high school career occurred in my own family. My cousin, Annie Mae, the daughter of my uncle Pheneas, had married a young man who was a mortician. As many undertakers, he usually drove Buicks, Cadillacs or other big cars. On one occasion while he was driving just outside Atlanta, he was stopped by two county sheriffs. The two sheriffs ordered him out of his car and following some questioning began to beat him with their clubs. He was beaten so severely that he could not drive his car and had to call someone else to drive him home. Had the law enforcement officers had any sense of concern they would have called the ambulance to take him to a hospital. But he was a black man and they could not have cared less about his condition.

Before the arrival of his friend, my cousin was finally able to stop a car and the driver agreed to drive him home. It just happened that the next morning I went to visit their home and I could not believe my eyes when I walked into the house and saw him in bed. I could not recognize him. His face was badly swollen from the blows and his eyes were tightly closed. It was only after I began to ask questions that I became aware of how badly he had been beaten and the severity of his wounds.

I was surprised and upset when I said to him, "Are you going to call the police and have these men charged?" He looked in my direction as if I was out of my mind and in a sense I suppose I was. He could only shake his head. I began to learn from other members of the family that it would be foolish to call the police. They would never arrest and charge their colleagues. Secondly, my cousin would have been subjected to additional harassment and beatings had he attempted to have the two men brought to justice. This incident led to a great deal of insecurity and anxiety in the family. We recognized that the law was not to protect us: it was in place to protect the power structure and the interests of the dominant white population. The events of that night made a lasting impression on my mind.

Nevertheless, even the provocation and brutality of police officers did not prevent most of us in the black community from enjoying a relatively quiet and peaceful life. I began, during my high school and college days, to view my community with some degree of concern regarding its possibilities for self-improvement. I thought, for example, there should be some recreational facilities for the children and teenagers. The boy scout movement was hopeful but only one example of an attempt to meet this need. There was no question that the black population was an oppressed and poverty-stricken group and there was general recognition that one result of this condition was an increasing crime level in that population. As often happens, when oppressed people cannot find a way to strike back at their oppressors, they easily learn to turn their anger and frustration against members of their own group. There were even sections of East Point where many of us simply would not go because of excessive levels of violent behaviour.

I felt that there was something we could do, as young adults, to improve some aspects of the many problems in our community. There were absolutely no facilities and space available for the recreation of young black kids in that community and they usually hung around on vacant lots, in the streets and either "behaved themselves" or got into trouble. Often it was the latter. Again there was nothing that could be done about this except to let the law run its course. Very rarely could a black person be acquitted once he or she was taken to court. The black individual could expect to be convicted and sentenced to at least the minimum period in jail. Sentences were not always very long: their function was simply a matter of keeping the black community in line.

There was a vacant lot behind our church which had never been used for any particular purpose so I decided that would be a good place to begin a recreational program. I called Marvin Coleman and some other friends together and we decided that space would be ideal for a basketball court. We arranged a few projects to raise money and were able, from the sum raised, to build a fairly playable basketball court. Many of us began our basketball careers on that outdoor basketball court. It became a focal point for many young boys who spent considerable time in a wholesome athletic activity.

Since the court was next to my house I probably spent more time shooting baskets than anyone else in the community. The result was that I became a top basketball player in that area. I was always chosen first when we got together for teams to play because I was the best shot on the team and perhaps even the best all-round player. We went so far as to challenge teams from Atlanta, College Park and other teams from out of town, a great experience for us because we travelled to other black communities which we would ordinarily never have seen. I also began my tennis career on that cleared-off ground. While I was unemployed Glenn and I practised almost every day and we became fairly proficient tennis players. The skills I had learned in East Point allowed me to participate in a few inter-club tournaments in Atlanta.

The small group of us, including Marvin Coleman, Coleman Robinson and Glenn, raised enough funds to buy cheap tennis racquets. The racquet strings, being of inferior quality, did not last very long, a problem solved by learning to replace them ourselves. The result was that the racquets were not very tightly strung, but they served our purpose. I became fairly skilled at stringing tennis racquets by holding them on my knee while the work was being done. On many occasions I ended up with badly bruised hands. But I made some good friends on that makeshift tennis court.

My final community activity came after I graduated from Tuskegee. The little playground and basketball court we had built next to my house was inadequate except for basketball and tennis. We needed a facility in which younger children could play and be supervised. Marvin and I began to look around the community to find a suitable vacant spot. We finally located a potential site which seemed suitable for our purposes. It was at the end of a dead-end street and a small creek flowed through it. While ideal in many respects, it would require a tremendous amount of hard work to become a suitable playground. We had very little money but were willing to do what was necessary to complete that project.

Several other adolescents and young adults joined the two of us to form a playground committee, later known as the East Point Community Club. I was elected as its first president. We then got the ministers of the local Methodist and, with some persuasion, the minister of my own church together. The Baptist minister did not live in our city and was not as available for meetings as the minister of the Methodist church. We drew up plans for the playground and then went to the various organizations in the community, most of which were church-related. We contacted social and civic clubs, and asked for support. We were pleased that these clubs fell in line very quickly and held many events for fundraising purposes including street fairs, bake sales, dances, fashion shows, and beauty contests. The result was we were able to buy the land after two or three months of active campaigning. That was the first time that all of the various organizations had joined together in a joint fundraising campaign. That, in itself, was almost a miracle!

The success of that money-raising campaign was celebrated by burning the mortgage at a special meeting called at the site of the playground. The community as a whole had made it possible to build the playground. The space was not large enough for a baseball diamond and other large areas that we would have liked. However, the playground was a total success and on its opening day, it was overflowing with parents and children. My colleagues and I were very proud of our success.

I saw that playground as one attempt to help the black community organize itself to provide for its own self-preservation and self-defence. The success of the Community Club and its playground had without question a positive effect on the total life of the black community.

Many of my friends felt very positive about the success we had achieved and looked upon me as a potential leader in the community. Unfortunately, I had no intention of remaining in the Deep South. I had made up my mind that I would be leaving the South as soon as I completed my college degree. I looked upon my stay in Atlanta and East Point as temporary stops in my desire to achieve self-realization and to make a bigger contribution to the black communities of the United States.

The situation in the Deep South was that of a black community under siege but not in the sense that the outside white community wanted to destroy us or to drive us out. Their progress and prosperity depended to a very large extent on their ability to exploit our labour and our brains. Their goal was to destroy our spirit, to impart a sense of hopelessness so that blacks would continue to occupy a position of subjugation and inferiority. The intensity of their pressure on us was such that it was very difficult to rise above that level. Their major purpose was first to teach blacks the futility of resistance to exploitation and second, to point out the likely results if blacks made an attempt to change their status.

The strategies outlined earlier developed by blacks to break out of this encirclement and assault basically involved education, employment and participation in religious and other aspects of community life. These attempts worked to some extent, but by no means fully. Certainly black people suffered discrimination and racism irrespective of accomplishments, status in their own community, educational or social level. The presidents of the various colleges and universities in Atlanta, doctors, lawyers, businessmen and others received precisely the same treatment as other blacks. The only criterion for being subjected to ill treatment was the colour of one's skin. One had to be extremely brave to openly struggle against this oppression. Jim Crow laws, customs, mores and every other aspect of life were mobilized to maintain the inferior social, economic and political status of blacks. The one-party system in the South at that time provided no political rights to blacks who were virtually excluded from voting and other aspects of political involvement.

And yet the struggle continued. Beyond the facade of smiles and attempts of friendliness between blacks and whites was another factor which was very rarely discussed openly, that is the myth of black acceptance of oppression which served as a defence against guilt. The southern black population was on the surface suitably intimidated and quiet when I left East Point for Tuskegee in the fall of 1937. Changes, however well hidden, were in the air. The war against Hitler's Germany, presumably sold to the public as a war against dictatorship and for democracy, was not far away. Soon young men, including blacks in segregated units, would be sent off to Europe to fight and perhaps "die for their country". That conflict set off a chain of events which led to increasing resistance to the obvious lack of democracy and freedom for blacks in the United States. The drive towards freedom and democracy, long delayed, reached full bloom in the massive marches and demonstrations during the 1950 and 1960 civil rights movement in both North and South. That movement was only one phase in the continuing struggle to create a fair and just society in the United States.

CHAPTER 4 Tuskegee Institute: An Educational Philosophy, Authority and Resistance

Following the termination of the American Civil War in 1865, there was a relatively rapid development of colleges and universities for blacks. Several colleges, including Fisk University in 1866, Taladega in Alabama in 1867, Atlanta University in Atlanta in 1867, Morehouse College, Atlanta in 1867 and Tuskegee Institute in 1881 were established by associations and religious groups such as the American Missionary Association. Hampton Institute in Virginia was established in 1864 but was not a degree-granting college at that time. Several other black colleges and trade schools had been established in the various southern states by the end of the century.

Since 1865 the federal government had made deals with the southern states to provide education to blacks and had therefore backed away from its commitment to equality of education and other aspects of American life, abandoning the black population to the tender mercies of the racist southern states. Under its Morrill Act of 1890, the federal government entered the area of providing education for black students. Over the next several years, 17 all-black land grant colleges were established in the 17 southern states, all of which were segregated and offered training in the agricultural and mechanical arts. This represented a backward movement from the American ideal of equality, freedom and democracy and it was further legitimized by the 1896 *Plessy v. Ferguson* Supreme Court ruling which stated that segregated institutions were legal if they were "equal". The "separate but equal" doctrine then, became the dominant ideology of the southern states. Every southern state then passed the "Jim Crow" laws in order to ensure the segregation of blacks in all aspects of southern life.

It was not until 1954 that another Supreme Court ruled that "separate but equal" was inherently unconstitutional. This decision was particularly applicable to the public school and college system of the various southern states. It meant, in theory at least, that, for the first time, blacks would be permitted to attend previously all-white schools where until then there had been virtually total segregation of blacks from participation in white institutions, with only a very few exceptions to this general rule.

The doctrine of "separate but equal" suited the economic interests of both the northern industrialists and southern landowners. The northern industrialists had won the Civil War and were looking for a period of calm and tranquillity in the Deep South. They viewed the South as a market for their manufactured and other goods and did not want to see it degenerate into instability, anarchy and unrest. They supported the philosophy of Booker T. Washington which called for black improvement in the economic and social arena, a philosophy which did not call for a struggle for equality and democracy through the political process. Northern industrialists were quite ready to invest money and energy in rebuilding the South.

Unlike the early founders of liberal arts colleges, this combination of industrialists, southern landowners and state governments was only interested in increasing the industrial and agricultural skills of black workers. It was this group which gave the initial and subsequent funding for Tuskegee Institute, initially labelled as Tuskegee Normal and Industrial Institute. It is within this context that Tuskegee Institute was born and received wide acclaim as an institution for the training of black students with the necessary skills for the future development of a revitalized South.

Tuskegee Institute was, in the words of the school song, "the pride of the swift growing South". Located in the rolling hills of Alabama, it was founded by Booker T. Washington in 1881 to provide an education for young rural blacks who had no opportunity to obtain high school and post-secondary education. Washington had graduated from Hampton Institute in Virginia before being asked to go to rural Alabama and set up a similar institution for black students. Washington was born in slavery and had some ideas of the difficulties he would face in establishing a school primarily for ex-slaves and the children of ex-slaves. He held a deep conviction of the essential value of work and study, or "learning by doing", as important and significant for young blacks. Shortly after arriving at Tuskegee and receiving a small grant from the state of Alabama, Washington opened his new school. Printing, brickmaking, carpentry and other skilled trades were immediately launched so that the school structures could be built by Washington, his staff and students. Many of these buildings constructed during that period still stand and provide housing, classrooms and other essential shelter for the students and staff of Tuskegee Institute.

The spacious campus and rolling hills often tax the energy and spirit of students who must dash from one class to another. Tuskegee was never intended to be a regular liberal arts college. Many programs, however, led to bachelor of science and other degrees. During the period I was in attendance at Tuskegee Institute, the school offered bachelor of science degrees in agriculture, home economics, commercial dietetics, industrial management, physical education, mechanical industries and education.

Each student was required to take at least one course in industrial arts. I selected photography as my required course in that area. My friend, Miss Chadwick, thought that it was a great opportunity as there was a possibility for me to earn a living through photography. At that time I did want the combination of courses Tuskegee offered, that is, the academic and the practical programs. Each student was expected to work at least eight hours per week, in return for which he was paid the "princely" sum of $25 per month. In 1937 that was not a bad salary for a student. Tuition was only $75 per year and room and board was also reasonable. Therefore it was possible for a student to earn almost all of his or her tuition plus living expenses on campus through this employment.

I arrived on campus in early September of 1937 and was immediately assigned to Rockefeller Hall, a residence hall for second year college students. It had been built by funds provided by the U.S. philanthropist John D. Rockefeller, who provided funds for building many of the facilities on black college campuses which usually included administration, residence halls, classroom buildings and libraries. I was pleased to be assigned to Rockefeller Hall, the building in which lived the famous black scientist, Dr. George Washington Carver. I have many memories of Dr. Carver coming down the hall to knock on the door of a student whom he thought was playing his radio too loudly. Dr. Carver would always say in his quiet voice, "Fellows, would you mind turning your radio down just a little bit? Dr. Carver is getting old and can't sleep." The offending student always complied. After all, Dr. Carver was recognized at that time as the world's most famous black scientist! Students considered it an honour to live near him.

The only area of unease in my mind when I contemplated going to Tuskegee Institute was the concern that Tuskegee Institute had a mandatory ROTC Training Program (Reserve Officers Training Corps). I had already decided that I would not participate in that program and as a result, I could be in for serious trouble. This is precisely what happened.

Certain activities, including chapel attendance and military drill were required of all male students who were also required to purchase and wear the traditional semi-military uniform. The uniform included all of the items of a standard military uniform: navy blue trousers and jacket, a military style cap, a belt and a white shirt. It was not necessary for me to buy all the items since I already made a pair of navy blue trousers while taking a class in tailoring at Washington High School. I had no particular difficulty with wearing the uniform, since uniforms were not that unusual among many schools at that time. They were seen by many as a method of developing a sense of equality, since students of all social and economic classes wore similar uniforms and consequently could not be distinguished by social class. However, I often wondered what wearing a semi-military uniform had to do with education. It seemed to me that the two are contradictory. The purpose of education was to develop creativity, critical thought and intellectual and physical growth whereas the purpose of military training was to prepare men or women to obey orders promptly, and if ordered, to kill the "enemy". Wearing a uniform and participating in military training was obviously an important part of the philosophy of Booker T. Washington and was probably an aspect of his attempt to instill character and discipline. From my perspective Washington had a distorted concept of the value of military training in developing the highest possibilities and potentialities of the black community. Enforced discipline, as found in drilling and other military training exercises, cannot possibly teach students how to live capably and fully in a democratic society where people must learn to make their own decisions rather than be subjected to orders, rules and regulations made by others. There was no evidence that wearing uniforms and participation in military training made better students or students who participated more effectively in campus life.

The most ludicrous aspect of the affair was the requirement that men and women wear their uniforms to chapel, marching into the chapel to the tune of "Onward Christian soldiers, Marching as to war". My limited studies in religious philosophy had not prepared me for this shift in philosophy. I had always heard that the Christian religious message was about love and forgiveness, but not at Tuskegee!

As expected, a problem quickly arose with the question of military training. Shortly after arriving and not attending the training programs, I was called to the office of the commandant, B.O. Davis Junior, a young lieutenant who was the first black man to graduate from the U.S. Army Officers Training Program. Lieutenant Davis welcomed me into his office and was already aware of my objection to accepting and participating in military training. We had a very informal chat in which he wanted to know why I refused the military training. I explained my reasons for not doing so. He gave the impression of a stern and strict young officer who was not interested in discussion. He wanted obedience. After 20 or 30 minutes of discussion, it finally became quite obvious that we would never agree and that another meeting would be necessary. He promised that he would call me in for a second meeting sometime in the next few weeks. Following discussions with school officials, it was agreed to drop the matter. For whatever reason, he never requested a second meeting.

In the meantime, I had a meeting with the dean of men, Captain Neeley, a strong-minded person who felt that either by persuasion or by the force of his personality, he could make young students follow his orders. In my case he found that his tactics did not work. I explained to him why I was not participating in the military training programs and he reminded me that this was a compulsory requirement at Tuskegee Institute. As in the case of Lieutenant Davis, there was no agreement. I began to feel that perhaps I had better start packing my bags and prepare to leave Tuskegee and return home.

I had taken my violin with me to Tuskegee and had joined the orchestra which practised every Monday, Wednesday and Friday evening, with no idea that playing the violin would have any influence on whether or not I would be excused from military training. In a meeting with the registrar, in which he asked what activities I was involved in, I casually mentioned that I was involved in the orchestra. He immediately picked up on that and said, "Well since you are playing the violin and are already practising with the orchestra, you shouldn't have to take military training". "I will", he stated, "write a note to the commandant excusing you from military training". He must have acted immediately because within a day or two I received an excuse from military training from the office of the registrar and the commandant.

I had moved in the direction of conscientious objection to military service, which was difficult for them to understand. My experience was unusual because other students involved in activities on the campus were not given the exemption. Perhaps they never demanded it. It seemed obvious to me that they had not wanted to force me to leave Tuskegee. Looking back on that experience, I am surprised at the strong and unyielding position I took on that matter. That experience was an unexpected test of my convictions. Obviously the officials were also surprised. From that point on I never backed down when challenged.

Tuskegee was more than an educational institution. It was an outgrowth of the life, philosophy, outlook, and ambitions of Booker T. Washington. Even though Washington had been dead for many years when I arrived on the campus, his spirit obviously still guided much of what took place at Tuskegee. A focus on developing the mind, body and character was not totally unique to Tuskegee, but it was a distinguishing feature of an institution which placed the highest values on those aspects of life. One result of this attitude was that the great majority of Tuskegee students were the children of parents who themselves had attended Tuskegee. This is not to say however that the "spirit of Tuskegee" reigned supreme at all times. There were challenges to the ideas of Washington and there were challenges to the programs offered by Tuskegee Institute. Some black leaders, and particularly W.E.B. Dubois, felt that Washington had placed too much emphasis on practical skills at the expense of a solid academic education for blacks.

Once I had achieved a solution to the question of military training, I settled into Tuskegee very easily and comfortably. In many respects Tuskegee students were quite different from what I had been used to at Morehouse and Morris Brown Colleges. In general those students reflected a higher social and economic status than those at Tuskegee. The bulk of Tuskegee students came from small towns and rural areas of the South with a small contingent from northern cities including Chicago, Pittsburgh, Philadelphia, New York and Boston. In general I found the students at Tuskegee much more willing to work hard to achieve their goals and I suspect that they valued post-secondary education more highly than did students who came from more privileged backgrounds.

My first work assignment was as an assistant to a psychology professor who in addition to his teaching responsibilities, also served as what was called the "secretary of labour" and was responsible for placing students in their various work opportunities on campus. I was initially assigned to work in his office on a part-time basis. I was later reassigned to work as a filing clerk with some other students in the office of the director of mechanical industries. I was assigned to work with Hollis Price, a professor of economics, in my second and third years at Tuskegee. I had taken two courses in economics with him in my first year and he thought I was a fairly good student in economics. I gladly accepted this new and exciting assignment. Anything would have been better than going back to the office of the director of mechanical industries! Professor Price was a very unusual man who related very easily and effectively to students. In addition he was very well known in labour circles in Alabama. I accompanied him on trips to Birmingham, the industrial and manufacturing centre of the state, on a number of occasions. He often met with union leaders and provided guidance and counselling during their deliberations. On a number of occasions he was asked a question by a union leader involved in a heated dispute with another member of the organization. He would give an opinion and it was accepted immediately. There was no further discussion once his opinion had been given. He obviously was a man for whom they had a great deal of respect. I was very pleased to have the opportunity to work as an assistant with a man of his demonstrated competence.

Most of his exams were based on so-called "objective tests", that is true/false, multiple choice and other similar type questions. I was assigned the responsibility for most of his marking. He would give me the papers received from his exams and the "key" which determined the correct responses and I would assume the sole responsibility for grading the papers. This was basically a mechanical job and of no great difficulty. However, later on in the season he began to give me his essay questions to mark as well. I found this to be a more difficult task since I had completed only two courses with him at that time. But, I was taking on the responsibility for grading the essays of all of his students, including his senior students.

The difficulty came however when students objected to the grades they had received. A few students occasionally asked him to look at their paper again because they wanted their grades increased. Instead of reviewing the grades, he sent the students to me and I found myself in some difficulties with some of my fellow students. I tried to be as accommodating as possible but there were occasions when the essays were inadequate and in all fairness the marks could not be changed. I began to learn some of the pitfalls regarding the exercise of power. I had never been in that position before and found that it was not altogether pleasant. There were times when I wished that the professor would do his own grading, particularly of the essay type questions. Some students whom I knew and liked became quite angry when I refused to change a mark.

I enroled in the school of education, the only section of the institute which provided a program very similar to that of a liberal arts college. Students registered in the school were required to take at least three or four courses in that particular discipline. However the bulk of my courses were in the fields of political science, economics, sociology and history with the major area of concentration in sociology. I was clear on my educational objectives and knew exactly what courses I wanted. As a result I took more than the required number of courses in those selected fields and I tried with only moderate success to avoid some of the courses I was not interested in. Among these were English Composition, English literature, French and other language courses. A few of those were required and, fortunately, they did not turn out to be as useless as I had feared. One of my English teachers who taught composition and literature also coached the dramatic club. I joined that club and participated in various aspects of several productions including acting in three one-act plays as well as serving as stage manager for two others. I also served as business manager of our "Little Theatre". Participation in dramatics was a very good experience and helped me to improve my public speaking ability before small and large groups. It also helped me to appreciate English and dramatic criticism.

Another of my English teachers served as coach of the debate society. I discovered debating to be tremendously exciting. One of the most important aspects of debating was to learn to understand and appreciate both sides of the assigned question. I recall the training we went through before we were permitted to engage in public debates. We had to learn to research and develop the best arguments we could in defence of our own side of the question. Once that had been done to a fairly high degree, we then were required to reverse positions and defend the other side of the argument. That was initially very difficult in that very few of us were accustomed to arguing the opposite side of a question. I have found that skill very helpful in later life.

My most striking memory of our experiences in debating was when we debated a team from Oxford University in England. We knew that team would be very good and we went to great lengths to prepare ourselves to defend our assigned topic. There were three members of each team, two who engaged in the actual debate and one resource person who sought to find weaknesses in the presentation of the opponent's arguments. The Oxford team graciously, or so we thought at the time, permitted us to present our arguments first. We thought we did a good job and had made a strong, solid and well documented argument which would be difficult to demolish. To our great surprise the young English students made no attempt to demolish our arguments. They instead engaged in a great deal of joking and comic relief activity. Their very funny jokes had the crowd practically rolling on the floor in laughter. There was no way we could deal with this kind of behaviour since our team had been expecting a very solid and intellectual type of debate. Instead we got a group of people who were extremely witty and humorous and the result was that we lost that debate hands down.

The debate club was one of the activities on campus in which students did a fair amount of travelling, usually by automobile, to other colleges and universities located in Florida, Tennessee, Mississippi, Louisiana, Georgia and other parts of Alabama. Often on lengthy trips we had to stop and buy a sandwich or a drink. It was very difficult for blacks to stop at a restaurant and eat a meal in the South because of segregation laws and discrimination. Fortunately we had Eddie Patterson, a young albino student, on our team who was of very fair complexion, with blue eyes, and very blond hair. Although he was defined as a black, he looked very white indeed. He was the obvious choice to go into restaurants and buy sandwiches or whatever we wanted. He brought food out to those of us waiting in the car which was parked some distance away from the restaurant. We would then drive around the block, park the car and eat our sandwiches and drink our soft drinks. It was almost impossible in the 1930s and 1940s for a black travelling by car to find a place where he or she could get a meal. There were very few black restaurants in most small cities in the South and consequently it was necessary to go to the back of a local restaurant, knock on the door and ask someone in the kitchen if they would make a sandwich and pass it out the back door. It was occasionally possible to find a black-owned restaurant where a traveller could purchase a meal. But with our albino friend with us this procedure was not necessary. I personally found these experiences annoying and frustrating, but we did enjoy the opportunity to "pull the wool over the eyes" of the system!

It was interesting and informative to read the history of capitalism as outlined in 1776 by Adam Smith in *The Wealth of Nations*. That book was intriguing and extremely informative since it helped me to formulate my thinking about the nature of the economic system under which we lived. Professor Price was not a classical free enterpriser, neither was he a classical Marxist. He had an inquiring and curious mind and often raised questions to encourage our input into class discussion. While I learned little about Marxism, I did learn that there were alternate approaches to making a living and to buying and selling goods. Professor Price's classes taught me how little I knew and how much more I wanted to know about the functions of economic systems, including those of other countries.

I had personally observed many aspects of exploitation in the system of free enterprise and capitalism in the South. I had seen people reduced almost to slavery, at the same time as they were presumed to be free. I had seen farmers, like my father, driven off the land not because they did not work but because they were paid so little for the work which they did. Many of the effects of capitalism appalled me. I had seen bananas dumped in the harbour of Mobile, Alabama in order to reduce the supply and thus keep the prices high at a time when many people, black and white, were living in semi-starvation in many cities and rural areas of the South.

I had been brought up to believe that the U.S. Civil War was fought to free the slaves. My father, my mother and almost everyone I knew believed that was true. Pictures of Abraham Lincoln appeared on the walls of living rooms of our house and the homes of friends of my parents. I thought he was the ugliest man I had ever seen, a feeling based largely on the fact that he wore a full beard and sideburns. My father and his friends were always clean shaven and as a child I had never seen a heavily bearded man. However, it was obvious that our parents and their friends greatly admired Mr. Lincoln as the hero who had "won the war and freed the slaves". As young children, we easily accepted that interpretation.

Mr. Reid, a history teacher at Tuskegee, was the first person I had known to question and challenge that particular interpretation of U.S. history. He pointed out that Lincoln himself had said that the Civil War was fought not necessarily to free the slaves but to "save the union". He is reported to have stated that if the union could be saved by freeing the slaves, he would do that. He also said that if he could save the union without freeing the slaves he would also do that. His function as president of the United States, as he saw it, was primarily to save the union. That was shocking news which contradicted almost everything I had read and heard about that aspect of American history. I found it very difficult to accept the statements of our teacher. However we listened to him and found his arguments convincing. In addition, he provided us with written material which supported his argument. Slowly but surely the class began to change and to accept a different view of that history. That incident was a very important learning experience for me; which helped me to understand certain aspects of history in a more profound way than previously.

Extra-Curricular Activities

When I look back at my student yearbook, the *Tuskeana*, of the class of 1940, I am amazed at the variety and nature of the activities in which I was engaged. I was a member of the Tuskegee Institute Orchestra, vice president of the social science club; secretary of the campus YMCA; a member of the Tuskegee Debate Society; business manager of the Little Theatre; managing editor of the *Campus Digest* (the student newspaper); chair of the Welfare Committee of the student council; and associate editor of the *Tuskeana*. In addition I was elected to membership in two prestigious organizations: "Who's Who among Students in American Colleges and Universities" and Alpha Kappa Mu, a national honour society.

The "Tuskegee Spirit" included a "commitment to the idea that character is more important than intellectual ability". Other aspects of that commitment included pride in the alma mater, Tuskegee Institute, determination to achieve goals, devotion to the heritage and culture of the black community and "service to God and mankind." Compulsory chapel attendance was one aspect of that commitment. Each year the school also brought on campus a highly regarded and respected theologian who lectured Monday through Friday evenings during "religious education week". I have a very fond memory of the intellectual stimulation brought to students by a Reverend William Borders who at that time was pastor of the Wheat Street Baptist Church in Atlanta. Other outstanding speakers came to the campus from time to time to participate in special meetings or in campus invocations. The attempt to bring "high culture" to the campus, however, was not always appreciated by students.

The Tuskegee chapel was the major setting for many of the social, religious and cultural events on campus. These included performances of the Tuskegee choir which had made its reputation through its outstanding concerts in many cities in different parts of the world, including Western Europe. Its director, William Dawson, was undoubtedly one of the outstanding choir directors in

North America. Sunday morning services and concerts often drew hundreds of people from afar and from surrounding areas.

The orchestra often held its rehearsals in combination with the choir. It was a great pleasure for me to be sitting in the pit and playing my violin while, at the same time, observing Mr. Dawson direct his choir. One of the most memorable spiritual experiences of my life was to listen to the choir sing the "Hallelujah Chorus" from Handel's Messiah. Even with that experience, however, questions often arose in my mind as to the effectiveness of compulsory activities including chapel service. Perhaps the students experienced ideas which they would not have learned otherwise. On the other hand, many students went to great lengths to avoid attending chapel. I was amazed at how many methods they devised to attain this goal. Attending chapel was not a problem for me — as a member of the orchestra, I had to be there anyway — but the choir itself was an attraction for me. Many young black students had been socialized to be ashamed and to avoid singing the negro spirituals. They wanted to sing the famous classics of the great European composers. I enjoyed and identified with the pathos, hope and often sadness of those spirituals because I recognized that they reflected the hopes of a people who had been subjected to slavery and oppression, first under slavery and, more recently, under the vicious "Jim Crow" laws in the southern states. Mr. Dawson, to his credit, insisted that his choir continue to sing these songs and keep them alive.

It was during the compulsory Sunday evening programs that Washington had espoused his philosophy of education and of life in general to Tuskegee students. There is little question that his ideas had great influence on the minds of these young men and women. His influence, however, extended far beyond the boundaries of Tuskegee Institute. His ideas, for example, the advent of black nationalism, and the black community's attempt to develop its own economic base and structures, penetrated into several different layers of the black community throughout the United States and particularly, in New York and Chicago. This idea of economic self-sufficiency was a direct aspect of Washington's thinking. The establishment of the American Reality Company in New York was a fruit of his thought. But Tuskegee was the major example of his energy and thought.

Other aspects of life at Tuskegee Institute have been recounted in novel form by other authors. Among the most critical and perhaps the most authentic is the novel *Invisible Man*, by Ralph Ellison. Ellison had been a student at Tuskegee during the years 1933–1936 and his experiences gave him a keen, if limited, insight into the inner workings of the institution as a whole. His portrayal of Tuskegee Institute as an institution under the domination and control of a president intent on deceiving both students and the white power structure was extremely unsettling. The president is portrayed in Ellison's novel as a man of tremendous interest in maintaining and extending his own power. Students in the institution were seen as simply one instrument in the achievement of this goal. There is no doubt in my mind that some members of the administration included individuals whose major concern was the maintenance and expansion of their own power and control.

The behaviour of the then dean of men met that criterion. He obviously was a man who enjoyed his power over the male student body. Ellison focused his attention on the behaviour of the total administrative structure but encapsulated that phenomenon in one individual. His physical description of Dr. Bledsoe, the person portrayed as the "founder" in the novel, resembled the physical description I have seen of the second President of Tuskegee Institute. I personally have seen evidences of black administrators, including higher officials, "bowing and scraping" before important white visitors from the North and particularly those who were on the board of trustees and who gave considerable sums of money to the institution. This behaviour was not simply an isolated incident: a considerable number of black leaders, whether in Atlanta, Tuskegee or any other setting, behaved in similar ways. That behaviour bothered me at that time and it still does.

The opportunity to demonstrate my feelings towards submissive behaviour came during the school year of 1938–1939. On that occasion, the president of the United States, Franklin D. Roosevelt was planning a brief visit to the campus. Before his arrival a number of secret service men including FBI agents arrived on campus, observed the layout and planned for the security of the president. That was understandable: however, in many respects I and other students resented this visit because it interfered with our classes and other activities. Tuskegee officials, however, cooperated wholeheartedly in this planning.

I had nothing personal against the president who was undoubtedly one of the greatest presidents in recent years. He was elected shortly after the beginning of the Great Depression and went to great lengths in his attempt to deal with the catastrophic aspects of the Depression in which thousands of people, black and white, were thrown out of work and became destitute. Roosevelt introduced a number of programs designed to improve their situation, including social security, pensions for the elderly and welfare reform for the indigent. This attempt to help poor people drew the wrath of both northern industrialists and southern agriculturalists who did not support federal programs designed to help the poor. They preferred having poor people in a destitute condition so that they could be hired to work more cheaply. Roosevelt was labelled a traitor to his class by many members of the ruling establishment but he did not give up. Regardless of the animosity from individuals of his own social class, he plunged ahead and pushed a number of these programs through congress. As a result, I had great respect and admiration for his tenacity and willingness to do what he thought was right.

I was managing editor of "The Campus Digest", the student newspaper and a group of editors was working on the next issue of the "Digest" when it was announced that the president was approaching. A motorcade had been sighted and we knew that the president would be in the middle of the motorcade. Everyone in the room, except another and I, left to view the motorcade. The others felt that it was a great privilege to see the president of the United States in person. I felt quite differently. My general feeling was "the president is not coming to see me, why should I run out to see him?"

Relationships

I met and associated with many students through various college activities and kept in close contact with several of these friends long after my graduation from Tuskegee. Robert Judkins, my best friend, was the individual with whom I was most closely associated on an extra-curricular basis. Although he took some courses in the liberal arts program, Robert was actually registered in the school of agriculture. He was a very intelligent man of many concerns and interests and was equally at ease in academic work as in the agricultural or mechanical aspects of the curriculum. His achievements in both sectors enabled him to develop a wide circle of friends who admired and respected him. His role as a campus leader was reflected in his participation in a wide variety of school activities including president of the student council. It has been largely through the efforts of Robert Judkins that the class of 1940 has continued to plan and initiate many outstanding events, including celebrations commemorating the date of its graduation.

In general my involvement with faculty was also very pleasing and satisfying. Of great interest was the friendly, challenging and intellectually stimulating discussions with professors in the fields of sociology and psychology and with Professor Price. In addition, my relationships with the administration, with two or three exceptions, were very good. After my refusal to accept military drill, I got along very well with the registrars, deans and others with whom I came in contact, including the directors of the department of education in which I was enroled.

In spite of the above comments however, not everything was 100 percent rosy at Tuskegee. There were times when certain difficulties loomed and I was not certain whether or not I would be forced to leave or would leave Tuskegee on my own volition. These grew specifically out of my challenging of certain administrative rules and regulations. My experiences led me to develop, slowly but inexorably, a resistance to what I considered authoritarian or unjust behaviour by administrators. That attitude often went even further into the town of Tuskegee. I tended to avoid most local discriminatory practices by rarely going to the small town. I only went to the local theatre on one occasion during my three years at Tuskegee and that was to take a girlfriend to see a movie. As was the usual custom in the South we had to sit in the upstairs balcony. That experience made it clear that I would never again return to that theatre.

During my senior year I was elected chairman of the welfare committee of the student council. This, of course, was a fairly high level position and one which brought me into contact with students who had complaints against the administration and other aspects of campus life. Many complaints were, as expected, focused on the food. In my view some of these complaints were not valid but in other situations they were very clearly justified. It was my responsibility to bring student complaints to the attention of appropriate officials and try to work out some satisfactory solutions. When my colleagues and I did not succeed in this effort I finally decided to go to the president himself.

I had had some contact with Dr. Patterson, the president, during my practice teaching as a part of requirements for a degree in the school of education. That assignment involved teaching students who attended a junior high school in a small rural area which contained about 40 families who had formed a cooperative as a result of a program sponsored by the federal government. The government had built a school and supplied funds for a teacher/supervisor. Arrangements were made for the Institute to employ Professor Deborah Cannon, a young new member of the faculty as teacher/principal to supervise the operation with other staff supplied by the Institute. The school of education agreed to dispatch five students to work at the school, including four women and me. Since I was the only member of our group who could drive a car, I became the unofficial chauffeur. The principal and the other student teachers lived in a large house near the school building. I lived with a farm family approximately a half mile from the school. Planning sessions were held during the evenings and following these I had to walk home on some very dark and even fearful evenings. Tuskegee had supplied us with a station wagon which I drove to Montgomery, a distance of 40 miles, for weekly shopping. The women actually did the shopping while I sat in the car and read or prepared lessons. The five students in our unit were very compatible and we functioned as a highly effective team, due in large part to the enthusiasm of our youthful supervisor.

On one occasion, Dr. Patterson, the president of Tuskegee, while on his way back from a trip, stopped by and talked with me about the progress of students and their needs. He also talked with some teachers and students and asked if there was anything he could do to be helpful. I suggested that many of the boys wanted to play football but did not have equipment. I suggested he provide us with a football. He agreed and a short time later he waved goodbye, got in his car and drove back to Tuskegee. We did not know what would happen and therefore were quite surprised a few days later when a box containing a brand new football arrived at the school. On behalf of the school and the students I wrote a letter of thanks to him. That occasion was my first direct contact with Dr. Patterson. A result of the visit and the gift to our school was a feeling that he was a friend whom we could trust.

Our group was extremely well-integrated and worked well together. Deborah was only slightly older than the students and it would have been difficult for an outside observer to identify who was the teacher and who were the field practice students. The experience was of only three months duration, and we regretfully said goodbye to the students and their families, with many of whom we had become friends. But the experience had taught us valuable lessons which enabled the five of us to question some of the ideas and concepts we were learning in our classes. I probably found it more difficult than others to leave because I had lived with a family, met and got to know their friends and children and participated in some of their activities. I was not only leaving the children, but also many members of the community. But the final two terms (six months) were hectic and in spite of my strong desires, it was not possible to visit students and families again. My only consolation was that I knew another group of five students would arrive within a few days for another three months.

Despite this experience with Dr. Patterson I had a few qualms about contacting him to complain about the food. However, I was not going to let those doubts stop me and I decided when the next problem arose, I would lead a delegation of three or four students to the president's home for a discussion of the problem. The spacious house was located on the edge of the campus and only a short distance from the dining hall. Two days later someone found some rotten potatoes at lunch and a group of us decided that it was a good opportunity for our visit. The president was quite surprised at our visit and complaint. He suggested that on the next occasion we bring a sample of the food for his examination. Following his examination he would take the appropriate next steps.

Two or three weeks later, students brought to me a plate of rotten potatoes from the dining hall. The students agreed to accompany me and the potatoes to the home of the president as he had suggested. When we arrived and knocked on the door, we found that he was having his lunch. He came to the door and was shocked to find that we were standing there with a plate of rotten potatoes in hand. Dr. Patterson was not amused and we were a bit embarrassed in that we had caught him at a time when he was having his own lunch. Nevertheless we insisted that the condition of these potatoes was not unusual and that this was only one example of a series of complaints which many students had filed during the course of that academic year. I cannot remember what the president said, but it definitely was not a friendly or accepting response. Two days later we learned that he had sent a memorandum to the director of the dining hall instructing him to keep a closer watch on the quality of the food he fed to students.

My final problem with the administration came during my senior year as managing editor of the *Campus Digest*. Many of us in leadership positions in many campus organizations, including the editor, had for some time criticized military training on campus. Many students had indicated their dislike of this equirement by finding every method possible to avoid participation. In fact the attitude of many students to military training was very similar to that of compulsory chapel attendance. The administration, however, remained committed to its military training program. In addition, a sizable amount of government funding was available to the institute to pay the costs of the military training personnel. This, of course, was a disincentive for administration to consider its abolition. Finally the staff of the *Campus Digest* decided to run a poll to determine the attitudes of male students regarding compulsory military training. We intended to run the poll by placing ballot boxes in the dining hall.

The results of the poll surprised even those of us who expected to find a considerable amount of opposition. The ballot count revealed that approximately 90 percent of male students voted for the abolition of compulsory military training on campus. These results were to be the basis of the lead article in the next issue of the *Campus Digest*. However, when the material for the next issue was sent to the on-campus printer, he refused to print the results of our poll. He thought that he would be in trouble with the administration if he printed the results of that poll. In spite of our efforts to talk to the appropriate officials in regards to this incident, we were not successful in getting the results of that poll printed in the *Campus Digest*.

As a result a group of students including all members of the editorial staff of the *Campus Digest* decided that we would have leaflets printed off campus and distribute them to students in the dining room. This was done. Again we found ourselves in some degree of difficulty, but the matter eventually blew over. I think the college administration did not want to tackle the *Campus Digest* staff on a matter for which there was massive student support. On the other hand, the results of the poll carried no weight with the school administration and compulsory military training was continued.

I am not certain how we managed to get away with that challenge to authority. We were lucky. One year later, after our senior class had graduated, the total student council and some 240 other students were expelled from Tuskegee Institute because of an incident involving a student strike and a confrontation between students and the administration. Only one member of the student council was permitted to remain on campus as a result of the intervention of his mother who persuaded officials to give him another chance.

This student thus survived that catastrophe and remained in the school until his own graduation a few months later. Tuskegee was not the only school that operated on the principle of "loco parentis", that is the school acting on behalf or in place of the parent. The school administration appeared to think that in many ways it actually was our parents, that it had the right to dictate what we should do, how we should dress and what we should eat. In this sense we were treated like children.

I previously referred to the Harlem Renaissance which occurred primarily in New York City during the 1920s and 30s. This new outbreak of a sense of pride, political participation and culture was defined as the appearance of the "New Negro". This new awakening of black culture was threatening to many people, including the individuals who operated public schools, high schools, colleges and universities. Tuskegee Institute was no exception to this new awakening of black consciousness and challenge to constituted authority. Captain Neely reacted to this development when he requested that all male students remain following the Sunday morning chapel services. Female students were permitted to leave. The men were then required to listen to the dean of men, who lectured on what he termed the ineffectiveness and lack of realistic approach to life of the "New Negro". Many students accepted this with a degree of resignation. Others had real difficulty with the content and tone of his lectures: however, there was no opportunity to respond or to question him. I and others felt that he would not have appreciated any attempt to question his conception of the "New Negro" and his assumed place in American society. We saw his lectures as "put downs" of any student who had aspirations of becoming an intelligent, creative or effective leader of the black community. Fortunately, the women students did not have to listen to a comparable disparaging lecture from the dean of women!

The strange thing about this episode was that the dean of men was delivering his lectures at the same time that a new mood was emerging in the black communities across the country, and particularly in the larger cities. A new militancy was developing among black journalists and in black institutions and organizations. For example, the NAACP, the Urban League and other black organizations were criticising the federal government for its lack of action in protecting the rights of black people. The Spanish Civil War and the rise of Hitler in Germany had resulted in increasing concerns about the lack of democracy and the role of black people within that context. The two largest black organizations, the NAACP and the Urban League, with chapters in all major U.S. cities, were beginning to reflect new militant roles. A new major national black organization, the National Negro Congress, was formed a few years earlier because many people felt that the NAACP and the Urban League were much too moderate.

The influence of the National Negro Congress was felt even at Tuskegee. A number of its speakers came to the campus and spoke to student groups, many of whom were quite impressed with their analyses of world conditions. They hammered away at the lack of democracy in the United States, the poor position of blacks and the rise of Franco in Spain and Hitler in Germany. A result of this ideological thrust was that a chapter of the Southern Youth Congress was organized at Tuskegee and many of us joined that organization.

One of my most exciting and exhilarating events at Tuskegee was attending a conference of the SYC held in New Orleans, Louisiana. That conference was a major event in the development of my political thought. For the first time I heard people expressing many of the ideas I had regarding the relationship of racism to bigotry, exploitation, underdevelopment and war. That conference was one of the last viable events held by the SYC since it was already in the state of dissolution and would only exist a few more years before its final demise. But I never forgot the passionate expression of views by young black men and women from various parts of the country who were attacking the racial policies of the various states and the government.

One rarely, if ever, heard these views expressed on the campuses of southern black colleges and universities, and certainly not at Tuskegee Institute. In my view, the opportunities for similar discussion and analysis should be one of the most important aspects of college life. Students should not be limited to learning from a few selected textbooks. The college or university could provide the best opportunities for students to learn as it can expose them to outstanding speakers and discussion leaders from outside its walls. In this sense one gets away from the concept of the ivory tower to the concept of the university or college as an integral part of the community with all of its myriad problems and possibilities. In spite of its rigidities and conventionalities, Tuskegee occasionally offered that possibility and for me it was very worthwhile.

I have been briefly discussing some of the problems associated with life at Tuskegee in the late 1930s and early 1940s but these problems were not unique to Tuskegee. Those who lived through that period will remember the many rules, restrictions and downright paternalism of black institutions. The powers of deans of men and women were almost absolute with little, if any, opportunity for appeals against unjust treatment. My criticisms of some aspects of life at Tuskegee can be viewed in two different ways. First the dissatisfaction with what I considered as arbitrary rules and regulations, and second my actual enjoyment of our effort to change these irritants. Win or lose, I enjoyed the struggles against entrenched authority.

I graduated from Tuskegee Institute with a bachelor of science degree (BSc) in education, with a major in sociology, in June, 1940. At this time war had come to Europe. Hitler's Germany had invaded Poland in August of 1939. Britain and France had already declared war and the United States was supporting the allies. It was also becoming clear that the United States would itself join in the conflict following the mobilization of public opinion through propaganda and other activities. The Selective Service Act requiring the registration of all males 18 years of age and over was enacted by Congress that fall. The U.S. armed forces, including the army, navy and air corps were strictly segregated in a manner similar to that of society as a whole. I knew that sooner or later I would have to make a major decision regarding my own participation or lack of it in the coming struggle.

In the meantime as a result of pressure by black organizations and newspapers, the government had established the 99th Pursuit Squadron, a separate all-black group for training pilots. Some members of my class were already receiving a limited degree of flight training at a nearby air field. My brother Glenn enroled in that organization and began his flight training in the summer of 1941. Apparently he did very well in his training program and was quickly promoted to the position of flight lieutenant. His honeymoon with the air force, however, did not last very long. Shortly after he received his commission as a lieutenant, he and some other black lieutenants decided one evening to visit the Officers' Club, a segregated club for whites only. Black officers were assigned to their own officers' club. Glenn and his friends entered the white officers' club and were quickly accosted by the officers in charge. They were told they would be arrested if they did not leave immediately. They refused to leave and the military police were called and the black officers were threatened with arrest. Glenn and his friends said they could not be arrested by an ordinary military police (MP). As officers they could only be arrested by other officers. The commanding officer at the base then called his own military police force who arrested Glenn and twenty-nine or thirty other black officers. The entire group was taken to the brig, a military term for a holding cell. Finally they were let out on bail and had to stand trial before a military court. All were convicted and some were demoted. Glenn was demoted from the rank of lieutenant to that of a "warrant officer".

His protest and that of the others was among the first confrontations of its kind between whites and blacks in the U.S. military forces. It was not to be the last. Glenn and the other officers were humiliated and embittered and their experience carried over into the remainder of their lives.

My other brothers, Frank and Marvin, were drafted by the military, Frank by the army and Marvin by the navy. The two boys did not protest their "1A" classification which meant that they were eligible for drafting into the armed forces. I was the only one of the four brothers who decided to challenge the system for the registration for the draft. Instead of accepting the 1A classification, I demanded to be given a "4E" classification, the classification for conscientious objection to military service. I was quite aware that the armed forces had no intention of providing me with that classification and that every effort would be made to force me to change my mind and to behave like a "good southern nigger should", that is to obey orders and do as I was told. I rejected that idea and prepared myself to face whatever consequences lay ahead. I had achieved an important goal, the earning of a bachelor's degree, but the future was still cloudy and uncertain. The approaching war would change the lives of millions of soldiers and civilians alike. The only certain factor was whatever happened, I would face the crisis as a civilian, not as a soldier conscripted to fight and to protect freedom and democracy, neither of which I had ever experienced in the United States.

CHAPTER 5 *Interracial Experiences*

A month or so prior to my graduation from Tuskegee Institute, I was called into the office of the secretary of the campus YMCA and was asked if I had any contact or association with the Quakers, also called the Society of Friends. I indicated that I had not and knew little or nothing about them except that William Penn, the founder of Pennsylvania, had been a Quaker. The director said that he had received an enquiry from the American Friends Service Committee (AFSC) in Philadelphia regarding the possible attendance of one or more black students to a work camp scheduled to be held in Chicago during the summer of 1940. I discussed this matter with him briefly and told him that I would think about it.

The next day I went back and told the secretary that I would be glad to accept. He immediately informed the organization of my acceptance and within two or three weeks, I received a letter from the office indicating that I had been accepted for the work camp and was to report within the next two or three weeks. This offer was quite a coincidence since I was already beginning to think about how I was going to prepare myself for the struggle ahead. Like most members of the graduating class, I had been giving some thought to employment and didn't really want to teach in some small southern town or large city segregated school. The summer work camp experience would give more time for seeking suitable employment.

I had some indication that I would be pleased with the opportunity to work with the Quakers since I learned they had a very good reputation for their non-violent and humanitarian work with people in various parts of the underdeveloped world. In addition I had already become severely disillusioned with the attitudes and practices of the southern Baptist church. The Service Committee said that I would be a part of a work camp located at George Williams College on the south side of Chicago on the border of an all-black ghetto. Our work would be to improve the social and economic conditions of the inhabitants. The work camp was to last eight weeks and would be composed of both blacks and whites, most of whom were students although a few, like myself, had recently graduated from college.

The project was directed by Tom Jones, president of Fisk University, an all-black university in Nashville, Tennessee. This was to be my first experience of living and working with whites and I looked forward to it with a considerable degree of both anxiety and anticipation. Travelling by train in a segregated all-black railway car, I arrived in Chicago in mid-June 1940.

I was one of the late arrivals. I later learned that my arrival was eagerly anticipated by other members because there were no others from the Deep South. There were 25 participants in the work camp of whom four were black, the remainder, including the director Tom Jones, being white. A black sociologist, Charles Johnson, also of Fisk University, served as a resource person to the group. I arrived in the late afternoon and before dinner we sat down for a fifteen to twenty minute period of silent meditation. I found that very difficult, having come from a society which spent much of its time in animated talk and very little time in listening. Our meditations involved sitting in a circle to increase self-awareness and sensitivity to others but I found myself feeling almost totally isolated. I had not yet learned how to sit silently and meditate. That was a learning experience I was to go through many times that summer.

Following the meditation and dinner we went through a period of orientation. Tom Jones gave us a quick history of Quakers dating back to their founding in England during the mid-18th century. This was a very fascinating experience since it was the first time many of us were told the basics of Quaker faith and belief which suggested that if God exists, he or she exists in every individual and therefore one cannot kill or harm another person. This belief is the basis of their non-violent behaviour. The implication of these principles required resistance to oppression and injustice, and engagement in a struggle against "evil" through non-violent means. I immediately began to feel a sense of relief because I was among people who apparently shared some of my basic beliefs. Quakers also believe in simplicity and oppose ostentation in dress, manners or speech and in personal relations. Titles are rarely used. Dr. Tom Jones was simply "Tom Jones". However, I was also very conscious of colour. It was very strange to be in a situation in which I was treated as an equal by white people and particularly people of the stature and prestige of Charles S. Johnson and Tom Jones.

The 25 campers, who included approximately seventeen or eighteen women and seven or eight men, were a cosmopolitan group, only four of whom lived in Chicago. The four black campers, three men and one woman, were only a small minority. It was generally assumed that we were "experts" in all areas of race relations simply because we were blacks; only Charles Johnson, however, could fill that bill. Wally Nelson, the one black who lived in Chicago, could at least provide the local background. Many other members of the group were highly educated, with degrees in theology, history, political science, psychology and sociology. I was surprised that only a minority of work campers were Quakers; a typical characteristic of most projects sponsored by the AFSC.

Our orientation focused on the nature of Quakerism, the basic values and goals of U.S. society, and the contradictions between the two. There was obviously considerable conflict in the basic philosophy of Quakers and North American society. While U.S. society was preparing for war in Europe, Quakers were preparing for the struggle against the basic concept of war. What, for example, were the possibilities if Quakers had to make a choice? Could they, for example, set up an alternative program to military service? The evening was exciting and challenging and I felt the work camp experiences were likely to change my life.

Our work assignment had been agreed upon in consultation between the community and our leaders and was to build playgrounds on vacant lots in the black community. At that time there were virtually no playgrounds or other recreational facilities for children in the black ghetto of Chicago. A work camp was usually based upon some form of physical labour and we often worked in the blazing hot sun clearing off a dirty vacant lot and preparing it for the installation of playground equipment. Although it was hard work, it was also an opportunity to talk. Work camps were occasions where blacks and whites "let their hair down" and began to talk about their real life experiences. Perhaps for the first time each group listened and learned from the other. White people, even those with lofty humanitarian impulses and attitudes, had little or no idea of how blacks were treated in the United States or how we felt about that treatment. Most blacks, in return, felt that all whites were bigots. We found that there were many whites in the United States who were probably as open and honest as we were. Certainly it was much easier for them to talk about their feelings than it was for us, presumably because we had more negative feelings.

In addition to providing work experience for the participants and some necessary services for the community, the work camp program revolved around education of participants and of the general community. The college residence in which we lived included adequate space for living, dining and for the various meetings which we had with members of the community. We often invited academics, university presidents, deans of theological schools, politicians and entrepreneurs to speak to us about various aspects of life in Chicago and in society as a whole.

Among other visitors and speakers, we met Horace Cayton and St. Clair Drake, authors of *Black Metropolis*, a history of the black community in Chicago, several local and national politicians and other community leaders. Although it was rather difficult to persuade them to attend we sometimes were successful in enticing a few local community people to our evening programs. Many of these people were very shy about participating in any activity involving white people, particularly strangers from out of town. By the end of the work camp, however, the situation had changed. Local blacks had come to know us as we worked on the playground, often observing and later joining with us in the work. Still later, they had become comfortable enough to join us in our evening programs which involved discussion and interracial socializing.

We were also visited frequently by staff and board members of the local branch of the AFSC. These were men and women of high ideals and a great sense of humanitarianism and I often felt that they may have been a bit too saintly. While the midwestern branch was located in Chicago, the central office of the Service Committee was in Philadelphia, and it appeared that Philadelphia was the central focus of the organization which we began to call the "mecca" of Quakerism!

Chicago offered a great number of opportunities for relaxation, socializing and recreation. We often went swimming on a Sunday afternoon at the lakefront beaches of Lake Michigan. Chicago had one of the longest and most attractive beaches in North America. Although the beach was not segregated, very few blacks chose to leave the ghetto and travel to the lakeshore for recreational purposes. In my eight weeks in Chicago, I rarely saw another black at the beach outside of our little group. Perhaps their memories of the Chicago race riots of 1919 were still strong and they did not want to risk a repetition of that murderous event. In effect, relationships between the racial groups in Chicago were virtually as bad as in the South. There was little or no mixing of the races, although from time to time one would find an interracial couple which usually elicited hostile glances and comments. However, there were a few interracial marriages and other relationships including St. Clair Drake and Richard Wright, both of whom were married to white women. Both suffered indignities and hostilities from some members of the local white population.

Two young white women, Mary and Kay, both of Minneapolis, had joined us about a week after the beginning of our camp after their assignment to a Methodist camp had fallen through. It was interesting that Mary and Kay showed no symptoms of racial prejudice or discrimination as both had lived in Minneapolis, and had never previously come in contact with a black person. As in any group of people, it is almost inevitable that small groups or cliques will form within the larger group. This happened in the Chicago work camp. I had met Wally Nelson, a black Chicagoan with whom I had become friendly. We were then joined by another black from Baltimore. That close relationship changed with the arrival of Mary and Kay who became my two closest friends. They joined easily into all of the group's activities and played a very important role in discussions. Kay was engaged to be married to a young student training for the ministry in the Methodist church. Their religious orientation and background was obviously much more liberal than that to which I had been accustomed. We had many discussions during and after work and during the trips we took from time to time but my most vivid memories of the relationship with those two young women resulted from a walk in the rain.

It was a very rainy night and everyone was sitting inside the building talking about the weather and feeling somewhat depressed because the rain interfered with the possibilities of going out. It was Kay who suggested we go for a walk. I looked at her with horror, but responded, "Are you suggesting that we go for a walk in this heavy rain?" She said, "Sure, of course, why not?" I sat there stunned. In my experience, one simply did not go for walks in the rain, particularly in a big city like Chicago. One only went for walks under those circumstances when the need was urgent, not merely for recreation!

Knowing something of the racial attitudes in Chicago, I had visions of being stopped on the street and perhaps attacked by hoodlums which could result because I was in the presence of two attractive young white women. We had already had some discussion about the racial attitudes in Chicago on previous evenings. One black camper who lived in Chicago related his experiences on the south side. He was a student at the University of Chicago and often on his return to the campus following a party or other evening event, he was stopped by the police who wanted to know where he was going and what he was doing in an all-white neighbourhood.

The police very rarely believed his explanation and usually insisted on him getting into the squad car and then driving him to the front of his building. They then waited until he unlocked the door and entered the building before they drove away, apparently satisfied that he actually lived in the university residence hall. This event, he informed us, occurred on many different occasions and he joked that he very rarely had to take a taxi home since he could always get a ride with the police!

Kay, Mary and I took that walk. We probably walked ten or fifteen blocks in a driving rain but protected to some extent by umbrellas, rain coats and boots. The two women were ecstatic with the idea of going out for a walk. I walked with watchful eyes and a certain amount of apprehension. I tried to ensure that they were not aware of how I was feeling. As usual, we became involved in a discussion around philosophy, religion and political issues. Apparently I succeeded in concealing my concerns because when we came home they happily informed the group of the wonderful time we had walking in the rain. We were not assaulted, which may indicate that it was safer to walk when the weather was unpleasant and few people were on the streets. Perhaps Chicago hoodlums don't like to go out and attack people in the rain! The event was astonishing and to me it was almost unbelievable that this kind of experience could happen only two or three weeks after leaving Tuskegee and the Deep South.

Another experience was the meeting with Richard Wright, the great black novelist who had recently written two controversial books: *Native Son* and *Black Boy*. Both books were somewhat autobiographical, in that Wright described his own life as a boy growing up in the South and Chicago and his experiences as a member of the Communist Party. Wright had left the party because it tried to dictate what he could and could not write. His two books were powerful indictments of racial discrimination in Chicago and in the South. However, he was not a very capable participant in discussions. In fact, it appeared that he was quite reluctant to respond to questions, responding only after a period of consideration. He spoke slowly, thoughtfully, and with great caution. I began to realize that he was a much better writer than a speaker. None of the fire and passion which characterized *Black Boy* and *Native Son* came through in his personal appearance and behaviour. Innocently, we had believed that he would be a man of strong personality. Unfortunately, we were wrong. The meeting was simply boring. However, we learned something worthwhile — that is one should not necessarily expect a very powerful writer to be also a powerful participant in group discussions.

Among our recreational and educational experiences were visits to a number of Chicago institutions including the Museum of Modern Man, art galleries, theatres, and the Rockefeller Chapel of the University of Chicago. Meeting and hearing speakers at the Rockefeller Chapel was an unforgettable experience for our group. Because of its reputation, the chapel attracted many of the world's premier theologians, philosophers and other eminent speakers but the two men who impressed me most were Howard Thurman and Albert Schweitzer. They had completely different approaches. Thurman was quiet, dignified and at the same time dynamic, charismatic and eloquent. In his own manner Thurman was a man of great intelligence and conviction. Schweitzer, on the other hand, was quiet spoken, "down to earth" and philosophical. His versatility, immense intelligence and commitment to the cause of helping suffering blacks in west African countries was awe inspiring. Like many others I felt that we were in the presence of truly great men.

We decided to spend the final night of our work camp at a Grant Park Concert. The feature was the Bach Violin concerto in "G" minor, a romantic and beautiful concerto. The music, plus the fact that we were going home the next day, created an atmosphere very difficult to describe. In the first place, we were sorry to be leaving each other. We had developed strong and positive relationships and were quite pleased with the work we had done in the community. We felt that we had achieved something constructive during that summer. At the same time, the beautiful music made the experience even more poignant. I came close to falling in love, not only with my two young friends but also with everyone else at the camp.

The next morning we said goodbye and left for our homes in various parts of the country. It was a sad occasion and, as one would expect, some tears were shed. However, the camp had come to an end and had provided a valuable service on behalf of the AFSC. We left with sadness but at the same time, a warm glow because of the appreciation which had been expressed to us by the citizens and the children for whom and with whom we had worked. A few of us kept in contact for several years. Over time, however, those contacts were gradually lost.

Warm Springs

I returned to Atlanta following the closing of the work camp and found a telegram offering me a job as a teacher/principal of a junior high school in Warm Springs, Georgia. The telegram was from the superintendent of education, who had obtained my transcript from Tuskegee and felt that I was the right person for the job. I had difficulty making up my mind since I had already been thinking about the possibility of enroling in a school of social work or law. I had already applied to the law school of the University of Georgia but this school, like all others in the South, was a totally segregated all-white institution. There were no law schools for blacks in Georgia or anywhere in the South. In fact there was only one law school in which blacks could enrol in the whole United States and that school was at Howard University in Washington, D.C.

My letter of application to the school of law was written in March of 1940, three months prior to my graduation from Tuskegee. I was aware that the school was segregated and that the chances of being accepted were nil. At the moment they received my transcript and recognized that I was a graduate of Tuskegee Institute, they would know that I was a black man since Tuskegee was one of the most famous of the black schools. As expected, I did not receive a reply to my application. In any event I decided two months later to write another letter and submit a second application. I did not receive a reply from that application either. I would have been shocked had I been accepted! In the meantime, I had already contacted the Atlanta University School of Social Work and had been accepted into the first year of a two-year master's program. I had to make a decision whether I would accept the job in Warm Springs or enter the School of Social Work.

I telephoned the superintendent of schools in Warm Springs and informed him that I would probably be going to the School of Social Work in the fall. He was disappointed but suggested that I might come down and work there for the first month or two and see how well I liked the job. He felt that I might find it challenging and might want to stay rather than attend the School of Social Work. I finally agreed to accept his offer, at least on a temporary basis, and went to Warm Springs shortly after the middle of August of 1940. I was to be principal of the segregated black junior high school and I accepted the offer in the full knowledge that the possibility of spending a year in Warm Springs was very small indeed. But I decided to give it a try.

The little, semi-rural town of Warm Springs had a population of between two and three thousand of whom probably fifty percent were black, with no economic or political power. The white population controlled everything, including the black schools. I was to work under the supervision of the white superintendent of schools in the town. The reputation of Warm Springs was based almost entirely on the fact that it was the summer home of President Franklin D. Roosevelt. This attracted many visitors and helped to improve the economy of the town. The black population, however, was entirely segregated and subjugated to the control of whites. The only possibility for blacks to earn a living in the city was to serve as waiters or waitresses at the summer home of President Roosevelt or to work for some white businesses or farms where blacks were often hired as non-skilled farm labourers with low wages, little or no responsibility and no control over their working conditions. The result was a black population totally disenchanted, alienated and with a sense of hopelessness and despair. The one structure which seemed to provide some hope for them, as I had found in other situations, was the church.

One of my responsibilities as principal of the school was to attend Sunday church services. These services were intense, emotional and very participatory. It was expected that members of the congregation would respond emotionally to remarks by the pastor and, as indicated earlier, I had already experienced this kind of religious service prior to coming to Warm Springs. I was surprised at the tremendous prestige and status given to two people in town: one was the pastor of the local church, the other was the principal of the junior high school, namely me!

I had never been in a position where I was called upon and expected to solve all problems and quarrels between members of the congregation or for that matter, anyone else in the town. I was boarding with one of the local families. I was already in bed when I suddenly heard a knock on the door. I was quite surprised at this and wondered why they were knocking on my door. Finally, I got up, went to the door and looked outside. A group of perhaps fifteen or twenty men were standing outside waiting for me to appear. One of them came up to the door and suggested that they would like me to come outside to settle an argument. He felt that unless I came outside there might be violence and someone might get hurt. I was a little hesitant about this request. In the first place I did not know these men and second, I wondered why they would want me to be the mediator between two warring factions. I expressed my hesitation and was assured that they would accept whatever decision I arrived at. Finally, after some discussion, I agreed to go out and listen to their argument.

Both sides presented their argument. I listened to them while they watched me. Very carefully and finally I said, "I think I have enough evidence now." I then made and explained my decision and stood there wondering what would happen next. Would the losing side attack me or the other side and, if so, would I be defended by the winning side or would I be left to fend for myself? It was a very tense moment for me. For them it was no problem whatsoever. They heard my decision, accepted it, and turned and walked away happily as if everything was settled. I stood there practically open mouthed and was amazed at this behaviour!

Not everything at the school, however, went as well as that particular encounter. One of the most important people in that school and the only male staff member was the teacher of agriculture. In this small rural community, the local politicians and entrepreneurs felt that all black children should become skilled and competent in agricultural pursuits since farm work was expected to be their major activity in life. This particular teacher had strong support among the white members of the population but the black population felt quite differently as they wanted their children to be taught and to excel in academic subjects. Prior to my arrival, the agriculture teacher had been acting principal and therefore was not overly pleased to see me arrive on the scene.

The superintendent had given him the responsibility for providing orientation to me, particularly regarding the attitudes and customs of the community. I felt that he was condescending and less helpful than he might have been because he was reluctant to give up his own control of the operation of the school. I gave full attention to the information he was providing, but at the same time made it clear that I would make the final decisions once I listened to the various points of view, including his own.

In the meantime it was becoming increasingly clear that I did not want to remain in that community. The educational level of the staff varied from grade eight to grade twelve. There was little or no intellectual stimulation from members of the staff or in the community. Neither were there people with whom I could discuss matters which were of concern to me. The overall background of students was generally poor, but there were exceptions. Because of limited educational background of teachers, it was necessary for me to teach two classes. Although I had never done so, one of the classes I taught was in health education. I felt this was necessary because so few students had any knowledge of nutrition, health or physical education. I decided to teach the first two of these as a part of my teaching load. Many students demonstrated strong interest in learning and were a joy to teach. However, I sensed that the general atmosphere of the town, including the clear indication that students should be trained only for employment as farm workers, would not be satisfying to me.

The superintendent and staff wanted me to remain, but I recognized that sooner or later I would come in conflict with the all-white power structure of the town and at that point I would have to leave, perhaps on the spur of the moment.

After one month, I informed the superintendent that by the end of the next two weeks I would be leaving to return to Atlanta. He was not very happy but had some indication that my decision was on its way. He had heard that I was not very satisfied in that situation. Having made my decision, I telephoned the director of the School of Social Work and informed him and his staff that I would be arriving for enrolment by the first week in October and would be two weeks late for classes. My tenure as principal of the Warm Springs Junior High School had lasted only six weeks.

In the final analysis, I could not accept the notion that my personal and professional life would be entirely dominated and controlled by representatives of the southern white aristocracy. I was expected to teach and indoctrinate black students to play their accustomed role as servants and unskilled workers in a semi-slave relationship. The idea that any of these students aspired to going to a southern black college would have been considered as heresy. In short, I left before my ideas were discovered with the probable consequence of being driven out of town. Nevertheless I admired the interest of these boys and girls in learning and improving the quality of their lives. It was a painful decision and I left them with deep regret.

Social Work Education

I returned to Atlanta and began attending the graduate School of Social Work in early October. I was quite surprised to find that this graduate work was quite different from my undergraduate work at Tuskegee Institute. In the first place the two-year program was divided into first and second-year classes. There were roughly thirty-five to forty students in the first-year class while the second-year class was somewhat smaller: perhaps twenty-five to thirty students. Approximately half of the students were from out of state because only a few southern states operated graduate schools of social work and none of this small number admitted blacks. However, even before the 1954 decision of the U.S. Supreme Court related to school segregation, the court had decided that the southern states must either admit blacks or make other arrangements for their post-graduate education. The southern states were thus required to find some other alternative where black students could obtain social work education. These states chose to pay the tuition and other living expenses of black students while they were attending schools in another state. Students from as far north as Kentucky, North Carolina and Tennessee, and from Florida, Alabama, South Carolina, Mississippi and Texas were enroled in the Atlanta University School. In this way it was possible to avoid the necessity of black students attending southern white universities. Their other alternative was the expensive proposition of building schools of social work for black students within their own borders.

Atlanta University School was my first experience studying under white teachers. Approximately twenty-five percent of the faculty were white. The director of the school, Forrester B. Washington, was a black man who had extensive experience having worked with several social service organizations including the National Urban League. The League's purpose was to provide employment counselling, training and placement services for black youths and adults, many of whom had migrated from the rural South. One of its major functions was to open new job opportunities so that qualified blacks could move into positions from which they had been systematically excluded.

Again, it was necessary for me to obtain employment to help pay my expenses. I had received a small scholarship from the school but that was not enough to finance my books and other incidental expenses. Following my first week in classes, the director, Mr. Washington, approached me and asked if I would like to serve as his administrative assistant. I was quite pleased because I had done similar work at Tuskegee and gladly accepted the opportunity. I was told that my work would be sporadic and that I would perform certain functions that he needed, but not on a regular schedule. One of the important tasks was to drive his car, to meet important people at the airport or at the train station and drive them to the school. I also served as a liaison person between the director and certain members of the faculty and the student organizations. This was important work and yet not too demanding. There were some weeks when I had nothing to do. Other weeks I would be taken out of class to carry out some important function for the director.

My decision to enter social work grew out of concern for social reform. In my view, it was much more important to try to change the system which initially created social problems. My interest in social work education was to learn as much as possible about community organization and development skills, effective work with small and large groups and possible approaches to changing the institutional structure of industrial society.

My initial assignment to a group work agency for field practice involved work with young people in a group setting, helping lead discussion groups, recreational activities and other adolescent and adult education programs. There was little new to me in the field practice courses since I had already achieved considerable experience in this area in previous voluntary activities. My second placement was working with tenants in a public housing project. This work with the tenants' organization involved supporting them in meeting problems of adjusting to life. The specific focus of my work was the attempt to develop, through adult education, some understanding of the need for a cooperative approach to their problems. A specific goal was the development of a cooperative store and/or a cooperative credit union. This step could be useful in facilitating a greater degree of what is currently called "empowerment". I had decided to write my MSW thesis in this area. I was particularly fortunate in both endeavours as the manager of the project was sympathetic to my intentions.

Participation in classes included raising many questions concerning social welfare. My questions had brought me to the attention of the professor of group-work, a woman of vast experience as a program director with the Young Women's Christian Association (YWCA) and other group-work agencies. We shared many of the same concerns and as a result, we became as good friends as was considered appropriate between a faculty member and a graduate student. I remember that she gave her name as Frankie V. Adams, with the addition of "V as in Victoria". She was considered by many as a committed radical who had no hesitation to discuss any matter of importance, whether social, political or economic. She was a great woman and one whom I strongly admired.

Talladega Conference

A few days before the end of the term Frankie "V" called me into her office for a brief meeting. She had been asked to recommend a student with at least one year of social work training who could provide social, educational and recreational programs for students who were to attend an interracial conference at Talladega College, one of the leading black institutions of higher education in the South. It was located in a small town in the heart of the state of Alabama. Dr. Gallagher, its president, was a prominent white liberal and was largely responsible for the high reputation of the college. Talladega was an ideal place for the interracial conference. This session was sponsored by the Student Christian Movement (SCM) and the YWCA. Its purpose was to bring black and white students together with outstanding adult leaders who could spend ten days examining various aspects of American society and focussing on the ethical, philosophical and religious foundations of North American culture. A part of this focus was on the question of racism and race relations in the U.S.A.

I was more than delighted to accept this invitation and within a week or so, following the termination of classes, I was on my way to Talladega College. More than one hundred and fifty students and twenty resource people, many of whom were part-time, participated in that unusual event. My job was to prepare informal educational and recreational programs which would enhance the interracial learning possibilities of students. Black students constituted about fifteen percent of this group, a higher percentage than I had seen in my experience with the Chicago work camp. This was an exceptionally intense experience. Students listened to a considerable number of speeches and participated in many workshops and panel discussions. At other times they were involved in small group discussions around specific topics outlined by the program planners. Students often served as chair people and recorders, as well as participants in the discussion groups.

It was at first very clear that a large gap existed between the black and white students. In almost every activity, black and white students initially sat separately in various parts of the room. It was only after the third or fourth day that they slowly began to interact on a fairly comfortable basis. For many students, this was a painful process. Some black students, by the end of the experience, ten days later, had achieved a commendable level of integration and interaction with some white students. However, a considerable number of frank and candid discussions had occurred before this result was achieved and many of these occasions brought forth tears, anger and to some extent, even bitterness. It must be kept in mind that these were southerners who had never experienced close interaction with members of the other group on a basis of equality and mutual respect. Although some students talked of leaving the conference, all remained. They had decided to stay and become more appreciative and understanding of the point of view and the experiences of others.

I had recruited a student program planning committee upon arrival at the conference and we organized a number of recreational and social activities between sessions. For example, picnics, hiking, visiting local communities and schools, visiting and participating in the services of a local black church (our interracial group could not possibly have gone to a white church), informal discussion and informal chatting. A major activity of the committee was to plan the evening events. This group, composed of both black and white students, in spite of some apprehension, worked together very well. We succeeded, often under great pressure, to plan and organize innovative programs following each of the formal evening events. Our final night was the highlight of the week. We developed an elaborate program which included group singing, poetry reading, dramatic skits and humorous "roastings" of several members of the faculty. The students had keenly observed the behaviour, mannerisms and speech patterns of each faculty member and a student mimicked the behaviour or accent of this particular faculty member, to the great enjoyment and laughter of all. That program ended with a good feeling on the part of everyone and with the suggestion that the entire group get together in the future.

My reaction to this event was somewhat different from my experience in the Chicago work camp. In the first place, we did not have to do any physical work. The focus was on intense discussion, understanding and appreciation of differences, based on ethnicity, culture and colour. As time went on, it became clear that my specific role was most effective if I helped the students to develop an effective planning mechanism. My relationship with young students was, for the most part, very positive. Occasionally, however, I was asked questions by black students which were very difficult to answer. They wanted to know about my own interracial experiences: how did I "really feel" about white people and did I have any prejudice or hostility towards them? It was easy enough to answer these questions but what was difficult, however, was when I was pressed as to why I, as a black individual, did not hate all whites? Usually these questions were asked by blacks and only came up during long hikes. Although there were many questions, I found that students were very rarely prepared to answer questions themselves. They would turn my questions back to me or to one of the white students. Their response was usually "What do you think?" I began to wonder how black people, who had been subjected to slavery and oppression by whites, could be expected to understand and appreciate the positions of whites, and particularly white students, in modern American society?

Whites were generally uncomfortable with the idea that blacks experienced degrees of distrust and hatred of them. Many white students clearly wanted understanding and appreciation of their position by blacks. These were bright and sensitive young people and a great deal of learning emerged from this seeking for answers to some very difficult questions.

I left that experience with a very warm feeling and I hoped that perhaps in the future positive relationships could be developed between black and white students throughout the United States and particularly in the Deep South. But past experiences had also made me extremely cautious on that point. I was keenly aware that both groups would be returning to a totally segregated society and only the most dedicated would be able to withstand the pressure to conform to the expected attitudes, behaviour and values. At best I could be only cautiously optimistic. As in Chicago I made some very good friends during that experience. After returning home, I received many letters of appreciation from students. It was interesting, however, that all letters were from white students.

Returning home, I decided to spend some time working with youth in my own local community. I organized a dramatic club and, based upon my experience at Tuskegee, decided to produce a series of one-act plays using local groups of young boys and girls between the ages of twelve and seventeen. We began to rehearse two different plays, both of which were presented during the latter part of the summer and were highly successful. I think participation in these activities made a big difference in the lives of these youths, most of whom had never had previous opportunity to receive acclaim for their own work. The praise of parents, friends and community leaders made a big difference in their self esteem. I was proud to have had the opportunity to lend a helping hand in this achievement. I also became involved in volunteer work with boys at the Butler Street YMCA, the black branch of the central YMCA. (Even the Young Men's Christian Association was segregated). In addition, I continued my studies of art and the violin with faculty members at Atlanta University.

With the coming of September, I entered my second and final year at the School of Social Work. This year was different from the first, in that there were fewer required courses and I had the opportunity of making a better selection of other courses. In addition to class requirements was the need to develop plans for a thesis. One had to select a topic and write out an outline for approval by the faculty. Once approved, it was necessary to begin the process of collecting and analyzing data and planning for writing the final report.

I was becoming increasingly concerned with the tremendous amount of apathy and lack of initiative among many of the young blacks living in the public housing project. A similar condition existed among their parents, that is, the tenants renting the units. I decided that perhaps one of the most important needs was to obtain a picture of how they felt about their condition and what they felt would be most useful in helping them to initiate programs designed to make living in a public housing project more positive and constructive. I had given much thought to this idea during the summer and I presented this idea to the thesis committee of the faculty for approval. Following the beginning of the school year, I began to develop a questionnaire to be administered to a sample of one hundred tenants living in the project. The information from this one hundred tenants became the basis of my master of social work thesis.

The experience was a very fruitful one and I got to know a considerable number of people who lived in the project and to understand many of their problems and concerns. The research enabled me to offer at least some help in the organization of programs for the benefit of their children and, in some instances, for the adults as well. As the project continued, I began to feel somewhat disillusioned because the faculty committee had permitted me to engage in a project which had little, if any, significance to social work theory and practice. There was really no need for a research study to confirm the obvious facts. However, my advisor told me it was not necessary for my study to have great social significance. It was a learning experience and the important thing, she felt, was that I learn how to do good research, not the significance of the findings. But like many other beginning researchers, I wanted my project to be significant and hopefully "world shaking". Unfortunately, that grandiose intention was not to be achieved.

In general, my experience at Atlanta University was positive and gratifying. I learned a great deal, although I was somewhat disappointed that the courses were not as difficult as I had expected. I had expected that the quality and volume of work in graduate school would be considerably higher than the undergraduate program at Tuskegee. However, the work in graduate school was no more difficult and in some cases even less so than I had experienced at Tuskegee and, in some situations, even less so than at the Washington High School. This was a surprise and somewhat of a shock. Since that time I have developed my own theory of higher education. I do not believe, for example, that higher education is necessarily "higher" in a qualitative sense than "lower" education. From my experience, much depends on the individual teacher and student involved. Some teachers in graduate school required a tremendous amount of work, some required very little, while other teachers showed tremendous commitment to their job and to their students. The percent of these teachers varied very little, if at all, whether in high school, college or university, in their commitment to students. I was to check out the validity of these observations some years later when I embarked on my PhD programs at the University of Chicago and at Ohio State University.

Social Context

All was not work. In Atlanta University, as previously at Tuskegee Institute, I was involved in a number of very interesting experiences. Some of these were on campus and others were experiences in the East Point and Atlanta communities. I have already mentioned that at Tuskegee Institute I had continued to play the violin. Immediately after arrival on the university campus, I looked up Kemper Harrell, my old violin teacher, regarding the possibilities of joining his orchestra. I told him that I had been playing in the Tuskegee orchestra during the last three years. He was more than happy to see me again, and quickly invited me to take my place in his small orchestral group. My relationship with Prof. Harrell and members of the university orchestra were among the highlights of my university experience. I was more pleased with that experience than with many of the classes in which I was enroled. My three years at Tuskegee had given me considerable experience in orchestral violin playing but it was very gratifying to be warmly welcomed and assigned a place among the first violinists.

Prof. Harrell also told me that he had recently organized a string quartet and wanted to know if I would be interested in playing with that group. I was very surprised to receive this invitation, which was a mark of his appreciation of the progress I had made since my earlier study under his direction. However, it simply would have been too demanding since I was spending two nights a week practising in the university orchestra and it would have required another two or three nights to practice for the string quartet. As a member of the University orchestra, however, I had the opportunity to play at a number of convocations and other special events on the campus.

As an individual who usually "did his own thing", I had little experience in accepting control and direction from others, including teachers. I usually studied in my own way, rather than in study groups. Playing in an orchestra required an accent on discipline which was good for me. It taught me the value of co-ordinated activity, particularly in some aspects of life. Playing in the orchestra required teamwork which could be an important asset in dealing with the many problems of life in a complex and rapidly changing society. I learned to value that discipline.

Thus far I have said very little of my relationship with women and have focused more on activities in which I was engaged irrespective of gender. Nevertheless, this does not mean that I was not interested in relationships with women. For the most part, however, these relationships were friendly and outgoing but not necessarily romantic. I was a bit slow or lacking in maturity as far as relationships with the opposite sex were concerned. With the exception of Jimmy, my high school friend, most of my other friends also operated in the same general manner. My first romantic interest in a female student occurred when I was in my second year at Tuskegee when I met a first year student. We spent a great deal of time together; however, this did not last for very long, since she dropped out of school and returned to her home in another city. I was not particularly annoyed or upset about her leaving the campus. Later in my third and final year at Tuskegee, I met another young woman whom I became very interested in and spent a considerable amount of time, mainly in activities in which we were both involved, including the student newspaper, "little theatre", the YWCA and on the tennis court. I really fell in love with this young woman for a time. But that was more of an infatuation than a deep and abiding relationship. It did not survive my graduation from Tuskegee and return to Atlanta.

As I look back on those experiences, it becomes fairly clear that I was avoiding any strong emotional entanglement and I had no interest whatsoever in the possibilities of marriage. At Tuskegee we joked about women coming to campus to not only get their B.A. degree but also to find a future husband. That may also have been true as far as some men were concerned. Tuskegee was a "happy hunting ground" for the women since they were outnumbered two to one and thus had an advantage if they were seeking a mate! In spite of my lack of interest, however, I certainly was keenly aware that other boys and girls were behaving quite differently. Some relationships were quite short and intense, lasting perhaps two or three months, others lasted through the university career and into a life-long attachment after graduation.

In part, my lack of interest in developing strong relationships with women was related to my precarious social/economic status. Like many other students, I was financially unable to take women to dances, parties and other social and recreational activities. Secondly, as indicated earlier, I was in principle opposed to elitist "Greek letter" organizations. The result of this attitude was that I did not have to invite girls to parties. I was usually invited by them. This gave me the opportunity to attend social and recreational activities without having to admit my inability to pay the tab.

This situation was somewhat different at Atlanta University. The student body in the graduate school was much smaller and personal contacts were much closer. It was almost impossible to avoid developing some kind of relationship with practically everyone in the class, both male and female. Again, I did not take the initiative in establishing these relationships. I was, in my first year, the beneficiary of the interest of two young women, both named Mary. I dated both at the same time. I am certain now that neither Mary was very comfortable or happy with the relationship. The relationship with one of the "Marys", did continue for a period after graduation. I had remained in Atlanta during the summer following graduation from the university and she had returned to her home in Kentucky. I visited her home on two occasions and we also met from time to time, at social work conferences and workshops. These and other relationships with women ended after graduate school when I entered a new phase of my life.

The U.S. had entered the Second World War and registration for the draft began in the fall of 1940. Strongly opposed to registration for the draft or participation in preparation for fighting a war, I did decide, finally, to register but I claimed conscientious objection which meant that I was objecting to participation in the Armed Forces. I was seeking the legal alternative to military service.

The government had, in its Selective Service Act, indicated that men opposed to fighting in the military services could claim a conscientious objection classification and could engage in "Work of National Importance." That status was what I sought.

I knew full well that I was not likely to be successful in achieving my claim and my goal. I had learned long ago that I had three strikes against me. First, the general opinion of people in the United States did not appreciate black people raising unconventional questions or engaging in non-conventional behaviour. Second, the South considered itself as the most militaristic part of the country and gloried in its past history of violence and warfare. Third, I challenged the government's right to draft me into an army with which I was in total disagreement partly because of the government's own policies of racial discrimination and segregation. Equally as important was my total abhorrence of fighting and killing.

I knew this would be a long and perhaps bitter struggle and was under no illusion that it would be easy to achieve the classification I sought. At the same time I was aware that it would be quite unlikely that many of my friends and neighbours would publicly support my position. It was not that they did not want to be helpful to me personally since I was well liked and I had support in the general community and among my friends at the university.

The fact, however, was that my friends and relatives were afraid. This fear clearly emerged when the Federal Bureau of Investigation (FBI) appeared on the scene to investigate my claims for conscientious objection. (All claimants for this status were investigated by the FBI and a report was written before a final decision was made by the local draft board.) Later I learned from those who had been contacted that they had told the officers that I was a person of good character and that, of course, I would go to the army, if called, to do my "patriotic duty". This investigation was the first time that most of my friends, relatives and associates knew of my claim for conscientious objection (CO) status. They had simply assumed that when the war came, like everyone else in my neighbourhood, I would go without complaint or contesting my classification.

It was at this point that I began to do some serious thinking about the steps which I had taken and which would be facing me in the future. I had completed only the first year in my social work education program at Atlanta University and felt that the chances were that I might not be called for several months, thus giving me the opportunity to complete my program. That was not to happen. My first draft call came in December, 1941, thus initiating a lengthy struggle with the federal government which lasted until October, 1942.

This struggle was indeed a lengthy one and it was conducted virtually alone. My mother had remarried and moved to Cincinnati, Ohio. My brother Glenn had volunteered for the air corps and was in training to become a pilot. Frank expected to be drafted into the army and Marvin was already in the navy. Minnie had graduated from Spelman College in Atlanta, had met and married one of my old Tuskegee friends and was living in Kentucky.

My situation with the U.S. military was not of great concern to me. I was facing the possibility of a five-year prison term if I failed to obtain the CO classification and continued to refuse induction into the army. I was living on the edge but it did not affect my academic or other activities. Life continued in its usual manner, but not for very long.

In the meantime the German army had overrun Poland and France and the war appeared to have reached a stalemate during the winter and spring of 1941. But that situation could not continue indefinitely. Although there was a considerable degree of opposition to U.S. involvement in the struggle in Europe, the administration under President Roosevelt was determined to enter the struggle against Japan and Italy both of whom had become allied with Germany. An increasing number of nations were entering on both sides and the Second World War was well underway, but the massive killing and destruction was to come later that year.

There was some turmoil in my mind during that period of relative inactivity and apparent calm in the United States. However, that lack of active involvement was deceiving. Thousands of individuals and groups were actively involved in "Keep America out of the War" movements and some prominent Americans actually supported the Germans. We knew very little of the persecution of Jews by Hitler at the time. I was, however, keenly aware of the brutal colonization of Africans and Asians by the British, French, Dutch, Portuguese and Spanish empires. Many American blacks, including myself, were actively engaged in "Free Africa Movements" and initially sympathized to some extent with the Germans. Although partly confused by obviously blatant anti-German propaganda, the facts gradually came to light and most, but not all, black leaders gave strong support to U.S. war preparation, partly because of opportunities for black workers to obtain jobs in war industries. Racial bigotry was strong and millions of white Americans were not prepared to work side by side with black men and women. Under threats by black leaders to stage a massive "March on Washington" of 100,000 men and women, blacks and whites persuaded the president to issue an executive order to establish a Fair Employment Practices Commission (FEPC) requiring an end to discrimination in corporations and agencies holding government contracts. This was a breakthrough which set into motion the beginning of the end to official discrimination. Executive orders, however, were limited in scope and only applied to war contractors.

Discrimination and segregation in the country and in the armed forces continued as usual.

My distaste for the overt discrimination prevalent in the United States made it difficult for me to cheer even these limited gains. But more important was my attitude toward war with its deliberate and highly efficient methods of mass killing and destruction. I was also keenly aware of the neo-colonialism of the United States initiated in the early days of the nation and including aggression and seizure of the territories of Mexico, Spain and the lands of the native people. The Japanese were newcomers to empire building who wanted their share in the exploitation of the resources and lands of other countries, many of which were under the control of western powers.

An unintended consequence of World War II was the devastation and weakening of Europe and its inability to hold its colonial empires. England, France, Portugal and the Netherlands were forced to surrender control of their colonial empires and to grant independence although they managed to maintain considerable economic control, a situation which continues to exist. From my perspective, the destruction of European colonialism was the only worthwhile achievement of the estimated 50 million men, women and children killed and billions of dollars spent on useless destruction. The old order has disappeared only to be replaced by the neo-American empire which controls and dominates much of the resources of the present world. The achievement of freedom, equality and democracy were as far from realization as in the past, and remained a part of the continuing struggle against tyranny and oppression everywhere.

CHAPTER 6 *Militarism and Non-violence: Making a Choice*

In this chapter I will discuss some of the considerations which guide my attitudes, opinions and behaviour. I recognize that militarism and non-violence have a number of meanings as defined by various individuals and groups. Very few countries, if any, will admit that they are essentially militaristic. They normally assume that the other side of any dispute is aggressive and that they must be prepared to defend themselves. The word "war", for example, has become almost obsolete. When I grew up in the United States the function of the "War Department", which included the army, navy and the air force, was open and above board: it left no doubt as to its function. Today that has all changed. We now have departments of "defense" to "defend" a country against another country's department of "defense".

My early interest in war was based on a sense of excitement and fascination with the drama of warfare. With the exception of the American Civil War, I had very little concern which nation was the victor or which suffered defeat. Slavery was involved in that conflict and I was 100 per cent for freeing the slaves!

My second interest in the study of war was based on increasing curiosity about the people who actually fought wars. I had read considerable material regarding the great generals but for me that was not enough. I wanted to know about the lives of the serfs, peasants, farmers, slaves and others who actually fought and died. I wanted to know what their lives were like, what was their relationship to the state, what were the factors that encouraged or forced them to join armed forces and the nature of the power structure. My reading of history taught me nothing about these concerns. What I did learn suggested that most wars are initiated by top military, the economic elite and government officials. Later I learned that ordinary people had little or nothing to say about wars. As the British author Kipling wrote, "Their's not to reason why, their's but to do or die."

My third motive for studying the history of wars was that I was beginning to experience some doubt about the effectiveness of wars as a method of settling disputes. The most powerful individual or the most powerful army might win a great victory but winning only means that one side had a more powerful army than the other. It says nothing about the justice of the situation. A victory did not mean that aggression was necessarily more effective, unless we accept the dictum that "might makes right". What I really wanted to know was did the ordinary people who suffered under the destructive aspects of war gain any worthwhile value or goal? My tentative answer was that they gained very little or nothing. There is scant evidence that the serfs in Europe or the slaves in the United States gained anything as a result of the wars fought by nation states. With respect to the U.S. and its revolution, the facts were that while the leadership changed, and independence from England was secured, there was very little difference in the lives of ordinary farmers or small entrepreneurs. They did not acquire the right to vote until many years later, and then only if they were property owners. A similar result can be observed when we study the French, Russian, Chinese and other revolutions in which the "common people" fought and died on behalf of their masters.

In spite of my extensive readings, however, I have very little knowledge of the men who killed and were killed in military conflicts or of the innocent civilians who suffered the devastation of organized warfare. They were the victims of war whether their country won or lost.

It was at this point that I began to gain some understanding of the nature and importance of propaganda in wartime. It is absolutely essential that the leaders of any country wishing to fight a war, identify an "enemy" against which it can arouse and mobilize its own population. The "enemy" must be defined as vicious, destructive, corrupt, brutal and bloodthirsty. The population, and particularly the young men, must be taught to believe that unless they fight and win, their own lives, their countries, and their families will be in mortal danger. In this respect the present world powers have developed "psychological warfare" to an unprecedented level of misinformation.

If propaganda does not work, then one must have other methods to entice or force young men, and more recently young women, into the armed forces. One method is the drafting of citizens into the armed forces. Practically every nation with an army has, during the last two hundred years, embarked on programs of drafting its young men. European armies were becoming larger and more destructive. In order to fill these increasingly large armies it was necessary for Napoleon to follow the program initiated by Frederick of Prussia and to initiate a similar arrangement in France. The American Civil War of 1860–1865 was another example of this growing trend. And of course World Wars I and II could not have been fought had it not been for the ability of various warring nations to draft their young men into their armed forces.

With the advent of nuclear weapons, the question of modern war becomes one of whether we wish to engage in the pursuit of mutual suicide. An analogy

I recently heard relates the story of two men in the basement of a house where the gas is escaping. They are arguing about who has the most matches, but they ignore the fact that striking only one match will blow up the entire building, including themselves!

Non-Violence

My first contact with pacifist thought and action came through my study of the early days of Christianity when I learned that many of the early Christians were pacifists and refused to participate in the armies of Rome. They were also communists in the sense that as children of God, they shared their possessions and other aspects of their lives. There was no need for the emergence of conflict based upon greed, lust for power and other forms of domination. According to some reports, the early Christians paid a heavy price for their refusal to serve in the Roman armies. The empire subjected them to severe punishment and even death. The Christians preserved their non-violent position and steadfastly refused to fight and defend the empire. It was only in the fourth century, during the reign of Constantine, that Christians and Romans reached an accommodation in which Christians agreed to serve in the Roman army. Persecution ceased and many Christians became Roman citizens. This submission to the power of Rome was, in my view, the most serious mistake made in its early history by the church. In spite of the Augustinian concept of "a just war", the impact of this error continues to plague many of the Christian churches to the present.

However, the spirit of pacifism has always existed in the Christian church — albeit as a very small minority position. Many of the other great religious groups — Buddhists, Hindus, Muslims and others — also contain elements of non-violence in their religious observances and philosophies. Mahatma Ghandi, the great Indian leader, was a leading proponent of pacifism and non-violence in the Hindu tradition.

Early contacts with non-violence as a philosophy came during my study of early U.S. history. During the 1840s the United States government declared war on Mexico. As a result of that war, the United States seized large portions of Mexican territory including what are now the states of California, Texas, New Mexico and Arizona. Henry Thoreau, a writer and naturalist, objected to that blatant and unprovoked attack on another country and was jailed for his refusal to support the war. According to reports, his good friend, the great American writer and philosopher, Ralph Waldo Emerson, visited him while he was in jail and wanted to know why Thoreau was there. Thoreau's response was "Why are you not in jail?"

It was during the period of his incarceration that Thoreau wrote his celebrated *Essay on Civil Disobedience*, a document which laid out the case for an individual to refuse to serve in the armed forces of a country engaged in a manifestly unjust war. It has become known worldwide, and has had a major impact on those of us who have become proponents of non-violent action against injustice.

The three historic "peace churches", the Mennonites, Brethren, and Society of Friends (Quakers), represent another aspect of religious pacifism. While their religious philosophies differ widely, they are united in that they do not support any form of organized violence or war.

Quakers were persecuted in England as were the Mennonites and Brethren in Russia and in Germany. In spite of religious persecution, and killings sanctioned by the state, Quakers persisted in their beliefs and behaviour. In the view of Quakers, it is more important to continue the search for truth than to submit to the dictates of the state. It is not their beliefs, however, which generate the high degree of acceptance and respect Quakers now enjoy in Canada and in the U.S. It is the fact that they live according to their beliefs and insist upon acting in the same light, whether or not their behaviour conforms to the dictates of the state.

The Struggle Begins

I had entered the school of social work in the fall of 1940 and had thought that perhaps I might have until the end of the school year, i.e., June of 1941, before I would be summoned by the Selective Service System to report for military service. By the spring of 1941, however, I had received their call to report for a pre-induction medical examination. There was some delay following the examination but, as noted earlier, I had requested the classification of a conscientious objector. I received, however, a "1A" classification, indicating the local draft board had rejected my request. I would be summoned for induction into the U.S. Army within a short time. The induction notice did not come immediately and I was therefore able to complete the first year of graduate study.

I immediately wrote to the Selective Service System appealing the classification given by my local draft board. For some time I did not hear from them but I began to hear rumours that the Federal Bureau of Investigation (FBI) and other police agencies were again engaged in an investigation of my character and my reputation in the community. My friends, teachers and relatives were among those questioned by the FBI. I waited to be interviewed by the police officers myself, but that never occurred. I was not too surprised about this phenomenon, however, because I was aware that anyone who claimed the "4-E" classification would be routinely investigated. My request for reclassification was again denied by the local draft board in Atlanta. Shortly after receiving that news, I appealed to the State Selective Service Headquarters to overturn the decision of the local draft board. I asked that the director award the classification I had requested. Within a very short time, probably no more than two or three weeks, I received a letter from the State Selective Service Headquarters, informing me that my request for an appeal had also been denied. I then had one other alternative, that was to appeal to the National Selective Service Headquarters in Washington, D.C. and request a review of my case.

At that time the national director of the Selective Service System was Brigadier General B.O. Davis, the first black general in American military history. Unfortunately, however, General Davis was a soldier who did not sympathize with my situation. He was also the father of Lieutenant B.O. Davis

Jr. with whom I had a minor problem at Tuskegee. A few weeks later, I received a letter from the general indicating that my final appeal had been denied and that the "1A" classification remained in effect. That denial was the beginning of an eleven-month struggle between the Selective Service System, the U.S. district attorney and myself. I was not prepared to accept my present classification and to simply sit back and wait until I was called by the U.S. military. I had made up my mind that I would resist that classification as far as possible, including the federal courts but I recognized that there was no further point in going to the local or national draft board in Atlanta or in Washington.

My first challenge to the "1A" classification was taken before the State Selective Service Headquarters. I called and made an appointment to see the officer in charge, a colonel in the U.S. Army. Upon arrival, following a wait of about fifteen minutes, I was ushered into his office by the colonel's secretary. He was standing and glaring at me. That began a very unfortunate and almost unbelievable interview. Before I could speak, the colonel launched into a passionate tirade against my position. One would have thought that I had committed the most heinous crime possible in American society. I listened to this tirade without attempting to speak. It was necessary for me to wait at least ten minutes before that opportunity came. I knew exactly how the colonel felt and decided that at the first opportunity I would cut in and explain my purpose for being there. His angry words appeared to me to reflect two basic attitudes. First, he was a career army man and could not understand my objection to military service. Second, I was an "uppity" black who was rejecting his submissive role in southern society. Finally, as a result of the commotion, the secretary rushed into the room to determine what was going on. She had heard the commotion inside and thought perhaps something dramatic had happened.

I was practically thrown out of the office and told that there was no point to even consider appealing this matter to anyone else. I should do as I was told and stop complaining. I left the office on the verge of laughter. I had thought that I would at least get a chance to express my point of view but the colonel made sure that opportunity never came. I left the office more determined than ever that no matter what the cost, I would take the next step. I am still not certain of my emotional state at the time, but I was not deterred from pursuing my usual activities in the school and in the community.

I began my second year classes at the School of Social Work in September 1941. Within the next month or so, I received a letter from the president which always contained the same message: "Greetings from the President of the United States, you are hereby instructed to report to camp ......" on a given date "...you have ten days to prepare yourself, to report and to be inducted into the U.S. Army".

The date of that letter was mid November, within two or three weeks of the Japanese attack on Pearl Harbour on December 6, 1941. That attack set the stage for U.S. formal entrance in World War II and all participants were mobilizing their armed forces and preparing for a bitter struggle which eventually led to the defeat of Germany and Japan and the victory of the allied forces.

I made my next move within a week following receipt of the letter from the president. I called the U.S. district attorney in Atlanta and made an appointment with his secretary. He received me in a sober but friendly manner. I think he was not quite aware of why I was there. I sat down at his suggestion and handed him the letter from the president. He read it and wanted to know what I wanted him to do with it. I said that he could keep the letter if he wished because I was not going to follow through on it. I cannot remember the exact words that were spoken during that interview, but what came through very clearly was his insistence that I take the letter back and report to the U.S. military base as ordered. As I recall, at that point, he began to talk about the consequences of my action, pointing out that I was a student, I had finished college and that I was taking the chance of forever ruining my life. My response was that I had read the Selective Service Act and was aware of the penalties for disobeying an order but had made up my mind. This discussion continued for fifteen or twenty minutes before we recognized that we were not likely to reach an agreement. At that point, I got up and said that he knew where to find me and that I would be available at any time he wanted me. I then walked out.

That incident was my first confrontation with the law, as represented by the district attorney of the United States government. The last comment he made before I left was, "You *will* report for induction into the United States Army! That is an order!" I said nothing but I was absolutely certain that I would not report.

The order for me to report to Fort Benning, Georgia for induction into the U.S. Army came in early 1942. The physical examination found me in good shape except for one minor ailment which they felt could be easily cleared up by using the appropriate medication. The examination had delayed the date for my reporting for induction by two or three weeks. I refused induction when the second order arrived. Instead I mailed that note to the district attorney informing him of our previous discussion and that he had my letter of induction which he could use if necessary. He could also use the second letter as evidence in the event of legal action against me.

Knowing that I would be investigated again and possibly arrested, I approached a number of people whom I thought might be able to provide bail on my behalf. To my surprise, none of my friends were able or willing to do so. They were afraid that if they put up bail for me they, themselves, might be under suspicion of law violation. This was the South and they had to be careful. Finally, I located two men who agreed to provide bail if required. They wanted to have some indication of how much money would be required for bail but I had no idea. One of the men was Forrest B. Washington, the director of the School of Social Work. The second man was the father of Jimmy Holloway, one of my high school friends. I had met Mr. Holloway, the owner of a jewellery store in downtown Atlanta, on a number of occasions when visiting Jimmy at his home. I decided to rely on him rather than on the director of the school. Obviously, I could not have raised the money for bail myself, neither could any of my relatives or close friends. Most did not own their homes or control other financial resources.

Some neighbours were waiting for me when I came home from school one evening about three or four weeks following the encounter with the district attorney. They told me that two white men in civilian clothes and one police officer had been at my house wanting to know where I was. They were told that I would probably be returning home late that evening. I knew precisely the meaning of that visit. For some strange reason I did not express any concern. My friends wanted to know what I thought was happening since I did not seem to be worried. I suggested that the situation was probably grave but that they should not worry about it.

The next morning, after arriving at school, I called the office of the district attorney and when the secretary answered, I asked to speak to him. She asked what I wanted to talk to him about. When I told her that I understood that the police had been looking for me the previous day, she checked with him and returned to say that he had no knowledge of the police action. They might want to consult with me or perhaps to pick me up for questioning. I accepted that, went back to my classes and finished the day without any particular concern.

The next day around 6:00 in the morning I was awakened by loud knocks at my front door. I knew what this meant and quickly got partly dressed, went to the door and found two men standing there with their hands on their guns. They asked me if I was Wilson Head. I said I was. They immediately grabbed me by the arms and started pulling me out of the house. I told them I had not finished dressing and wished to go back into the house and complete dressing. They reluctantly agreed and waited. I happened to look out the back door and noticed a city policeman standing with his gun drawn. Obviously, they expected some kind of ruckus with me and were quite prepared to deal violently with whatever happened. Strangely enough, I felt very calm and I took my time getting dressed and walked out to meet the men at my front door. I was immediately taken to their car and pushed into the back seat. One man sat in the front seat with the driver and two other men sat in the back seat, one on each side of me. Strangely enough, I went through this process very calmly. When we arrived, I was taken to one of the upper floors of the court house.

I was not permitted to walk but was pushed into a small cell adjoining the court room which was used to hold people prior to their appearance for bail or for detaining until such time as a trial could be arranged. Upon entrance to the building, I had used a telephone to call Mr. Holloway and asked if he would come down to provide the bail, as we had previously arranged. He agreed to do so. I was taken from the cell to the office of the district attorney where I met with him and six additional people, one of whom was a "bailsman" who would provide bail, if needed. Providing bail for detainees was a business which helped those not having ready cash. Mr. Holloway arrived shortly after we entered the office of the district attorney and we were taken to a justice of the peace who set the bail at $2,000. Mr. Holloway signed a cheque for that amount and deposited it with this gentleman. I was immediately released and went back to school and continued in my afternoon classes.

I said nothing to anyone about what had happened at that time. It was only some two or three weeks later that I began to inform my classmates, my teachers and others that I had been arrested and was out on bail because I had refused induction into the U.S. Army, thereby violating the Selective Service Act.

From my perspective, two significant events had occurred during those months. The first was when I handed my notice to report for induction into the United States Army to the district attorney and the second was when I was finally arrested and taken before a district attorney and a magistrate to arrange for bail as a result of violating the Act. I was experiencing a strange sense of calmness and a feeling of absolute freedom. I clearly recall comparing my situation to that of Julius Caesar when he faced the possibility of victory or defeat before crossing the Rubicon, a small river in northern Italy which separated the two warring armies. Caesar had debated for some time whether or not to cross the river and to attack his enemy. Finally he made the decision to do so. When Caesar crossed the Rubicon he knew there was no turning back. It was either victory or defeat. I knew that it would be either finding some way to obtain a change in my classification or to be subjected to prosecution and perhaps sentenced to a federal penitentiary.

I was aware that the term of imprisonment for violation of the Selective Service Act was between one and five years. At that time very few people had gone to jail because of refusal to obey the Act. Those who had gone, however, had often received the maximum prison sentence because judges and other officials often saw a refusal to obey the army as a more serious crime than breaking and entry, theft or other crimes. I knew that some time would elapse between when I was arrested and the actual date of the trial. I felt there was a good possibility of remaining in school until June and completing my master of social work (MSW) degree before I was actually called before the federal court.

I did not fully understand the reason, but the district attorney did not immediately choose to have me arraigned. Instead, he began a process of calling me in for consultations. Over the period of January to October 1942, I was probably called into the office of the district attorney at least eight times. Each meeting began with a determined attempt by those present to break my will, to get me to recognize that I had made a terrible mistake and that this mistake could be rectified only if I changed my mind and agreed to be inducted into the United States armed forces. This scenario was played in many different ways. The number of men involved in these discussions ranged between five and eight and always included the district attorney, FBI agents, city police officers, assistant district attorneys and other individuals. I was informed that being a university student and a person about to receive a degree in social work,

I could get a high position in the military services and would not have to go on the battlefield as an ordinary soldier. I could play a role, for example, in the personnel department or in the recruiting and selection department, or some other branch of the armed services. On one occasion, I was told that I could go into the navy and play a musical instrument in the navy band! I laughingly told the navy captain that I could not play in the navy band because I played a violin and that bands did not include violins. The important thing was that they were trying to get me to accept some compromise and that I could go into the military services without necessarily having to be a fighting soldier.

As these interviews continued over the weeks and months, I began to really enjoy them. I had no sense of fear that I was in any great danger, I simply enjoyed the discussions. It was almost like a game; they were trying to convince me of the errors of my ways and I was stubbornly insisting that I was doing what was the right thing for me and that I intended to follow through no matter what the consequences.

In the meantime, during the summer of 1942, I had graduated from the School of Social Work and received my degree. Shortly afterwards I accepted a temporary position with the Butler Street YMCA as a recreation and group work adviser to youth clubs. It was not advisable for me to seek permanent employment since I could not be certain how long I would be free to work and the temporary position was quite appropriate.

Two other incidents occurred during the summer of 1942 which heightened my determination to leave the South. One was that on two occasions I had written letters to the minister of the First Baptist Church of East Point suggesting that since there was a war going on against fascism in Europe and in support of democracy, perhaps it would be a good idea if our young people would get together. As Baptists and Christians, perhaps we would find something in common to discuss, particularly around the subject of building a more democratic and less racist society. I had no response to that letter so three or four weeks later I repeated the process, writing another letter suggesting that we would be pleased to invite his group to our church since there might be some difficulty of blacks attending his church. Again, I had no response.

However, a short time later an unusual incident occurred. One night when I came home from the school library, I found the remains of a burning cross on my front lawn. Obviously the KKK had been at my house but fortunately, I was not present when they arrived. I have no idea how many there were but I suspect two or three car loads of KKK members had been there. That was quite surprising for I had no idea that the KKK was operating in East Point or Atlanta since it was unusual for it to operate in large urban areas. Nevertheless, the evidence was clear, the KKK had left a cross burning on my lawn and I was well aware of the significance of the act. It was a warning and was recognized as such by friends and neighbours.

The second incident occurred when I was coming home one afternoon. As I had stopped in the downtown section of Atlanta to transfer from a streetcar to a bus, I found, at the point of the transfer, a large crowd of people standing around, listening to a speaker promoting the sale of war bonds. The bonds were not selling well and the speaker was trying to encourage as many people as possible to buy them in support of the war effort. The speaker was also focussing on the idea that war bonds were "helping our army to destroy fascism and promoting 'freedom and democracy' all over the world". The crowd was almost entirely white. At most, I saw two or three blacks among the crowd of two or three hundred people. I was standing on the periphery of the crowd listening to his remarks. The speaker asked if there were any questions. Two or three people did ask questions about the cost and where bonds were available. I raised my hand and asked if his concern about democracy also included democracy and freedom for black people in Atlanta? I asked this question on the spur of the moment and without giving it any thought or considering the possible ramifications. Suddenly I noticed that the crowd was turning silent and that a number of police officers was gathering around me. Two of them came up to me and asked me why I made such a stupid remark? I was so oblivious to what was going on that I was not quite aware of what he was talking about. Looking into their faces and their expression of hostility, it suddenly occurred to me that my remarks were totally unacceptable in their concept of the proper and acceptable behaviour of blacks. White people did not want to hear black people talking about liberty, freedom or democracy. The policeman suggested that I should leave that area very quickly and say nothing else. I was more than happy to oblige and left rapidly, I thereby avoided what might have become an ugly incident and perhaps even a riot. I had to admit that under the circumstance the question had not been a wise one.

By the beginning of September I had come to the conclusion that my discussion with the D.A. and others had gone on long enough and that it was time for them to either take me to court, have a trial and get it over with or I would take another approach. I had decided to challenge the Selective Service System itself and had reread the Act and was struck by the fact that anyone had the right to examine their own file if a request for a specific classification had been denied. I checked with a lawyer to ensure that my interpretation of the Act was correct. He assured me that it was true, however, he had not noticed that particular item in the Selective Service Act. I suspected that many other lawyers were also not aware of that clause. My challenge was the first of its kind in the area.

At our next session with the district attorney and his friends, I raised the question. By that time we had held probably seven or eight friendly but unproductive meetings. I informed them that I had on a number of occasions asked to examine my file regarding the evidence they had against me and which prevented the possibility of reclassification. He was quite surprised when I stated that this denial had occurred and suggested further that I was going to take the matter to court since I felt my rights had been violated. He and his colleagues were apparently quite surprised. He looked at the others; they looked puzzled.

The meeting was terminated and I was quickly asked to leave the room. I assumed that after I left the group entered into a fairly detailed discussion of my claims. Someone must have brought a copy of the Act out and shown them exactly what I was referring to. Of course, I will never know exactly what happened but within three or four days I was called back to a further meeting and asked the question; "If we help you to go to the 'concentration' camp you have been speaking about, would you go without any further trouble?" I laughed at that idea because I had not been talking about a "concentration camp" but about a Civilian Public Camp (CPS) set up on behalf of conscientious objectors by the American Friends Service Committee and other "peace churches". They had taken the responsibility for supporting men who were given the "4-E" classification as conscientious objectors to military service. Men with that classification were not under the supervision of the army, navy or air corps but under the direct supervision of one of the three "historic peace churches".

I had selected a camp operated by the Service Committee (AFSC), the service arm of the Society of Friends (Quakers). So I told the group that I would be very happy indeed to go to one of these camps since that is what I had been seeking. Shortly following that discussion the district attorney terminated the meeting and said they would be in touch with me soon.

A few days later I received a letter from a local draft board informing me that I had been given the "4-E" classification I had been seeking for more than a year. The camp at Kane, Pennsylvania, however, was not operated by the AFSC, but by the Church of the Brethren. I was not overly happy with the assignment but I was satisfied to have the struggle over. I preferred a Quaker Camp, simply because my philosophy of life was closer to theirs than to the relatively unknown Church of the Brethren. I left Atlanta by train in mid October and arrived at Kane the next day to be met by members of the administration and a few campers.

That assignment was my farewell to Atlanta, and to the Deep South. Upon leaving, I was quite aware that I would never return and resume living in the South. I was entering a new phase of life in a new environment and a totally different society and milieu than I had been accustomed to in the past. There were very few blacks in the CPS program. I expected that a large majority of the people would be whites but they would be individuals of high intelligence, commitment to service and non-violence. I looked forward to this new challenge with eagerness and great anticipation.

The news of my leaving the city to go north to participate in a program for conscientious objectors spread very rapidly throughout the Atlanta community. It was very interesting to ascertain the reactions of many people to the position I had taken. Some people seemed to feel that my leaving was almost the same as going to a "concentration camp". They had never heard of Quakers, work camps, non-violence or pacifism. These people felt sorry for me and wondered how a person like myself, with my education, could manage to get into such a state. Others knowing and having worked with me felt that there must be more to the situation than met the eye. They had some understanding of my attitudes toward war and violence from my discussions in high school and in university. I had informed many people of my position while at Tuskegee, including my reasons for refusing to accept military training in the Reserve Officer's Training Corps (ROTC). At least a few of my friends and neighbours had some appreciation and understanding of my position. The fear of the FBI, however, and a generalized feeling that one can not 'buck the government' was very prevalent. The result was that while I had some sympathy and understanding, I received very little practical support from my friends, colleagues and neighbours. Even the pastor of my local Baptist church was noncommittal.

I found that my abhorrence of the killings, destruction and hatred engendered by participation in modern warfare, predated the philosophical, moral and ethical arguments in favour of pacifism.

Encouragement and Support

I was not alone in this struggle. Unexpectedly three men, one from the Fellowship of Reconciliation (FOR) in New York City and two from the AFSC in Philadelphia, came to consult and support me during the episode. The two Quakers from Philadelphia came to offer information, counselling and any other help I needed. Both organizations had strong commitment and dedication to non-violence and non-participation in wars. Through channels of which I am not aware, they had learned of my situation and had made the decision to come south to stand with me in a time of need. Among the many activities in the cause of peace the AFSC had also accepted responsibility for the administration of many of the Civilian Public Service Camps.

The Fellowship of Reconciliation operated very few active educational programs, such as work camps. Basically it was an educational and advocacy organization that saw its principal function as that of spreading the message of pacifism and non-violence. This work was done primarily through its contacts in churches, colleges, universities and other organizations including the YMCA, YWCA and the Student Christian Movement (SCM). Both organizations were founded in reaction to the terrible devastation of the First World War. They had considerable experience in working with many individuals and organizations whose ideas and values were at odds with those of the majority of Americans. The attitudes and actions of most people, they said, were not based on a non-violent perspective. They taught me how to behave non-violently in the event that I encountered verbal or physical violence from the general public. Reading materials on the history, philosophy and values of non-violence were made available by members of both groups. I felt that I had realistic and effective support and was fairly well prepared to face any problem I might encounter. Occasional contacts were maintained with both organizations during the long period in which I went through the struggle to obtain the 4-E classification. My contacts with those organizations continued through my CPS career and several years after that episode.

I had lived through some important experiences during the brief period between my graduation from Tuskegee Institute in 1940 and from Atlanta University in 1942. The most significant, and memorable of these experiences were the encounters with the U.S. district attorney and his colleagues. From one point of view, I was more than pleased that the experience proved to be a successful one. I had achieved a long-sought goal, but those experiences could also have been times of considerable danger. As far as relations between the white and black populations were concerned, blacks were still powerless and had no protection against constant harassment, humiliation and verbal and physical abuse. Had I been home when the cross was burned on my front lawn presumably by the KKK, there is no certainty of what might have happened, but the one sure thing is that it would not have been pleasant.

I have often wondered why I was able to face these possibilities with apparent calm and lack of concern rather than outright anxiety and fear. My only answer to my questions is that I must have, somewhere along the way, developed a sense of fatalism which enabled me to carry on my community and educational activities in the absence of disabling fear.

It was a bright sunny day and I remember marching across the campus of Spelman College to Sisters Chapel where our graduation exercises were held. I wondered, as we marched, what the cheering crowd would have thought if the FBI and city police had swooped down on the line of march, yanked me out and driven me off to the city jail. I'm sure that a puckish smile crossed my face during the remainder of that march, and as we sat in the Chapel listening to speeches before receiving our degrees! However that aspect of the ordeal was over. I had achieved the goal of obtaining the desired qualification and was now ready to face new prospects and new challenges in a strange and distant environment. In many respects, that prospect was quite exciting!

PART II

North to the Promised Land

CHAPTER 7 *World War II:*
A Personal Journey

I always had the vague goal of leaving the South. Many southerners thought of the North as a place of opportunity with a lack of bigotry, prejudice and discrimination. That intent to leave was not very firm, however, since we had no idea what we would do even if we did go north. Further, as young children we were tied to our families by attitudes, practice and by our various identifications with them. Going north would have meant a separation from our families and friends. We might have been able to develop social relationships, integration and acceptance but we were not certain of that. My father's brother lived in Cleveland and my father had lived with relatives for several months before returning to the South. My friends Charlie and Forrest Green also had an uncle living in Detroit and other relatives living in Pittsburgh. We often talked about the possibility of going north and living with our uncles, finding a job, becoming established and then sending for our families to join us.

We saw ourselves as part of a "stream of migrants" from the rural South moving to the urban North. Many of our forefathers and other relatives had taken that path. The result was that Detroit, Chicago, New York, Cincinnati, Cleveland and Pittsburgh were largely populated, particularly in the black community, by ex-southerners. Our dream was to escape from the bigotry and poverty of the South to what we thought were the golden cities of the North.

I was not quite so optimistic about this as some of my friends. I had spent the summer of 1940 in Chicago and had seen with my own eyes the poverty, homelessness, crowded conditions, poor job opportunities and the heavy crime rate among blacks. I knew there would be no "promised land". But I also knew that there were more opportunities for black people than in Atlanta, or anywhere else in the Deep South. Being drafted into the Civilian Public Service and doing "work of national importance", instead of military service, gave me that opportunity. I seized it eagerly.

The approaching military crisis in Europe led to the closing of the Civilian Conservation Camps (CCC) which later were chosen to house the newly established CPS units. Establishing an alternative program for conscientious objectors to military service was not an easy task. The process, including the

Mennonites, Brethren and Friends, began before the German invasion of Poland in the summer of 1939 and continued well into 1941. The Historic Peace Churches were interested in providing an opportunity for their young men to demonstrate their rejection of war as a solution to human and national problems but the Selective Service System was interested in keeping the men out of sight because all army officers were afraid of public outrage if the men were too visible. The availability of CCC facilities helped to resolve the housing problem. These facilities had been constructed as a part of the Roosevelt plan to provide employment for unemployed youth during the Depression of the 1930s and had been abandoned as young men were drafted into military service.

As noted earlier, I was not called for service in the CPS until 1942 and was not a part of these negotiations. But I met and talked at considerable length with Paul French, Paul Furnas and other Friends who were involved from the beginning along with representatives of the Mennonites and Brethren Committees. Agreement was finally reached and the first CPS camp was opened in May, 1941.

At Kane, for the most part, the men had come from Brethren churches in Ohio, Indiana, Illinois and other parts of the mid-west. Many of them were not very well educated, having been raised on farms or in small towns. Their farm background gave them a major advantage over those of us who had come from an urban setting since they were accustomed to hard work. Every attempt by the management and administration of the camp was made to meet the spiritual, social and physical needs of the men, even though, in some situations, this came in conflict with government regulations. For example, the government tried to control the time when men would be away on leave. The Brethren would not cooperate with that attempt to undermine their project and they insisted that they would control their camps. They would make the rules and regulations. Running the camp would not be any of the government's business and more specifically, not the business of the United States military.

I was only in that setting for a matter of three or four weeks. A letter from the AFSC inquiring about my interest in transferring to a "detached unit" was welcomed. "Detached units" were basically projects in institutional settings such as mental hospitals, training schools for "delinquent" boys, schools for the mentally retarded, and a number of experimental projects. This unit, the Cheltenham School, a reform school for black boys, was located only twenty-five miles from Washington, D.C., an area normally considered a part of the "South". Although having some mixed feelings about returning to any part of the South, I decided to accept the assignment because I realized that this was an opportunity to provide a much-needed service, under the supervision of the AFSC.

I said goodbye to the new friends I had made at Kane and boarded a train for Philadelphia where I was then given a period of orientation at the office of the Service Committee. Plans were made for me to depart the next day for Washington, D.C., where I would be picked up and driven to the Cheltenham School which was located in rolling farm lands of western Maryland. The buildings were constructed of brick and were relatively well-cared for. Approaching it from the highway, one would get the impression that the institution might have been a well-kept college or university campus. However, it was quite different once one was inside. It housed approximately two hundred young black boys sent there by juvenile court judges on convictions of delinquent behaviour. These children ranged in age from eight to sixteen. The delinquent acts for which they were sent to the school ranged from simply skipping school, disobeying their parents or running away from home, to more serious acts such as stealing cars or breaking into homes. Most of them were away from home for the first time and were simply lonely, frightened and only wished to return to their parents and homes. From time to time, some young boy would try to run away from the school and most often, they were caught and brought back to the school which provided $5 to any farmer in the neighbourhood who caught an escaping boy and returned him to the school.

The superintendent, most professional staff, clerical and middle level staff were all white. Only a few cooks, cottage parents and janitors were black. The arrival of our CPS group changed the entire complexion of the school since our group was composed of twenty-five young, well-educated men, twenty-three of whom were white and two of whom were black. The two blacks included Wally Nelson and myself. I had met Wally previously in the 1940 Chicago work camp. We were not at Cheltenham because we were wanted by the superintendent and his administration, but because no other males were available. Most of the previous workers had been drafted into military services and were therefore unavailable. Consequently, the superintendent had to look to some other source for workers in order to keep the school in operation. The superintendent obviously had some concerns about our coming based on the fact that we were conscientious objectors.

The fears of the superintendent were realized shortly after our arrival. There were more than adequate reasons for his concern. We arrived at the institution in groups of twos, threes and fours over a period of four days. Once all of us had arrived, we had our first unit meeting. The first question that came up was that we were housed in different buildings. All of the white CPSers were placed in two buildings separate from the building to which Wally and I were assigned. We agreed at that meeting that we would approach the superintendent and ask what the policy of the school was and why our unit could not live together. The superintendent found himself in a very difficult situation. We were essential to the operation of his school but the practices and the laws of the state of Maryland were based on segregation of the races. He felt he could not change that practice, even though he would like to have done so. We understood his position but were not satisfied. There began a continuous series of meetings and confrontations which lasted over a period of several weeks.

Wally and I filed a strongly worded letter of protest to the superintendent. Our colleagues joined us in this protest which made the matter even more difficult. Segregation extended into the dining areas with one dining room for blacks and one for whites. The few black staff members and the two of us ate in the "black" dining room while the whites ate in the "white" dining room. Following our letter, our group met to decide strategies for dealing with this unacceptable situation. After a considerable amount of discussion, we came to the conclusion that the white members of our group might begin eating in the "black" dining room with the expectation that "all hell would break loose" when this was done.

Our third complaint revolved around the fact that a new unit of four of our men were appointed to serve as a new "professional department" which was to include social work, education and psychology. One of our men was a professional psychologist but I was the only person in the group who had a master's degree in social work. I was not appointed to that special unit. This again raised considerable anger and concern. The result was that a number of meetings were held in which the superintendent became quite upset. He felt that we were pushing too hard and charged us with not being able to understand his position and trying to force him to violate the laws of the State of Maryland.

During this conflict our unit had to become familiar with its new jobs, learn the procedures and become acquainted with the boys we were supervising. Usually they served terms varying from three months to as long as two years. The result was there was a constant turnover, some boys being discharged and others arriving for their time in the training school.

There was not much actual "training" taking place in the school because there was very little work to be done, very few educational programs and the boys spent most of the time in their residential cottages. It required much ingenuity and skill to develop adequate programs and games to keep the boys busy. Our unit was fairly successful in doing this and were told by some of the old staff that we had done a much better job than the previous staff, many of whom had worked in the institution for many years. This praise, however, did not add to our popularity. Many of the older staff appeared envious and resentful of the fact that our unit had a good relationship with the boys. Our unit had reduced the number of runaways as well as the number of physical and verbal conflicts between boys in the cottages. We had created a more positive atmosphere in the entire institution. One would have thought that this would have been appreciated but it was not.

The work with the boys, plus the tension and conflict with the administration led to an increasing number of meetings, many of which lasted until early morning. Wally Nelson and I continued to insist that we would not remain in a segregated living situation. We preferred returning to the CPS camp than to live in a segregated environment. Our colleagues agreed with this sentiment and kept the pressure on the administration to make necessary changes. The superintendent kept stalling and insisting that he was doing all he could.

Finally, the situation became so tense that the superintendent felt that we would have to go. There was, under the circumstances, no way he could keep us at the school. He then called Philadelphia and asked the Service Committee to rescind his request and to remove the unit. The next morning, however, he got on the phone again and called the Service Committee indicating that he had changed his mind. After second thoughts, he had realized that without us it would be impossible for him to operate the school and it would have to close. Within a day or two the Service Committee despatched two of its officers to meet with us and with the superintendent to see if the conflict could be resolved.

Apparently the separate meeting between the AFSC emissaries and the superintendent went well. However, no decision was arrived at following that meeting. The superintendent was fully aware of his predicament and was willing to make a few concessions, but he was not willing to accept basic changes in the segregated structure of the living and dining arrangements. As a result a meeting of the entire CPS unit was called for that evening and for some reason I was unanimously elected to chair that meeting. By that time two other AFSC executives had arrived on the scene. The CPS unit at the Cheltenham School was obviously considered a desirable "detached unit" and neither the superintendents nor AFSC wanted to see it disbanded.

The meeting was called for late in the evening so that all members of the unit could attend. The superintendent did not attend and the tension in the air was palpable. One member of the unit, commenting on the meeting, noted that one could almost cut the air with a knife. I decided not to open the meeting for several minutes so that hopefully participants could have the opportunity to relax and talk informally before the heavy discussions got underway. Finally I called the meeting to order but there was total silence for a brief moment; one that seemed like an hour to me. Finally a member of our unit asked the emissaries to relate the nature of their conversation with the superintendent. They made a valiant attempt to place the meeting with the superintendent in as positive a light as possible, but it was clear that little or no significant progress had been made. The young, white psychologist leaned toward me stating, "What's the use? Why don't you end the meeting?" However, I was not ready to terminate the meeting at that point because I felt that all members should have an opportunity to have their say.

The anger which had been building over several weeks simply exploded. I felt sorry for the AFSC emissaries who were doing what they could in their own calm and peaceful manner. Wally Nelson led the attack on the institution noting that he preferred to return to Big Flats. Most of our white colleagues supported his stand. I was barely able to keep the meeting under some degree of control but succeeded in ensuring that all who wanted to speak had that opportunity.

It was clear, however, that some members were uncertain of the position taken by the majority of the unit. They were reluctant to see the unit closed. Nevertheless they supported the majority position that either substantial changes be achieved or we would close down the project. We had reached an impasse and it was apparent that there was little value in continuing the discussion. The meeting was terminated inconclusively but with the stated intent of some members to take action on their own behalf.

The next day several white unit members walked out of the dining room for white staff and entered the black dining room. State regulation prohibited blacks from entering white dining rooms but said nothing about whites entering dining rooms for blacks. This action created total consternation for the superintendent and other members of the regular white staff. We began to face the very strong hostility of other members of the white staff. The black staff members were very happy to have our white colleagues come into their dining room and eat with them. The whites, on the other hand, felt this was totally inappropriate, a violation of the mores and customs of the institution. Strangely, most of the hostility was not directed at the two of us blacks but at the white men who violated the culture of that institutional structure. The hostility was intense but they had no way of dealing with examples of civil disobedience. Aside from continuous hostility, the status quo remained and our white members continued to dine in the "black dining room".

Shortly after that incident I was approached by the staff of the AFSC and asked if I would be interested in serving in a newly established "China Unit" (CPS #99), a group of CPS men to be trained for relief and rehabilitation work in China. The possibility appeared exciting and I agreed to accept the transfer. My colleagues at Cheltenham stated their regret at my leaving but supported me in the move. The struggle for equality and freedom was not over and I was assured that it would continue. Although pleased that I had been offered the new assignment, I was also unhappy with the idea of leaving my colleagues in a continuing struggle.

I left Cheltenham in early 1943 and joined the China Unit which was to receive language and technical training at Pendle Hill, a Quaker religious and educational centre in Wallingford, near Philadelphia. The China Unit was scheduled to be based in Chungking, China. It was considered to be one of the prized locations of the system and assignments were eagerly sought. Two units of eight men each were selected by AFSC for the project from applicants from across the country. I was chosen as a member of the second group and immediately was dispatched to Pendle Hill for training. The Pendle Hill experience was to become one of the highlights of my life.

Pendle Hill

The directors of Pendle Hill, Howard and Anna Brinton, were great inspirations to those who were studying not only Chinese but also Quaker history, philosophy and values. Both people were deeply involved themselves and both could be considered philosophers. Both had done considerable writing and therefore were well known in Quaker circles in the United States and in England. They were bright, intelligent, knowledgable and sensitive.

It was at Pendle Hill that I met a few "Weighty Friends", meaning Friends who were somewhat more influential than others. Among these were Douglas Steere and Clarence Pickett, who at that time was Executive Director of the

AFSC. I also came into contact with the writings of Rufus Jones. In addition, outside speakers presented a wide variety of points of view. One of the most imposing from my perspective was Scott Nearing who was a former Communist and at that time a practising anarchist. His critique of much of religious practice was devastating. Many of us who had previously not heard this type of critique sat in awe of a man who had such wide knowledge and experience, not only in philosophical terms, but also in practical living. He and his wife lived cooperatively on a farm in New Hampshire with several other people who were attempting to put into practise what they believed. I learned a great deal about the attitudes, practices and philosophy of cooperative living from Scott Nearing.

After four or five months of study and planning at Pendle Hill, preparation was made by AFSC for our group of eight to embark on our trip to China. The first group of eight had already departed from Philadelphia and had arrived at Durban, South Africa for a brief rest on their trip. We learned, to our amazement, that they had been held up at Durban and in the absence of further negotiations, would not be permitted to go further. That raised some questions about our own status.

In the United States, a legislative bill unable to pass through Congress on its own merits could often be attached to another bill which had a better chance of approval. This was often done even when the two bills were totally unrelated. This strategy was used in connection with our planned trip. A representative of the state of Alabama, Congressman Starmes, had proposed a bill which had little chance of acceptance. That bill was designed to block the ability of conscientious objectors to travel abroad. Mr. Starmes then used the procedures mentioned above and had this bill attached to an appropriation bill which was almost certain to pass. Thus when that bill passed through Congress, Mr. Starmes' bill also passed with it. Congressman Starmes was able to manoeuvre to block the continuation of our trip and our group never made it to China. The first group who had arrived at Durham eventually had to take the next available ship and return to Philadelphia. Initially we were unaware why Mr Starmes was so hostile to our project but we learned later that he was a "hawk" who would do all he could to conceal the fact that conscientious objectors existed in the United States. It became clear that we had few friends in Congress.

That was a terrific blow to all of us. We experiencing great anxiety and hoped that the situation could be changed. Our informal leader, Nelson Fuson, spent much of his time in Philadelphia working with Service Committee personnel trying to arrange a reversal of that decision. Even Mrs. Roosevelt, the wife of the American president, who intervened on our behalf, was unable to secure a reversal of that bill. Members of Congress and legislators everywhere were generally reluctant to reverse already approved bills. The repeal of legislation in the United States at that time was very rarely accomplished.

Those of us who remained at Pendle Hill were despondent and disappointed. Even though we were aware that continuing efforts were being made to change the requirements of the bill, we realized that the chances were very small. We were then transferred to Big Flats, New York, a CPS camp located near Ithaca and Elmira.

On arrival at Big Flats our group decided that in addition to our regular work at the camp we would remain together as a unit and continue our study of Chinese history, philosophy and language. Nelson Fuson played a leading role in this activity. Here we continued the cohesiveness and close personal ties we had developed at Pendle Hill. This experience lasted for five months before it became obvious that we would never have the opportunity to provide a civilian rather than military service to the people of China. At that point some of our members transferred to other camps or detached service units. The Big Flats camp was designated as a reception camp, that is one to which all men assigned through AFSC would initially be sent for several weeks before being transferred to other camps scattered throughout the country. We remained at Big Flats for a period varying from six months to more than a year.

The training period not only included intellectual aspects: it had also included a practical dimension. Three of us, one from each of the peace churches, were chosen from the group and sent to Indianapolis, Indiana to gain experience in an AFSC work camp in which twenty-five students left their college campus and lived and worked in a local all-black ghetto. The work camp was attached to Flanner House, an adult education and recreation centre which provided a nursery school, adult education programs, social and health and many other services needed by residents of its local community.

Jim, Ralph and I, three members of our China Unit, were assigned to the work camp in the summer of 1943 and arrived a week after the camp had started. The original work campers included approximately two-thirds women and one-third men. We received the impression that we were considered as heroes, a status in which we were not very comfortable. One young woman and I were the only black workers. It was clear that she was ill at ease in the group of white middle-class students. We joined the other work campers and immediately began to work on a project involving cleaning second-hand bricks which had been recovered from the destruction of an old warehouse. Flanner House was in the process of trying to move out of its extremely inadequate premises into a new, more suitable building. It did not have the necessary funds to build a new building, thus the use of used bricks. Our job for the summer was, with the use of hammers and other tools, to clean the old mortar off those bricks and make them available for use in building the new Flanner House.

The great majority of participants in this work camp were younger people, varying from 18 to 25 years of age. They were selected by the AFSC from a list of several hundred applicants and were a highly motivated, intelligent and very energetic group. It was difficult to understand the significance of the work we were doing as we sat in the hot sun, with temperatures ranging from 80 to 90 degrees fahrenheit, cleaning bricks. It required stamina, determination and willingness to achieve small goals for a larger and more significant purpose.

The males lived in a large old house located in an all-black poverty stricken area. Indianapolis imposed a pattern of residential segregation similar to that found in the South. The black population was confined to a small ghetto west of the downtown area and, as in other ghettoes throughout the United States, this small area had developed its own infrastructure, including its social and civic agencies and a small group of doctors, lawyers, accountants and other professionals. It had elected one or two members to the Indiana State Legislature and also had its own business establishments. However, the infrastructure was inadequate, inefficient and certainly unequal. The Indianapolis black business and professional communities could not compete with their downtown counterparts because of racism. Many blacks in Indianapolis, as elsewhere, could not believe that black business or professional people could be equal to whites. The result was that a black entrepreneur or professional was left with a very limited clientele: neither whites nor blacks would be customers.

In addition, many of the blacks who lived in the black ghetto had come from the rural South and possessed very few skills useful in an urban setting. The result was widespread poverty and deprivation. Even the school system was segregated.

Living in an all-black area was quite a different experience from what our young, white work campers had experienced in their past histories. Most had grown up in middle class homes of parents who had attained college or university degrees. These students were achievers and were working toward college degrees themselves, and in a few instances had already achieved that status. Now they were living among people who had very few resources. Most blacks lived in poor housing, had low paying jobs and low educational levels.

The one institution to which they were attached, as in the South, was the church. The city of Indianapolis contained a large number of churches of various denominations. The Director of Flanner House, Cleo Blackburn, a minister in his own church, was a man who possessed the ability to persuade and charm a wide variety of people. He often demonstrated that he could succeed in manipulating the white power structure for the benefit of Flanner House, an ability which did not always lead to improving relations with other people in the same field. Other agency directors, who were suffering from lack of adequate funding, were dependent upon the United Way for financial support and never received enough to carry out the programs they felt were necessary. However, because of his close identification with the white power structure, Cleo could always extract extra money from funding agencies.

It was interesting to look at the relationship between Flanner House and the larger white community. On its board of directors sat some of the leading financial figures in the city: people from the banks, major industries, major pharmaceutical concerns, the automobile industry, and other business establishments. The board of directors was clearly dominated by members of the white power structure. While providing services to the black community, the board made certain that these programs did not threaten their financial and other interests. The concept that people receiving help should have some voice in the delivery of that service had not yet reached Indianapolis. It was not to do so for many years.

The small group of blacks who had attained some position of importance in the city were almost totally powerless. One of the state legislators, a black who was well entrenched, had attained the position of an elected senator. However, his influence had been undermined by the majority white community. When the blacks were in need of support for various projects, the senator was of little or no use. He had to check first with his white colleagues before he could make any decisions. The result was a community characterized by apathy, powerlessness and alienation.

These and similar issues were often discussed by work campers following the day's work on the playground. Often we were up after midnight discussing the relationship between poverty and education, race and economic and social structures. The relationship between poverty and inequality was also the subject of intense debates. But chipping mortars off second-hand bricks was not designed to make one alert and energetic late in the evening. Often work campers would gradually leave the meeting, go up the stairs and to bed out of sheer fatigue. The few who remained downstairs often continued these discussions far into the night.

As at Pendle Hill we arranged our own program and often brought in speakers from the community or the local office of the AFSC. We were constantly the focus of attention by politicians, ministers, and other community leaders. Community leaders often asked to be invited to meet with us. They were very curious as to what actually was going on at Flanner House. Some people in the neighbourhood went so far as to suggest that they suspected we were running a house of prostitution! They felt that any house with a large number of young people, most of whom were white, and most of whom were women must be a house of ill repute! Occasionally a young black man would stop at the house, knock on the door, and ask if he could have one of the women living there. Our standard reply to this kind of question was that we all were together. If he wanted to associate with one of us, he had to associate with all of us. That response usually solved the problem since the visitor had little or no idea how to respond to that statement.

Group Development

Within a short time we became a very close-knit group and made far fewer outside trips than I had enjoyed during the summer in the Chicago work camp. Most of our social and educational activities were enjoyed in the house where we lived. This was not a problem for me. In the first place, I did not care about association with the local community. Many people in the local community, in addition to poverty and deprivation, were also allegedly involved in criminal activities. A considerable number of breaking and entering, muggings and other crimes were committed within a block or two of where we lived. At the same time Indianapolis was noted for its large number of churches. This subject was always a source of considerable discussion: how could there be such fervent religiosity in the city and, at the same time, so much bitterness, hatred and crime, particularly among many young blacks?

The white campers were more accepting than I was of this behaviour. I tended to be more critical of many young blacks because I often felt embarrassed by their behaviour. Secondly, I often did not appreciate the manner in which the women in our group were approached by some individuals from that socio-economic group. I realized that we were there for the purpose of helping them to improve their condition. But the help we could give was related almost entirely to the possibility of cooperative work on the construction of the new Flanner House. It was impossible to believe that the young white work campers could understand or deal with the many problems faced by the black population. On the other hand, I suspected that although a trained social worker, I would not be very effective in dealing with that group in their own social milieu. I simply felt uncomfortable with the prospect of relating to people whom I suspected were involved in various activities of which I did not approve. My professional training in social work was coming into direct conflict with the religious and philosophical attitudes which had been developed throughout my life. I discovered that I was more comfortable with my work camp friends than with members of the black community who reflected a completely different life style and patterns of behaviour. This recognition was somewhat sobering!

On one occasion our group was invited to a dance at the old Flanner House. We all got dressed up, in preparation for the event. Many of the women put on makeup, had their hair done and made other efforts to look their best. When we arrived at the old Flanner House, we ran into a group of black youths who were dressed in shabby clothing, wearing their overcoats and hats and were generally unruly. As soon as the music began playing, a few of these guys went over to the side of the room where our group was sitting, grabbed some of the women and practically dragged them out onto the floor. They violently pulled the women into a very close embrace. The women were not sure how to react and their discomfort was obvious. Their worried glances at us indicated that they wanted to be rescued. We men did not feel that we had the responsibility for rescuing the women from their hosts. As the crowd grew larger, with more people entering the small space, we began to feel that we had to take some steps to protect these women from unwanted behaviour. However, we were still not sure what we should do. Jim, Ralph and I got together on the sidelines for a little conference. Unable to arrive at what we considered to be a socially appropriate solution to the problem, we suggested that perhaps it was time for our group to leave and return home. We suggested, much to the relief of some of the women, that all of us should leave. That suggestion was quickly agreed upon.

This incident reflects some of the problems felt by young middle-class university students coming into contact with a lower class sub-culture. A constructive solution to differences in culture and social/economic status requires skill and sensitivity and we had not found those qualities in sufficient amounts at that time. Our behaviour on that evening received a great deal of discussion by our group over the next several days.

Intergroup Relationships

We developed strong personal relationships due to living in very close quarters. Because of limited space, it was necessary to have bunk beds in each of the small bedrooms. As many as four or five of us slept on bunks in the same room. Although we were crowded, this did not seem to be a serious problem. The high morale in our group contributed to our ability to live and interact positively under extremely overcrowded conditions.

I had developed, within a week or so after our arrival, a very close and satisfying relationship with Phyllis and Norma. They came from entirely different backgrounds, Phyllis from a middle-sized city in the mid-western state of Iowa, and Norma from a large eastern city. They adopted me as a part of their "twosome" and it quickly became a "threesome". My experiences with Kay and Mary in Chicago, and in the CPS had prepared me for comfortable interracial relationships which would have been impossible some years earlier. But I still had some concerns with what I felt would be the reactions of the local black and white communities. There was reality to these concerns: we often received hostile glances when working on the project or walking in the nearby, all-black neighbourhood. My two young friends were always on the go. They had tremendous energy. As soon as the work day was over they were always ready to go other places. We did not feel it was very safe for our young women to go out alone in that neighbourhood. They needed escorts, and often some of the men in the group would take up the challenge and accompany them on their various travels. We were fortunate in that few negative encounters occurred.

Following that work camp and for several years I kept in contact with a number of the young women and two of the male work campers. The experience had been an extremely positive one. I will never forget the many intense and friendly discussions in which we were often engaged. Unfortunately, in spite of our best efforts we did not succeed in solving the many problems of our world! Eventually and following a period of time, I married Phyllis!

The summer work camp completed its eight weeks of operations by mid-August. Campers, often tearfully, prepared to leave and to return home or to some other destination. Some were preparing to return to university or colleges in the fall. By that time, it was obvious that Jim, Ralph and I would not be going to China. With the closing of the work camp we were reassigned to our respective camps. My assignment was to the Quaker-operated Big Flats CPS camp #46 in New York State.

That second work camp experience was a very significant aspect of my life. My experiences gave me the opportunity to interact on a close personal and equal level with young, educated, white people from middle-class backgrounds. The only way we had been able to associate with whites in the South was on an impersonal level in some variety of a master-servant relationship.

I was often surprised and pleased at my ability to fit into and adapt to this new reality. I found these interactions pleasant, productive, emotionally and intellectually stimulating. These young men and women had been among the brightest I had ever met. I had wished in the past, and particularly in my university experiences, that I could have met people of this calibre. They were not available simply because many young blacks had not had the opportunity to develop original, sensitive, cultivated and intellectual insights. In spite of all the talk to the contrary, educational programs in the South, whether in the college, university or in high schools, were generally inferior to those of whites.

Big Flats (CPS #46)

I left Indianapolis in late August and arrived at Big Flats in early September of 1943. The facilities were ideal for a CPS camp. They included four dormitories containing 30 beds each. In addition, other buildings, including a dining hall, meeting hall, library, small medical clinic and a house suitable for the director of the camp and his family were available. The Big Flats camp was located in a rural area and its major focus was planting and cultivating trees in a tree nursery. This was my first opportunity to be a part of a reforestation project.

Most of the men in the camp were assigned to useful work in the tree nursery. However, the nursery could not utilize the entire camp population. Some men had to be driven out to a nearby forest area to perform work similar to that done at the Kane camp, including clearing paths and underbrush, as well as cutting deadwood in conservation areas. These were necessary tasks, which had not been done in the past because of cost.

After three or four weeks at Big Flats, I was asked by one of our men if I would be interested in being transferred to kitchen and dining room service. The job involved cleaning the dining room after meals, washing dishes, and other related activities. Having had some experience working in restaurants in Atlanta, the work would not be a new experience for me. I accepted that opportunity for two reasons. It gave me a lot of free time during the day. It also meant that I would be inside during the cold New York winter months! I had enjoyed those late summer days in the outdoors but as a southerner, I preferred the warm climate of an inside job! I began my new assignment in October, 1943. I had no idea that I would remain in that assignment for a year and a half, or until the spring of 1945.

I found myself in the company of the most multicultural group of people I'd ever seen. The men were from all over the United States including New York, Boston, Chicago, Philadelphia and as far west as Los Angeles, California. There were even a few from the southern states. What initially surprised me most, however, was that Quakers in this Quaker-operated camp were a minority and the largest group of men were members of the Methodist church. This was of course partly a reflection of the fact that the Methodist church was much larger than the Quakers.

This extremely well educated group reflected a wide variety of interests. It included people trained in physical sciences and others trained in languages, humanities, music, social sciences, mathematics, philosophy and theology. The one factor that they held in common was their mutual and unwavering opposition to participation in military service. The old saying that "it is educated people who tend to seek more education" was certainly true at Big Flats. At one time the camp included seven Ph.Ds, and more than twenty men with master's degrees in various fields of study. The high level of education resulted in the organization of a wide variety of evening study programs. During my second week, I joined a group focussing on the study of Marxism. That was my first opportunity to obtain some insight into the nature of orthodox Marxism and its various branches. The teacher of this course was from Philadelphia and a Marxist himself. He also was well versed in the perspective of the Socialist Workers' Party, a perspective which differed considerably from that of some other branches of Marxism. I was attracted to that part of Marxism which seemed to be closely allied to the concept of democratization and equality. The reading of the Communist Manifesto sounded much like some parts of the American Declaration of Independence. On the other hand, I was repelled by the fact that the communist parties of that time felt that they were the "vanguard" and that everyone should fall in line and follow their leadership. I knew that I could not accept that idea. Moreover I was particularly disturbed about the concept of a "dictatorship of the proletariat" since I reacted negatively to any concept involving the word "dictatorship"! I wanted to study Marxism from the point of view of learning Marxist principles, their development and the context in which that development had occurred.

I learned to open my mind to a wide variety of economic and political ideas which I had never previously considered. The clash between traditional capitalist and Marxist ideas was an exciting and stimulating experience.

I also began an informal study of philosophy during my period at Big Flats. I had only taken one course in philosophy in my first year at Morris Brown College. The experience had stimulated my appetite but I had no further opportunity to follow up on that initial interest. At Big Flats we had a considerable amount of time to pursue our interests and we had a relatively good on-site library. In addition, we could borrow books from local college and university libraries. We were relatively close to Cornell University in Ithaca and to Elmira College.

CPS men had made the decision to refuse military service and were committed to that course of action. The result was a very cooperative and closely knit working group and a total commitment to non-violent behaviour. It was that belief which enabled a highly diverse group to work together with a high degree of cooperation and harmony. I experienced a complete lack of racism and was completely at home in that group. From my perspective, however, it was unfortunate that only one or two blacks were ever in Big Flats at any given time.

My earlier decision regarding my work assignment was accurate and my days were relatively free. I could engage in considerable individual study and in some group seminars. I could also practise my violin which I had brought from Atlanta. I met a young violinist who had played with the New York City Symphony Orchestra and found him a very generous individual with his time. He also worked on the kitchen detail and as a result he and I had time off together, to practise on our violins. My improvement was largely due to the fact that he was a professional and we could play together on a daily basis.

While the CPS men reflected a high degree of intelligence and educational achievement, music was not one of their achievements. Although a few of us were very interested in music and played a number of different instruments, we never had enough men to form an orchestra. In addition, many of the men were constantly moving in and out and did not remain long enough for us to develop a highly cohesive group. At various times, there were a number of good singers in the camp but again, we were never able to form a choir or even a quartet. Many of our men travelled into Elmira to sing in the choir of the local Baptist Church.

Men in the camp associated closely with local people in a variety of ways. At harvest time, many of our men helped the local farmers and fruit growers. Many farmers grew hundreds of bushels of apples, but because many men were in military service, farmers had little help in getting these apples from the trees, into crates or baskets, and ready for the market. Our men helped the farmers on a voluntary basis and in return they were often given bushels of apples to bring to camp in lieu of pay. We often had apples two or three times a day and in a variety of forms including pies, strudels, rolls and cakes.

Another method of interaction with the community was through volunteer work in local hospitals. There were two major hospitals in Elmira and many would drive into town four times per week to work at one or both of those hospitals. I spent some evenings in volunteer work at the Elmira Catholic hospital.

The free time at Big Flats enabled me to engage in pursuits which I would not have been able to do had I been employed on a nine to five schedule. My major satisfaction, however, was to become chairman of the camp's education committee. I was responsible for organizing Sunday morning and other educational programs. Our camp, with its extremely diverse population, did not organize the traditional Sunday morning religious programs. No single religious program would have been appropriate for so diverse a group. The large Methodist group was not interested in initiating their own religious program. I organized a program committee designed to reflect the various tastes and interests of the men in the camp. The committee initiated Sunday morning discussion topics which included problems related to science and religion, education, philosophy, social structures, psychological theories of human behaviour, cultural anthropology, criminology, democracy and equality and a broad range of other topics. These programs included speakers from within and outside of the camp who gave brief presentations and then sat in the "hot seat" to defend their position. Alternately, three or four campers participated in panel discussion.

Out-of-town speakers were also invited to visit the camp. Speakers from Philadelphia, New York, or from some of the nearby colleges and universities were invited and this option gave us a wide variety of experts upon whom we could draw. I recall on one occasion a Methodist Bishop from New York City spoke on a Sunday afternoon. The intention was that he would speak for perhaps a half hour and that another half hour would be available for discussion. The men were so enthralled with him, however, that he spoke for one and a half hours and then was asked to continue the discussion for another hour. This meeting had a tremendous influence and was the subject of considerable debate over the next several weeks. Other speakers included the president of the Fellowship of Reconciliation (FOR) and Clarence Pickett, the Executive Director of the AFSC. In addition, from time to time local ministers, professors and chaplains from Cornell University and other local colleges visited us for Sunday afternoon programs.

Social and Recreational Programs

American military personnel had access to social and recreational activities organized by groups of women who provided programs for off-duty soldiers and those on active duty. These groups provided members of the armed forces with opportunities for parties, dances and other activities which we sorely missed at Big Flats. The only women in the camp were the wife of the director, the head cook and the nurse. A few of the men, perhaps a half dozen or so, had wives living in the nearby city of Elmira. From time to time these men went into town to visit their wives, or their wives visited them. Single men were occasionally invited to share a dinner with these men and their wives. Otherwise our relationships with women were restricted to volunteer work in the community. The question of co-ed activities was discussed from time to time but nothing concrete had ever been done. As a result a group of us formed a committee to examine what could be done to provide a recreational program involving women at our camp.

I was one of the few men who possessed previous experience in this area. My experience in East Point, at Talledega College and at Tuskegee Institute enabled me to provide leadership in helping the committee to organize programs to attract nearby college women to visit the camp and to join us in a variety of social activities. The men at the camp were very pleased that, on the first occasion, thirty young women from Elmira College came to the camp to spend a weekend with us. I observed, for the first time, the great differences in the behaviour of men in an all male group, as opposed to their behaviour in the presence of women. The women were treated with great respect, appreciation, and consideration of their every want and need. The men eagerly joined in the activities. My suspicion is that the women themselves felt the need for such activities. They were living in communities, or attending universities and colleges, in which few males were available. The opportunity to visit and associate with the group of highly educated men was, in all likelihood, a highly valued experience for them as well.

Dave, one of my best friends, and I became somewhat involved with two young women early in the program. Joan and Karen were students at Cornell University in Ithaca and they attended practically all of our early programs. On occasion he and I hitch-hiked to visit them. On one visit Dave and I encountered what could have been a very embarrassing situation. In the early evening we were trying to hitch-hike back to camp and had no luck whatsoever. We then walked to the edge of the town, crossed to the other side of the road and planned to return to Ithaca. After a lengthy wait for a ride, we contacted a local minister who promised to help us find a place to stay over night. After a few unsuccessful attempts we were more than grateful when he agreed to have us to stay with him for the night.

The next morning we were more successful and were able to arrive at the camp before noon. Needless to say, on telling our story we became the laughing stock of the camp. Several days passed before we were permitted to forget that incident!

The Saturday evening dances were the highlights of the week. Often we would have as many as forty young women visiting for the weekend. The college women usually remained overnight and participated in the educational programs on Sunday morning. Many young women were somewhat shy about participating in discussions with older and more highly educated men but others were quite eager to jump into these discussions. Often their contributions were quite unique because they were speaking from a female perspective. Many expressed their appreciation for that opportunity and some expressed regret that the discussions on university campuses were not nearly so exhilarating and exciting as those at Big Flats.

Some students were regular attendants at our bi-monthly programs. We made specific efforts to attract students from the wide variety of colleges located in mid and upper New York State. Most young women were recruited through the campus YWCA, and the Student Christian Movement (SCM). With their support, we could recruit an adequate number of young women to make the Saturday night parties a very pleasant experience.

The FOR

During the following spring, I was contacted by the Fellowship of Reconciliation (FOR) and asked to serve as a part-time staff person with responsibility for visiting and speaking to student groups on campuses and other institutions in the Middle Atlantic region, primarily the states of New York, Pennsylvania and New Jersey. Although I had a heavy schedule at Big Flats, I felt that this was an important task and I was pleased to be invited to take on the responsibility. The Fellowship, located in close proximity to New York City, was initially established in early 20th century England as a result of the experiences of the First World War. The appalling death and destruction of that war had generated the idea, shared by many sensitive individuals, that an organization should be established for the purpose of preventing future wars. The focus was on finding solutions to international conflicts by mediation, conciliation and other forms of non-violent action. More significantly, however, was its focus on individual, community, national and international non-violent philosophy and practice. I was to support the campus YMCA, YWCA and the ShM in their effort to develop a more just society, nationally and internationally and also on their own campuses.

Before arranging my schedule so that I had every other weekend free, I thought that it would be useful to go to New York City to visit the office of the FOR and meet some of its leaders. I had previously met a FOR staff member who had visited Big Flats. Another staff member had visited and provided much needed support during my struggles with the selective service system. This was to be an opportunity to get deeply involved in the structure, functions and goals of the organization so that I could adequately represent it on various college campuses of the region.

The FOR was an advocacy organization which lobbied on behalf of peace. My work in the field of peace and human rights education had, until this occasion, never involved actual protest in public marches and demonstrations but it was one part of the program of the Fellowship to support the independence movement of the Puerto Rican community living in New York City during the 1940s.

It was a frosty winter morning in late November when a group of approximately thirty men and women joined about 150 to 200 Puerto Ricans attempting to influence American government policies. Many residents of Puerto Rico had fled when the Americans seized their land from Spain. Neither the Puerto Ricans nor people of other Spanish territories wanted to be conquered by the Americans. They wanted freedom from Spain but not at the expense of subjugation by another foreign country.

Many Americans sympathized with people struggling for freedom and independence from foreign rule. Marches and demonstrations on the streets of New York City were one method of expressing that support. I was very pleased to have the opportunity to support the struggles of another people for the freedom which had been denied to my family and friends. However, this was not a mere discussion or debate about ideas, philosophies or opinions. This was to be a real test of how well others and I would behave in the face of possible opposition and physical violence. We were aware that numerous police officers would be present presumably to protect us, but none of the marchers believed that. The police on other occasions in which I was not involved, had actually provoked violence, thus discrediting the protesters. For whatever reason, the number of police present was clearly excessive since we marched in an orderly fashion, with our own "marshals" making sure that no incident occurred and leaving the police officers with nothing to do except to express their distaste by stormy stares and negative comments.

Although time was limited, I nevertheless visited many campuses in my assigned region. Many were within a short distance, such as Cornell University. Other visits were made travelling by train or bus. I usually left the camp on

Friday night or Saturday morning, and arrived on campus for a session on Saturday afternoon or evening. Often I stayed over for Sunday morning programs with student groups. Most campuses in that area of the country held chapel services on Sunday mornings, many of which were compulsory.

I often found these sessions utterly amazing. I faced a wide variety of attitudes and behaviours by students and faculty members. In some situations I received a very warm welcome and very strong agreement between what I was saying and what students felt. On other occasions I ran into a considerable amount of opposition and disagreement, which was quite understandable. The country was at war and there was tremendous pressure on everyone, including students in colleges and universities, to conform and to demonstrate a high degree of patriotism. There were often long sessions with very heated debates following my presentations. In general, I found that students were far more liberal in their thinking than were their faculty members. I suspect this was because students had little to lose. Faculty members had much to lose, including their jobs, if it appeared that they were advocating positions opposed to those of the government.

Nevertheless I look back upon those occasions with a great deal of satisfaction and appreciation. I had a chance to help students probe into their basic beliefs, including why they believed as they did and how they justified and supported those beliefs. Some students were willing and able to enter comfortably into the probing into which I was leading them. Others found these probes too threatening. One of the generalizations I made regarding those visits, is that women students tended to be considerably more liberal in their thinking than male students. This may be related to the fact that many male students were awaiting the draft at the end of the university year, or as soon as they graduated. However this was not a unique situation. My subsequent experience also reinforced the same view. I have found that women are generally more liberal regarding social and economic issues including peace, war, racism, poverty and inequality.

AFSC Programs

The AFSC did not simply operate camps for conscientious objectors. The organization was frequently involved in presenting programs by conscientious objectors at the camps themselves or in Philadelphia or other locations. Many Quakers and non-Quakers had adequate opportunity to learn the values, goals and the religious ideology of Quakerism. On occasion a group of non-Quakers would take a car owned by one of the campers and drive to Philadelphia for meetings. It was a great pleasure to meet the leaders, staff and supporters of AFSC and some of the leaders of the two major branches of Quakerism. Those of us who were non-Quaker objectors were always welcomed and enjoyed participation, particularly in social and educational activities sponsored by Young Friends, under the age of thirty-five. We were free to attend their dances, parties, workshops and other social and intellectual events. These trips to Philadelphia became a desired aspect of life in the camps. It was important for us to get away for a weekend in Philadelphia, and return Sunday evening ready for work on Monday mornings.

These were exciting times and elicited the feeling that some minds were opening up to new and even radical ideas. I was quite aware that the college or university students were exposed to a variety of new ideas and approaches to life. That exposure, however, did not necessarily mean that concrete action would result. For me the new ideas, philosophies, and attitudes led directly to the types of action in which I was engaged. The march for Puerto Rican independence was the first of several dozen rallies, marches, demonstrations and vigils in support of disarmament, peace and independence. I hoped that at least a few individuals, based on our experiences together would also struggle for similar goals.

It was during this period of frequent visitation that I made the first of two visits to Keuka College, a small and exclusive all-girls college in upper New York state. I was invited by June Johnson and a friend who represented the Student Christian Movement on campus. They had also arranged for me to speak at the Sunday morning service of a local church attended by many students.

I became close friends with my sponsors, and especially with June. But it was June who spent most of her time as my guide including escorting and introducing me to the various activities in which I was expected to participate. I thoroughly enjoyed her company and we gradually developed an unusually close relationship which continued for a period following her graduation. The relationship was basically a result of mutual admiration, friendship and a simple enjoyment in being together.

June was a senior and graduated several months after our initial meeting but we continued contact through the mails. She obtained a position as a program secretary with the YWCA (Young Women's Christian Association) of Boston while I remained at Big Flats until I obtained my long delayed "detached service" assignment some months later.

Subsequently, I learned that June was planning to be in New York City for a few days and I immediately made plans to meet her there. It was a cold, bleak winter day when we met. She was attending a conference and did not have much time so we decided to visit the Statue of Liberty in New York Harbour. It was really cold and there was little shelter on the ferry from Manhattan to the Island on which the statue is located. It was equally cold but less windy as we climbed the more than 150 foot high bronze statue of a crowned woman holding a torch in her upright hand. The statue, a gift to the United States by the French government, was famous as a symbol of freedom and liberty in the newly established union. The inscription beneath the statue reads as follows:

> Give me your tired, your poor, your huddled masses yearning to breathe free, the wretched refuse of your teeming shore. Send these, the homeless, tempest tossed to me, I lift my lamp beside the golden door!

The statue, looking out to Europe, ignored the millions of blacks not seeking the "golden door" but rather the freedom from the horrors of American oppression and slavery. The promise related only to those Europeans whose skins were white.

I had read and admired those words while in high school and in one sense found them inspiring and worthy of memorization. Recognizing that the reality of the American dream of equality and freedom was little more than a myth, I found myself caught between my desire for the realization of that dream while knowing it was only an illusion. I recall not wanting to destroy the symbolic dream. I did not express my feelings to June but wondered what she was thinking as we stood in the biting cold and read those noble words. We walked down the tight winding staircase and took the next ferry to the city and found a restaurant where we could thaw out with a cup of hot chocolate and a doughnut.

Although our correspondence continued for more than a year, that was the last time I saw June. I was sorry that the relationship cooled. It had been a wonderful and satisfying relationship but in wartime, everything is focused on winning the war. Relationships tend to be rapidly formed, and often as rapidly broken off as the struggle against the "enemy" demands primary attention. It is difficult to maintain strong personal relations under those conditions and the everpresent threat of death focuses the mind to deal with that issue at the cost of other equally important human experiences.

In the meantime I was taking advantage of experiences beyond anything I could have imagined prior to the CPS experience. I had heard and read of the magic and excitement of Harlem and the Cotton Club where Cab Calloway, Duke Ellington and other famous black musicians had performed. Exploring Harlem was expected to be a highlight of my life. It most definitely was not. Two of my friends agreed to take me and a few other men to see the famous Cotton Club, again a great disappointment. Its fabulous shows, many including black performers, did not admit black patrons. My white friends, had they wished, could have bought tickets and enjoyed the best of entertainment. But I was excluded solely because of the colour of my skin. That was a galling experience and one which I never forgot. But anger and bitterness do not exist forever, and life must go on.

The CPS camps were no great hardship for me and I enjoyed my experience even though we had a great number of arguments about the contents and structure of the program. Many men felt the Service Committee should not be involved at all since we had been drafted through the Selective Service System, the same system that drafted young men into the armed forces. The Service Committee or any other organization, according to this thinking, should have nothing to do with anything remotely related to the military system. They felt that the Service Committee should remove itself from the operation of camps and return them to the Selective Service System. The men could then raise their objections and concerns directly with the government agency which indirectly controlled some aspects of the camps. The vast majority of men, however, were quite content to have the AFSC continue its direction and administration of the camps. I was identified with this group. Some men in the camps were unconcerned. An example that reflects this situation is the behaviour of a young black man whom everyone called "Pete". He was always joking, laughing and teasing other campers. On one occasion, we had a visit from a Colonel Kosch, the officer responsible for liaising between the system and the CPS camps. Pete was sitting down under a tree, reading a book. Pete was enjoying himself while other men were working but when the men noticed the approach of the colonel, somebody said to Pete that he should get up and start working so that he would not cause any trouble. Pete smiled and said he would handle the matter in his own way.

As the colonel approached Pete waved for him to come over. The colonel slowly walked over whereby Pete showed him a passage in the book. He was laughing and said "Look Colonel, you will enjoy reading this passage." Colonel Kosch looked surprised but read the passage and also started laughing. The rest of us stood there with our mouths practically wide open at this blatant disregard for the power and authority of the colonel. It was at this point that I also lost what little respect and fear I still had for arbitrary authority. I was one of the people who initially thought that Pete should get up and get to work. I learned later that my view was not the view of the majority of the men at Big Flats.

It became apparent, as time went on, that it would be more difficult for military men to visit our camp. While the outside public probably viewed military men with great respect and admiration for their military service, the men in CPS camps often viewed them with contempt. While some of our men could be completely non-violent in their physical behaviour, their verbal attacks on military men were often aggressive.

Gatlinburg (CPS # 108)

I was quite surprised when AFSC asked me to visit and meet with the men at Gatlinburg. Although I was active in campus visitations and busy with the educational program at Big Flats, officials summoned me for a "mini-conference" at AFSC headquarters. I had no idea of the reason for this unusual occurrence: the usual practice was for groups of CPS men to be invited, drive down, and remain for some official activity. However, my relations with AFSC officials were warm and friendly and I could only guess the nature of the meeting.

Upon arrival I was warmly welcomed and without further preliminaries, I was asked to visit Gatlinburg for a period of three or four days. Gatlinburg was composed primarily of southerners, most of whom were also rural farm boys and men, who, irrespective of their pacifist leanings, might still possess the basic racial attitudes of the Deep South. In spite of my apprehensions, I did not hesitate in accepting their invitation. I was not given any specific instructions, only to visit and interact with the campers. I was to be an unofficial visitor representing the multicultural camp at Big Flats, which by that time was well known throughout AFSC circles as a hotbed of controversy and radicalism.

Graduation, Masters Degree in Social Work

Wilson and Phyllis, shortly after marrying

Wilson in front of Flanner House, Indianapolis, 1946-47

Wilson washing the family car in Indianapolis

Wilson on right, brothers Glen on left and Marvin in centre

Receiving Doctorate degree from Ohio State University in Columbus, with sons Gregory (left) and Norman (right)

Now there are three! Wilson with Gregory, Renée and Norman (left to right)

Wilson, Phyllis and son Norman in Chicago

Wilson with T. Eberlie, J. Marshall and Dan Hill

A fond farewell, as Wilson leaves his position with the United Appeal in Windsor

Wilson in Toronto, 1968

Wilson, with his research staff at the Social Planning Council in Toronto, 1970

Playing the violin was another love

Wilson and Sandy enjoying recreational folk dancing

Katherine Cook Chaplain, with Wilson and his second wife Sandy, 1976

Honourary Doctor of Laws degree, conferred by York University, 1982, with Dorothy Herberg

Lincoln Alexander, Lieutenant Governor of Ontario and Audi Dharmalingam in 1986

With his four children, Cindy, Renée, Gregory and Norman, at a family reunion in Cincinnati, June 1993

The camp at Gatlinburg was located in an extremely attractive mountainous area of the state. The beauty of the trip with mountain streams flowing downhill, tiny waterfalls and the cascading of rapidly flowing water over rocks was almost enough to make me forget that I was sitting in the back of a segregated bus. I arrived at Gatlinburg about an hour after leaving Knoxville and was greeted by the camp director and several campers. I was given a hearty welcome by campers, a somewhat unexpected occurrence. I was immediately ushered into the dining hall for an impromptu session, questioned about my background and CPS experience and generally made to feel welcome. Had I not known my location I would never have guessed that I was in the Deep South and among southerners.

I remember little of the details of my sessions with campers but cannot forget the warmth of my welcome. We discussed almost every conceivable topic including my experiences growing up in the South, my reactions to the northern states, and how I arrived at a CO position in that atmosphere. Aside from the usual southern "drawl", there was little to distinguish them from northerners except that the southerners tended to be somewhat older and more socially conservative. It appeared to me that the general educational level of the men was considerably lower than at Big Flats and this general condition did not encourage philosophical discussion of any great depth. But these men were "down to earth" and there could be no doubt of their deep commitment to non-violence. In many respects, their sincerity, deeply held beliefs and behaviours were more convincing than many of the abstract discussions engaged in by the more highly educated campers at Big Flats.

Three days later I was given a warm "send-off" and again enjoyed the spectacular views of the rugged mountains of eastern Tennessee. Aside from our racial backgrounds, we had much in common since many white campers could identify with my experiences in obtaining the 4E classification from their local draft boards, and many had to undergo considerable criticism and hostility as a result of being charged as "unpatriotic". These men, through their non-racist and accepting behaviour, did much to mitigate negative attitudes resulting from my southern background. The Gatlinburg experience was one of the highlights of my CPS career.

New Haven Unit

Although I had enjoyed my stay at Big Flats, aside from my part-time work for the FOR on campus visitations, I was not engaged in work which was contributing very strongly to the well being of society or to the development of a more peaceful way of life. I had viewed work in the dining hall as one method of finding time to engage in other activities such as my work on college campuses, voluntary work at a local hospital and my educational leadership at the camp. This, however, began to wear thin: I had remained at Big Flats far longer than I had intended. Initially, when we left the China Unit we had expected to be at Big Flats only a short time and then, hopefully, move into some other detached services unit. For most of us that development did not occur.

Finally, in the spring of 1945, another opportunity arose which I gladly accepted. A newly established unit (CPS #140) was recruiting men for experimental purposes. They were needed to serve as "guinea pigs" in medical experiments. There was some danger of serious injury or even death in some experiments. Men in the CPS units were very anxious for the public to recognize that they were not avoiding military service because of fear. Conscientious objectors wanted to make it very clear that they were equally as brave, if not more so than soldiers in military service. Certainly, it took tremendous courage for most men to defy the mores, customs and attitudes of their society and to demand exemption from military service rather than submitting to it. Volunteering for these dangerous experiments was one way by which conscientious objectors could indicate to the general public that they were not afraid, but were not ready to demonstrate this courage by submitting to military authority. They were determined to obey what Quakers called the "inner light" or their individual conscience. My earlier struggle for the right of a CO reflected my agreement with this point of view and philosophy.

The detached service unit in which I volunteered to serve was the "New Haven Jaundice Unit". Jaundice was a disease which was expected to develop rapidly in Europe following the end of World War II. At that time little was known about how jaundice was transmitted or how it could be cured. The purpose of the experiment then was to subject men to various potential methods of transmitting the disease. Our group of thirty volunteers arrived in New Haven in the spring of 1945. The Service Committee had arranged for us to live in a fraternity house which was free until the fall. The thirty of us had been recruited from various CPS camps across the country including a few from the southern states. I was the only black in the group.

After arriving, we went through a period of four days of orientation given by medical staff at the Yale University hospital. Initially we had two visits from Service Committee staff and from the Selective Service System. Our liaison person was not the colonel but a general who was involved in training military personnel. The experiment itself did not take a great deal of time and in general, we were expected to live a relatively normal life. The hospital had a number of available jobs open which men could accept if they chose to do so. Having had some photographic experience at Tuskegee Institute, I could bring this skill to the hospital when to my surprise, I found that there was an opening for a staff photographer in the hospital. Many of the people who had been on staff had been drafted into the military services and therefore, were not available. Consequently, the labour of many of our group was highly appreciated.

For the experiment we were divided into three groups of ten and each group was to take a certain substance which might include a suspected type of bacteria. This would test whether or not the bacteria would cause the subjects to become ill with jaundice. I remember the morning when we were to see a doctor and be assigned to our particular group. The ten of us in my group were asked to take a substance from a spoon, given by the doctor. I swallowed this substance with a very strange feeling. At that time we had no knowledge of the nature and content of the medicine or bacteria in the spoon. It was also possible that some might suffer severe illness or death, or alternately nothing at all would happen. The medical staff had simply informed us that each group would get a different kind of bacteria.

A few days later some of us began to feel the effects of what we had taken. Eight of the men in the first group became ill in varied degrees. Two of them became seriously ill and almost reached the point of death. They were placed under emergency care in the intensive care unit. Other men were less ill and survived without too much difficulty. Some discomfort was experienced by some men in the second group but nothing serious. However, it was quite possible that they might become ill at a later time.

We, in the third group, were the lucky ones and none of us became ill. However, we too were uncertain how long this good fortune would last as it was quite possible that an illness might develop over a period of several weeks or months. Fortunately, this possibility did not occur. Those of us who had escaped illness and danger were relieved that we were not victims. Our sympathy and best wishes for the victims did not entirely cover up that fact. The two men in the first group who had become seriously ill, remained in the hospital throughout the duration of the project and one remained under care for some time after the project had been terminated. We never learned the exact fate of our fellow "guinea pig".

Most of my work as a photographer focused on the surgical wards. I was asked to photograph various stages of operations, particularly when the surgery involved the removal of an organ. Pictures were required from a variety of perspectives. In addition to photographing the operations, I was asked to photograph patients who had certain types of illnesses. This would involve a closeup, often with the camera no more than six or eight inches from the face of the patient. From these and other experiences, I became acquainted with the doctors, nurses and other staff members. I was also called upon to take pictures in situations having little to do with surgical or any other operation. On one occasion, I was asked to take pictures of a group of visiting generals and other high-ranking government officials. The hospital also served certain military personnel who had been wounded or who were suffering from stress and a variety of illnesses. At the end of their visit, it was suggested they would like to have pictures of themselves and I was asked to take those pictures. I had the unusual opportunity of giving orders to military men. For example, I would say, "General, stand over there", "General, get your chest out and your stomach in" and, "General, let's see a little smile". Like little children they always obeyed. This was a very unusual experience for me as I had never been in a situation where I could give orders and have them instantly obeyed, particularly by high-ranking military men. Needless to say, those were occasions which I thoroughly enjoyed and apparently the enjoyment was mutual. Some time later, after the pictures had been developed and distributed, I had notes from some of these men indicating how pleased they were with the results of my photography. They probably were not aware that I was an objector to military service!

Aside from the fact that we had to check into the hospital once or twice a week, for a 15-minute checkup, we had little to do. My work as a photographer did not require all of my time. The result was we had lots of time for socialization among ourselves and with the hospital staff and several of us took advantage of this opportunity. Many of us became quite friendly with physicians, administrators, nurses and other hospital personnel. The Yale University Drug Addiction Research Program invited us to attend a three-week work shop on addictions and we were given the privilege of participating in many of the sessions. Many others and I gained considerable information about the problem of alcohol addiction in American society. We knew friends and others who drank too much and suffered the consequences, however, we were not fully aware of the parameters of this problem and its negative and destructive effects.

At the same time, several of us became active participants in community programs operated by the Yale University Divinity School. We became acquainted with the professors and a considerable number of students. Many young Methodist students attending the Divinity School were pacifists. In our meetings we discussed the war effort, the meaning of the conflict and its ultimate impact on society. As a result of their enrolment in divinity school, the young men had been given deferment from the military draft for the duration of the war. Nevertheless there was very strong opposition to Franklin Roosevelt and his policies which had led to American involvement in the Second World War. One student often led an irreverent song which the students enjoyed very much. I still remember, at least in part, the words which are as follows:

> Franklin Roosevelt told the people how he felt,
> and they darn near believed what he said.
> He said I hate war, and so does Eleanor,
> but we won't be safe till everybody's dead!

Many students were women. I was quite surprised to find that these women were going into the ministry of the Methodist Church but it was only after I asked what potential female ministers were going to do, that I found that they were really not training for the ministry as such, but rather for positions as directors of religious education in local Methodist churches. These young people were lively, intelligent, full of enthusiasm and interested in having a good time at parties, dances, picnics and other social activities. Two of their favourite activities were square dancing and group games. They also liked to go to the beach for beach parties. The result was that four or five of us CPSers became very interested in some of the women and were invited to attend many of the events sponsored by the female divinity students.

I became involved at Dixwell House, a social settlement agency serving the New Haven black population. I had no idea that New Haven, at that time, was a strictly segregated community and the black population was essentially living in a northern ghetto with all aspects of life, churches, schools, recreational and other activities strictly segregated. Many of the students at the divinity school were involved as volunteers in Dixwell House in an effort to help the black community solve some of its many social and economic problems. In general, meetings were held every two or three weeks at the divinity school or at Dixwell House. The house was located in a community very near a segregated all-black public housing project. The black population was relatively small and constituted less than 10 per cent of the total population of the city.

I was not prepared to discover that, in New Haven, Connecticut, we would encounter a situation of this type. It had been my general impression that New Haven was a very progressive and middle-class university city. I also felt that the large and prestigious Yale University would exercise a positive impact on the life of the community as a whole. That did not turn out to be the case. There was a variety of ethnic and racial groups in New Haven but much to my surprise, the dominant group was the Italian community. It appeared to me that except in the area of employment, the leadership and members of Dixwell House were not overly concerned with the level of segregation and discrimination faced by blacks. It was extremely difficult, if not impossible, for most blacks to find other than menial employment. The result was that the black population was generally poor, of limited education, and occupied the bottom social and economic strata of New Haven society.

The divinity students felt that they could bring their enthusiasm, youthfulness and education to bear on the problems of blacks. Their commitment to the cause of equality reminded me of the efforts of the early founders of the settlement movement of the late nineteenth and early twentieth centuries. The impact of the group, however was minimal. Meetings were held frequently but almost invariably three quarters of those attending were white students from the Divinity School. Less than 15% were members of the black community. My influence in the community was somewhat better than that of my colleagues, simply because I was black and people had learned that I had a degree in social work. As a result there was a slow movement toward calling on me to provide some leadership in the community. I knew this would not be possible on a continuous basis because our project was for only a period of four months. Approximately one half of that time had already transpired before my involvement.

Beginning efforts were made by others and myself to organize youth clubs since we felt it was important to get the youths off the streets and to develop programs which would help keep them in school. Many youths felt this attempt was useless simply because there would be no jobs available upon graduation. Interestingly enough, I learned that Yale University did not enrol a single black student who lived in New Haven.

The second problem in relationship to working with the community was a lack of effective local black leadership. The only leadership in the community came from the black church. The black churches in New Haven, unlike those in the Deep South, had very little interest in social, economic or political concerns. Some members of black churches even expressed opposition to the fact that divinity school students were trying to help organize their young people. They felt that the students might be labelled as communists or other undesirables. This attitude was very hard for me to accept since I lived with the people in our unit and was getting to know and enjoy my relationships with the students and I was quite aware of the depth of their commitment. A result of the attempt, however, was that the students from the divinity school became well aware of the social and economic conditions of the black community. Many of them had never met a black person and initially felt some uneasiness in these relationships.

I was often asked to serve as an informal consultant to the divinity students and to help them in their attempt to make a real impact in the black community. I accepted this invitation and was asked on a number of occasions to speak to the entire student body and faculty of the school. However, I did not feel that I could play this role adequately unless I became more closely identified with that community. I made an effort but only achieved a limited degree of success because it is virtually impossible for an outsider to adequately represent the attitudes, values and interrelationships of a community on the basis of a few months of contact.

In the meantime I had become a close friend of the young woman who was the secretary to the Dean of the Divinity School. We often discussed the problems we faced in both situations, she as a secretary to a demanding dean and me in my attempts to become involved in the black community. It happened that both of us played the violin and we quite frequently practised together in one of the music rooms of the divinity school. We were practising the Bach Concerto for Two Violins when we received word of the death of Franklin D. Roosevelt, then president of the United States. Roosevelt was held in very high regard in the country and his death resulted in an outpouring of grief and concern for the future of the country. Truman, his successor, made a major impact on the country in 1946 when he abolished segregation in the armed forces based on race. Roosevelt and his predecessors had refused to take that step.

I made many good friends at New Haven and had enjoyed working with my colleagues in the project and with the students and faculty at the divinity school. A year or two later I met some of these young students after they had graduated and were attending a conference at the Union Theological Seminary in New York City. Many of these young people had tremendous potential and I was certain they would become leaders in the field of civil and human rights and in religious leadership during the next several years. Unfortunately with two or three exceptions, my relationships with these men and women were terminated when the project came to an end in September 1945.

CHAPTER 8 *CPS: A Final Assignment and a New Adventure*

My commitment to non-violence was further tested in my next assignment at the Philadelphia State Hospital, my final assignment in the CPS. The hospital, sometimes known as "Byberry", was an extremely large mental hospital, probably the largest in the United States at that time. The 7,000 bed hospital was located in a farming area, five miles from the nearest small town, making it a difficult place to reach unless one had access to a car, for there was no public transportation providing direct service to Byberry.

The hospital included approximately 30 large buildings in which the patients and staff were housed. In addition, there were several smaller buildings, including the administration building, a professional staff building, a kitchen and a laundry. The institution also included a large farm on which many of the inmates were assigned to work, an assignment labelled as "occupational therapy". Some inmates and staff expressed concern regarding the practice of assigning inmates to unpaid work. It was not considered "treatment" by some, but as the exploitation of the labour of inmates. The State Hospital was not unique in this respect: many other mental hospitals utilized the labour of inmates.

The common complaint that ran through the entire institution was that it was under-staffed and there was a need for more of everything. As at Cheltenham, the staff who had previously worked in institutions had left for better paying jobs in war industries or had been drafted for military service. This depletion of the attendant staff was the major reason for requesting our unit. The Service Committee was asked if it could provide a group of men and women to staff some units. The men were recruited largely from the various CPS camps widely scattered across the United States. The number varied from 12 to 160 men at the hospital at any one time. In addition, the Committee was also successful in recruiting 25 women who agreed to work in cooperation with the CPS unit. I believe this was the only female unit organized to work voluntarily in a mental hospital.

The Civilian Public Service Unit (CPS #49)

I was not among the first to arrive as a member of the CPS unit at the hospital. The unit had been established several months prior to my arrival and the program was already in operation. The assignment of CPS men was made after consultation between the hospital administration and directors of the AFSC program in Philadelphia. Most men in the Philadelphia State unit had come directly from the reception camp at Big Flats, N.Y. but were originally from towns and cities from across the country.

Initially men in the CPS unit were assigned to work in cooperation with other members of the regular staff. This plan did not work out well in practice but it did give CPS men an opportunity to learn necessary skills in working with mental patients. Only a few of the men had previous experience working in a mental hospital. Like the public in general, most of us had great trepidation with the idea. The general view, shared by many of the men in the unit, was that mental patients were dangerous, violent and had to be watched carefully. To some extent this attitude towards mental patients still exists today.

The CPS unit, at its request, was assigned to a residence. We ate with the patients while on duty and while off duty in a central dining room shared by the other members of the staff. Living accommodations were simple but adequate. As usual in institutions, there were complaints about the food. However, I found the food better than the ordinary diet in most public institutions.

The surrounding area was quite pleasant and attractive. The buildings, grounds, and the outlying areas gave the impression that they were under constant attention and cultivation. The large number of inmates in the institution provided an adequate number of workers to keep everything in tip-top shape.

Staffing

The general attendant staff of the institution was inadequately trained and supervised. Aside from a few psychiatrists, psychologists and nurses, the workers engaged in day-to-day work with the patients probably had no more than a grade 8–12 level of education and operated primarily as custodians, in a manner similar to that of prison guards. Their job was to keep the patients under control and available for whatever treatment they were to receive. The result was a heavy emphasis on security, preventing patients from escaping or from physically attacking others. The number of professional staff was extremely limited. I saw no more than three psychiatrists during my seven months of employment. The best trained and equipped professionals in the area were drawn into providing services in support of the war effort. The army needed doctors, psychologists, psychiatrists, teachers and other people who normally would have been working in the mental health field. The treatment of the patients reflected the lack of adequately trained staff.

Most of the men in the CPS unit were highly educated individuals and their education covered a wide spectrum, including the social and physical sciences, medicine, law, and a variety of other fields. Members of our unit believed in a non-violent approach to the problems of individuals and were not very pleased with the treatment of inmates in the hospital. It was not very long after the establishment of CPS unit #49 that conflict developed in the relationship between the CPS unit and the regular hospital staff. Conflicts centred principally on the fact that the CPS men tried to view patients as people who were ill and who should be treated with respect, dignity and humanity. As a result it was necessary to find innovative methods of working out differences in attitudes, opinion and behaviour in this specific field.

Meetings were held with the administration and the professional staff in an attempt to establish a cooperative collaboration between the two staff groups.

That attempt failed and increasing hostilities began to develop. Many members of the staff, including attendants and even some professional staff members, expressed extreme anger towards some members of the CPS unit. On one occasion I was walking across the campus with several friends and was accosted by an angry group of regular staff people. The hostility was expressed through obscenities, curses, threats and attempts at intimidation. On another occasion, a bus load of female staff workers, on their way to work, had the bus stopped while they raised the windows and shouted obscenities at a group of men from the CPS unit.

In the meantime, several of us from the unit had become good friends with members of the AFSC Women's Group and when off duty, frequently attended various social activities together. These friendly relationships between the men and women of the two groups did not sit very well with most members of the regular staff and even of some patients. These co-ed relationships were probably the most important single reason for open hostility from regular staff members.

The result of this negative behaviour was that we increasingly began to think of some type of separation from the normal staff of the hospital and decided that we should request discussion of the problem with the administration. We suggested that the CPS unit take over exclusive possession of one or more buildings which meant that we would not be working in collaboration with other staff members, but would be the exclusive staff in the buildings assigned to us. Eventually our proposal was accepted by the hospital administration and CPS staff were shifted from other assignments in order to achieve our goal.

In addition, a group had already begun to envision the possibility of establishing a small professional unit which would investigate developing better policies and practices in the treatment of patients but the increasing hostility between our unit and the regular staff made it very difficult indeed to work out a more positive arrangement. We felt that the separation of our services to patients was a worthwhile experiment.

A group of five CPS men were withdrawn from work on the wards and assigned to this new unit located in the administration building. They remained there, not only until the termination of the project, but for some months beyond. Although I was the only member of our unit with training in social work, including mental health, as at Cheltenham, I was not chosen as a member of that elite unit! Members of the unit and I could only speculate regarding the reasons for this omission but the most likely reason was a carefully concealed instance of racism.

Assignments

My first assignment after arriving at the hospital was to a geriatric ward where I worked with men mostly between 60 and 80 years of age who were, for the most part, depressed, inactive and spent much of their time simply sitting silently or chatting among themselves. The three of us who were assigned to that ward had very little work to do. Most of our activities were concerned with trying to keep patients more active. We encouraged them to take walks, to play games and to interact more with each other in small groups. These men were not dangerous, but apathetic and lethargic.

I spent only one month on that ward because plans for setting aside a building for the first all-CPS unit had been activated. In cooperation with administration officials, our unit had selected the most violent and unattractive ward in the hospital. We had some concern about this assignment but wanted to prove that we were not afraid of mental patients, including the most violent ones. We felt that our humane and active approach would help the patients to slowly obtain some sense of their own competence, dignity and worth. We thought that our approach might also help patients to recover their normal mental functioning. Once all arrangements had been made, practically all members of our unit were transferred to the selected buildings.

Upon arrival, I was appalled to see how the men on the wards were treated. Many of them were kept strapped down to their beds throughout the day and night. I could not believe that men in a mental hospital would be kept as if they were dangerous animals. That evening, most of us who had volunteered to work on that ward met to discuss the situation and to decide upon an approach to be taken in resolving the matter. After a short discussion, we arrived at the unanimous agreement that the first step would be to remove the straps. Professional staff would be present from time to time, but this was to be our responsibility and our challenge. We agreed that it would be desirable to inform the whole unit of our decision and to get their agreement. Agreement and support came very quickly and without any further discussion.

The problem came, however, when our decision was announced to the institution as a whole. We had expected hostility and opposition from the regular attendant staff but had not expected the same level of hostility from the psychiatrists and other professional staff. We were quite surprised and dismayed at the attitude of psychiatrists, psychologists, nurses and special education teachers. We were told that we would be responsible for any damage done to the property, injury to patients and other staff members. We were also told that our action would damage the morale of other members of the institutional staff. We may have been a bit naive but we were confident that we could handle the situation. The little experience we had gave us some indication that things were not as bad as they were being portrayed.

CPS: A Final Assignment and a New Adventure

My first day in that building, as a member of the staff of the "not-so-violent" ward, was in the "day room". A group of up to 200 men wandered aimlessly, with others sitting and doing nothing. A few patients, perhaps a half dozen, had no interest in what was happening in the room. These patients, labelled as catatonics, simply stared off into space and seemed to be completely oblivious of anything going on around them. This group was perhaps the most difficult to work with. They stood in a rigid posture and refused to participate in any form of activity. When spoken to they simply stared at the speaker or into space.

I had taken one specific course in psychiatric social work as a student and the psychiatrist teaching the course had given us considerable information based on psychological and psychiatric theory. I labelled him as a "Neo-Freudian" classical analyst, as he believed implicitly in the theories and ideas of Sigmund Freud. We did not focus on Freud alone, however, but also on several other classical theorists who lived and worked in the early twentieth century. However, we found that little, if any, of this theorizing was of any practical use to us in our work with psychiatric patients. We learned, for example, that at times many of our patients were quite lucid and intelligent. Some had remarkable memories in connection with certain past events. For example, one man who was forty-five years of age could remember every winning pitcher in every world series baseball game since the 1920s. When asked questions, for example, he could give the exact name of the winning team, the pitcher and the score. On the other hand, he could not remember what happened the previous day or week. This ability to recall specific events is a perfect example of what is sometimes labelled as "selective memory".

However, the situation was not always well in the day room. Occasionally there were "scuffles" of one kind or another. On one occasion a big black man made an attempt to attack me. One of my CPS colleagues stepped between us and he simply walked away totally forgetting what had happened. I observed brief flare-ups on a number of occasions.

A group of patients on the ward was considered too violent to be permitted in the "day room". We labelled the day-room group as the "not-so-violent" patients and the others the "super-violent". I later worked on the day shift with the latter group. This room included twenty-five men strapped down in their beds at their ankles and wrists who were not permitted, except in unusual circumstances, to go into the day-room and associate with other patients. They had to be unstrapped whenever they wanted to go to the bathroom, the dining room or to any other part of the building. In this instance, two attendants held them by each arm and walked with them to their destination. This was, in my view, a very degrading situation so one of the first things our group did, following our assignment to that small subgroup, was to remove the straps and unlock any other restraining devices around the bodies of these men. We got the impression that the entire institution was holding its breath, waiting to see what would happen next. The expectation was that "all hell would break loose" but nothing happened except the men were very pleased to be out of the restraints and to be able to circulate freely around the day-room. A few even wanted to participate in activities of various kinds.

Our problem was not the behaviour of the men, but to find something in which they could utilize their time in a constructive way during the day. Having been restrained on beds all day, there had been nothing to do. We had to develop appropriate programs once they were given freedom of movement but this task taxed our minds and imagination, primarily because there were so few available resources in the hospital. As indicated earlier, this hospital contained very few facilities for occupational, educational or recreational programs.

The men were only seen by a doctor and a psychiatrist once every two or three months. Treatment was virtually non-existent. When I left the hospital, we had not completely solved this problem; however, some progress had been made and the men were getting involved in a few activities which in the past, would have been totally unavailable. We, in the CPS unit, were relieved and pleased at the progress which had been made under our new approach and attitude.

Even with the hostility we had encountered from the regular staff, we still felt that our success would result in some changes in their negative attitudes. We had believed that we would be better accepted by the total staff of the institution but this change did not occur. Our unit found that with our limited success even more hostility was directed toward us. After all, we had demonstrated that the rigidity and punitive attitudes of the staff were not only unhelpful, but indeed counter-productive and harmful. The behaviour of regular staff, however, should not be judged too harshly. Their behaviour was compatible with the attitudes of the general public and they had little support from the professional staff who should have recognized the importance of humane treatment of patients.

There were some rules which we could not change. For example, nurses came in every night and injected a drug in the men to insure that they would sleep throughout the night. Although we were not in agreement with this routine action, we did not have the power to overrule the medical staff.

I have a vivid memory of an ex-marine, probably eighteen or nineteen years of age, who had been committed as a result of psychological problems. Apparently, like many others, he had been under continuous fire for several months and had broken down completely and was now a psychotic war casualty. The medical staff was well aware of his behaviour and his attitudes toward them. The female nurse was accompanied by two or three attendants when she came to give him his "needle" each night. These attendants held this man down while she stuck the needle in his arm. It became almost a ritual to watch this event. The young man could not resist effectively because of his physical restraint, but he reacted in the only way he could. He spat in her face as she bent over to give him the needle. This procedure of giving the man a drug each night was ordered by the ward psychiatrist. I personally would like to have seen what would have happened had the needle not been given and the young man allowed an opportunity to go to sleep on his own volition. It might have been dangerous to do this but my colleagues and I would have liked the opportunity to test the idea. We had already removed other restraints and had no fear of hostile behaviour.

The unpredictability of the work, however, could not be denied. On one occasion, during the night shift, one of our men was attacked by a patient whom he thought was asleep. As he walked past the bed, he was grabbed from behind and the patient attempted to strangle him. This act caused quite a commotion as the two men struggled around the room. Beds and chairs were overturned and the ensuing commotion woke up other people in the nearby part of the building. Two of our CPS men ran over, broke up the struggle and restored order. It is difficult to know what would have happened had CPS staff not been available. Obviously this man, a psychotic patient, was going through a stage in which he felt that he was in danger and had to protect himself. Based on past experience, it is possible that the struggle might have ended abruptly and the patient might have simply forgotten what had occurred and gone back to bed.

The attack and struggle brought home to us that humane treatment alone is not enough in many instances. We had, however, demonstrated that even with its limitations, it is a more constructive approach than the methods that were in use in most mental hospitals at that time.

In the meantime, the little group of men who were transferred from the wards to a small professional unit had begun its work. The purpose was to study and attempt to develop new methods of treating the mentally ill. This group made a comprehensive study of the treatment of mental patients in several countries. From these studies they recommended an innovative policy to the administration based on the model which we had developed and utilized. At the same time, we recognized the need to know much more about the phenomenon of mental illness itself. We had not been even slightly impressed with the quality of nursing and psychiatric services at the Philadelphia State Hospital and it was our strong belief that this hospital was not serving the needs of patients, but was a warehouse to keep them out of mainstream society. The lack of adequate trained professionals was a major aspect of the problem.

Another problem was the prevalence of racism. It was not coincidental that forty to fifty percent of the patients were black and yet the black population of the United States, at that time, was between ten and twelve percent. I was keenly interested in why this factor was never taken into account in diagnosis and treatment plans. There was neither interest nor concern within the hospital administration and professional staff. On one occasion, I raised the question with the superintendent and other top administrators. "Is the disproportionate number of blacks a result of a social and economic condition or is it based upon the assumption that black people are more prone to mental illness than others?" They were reluctant to respond to this question because they had no evidence that black people were more prone to mental illness than other groups in society.

The self-segregation of groups in the hospital was also an interesting phenomenon because even though technically the hospital was not segregated, patients tended to stay in their own racial or ethnic groups. Even in the day room, which was open to all on a non-segregated basis, black and white patients still could not break out of the pattern of segregation to which they had become accustomed in the outside world. The northern state of Pennsylvania included a pattern of housing ghettoization, segregation and discrimination based on race. One of the biggest problems for the staff was dealing with that situation within the institution itself. I was certain that as long as this system of oppression existed in the outside world, it would be very difficult to instill positive changes in the institutional setting. In my view, closed institutions had no answer to that problem, but simply repeated and reinforced it.

Social, Educational, and Recreational Activities

As noted earlier, the CPS unit at Philadelphia State was in operation for some time prior to my arrival. A limited number of recreational and social programs had already been initiated by a few of the men. While some were dissatisfied with the inadequacy of educational and recreational programs, others were not too concerned, primarily because the hospital was located fairly near the city of Philadelphia and it was easy for them to get rides and enjoy the various social, education, and recreational facilities of the big city. In addition, the city also offered the advantages of several good colleges and universities. Many of these men, however, had also participated in the programs which I had helped to develop at Big Flats. They felt the need for something similar to that program at the hospital.

To organize this program was much more difficult than it appeared on the surface. In the first place, the men in our unit were operating on a three-shift basis and many were not available. At Big Flats all had operated on the same shift. The CPS unit at the hospital had the advantage, however, of having a women's unit. When I arrived, there had been very little contact, at least on a group basis, between the two units. It was quite acceptable for men to go into the city singly or in small groups but the same freedom at that time was not generally available to women. Consequently, the women might be even more interested in social and educational experiences on a joint basis than the men. This idea was borne out by later developments.

I called together a small group of women, to meet with a group of us, to discuss the possibility of establishing a committee to plan social, educational and recreational activities, including dances, parties and outings. The idea received unanimous support and it was agreed that these activities be sponsored on an informal or a "drop-in" basis. In this way the individual could feel free to come at the time that was most convenient and to leave depending on his or her schedule and other considerations. Even with this arrangement, however, attendance was not as good as at Big Flats. That program had attracted virtually all members of the camp. These programs, however, were effective in providing socialization opportunities for men and women who had very few other alternatives. Many valuable friendships were formed among the men and between the men and the women, many of which lasted during the course of the project and, in some instances, considerably longer.

One woman, a student at the University of North Carolina, and I became very fast friends, not in a romantic sense but in the sense of having much in common because of our southern backgrounds. I was from Atlanta and she was from North Carolina, one of the most liberal southern states. Margaret came from a "well-to-do" southern plantation family and grew up with many black servants around, many of whom she felt emotionally closer to than to her own family. Her family, like most southern families at the time, was very conservative and strongly opposed to any relationship between blacks and whites, except in the usual situation, that is, blacks as subordinates and submissive. Although her mother could be quite kind and generous to blacks, the idea that her daughter could be a good friend and a dancing partner with a black man would have been totally unacceptable.

Visiting Friends

Very few in our unit attended the religious services on campus sponsored by the hospital staff. Most of the people who attended were patients in the hospital. It was our feeling that these services, under the hospital chaplain, were designed to keep patients in contact with religious activities and perhaps with their own churches back home. We also felt that these services were inane and not designed to raise serious questions about the nature of society, the personal and social implications of their illness, the impact of negative social relationships and certainly not about war and peace. To some extent these services would have supported the estimation of Karl Marx that "religion is the opium of the people." Very few of our men or women were interested in this kind of religious exercise with the result that many chose to travel to Philadelphia for various religious services on Sunday mornings. I had recently become a member of the Quakers. I joined the Florida Avenue meeting in Washington D.C. which was designated as one which accepted members from outside the community in which they lived.

The favourite meeting for members of our unit was the Frankfort Friends Meeting in suburban Philadelphia which was much closer to the hospital. That meeting was particularly congenial and I attended it quite frequently. During one of my visits to Philadelphia and to the office of the AFSC, I had met Mae, a young woman who later became one of my best friends. I had earlier met her during one of the trips from Big Flats to attend a meeting at the office of the Service Committee, where she worked. We had lunch together on a few occasions and talked about the possibility of my obtaining a placement at the office of the Service Committee itself. This did not work out in the way which we had hoped. However, I did continue as a volunteer staff person for the Service Committee on a part-time basis. My function was to contact and visit students on college and university campuses throughout the Atlantic Region in cooperation with the FOR. Much of that activity ended when I was assigned to the hospital.

Mae and I re-established our acquaintanceship when I moved to the Philadelphia State Hospital. She also attended the Frankfort Friends meeting and we met there on several occasions. A very shocking experience awaited us on one of these occasions. Friends meetings are usually based on involvement in group meditation. If the situation is convenient, Friends will usually sit in a circle so they can face each other. The purpose is to invoke a sense of quietness and meditation so that one may develop sensitivity to his or her "inner light" or consciousness to religious values. The end of the meeting is signalled by the clerk and others shaking hands. In most meetings, it is at this point that the clerk asks if there are announcements. To our great surprise, Mae's mother stood up and announced to everyone that she was pleased that her daughter and I were engaged to be married. This was a complete shock to us and we faced each other with consternation. People gathered around to congratulate us and what could we say? So we simply faced the group and shook hands with those who were congratulating us and left the meeting as quickly as possible.

The interesting aspect of this story is that Mae's mother actually believed that we were engaged. She had arrived at the conclusion because we were seeing each other fairly often so our relationship was more than friendship. Obviously, she welcomed this prospect. To demonstrate her satisfaction and happiness with the arrangement, she offered us a sum of $15,000.00 for us to make a down payment on a house and to begin our family life.

In the meantime, things were beginning to wind down, as far as the unit was concerned at Philadelphia State Hospital. The war in Europe was over and the men from the CPS units were being discharged. By the winter of 1945–46 the unit had been reduced by at least 25% with several men leaving almost every week. The women's unit was also closed in the early spring of 1946. I had begun to make plans for my own termination but I realized that I would not be in the first group as I had been assigned to CPS in late 1942. By April 1st, however, it became clear that I would be among the next group to be discharged and the notice actually arrived on April 6, 1946. I had paid my dues, although not in the manner my country desired.

My career as a civilian public serviceman was finally over and I was free to return to regular civilian life. I looked back on the experience with a degree of satisfaction as well as some disappointment. I was not mistreated. Even the visits of Colonel Kosch were not unpleasant experiences. On occasion I was somewhat embarrassed at the manner in which he was treated by my colleagues who delighted in teasing him. For example, they would say, "How many Germans and Japanese did you kill today, Colonel?" I was not overly concerned that we were engaged in unpaid labour, but that matter became an issue as many men began to consider the broader issue of "slave labour" — an issue which dominated much of the camp discussion during the last year of the program. This issue was intensified by the knowledge that German prisoners of war were paid a small daily wage for their work. I agreed with the position of those who felt strongly about this matter but did not agree with the idea of removing administration of the camps from the peace churches and into the tender mercies and care of the Selective Service System. I had enough of that military organization prior to leaving Atlanta!

The experience had been a significant one. Aside from its compulsory nature, many aspects of the CPS experience were enjoyable and valuable. I had learned much about life and about myself, but now it was time for new challenges. At the invitation of my future "mother-in-law", I decided to spend a few weeks at their home in order to begin my re-introduction to ordinary civilian life. I would be looking for opportunities for employment in the field of social work, peace education or regular high school or university education in a northern community.

After exploring possibilities for employment in the Philadelphia area, including potentialities with the Service Committee or going to New York City and working with the FOR, I decided that perhaps I should return to regular civilian work. Since the work I had done in peace education had been entirely voluntary, I felt I could continue that work while seeking more suitable full time employment. At the end of two or three weeks, I had not found suitable employment in Philadelphia. However, another opportunity arose. On one of my visits to the office of the Service Committee I was asked if I would be interested in going to Poland with the United Nations Relief Agency which was shipping farm equipment and animals to Poland. The shipment required the services of perhaps thirty men. Since I was unemployed at the time, I quickly accepted this opportunity to observe life in another country and particularly a European country devastated by war.

My agreement to travel to Europe on a victory ship loaded with wheat, equipment, seeds and horses for Poland could be interpreted in a number of ways. It could be interpreted as interest in going on an exciting trip to a part of the world I had not previously visited; or it could be interpreted as my attempt to get away from an unfortunate situation regarding my "engagement" to Mae. (We were compatible and really enjoyed being with each other, but I was not interested in marriage.) It was also a desire to examine the devastation of Europe from a war in which I had refused to serve. Human behaviour is rarely activated by only one motivation: in most situations there are combinations of motivations, any of which might be considered the primary one. However, humans tend to select and express the motive which enhances their reputation and status among friends and family. I suspect my trip was based on all three.

We sailed for twelve days on a "Victory" ship over the Atlantic Ocean, through the English Channel and into the Baltic Sea and landed at Gdansk, a Polish port. The harbour was filled with the litter of ships which had been bombed and sunk. That was my first view of what a battlefield was like, on both land and sea. At least 90 percent of the buildings in Gdansk had been bombed to rubble. One had to pick one's way through the rubble in the streets. The railroad station had also been bombed, although the walls still stood. We remained in Gdansk for several days while the ship was unloading and preparing to return to the United States. In the meantime, several of us visited Warsaw and other Polish towns and cities. I had never seen such wholesale destruction in my life. It was indeed difficult to find a building which had not been bombed into oblivion or destroyed by artillery fire.

The condition of the people was even worse. The impact of the war on health was enormous and evidence of semi-starvation could be seen in the appearance of individuals, and particularly the women whose arms and legs exhibited sores of different sizes and shapes. Another surprising fact was that most of the hard work, digging sewers and clearing away the rubble created by the war, was performed by women. I had seen my mother and other women helping their husbands in the fields when living on a farm in the South. However, I had not seen women digging ditches, lifting heavy loads of rubble, driving huge trucks and operating other large machinery. But the men were away, mostly in prisoner of war camps, and Poland had been the victim of heavy fighting. It had paid a heavy price in that struggle between two military giants. But its people were making a gallant effort to recover from that catastrophic event. A large number of soldiers, some of whom were Russians, were guarding the cities. By that time the Germans had been defeated and driven out of Poland, but the Russians remained.

The members of the former CPS unit were not the entire staff of the ship. Perhaps 25 percent of the crew had been recruited from the local community of Newport News, Virginia. We were a motley crew, including our contingent of conscientious objectors. The regular crew of sailors contained men from all parts of the world and a small contingent of black Americans who were recruited because they were unemployed and looking for work. The CPS contingent stuck together and insisted upon permission to leave the ship to visit the countryside, the towns and the cities.

Our little group of six ex-CPS men were able to obtain transportation and travel around the country. Everywhere there was devastation, ruins and starvation. Burnt-out and destroyed tanks littered the countryside and many of the cities. These were Russian as well as German tanks that had destroyed each other. We observed animals which had been killed in the fighting or had died of starvation but had not yet been buried. Poland was an example of utter destruction and despair.

We had initially gone aboard for meals every day while the ship was in port. Later we decided to skip meals because we could not get back in time to board the ship for dinner. Our opportunities to explore the countryside were limited by the fact that there were very few transportation facilities. Many of the railroads and highways had been destroyed. However, we did enjoy the opportunities which were available. My ex-CPS friends and I became fairly familiar with the cities of Gdansk and Warsaw. Unfortunately, none of the men in our group spoke Polish and we found very few Poles who could speak English. But we learned a few of the essential terms, such as the words for restaurant, transportation, and directions.

In addition, we had to change American money into Polish zlotys. Changing American for Polish funds was the official requirement: however, one did not have to have zlotys. In Poland, there was a thriving black market operating in cigarettes. It also operated on our own ship. One pack of cigarettes was worth two or three U.S. dollars. Cigarettes in the United States were selling for forty cents a package. A camera which would have cost me a hundred dollars or more in the United States was only three packs of cigarettes. In view of the fact that many Polish people were unable to buy the basic necessities of life, such as food, clothing and shelter, this was a curious phenomenon for me.

One incident that stands out in my mind was contact with a group of Polish parents and children around a water fountain. I was standing drinking water along with my other ex-CPS friends, when a young mother and her two children came up. The children were five or six years of age. One young girl spoke excitedly to her mother. We were fortunate to find someone who could translate as none of us could speak Polish. He pointed to me and said "She says you have not washed your hands." For a moment, I was puzzled about what this meant. Then it suddenly dawned on me that this little girl had probably never seen a black person before. She saw that the colour of my hands was brown rather than white, thus she drew the conclusion that my hands were dirty. So I went over to the fountain, turned on the tap and began to run water over my hands. She watched closely and could see that the brown skin did not wash off. That seemed to satisfy her and she went skipping away along with her sister and her mother. The interesting aspect of this encounter was that she did not notice my face: she only noticed my hands. The little girl was extremely curious but not hostile. She had not been socialized by her culture to look down on anyone whose skin colour was different from her own. As far as she was concerned, I was just a man who had not taken the ordinary precautions to keep himself and particularly his hands clean!

During my travels while at Big Flats, New Haven and Philadelphia State Hospital, I often received invitations for dinner after a Sunday morning service. Some families had young children and I found a situation similar to that in Poland. The children had no fear of me whatsoever. Their curiosity would lead them to come over to look at me and to ask questions. I was friendly toward them and they would ask my name, my home, and my purpose for being there. I found this very interesting because instead of showing fear, they often wanted to climb up on my lap and have me hold them for a few minutes. This behaviour does not support the popular notion that humans are fearful of strangers or someone who is different. The children would tell me all about their friends. The almost total naivety and honesty of young children was refreshing but honesty and innocence do not last indefinitely. The North American culture and community values make certain that children are taught certain basic attitudes and values, one being an ability to conceal feelings and attitudes.

We left Poland on a bright sunny day in the late summer of 1946. Our trip back was uneventful except for one incident. The lookout on the ship's tower thought he had spotted a mine which carry a tremendous amount of explosive power. Many ships had been sunk during the war when they struck mines. All alarm systems on the ship were activated; bells were ringing, horns were blowing and the ship began to slow down. As we approached the object, moving slowly around it, we noticed that it was merely a piece of a black painted barrel floating in the water. Everyone gave a sigh of relief and the ship resumed speed. However, we were due for another surprise.

When we came near New York City we received a message ordering the ship to dock at Mobile, Alabama. We were to spend three or four additional days sailing down the east coast of the United States, around the tip of Florida and up into the Gulf of Mexico where Mobile is located. The ship docked at Mobile in the early evening and our ex-CPS group decided to remain on the ship, eat dinner and use its facilities until the next day. We could then arrange for transportation to our several home towns. However, it had been a long journey and we decided to leave the ship to take a look at the town during that evening. I was the only black among the group of six. The first place we went to was a restaurant and we immediately ran into the problem of southern discrimination. We had never faced a single instance of bigotry or racism on the ship or during our travels in Poland. But we were now back in the United States, with all that implies. The waiter came over and informed our group that all could be served except me. The restaurant, he said, did not serve black people. If I was looking for something to eat I could find a restaurant in the black community. One of my friends said that we did not want to be separated. But the waiter was adamant. The restaurant would not serve a black man. Following that discussion, we went outside for a few minutes to plan our next step. It was agreed that my white friends would speak on my behalf, indicating that I was not an American, but a foreign-born person. I was supposed to say a few words in French. This ploy would be great fun, or so we thought. Since we suspected that none of them could speak French, it did not matter what I said. However, that gimmick did not work. We were told that either I would have to go or the whole group would have to go. The whole group chose to go!

The reason we had chosen that particular ploy, was that we had information that foreign blacks were treated quite differently from American born blacks. A Nigerian or a diplomat at the United Nations in New York city would be treated very well. Had I gone into that restaurant dressed in a Nigerian or Ghanian costume, I probably would have been served. But as an American-born black, service was automatically denied. Although we strolled around several blocks we could not find a restaurant which would serve our group. We finally had to return to the ship for a snack.

The next morning we were discharged by the American merchant marine and were free to go our separate ways. We said goodbye to each other and made our separate arrangements for transportation back to the northern states. It was difficult to leave those men. We had gone through a lot together, both on the ship, in Poland, and the experience in Mobile. Our tour in the CPS System and with the American merchant marine was over. Some of us talked of keeping in contact but that never happened. Such is life.

I travelled by bus from Mobile, to Atlanta, my old home where I spent several days before going on to Philadelphia. I had a chance to visit some of my old friends, to meet people I had not seen for several years and to tell them some of my many experiences since leaving the South. There was great curiosity about what I had been doing because very few people had any first-hand knowledge of my activities since I had left Atlanta in 1942.

My brother Marvin was released from the navy about the same time. I had not seen Marvin for more than six years. He had grown a great deal since I had last seen him as a senior in the Washington High School. I tried, during that visit, to talk with my brothers about their experiences in the military services but with the exception of Glenn, there was some reluctance to talk about them. I believe these experiences were too painful for them to want to re-open old wounds and they preferred to not speak of them. The humiliation which Glenn had suffered when he was arrested for entering a white officer's club still rankled very deeply. His anger was still as strong as when the incident had occurred.

In subsequent discussions with Frank several years later, I learned a little of his experiences in Europe. One of the most gripping was his reaction to the racial discrimination he had suffered in the army. Blacks were not permitted to fight in battle beside white soldiers, but they had been drafted to do some of the unskilled work, such as cooking in the mess halls, digging trenches, driving trucks carrying supplies and other similar jobs. Frank was assigned to drive a truck which supplied gas to the tanks operating at the front.

The southern "Jim Crow" laws were still in effect when I boarded the bus. That meant that as a black, I was required by law to sit in the back of the bus. I did that between Atlanta and North Carolina where I planned to stop at Chapel Hill for a visit with Margaret, my young friend from the Philadelphia women's unit who was attending the University of North Carolina. She had returned home when the women's unit closed at the hospital and had married her fiance. I had been invited to the wedding but could not attend. In fact, I would not have attended even had it been convenient, simply because I was much more aware than she of what would happen. I knew that I would not be accepted, unless I played the role of a servant of one kind or another. In a southern city, it would have been unprecedented for a black man to attend a wedding of a young white woman and a white man as an honoured guest. That would have been considered totally inappropriate and would have aroused a tremendous amount of hostility and perhaps physical violence. Margaret was not aware of this possibility. She had been raised in a protected environment and had very little understanding of the nature of race relations in the southern states. I was nevertheless going to stop at Chapel Hill and visit her and her husband, because I had been invited and because I wanted to meet her husband and Reverend Jones, the minister of her church about whom I had heard much while at the hospital. Reverend Jones was considered to be one of the most liberal-minded individuals in North Carolina.

She and Jack met me at the bus station and we walked through the streets to the stares and some hostile remarks of passing shoppers. Margaret and Jack did not appear to notice but I was very conscious of them and was somewhat ill at ease. After all, I was the only black person in a large crowd of white people on the streets of a small southern town. I was also aware that if I were violently attacked by the crowd, there would be little or no protection for me by the local police. We were lucky and arrived at the church and were met by Rev. Jones. We enjoyed dinner with him and following an evening of animated conversation, I stayed at his home that night.

Rev. Jones was an unusual man in that he spoke his mind in the midst of an extremely conservative community. Chapel Hill was probably one of the best university towns in the South. It was instructive to learn that a university town does not necessarily mean a liberal-minded town. There may be a vast gulf between the commercial and the academic aspects of community life. Rev. Jones was therefore, under constant attack for the liberal positions he usually took on racial, social and political issues. While some members of his church, including my friends, supported him, many others would have been very happy to see him leave town. These attitudes did not deter him and he continued to project a strong liberal approach to the political, social, religious, and the academic arena of community life. He welcomed me with open arms as his guest. It was apparent that he and I held compatible views on many issues.

Following breakfast the next morning, Jack and Margaret invited me to take a walk with them to his laboratory on the University of North Carolina campus where Jack was studying for a master's degree in chemistry. Again we walked down the streets, to the curious and hostile glances of many pedestrians and were always pleased to meet people who paid no attention to us. There was, however, considerable commotion when I entered the chemistry building since it was obvious by the way I was dressed that I was not one of the blacks who worked on the lawns of the university. There were no incidents although many students did stare at me in a curious way. On the campus I did not feel the same tension and hostility I had felt earlier. We stopped at one store and bought a few items, and again there were curious glances, but no hostile behaviour.

My bus for Washington D.C. and Philadelphia was leaving that evening, and around 7:00 p.m. Jack and Margaret decided to accompany me to the station. Most of the people who were strolling on the streets appeared to have little interest in us. Some looked at us but not in any particularly hostile manner, until we arrived at the bus station. We arrived fifteen minutes early to continue our discussions while awaiting the bus. It is at that point that we began to sense that trouble was brewing.

Encounter With Police

The Chapel Hill bus station was located across the street from the city police department. We noticed a group of people standing across the street observing us but apparently with no particular hostile intent. Within a few minutes of our arrival, however, two policemen came out of the station and approached us. They wanted to know who we were and where we were from. My two friends said that they were students at the University of North Carolina and also members of a Methodist church. The policemen then turned to me and wanted to know my identity. I told them I was on my way from Mobile to Philadelphia. They wanted to know why we were walking down the streets together. I decided to say nothing but leave any explanation to my friends. They responded immediately by indicating their resentment in being questioned in the absence of any misbehaviour. It became quite obvious that the policemen were not interested in discussing misbehaviour. We had not violated any law and as far as we knew there had been no complaint by anyone suggesting that we had committed a violation of any law. What was apparent was that we had committed a violation of a southern custom in which blacks and whites do not associate as equals. From the perspective of the police and other southerners, this violation was as serious a matter as if we had actually committed a crime. Even "Jim Crow" laws did not prohibit blacks and whites walking on the streets of southern towns and cities!

Jack finally decided to go into the bus station and telephone his minister, the Rev. Jones. who immediately came down to inquire as to what was going on. Unfortunately, the bus came at that time and I had to leave my friends standing on the sidewalk talking to the minister and to the two policemen. Later I learned through correspondence that the conversation continued for a half hour after my departure. It was clear that the two policemen were angry at my two friends and the minister.

This incident raises one of the questions endemic to the South: why the extreme hostility and even hatred of white people who offer the slightest support to the aspirations of black people? White people who seem to be even casually friendly to blacks are often labelled as "nigger lovers" and are usually considered as traitors to their race and unwilling to uphold the ideal of white superiority. Whites who were friendly to blacks often lost their jobs and their friends and suffered considerable ostracism. This is a very difficult experience for the white individual living in a small town. I was pleased and appreciative of the principled stand my friends had taken but at the same time worried about their future as residents and students in Mobile. Apparently, the matter blew over quickly and no adverse impact was felt in their day-to-day existence.

However, I was getting increasingly angry with those two policemen and the behaviour which had been directed towards me and my friends. I was fuming with anger when I entered that bus and decided to make the trip a test case on the implementation of the Supreme Court decision outlawing segregation in interstate travel. In retrospect, it is obvious that a test case in this circumstance could have been quite dangerous. After all, the Irene Brown decision was a recent one and a considerable number of people had never heard of it. In addition, the police thought they were enforcing the laws of the state of North Carolina requiring segregation on interstate travel. That meant, as far as buses were concerned, blacks were required to sit at the back. Much can happen and people can be seriously injured during the time elapsing between a Supreme Court decision and the actual implementation of that decision in practice.

The second difficulty was that I would have to get a lawyer and file a case which would have to make its way through the lower courts, a process which would be time-consuming and expensive. In all probability it would require at least two or three years before a case of this kind could be finally settled by the U.S. Supreme Court. The southern states, as they were to demonstrate during the civil rights revolution in the 1960s, were extremely reluctant to give up their "Jim Crow" laws.

A Bus Ride

I boarded the bus in Chapel Hill and took a seat in the middle of the vehicle. The bus driver entered the bus and took a look at the passengers and quickly noticed me but made no comment. He might have become very angry and ordered me to move and if I refused, he could have gone outside the bus and called the police — the same police with whom I had been in confrontation only a few minutes earlier. At that point, it is difficult to know what would have happened. It's likely that I would have been dragged off the bus and into the police station and booked for violating the segregation laws of the state of North Carolina. During that process, I could have been roughed up by the police and even subjected to serious physical violence. In any case, I would have had to secure bail probably from someone in Philadelphia or New York since I knew no one in North Carolina, except my two student friends and a Methodist minister whom I had just met.

The trip, however, was uneventful until we reached Richmond, Virginia. The bus made a rest stop and I was approached by the bus driver and told I would have to move to the back of the bus. I told him that segregation in interstate travel had been ruled illegal by the U.S. Supreme Court. He had not heard anything of that and said he was enforcing state laws. I said that he should be aware that I was travelling by an interstate bus. I had entered his bus in North Carolina: we were now in Virginia. Obviously, we had crossed state lines and were therefore subject to the ruling of the Supreme Court. Then I sat back and waited to see what would happen next. The bus driver left the bus and went into the station while I waited. A few minutes later he came out, sat down at his wheel and drove off. Nothing had happened and I breathed a sigh of relief. I am still not sure why nothing happened but my suspicion was that because the bus was not crowded, he saw no reason to make a fuss out of a very small matter. Had the bus been filled and I had refused to go to the back, it's quite likely that the situation would have turned out differently. Or perhaps he had checked with the bus headquarters and been instructed to leave the matter as it was.

Richmond was the capital of the old southern confederacy, the southern states which had rebelled and fought the northern states in a vicious civil war. By reputation, it was one of the most racist cities in the South and had been the centre of the rebellion. It occurred to me that I was travelling in a state which had bitterly objected to any change in the status of blacks in its society.

Among other issues, the southern states had fought to maintain slavery. However, I was only a few miles from Washington D.C. where I would cross the Potomac River and into the national capital. At that point, I would be in the capital of the United States and a part of the country which was supposedly democratic and free. However, it was not as democratic or as "free" as was claimed. Washington was as racist as any of the southern cities.

In the early morning, we entered the Washington bus station. Washington was also a segregated city: however, my early morning arrival and departure from the city occurred without incident. I settled down in the bus and slept most of the way to Philadelphia.

Quakers were among the early settlers and established themselves first in Philadelphia and later throughout the colony. Increasingly, however, immigrants of other background and religious faiths moved into Pennsylvania and as those numbers increased it became more difficult for Quakers to maintain the peaceful relationships they had established over a long period. By the mid-nineteenth century, the Quaker principle of tolerance, respect, and non-violence had been overcome by the ideology of capitalism and "free enterprise". The rapid industrialization in the northern and eastern United States and the spread of capitalist ideology gradually pushed aside the concepts and ideas of Quakers who became a minority. By the beginning of the twentieth century, Pennsylvania could claim few, if any, features which distinguish it from other northern states. One aspect of Quakerism which did receive public recognition was the quality of its schools. Many excellent high schools and colleges were located within the city and in surrounding areas but apart from educational institutions, I detected little Quaker influence of any significance on the education, commercial, political and social life of Philadelphia.

Immediately after returning to Philadelphia, I re-established contact with many of my friends and colleagues whom I had known in previous years. I became active again, in high school, university and college visitation for the AFSC and FOR. I found a very receptive audience to much of what I said during these visits. There was a feeling that, the war being over, people were tired and wanted to get on with their lives. Many would have liked to forget that the war had ever happened. Many young people were quite sceptical of the values they were being taught in schools and other circles. People were beginning to read and hear about the cruelty and barbarism of modern war. In addition, young people were becoming aware of the vast scope of the holocaust. Questions were raised about the values of society and so-called "good Christians" were increasingly engaged in support of these critical and analytical activities. The Service Committee was taking advantage of this new opportunity and significantly expanded its own peace education programs.

Leaving Philadelphia

Mae had gone to Toronto to spend a few weeks alone. We had agreed that this step might be useful in dealing with her mother, who was still insisting that we were going to get married and wanting to help us in any way she could.

Neither of us had agreed to get married and yet we were under constant pressure from her mother to do so. So the trip away, we thought, would be a time for things to cool off and for her mother to get a better perspective on the actual situation and the future of our relationship. I was still seeking work in social work, my chosen profession. The type of social work I was looking for, however, was not immediately available. What was available involved determining eligibility to receive social welfare assistance. That was an investigative function and one which was not to my taste. It would have involved "snooping" into the affairs of vulnerable people and I felt that such investigations would subject clients to unreasonable and humiliating treatment and I wanted no part in that type of social work practice.

In late summer I received a telegram from Cleo Blackburn, the Executive Director of Flanner House in Indianapolis, the setting of my 1943 summer work camp. I was offered the position of director of community organization and development at the community centre. I did not reply immediately because I felt the need to think over the implications of moving to Indianapolis. Having been a participant in the summer work camp, I was aware of the work of Flanner House. I was also aware of the area in which Flanner House was located: a slum neighbourhood, populated primarily by poor and indigent black people.

I learned later that my almost idyllic existence during the years in CPS and the stimulating contacts I had with the Quakers, FOR and others had partly blinded me to the reality of racism in northern cities. I lived almost entirely in a white world and my associates were predominately friendly and liberal minded people. It was my intention to leave the racist societies of the South and aside from the Cheltenham experience I had apparently succeeded in that goal. The programs of the Service Committee were focused primarily on peace and justice issues and rarely on specific racial issues. This was not intentional; it was an almost inevitable aspect of a program designed for conscientious objectors, not on race relations. There were too few of us non-whites for race to become an issue except at Cheltenham, and even there we were only two of a unit of approximately thirty men.

I agreed to accept the position at Flanner House. I was enjoying a very pleasant and stimulating life in Philadelphia and other parts of the North but I felt the time had come to re-establish relationships with black communities in the United States. I knew that Flanner House would provide an opportunity to achieve that goal. In the meantime, Mae, my girlfriend, had returned from Toronto a few days before I left Philadelphia. She had found interesting work in Toronto, but in her opinion the people were cold and unfriendly. She returned to Philadelphia to resume her life in "the city of brotherly love". My plans and commitment had been made and a few days later I embarked by train on the trip to Indianapolis.

Leaving Philadelphia was one of the most complex and difficult decisions I had ever made. I had enjoyed visiting the city when involved in the CPS program at Big Flats and following my discharge from that assignment, I had many good friends in Philadelphia and regretted the possibility of leaving. But the lack of suitable employment was a valid reason for leaving and once the decision was made, there was no turning back.

CHAPTER 9

Community Development and Civil Rights: A North/South Experience and Perspective (Indianapolis)

In the mid 1940s Indianapolis was a city of almost 400,000 individuals. It had the unique reputation of being the "largest southern city in a northern state". Although Indiana is a northern state, the population of Indianapolis was, to a large extent, southern born and many of its residents came from Kentucky, North Carolina, Tennessee, Virginia and West Virginia.

Segregation and other forms of racial discrimination were as complete and intense as in any city in the Deep South. It was reported that during the 1920s and 1930s, one of its previous governors was a member of the Ku Klux Klan. There were only three restaurants in downtown Indianapolis where a black could eat: the YWCA, the YMCA, and Union Station. All public schools were segregated and there was only one high school where black students could attend: the Crispus Attucks High School. (The school was named after a black man who was the first individual killed by British troops at the beginning of the revolutionary war in 1776). There was no independence and certainly very little freedom in the schools, employment, public services and other systems for blacks. Blacks occupied the lowest economic levels and very few were engaged in business or professional occupations.

Even in this situation, however, a few blacks had done well. For example, a black senator had been elected to the state legislature by a largely white constituency. He represented one of the most important financial districts in the city. In addition, there were a few blacks on the police force and one or two blacks in the business world. An undertaker was probably one of the most prominent blacks in the city. The executive director of the black branch of the YMCA was also considered a leading citizen. His reputation was based, to a large extent, upon his ability to attract outstanding black speakers from across the country. On a number of occasions, he brought A. Philip Randolph, President

178

of the Brotherhood of Sleeping Car Porters, the president of Howard University, outstanding theologians and other visitors to speak at the YMCA lecture series.

These men, however prominent in the black community, were largely powerless. The real power in the city of Indianapolis rested almost exclusively with a small group of high-powered entrepreneurs, among which were representatives of the automobile industry; Ely Lilly, a large pharmaceutical company; banks; and Blocks, a large department store.

Blacks made up roughly 20 per cent of the population. They were hedged into a black ghetto from which very few were able to escape. One result was the emergence of a small black middle class of professional and small business people who had established their own small offices, shops and stores, simply because they were not welcome in the downtown establishment facilities. With one exception, these black establishments were small, marginal and powerless. The exception was the Madam C.J. Walker Beauty Products, a company which made creams and other beauty products designed for black women. The most popular of these products and the best selling item was a cream developed for the purpose of lightening the skin of black women. This would, of course, mean that black women could look more like white women. The Walker products were very popular and sold extremely well in black communities throughout the United States. Their effectiveness in achieving their goal was another matter.

Aside from the churches, Flanner House, the YMCA and the YWCA were among the most important institutions for blacks in Indianapolis and the social services agencies dominated the social and economic structures of the black population. In addition, Flanner House received most of its funding from the United Way which was controlled by the Chamber of Commerce. Cleo Blackburn was among the most prominent black citizens. I had met and come to know him slightly when I was a member of the 1943 Quaker work camp in Indianapolis. He was a very charismatic man and an extremely powerful speaker. He had established strong relationships among both blacks and whites and was highly regarded among the black population and to some extent the leaders of the white population. Consequently, Flanner House was well financed, largely through his contacts and influence.

I first noticed that construction had been completed on the new Flanner House building which was built from the bricks the work campers had cleaned during the summer of 1943. It was a modern building and well-equipped for a day care centre, programs for adolescents, after-school programs for younger children, senior citizens and community meetings. I was met at the train by the Executive Director and escorted to Flanner House where I was introduced to the staff. My position was second to that of the Executive Director. Shortly after my arrival, I was promoted to the position of Program Director and Director of Community Organization and Development. The staff of Flanner House included nurses, school teachers, a family social worker, a housing coordinator employed to develop cooperative housing projects, a director for senior citizen programs and several part-time recreational leaders for teenage after-school programs.

Although its program thrust was largely that of social group work, recreation, and adult education, its major theoretical focus was the concept of "self-help". The ideological model of Booker T. Washington provided the rationale for much of the program at Flanner House. One example of this approach was the operation of a cannery, a facility in which women could bring their produce from their gardens and can them for use during the winter months. Growing and canning food was viewed as a method of reducing reliance upon the major stores in the downtown area. Blacks were helping themselves. In like manner, the cooperative housing staff was expected to develop a sense of cooperation among blacks which was expected to result in the development of co-op housing. Unemployed members or those working only part-time, were to be trained as carpenters, masons, plumbers, electricians and other skilled workers to work cooperatively in building their own homes. This project, co-sponsored by the AFSC, was expected to provide employment for members of the black community.

The ability of Cleo Blackburn to raise funds in the majority white community to help these projects become a reality was legendary. However, it must be admitted that in no case did these projects provide very much employment and the employment created had little impact on the total picture of black unemployment and poverty in the city.

The publicity received by Cleo Blackburn created a major impact on national social welfare organizations. Blackburn was invited to become involved in the National Federation of Settlements and Neighbourhood Centres. The federation was an umbrella organization which included members from most of the major cities in the United States including five member organizations in Indianapolis alone. In the mid-40s Blackburn was elected vice-president of the National Federation. In addition, in 1946 he was featured in a major article in *Reader's Digest* in which he was lauded as an outstanding black leader who could be compared favourably with Douglass, Washington, DuBois and others. This national acclaim, however, did not endear him to some members of the Indianapolis black community, who saw him as being too close to the power structure in downtown Indianapolis and too interested in his own advancement. But there is no denying the charismatic character of Cleo Blackburn and his ability to charm and to influence members of the white power structure.

Two incidents began undermining the confidence of the staff in regard to his relationship to the white power structure. On one morning, he came to a staff meeting in a high state of agitation and pointed out that during the previous evening, a black had killed a white man in an argument and a resulting fight. He thought that something had to be done about this incident. We did not understand what he meant. It appeared to us that a black man was alleged to have killed a white man, he had been caught and charged by the police and why not simply let justice take its course?

Blackburn, however, was not satisfied with this attitude and felt that we had to go much further. He wanted the staff to develop a statement, hold a press conference and announce to the community that Flanner House did not approve of crimes committed by blacks against white people. The staff looked at each other in amazement. We could not believe that we were being told that Flanner House should take on its shoulders the burden of protecting the white community against an alleged black criminal. Other members of the staff and I felt that it was a problem for the law and in this case the law had worked efficiently and had already caught the culprit. Why did we have to say anything further? But Blackburn insisted upon going ahead with his project. Obviously we could not stop him — after all he was the executive director of the organization and he did what he felt he had to do. However, this incident severely undermined my confidence in him.

From my perspective the second event was even more damaging. In this case Blackburn told the story (in a staff meeting) of a black person who had gone to the front door of a white farmer and asked him if he was willing to sell or give him a few tomato plants. The white farmer had said, No, he did not have any tomato plants. The black man did not contest the fact, he simply left and returned home. We were then asked by our executive director if we knew why the black man had not obtained the tomato plants? We shook our heads: we did not know why. Cleo proceeded to tell us that the black man should have gone around to the back door, knocked and when the white man came out said, "Boss, this nigger understands that you have some tomato plants. I would like very much, if you don't mind sir, to have a few for my garden." Blackburn then pointed out that the white man would have gone outside, dug up the plants and gladly given them to the black man!

From listening to the story, we were supposed to have learned a lesson about how to deal with white people. It became clear that the reservations that some blacks in the community had toward Blackburn were based on a true assessment of his approach to the white population. I was surprised and dismayed. Even in the South I had never heard such a blatant reflection of acceptance of self-abasement. From accounts it is true that Washington urged blacks to develop a "modus operandi" in their relations with the southern white man, but never at the expense of human dignity, mutual respect and a sense of equality. Booker T. Washington and W.E.B. DuBois approached these goals by different routes but, in my opinion, neither would have advocated the approach of our executive director!

One of my responsibilities at Flanner House was to go around the community, knock on doors and meet the people who lived in the nearby neighbourhoods. I made it a habit of visiting many local residences and listening to their concerns, interests, and evaluation of the problems. I also encouraged them to think of possible solutions they would like to see implemented. Blackburn supported me in this activity. Many people were upset about the lack of traffic lights where their children crossed a busy street to go to school; and the lack of adequate sanitation and garbage removal. After three or four months of listening to problems I felt that the time had come to suggest that a meeting be called for a community discussion of these issues.

That suggestion was eagerly accepted by many of the people in the community. Several men and women met to discuss the possibility of inviting the mayor to attend and listen and respond to the complaints of the residents. This idea was enthusiastically accepted. I contacted the mayor and he agreed to attend. There was a good discussion of issues on the night of the meeting. The mayor had arrived early and walked around the community prior to the beginning of the meeting itself. He listened carefully to the discussion, made notes and promised that he would take action to address the problems raised by community members. Everyone left the meeting in a very good mood. People were feeling optimistic that, perhaps for the first time, some progress was being made.

Cleo Blackburn had been out of town at the time of the meeting and when he returned, I reported what had happened and how happy the people were. To my surprise, instead of being pleased and satisfied, he was obviously very upset. He felt that I should not have called a meeting with the mayor, he should have called it. I should not deal with people at the top level of the city administration, certainly not the mayor. This should be done by him on behalf of the people. While I had been hired to promote community organization and development, Cleo wanted the credit for anything that was positive and constructive. He was not satisfied that I had already achieved that result. This incident created tension which never fully evaporated during my stay at Flanner House.

Following these experiences, it became clear that I would not remain at Flanner House very much longer. Two other incidents occurred which contributed to my difficulties at Flanner House. I had been from the beginning very much involved in working with students from the local university. Earlier I had been a part of the emerging civil rights movement in Philadelphia and had sat in restaurants and picketed drug stores and other institutions which refused to serve blacks. Following my orientation to the city and my evaluation of the impact of its policies, I had decided that something had to be done about the racial situation, even if it did not succeed. Consequently, I called a meeting of a group of white and black students from Butler University and laid before them the possibility of taking direct action against racial practices. The first meeting of students was held at the black branch of the Indianapolis YMCA. (We could not have met at the main YMCA because it was segregated.)

At the first meeting I gained their attention by talking about a "gentleman" who existed in our society, but whom we never saw directly. The name of that gentleman was Mr. James W. Crow. The students looked at me with a degree of puzzlement. They could not imagine to whom I was referring. I then identified the real phenomenon. I was talking about "Jim Crow", the pattern of legal segregation in the South and in some northern states including the state of Indiana. Following animated discussion, it was agreed that the students would meet with me again and map out a plan of action. I was quite aware of the limitation of students as far as social action was concerned, but felt that this particular group had great potential. It might, in time, become one of the most important forces for social change in the city.

Several new students, including three or four from the University of Indiana, fifty miles away, attended the second meeting. Several students had read about a similar project in Chicago. The Congress on Race Equality (CORE) was organized for the purpose of challenging restaurant discrimination. Black and white students and citizens were engaging in "sit ins" involving restaurants and other places of public accommodation and demanding that the total group be served. It was agreed that our group would embark on a similar program but focussing on downtown restaurants because we felt there would be less danger of physical attacks by hoodlums in the downtown area. We were aware that there had been some attacks on blacks when testing restaurants in Chicago and we wanted to avoid this kind of behaviour in our campaign, especially in the initial stages.

The Campaign Begins

We agreed to hold our first testing sessions on a Saturday morning, since most of the young people were either students or workers. Those who were employed in the downtown area demonstrated a certain amount of anxiety regarding their role in the project. This attitude was quite understandable in view of the fact that, had they been recognized many would probably have been fired from their jobs. I also had some uncertainty about my own role as far as the attitude of Flanner House was concerned. Our testing of restaurants and other business places would be a direct challenge to the attitudes and behaviour of many of the leading citizens of the white community; nevertheless, I decided to go ahead. If the young people were ready to take that risk then I must also be ready. We were not aware of it at the time, but we were among the pioneers who initiated campaigns against racial discrimination in several northern cities. The larger movement began in the southern states a decade later.

I felt, and the group agreed, that perhaps it would be better to begin our testing in a situation which would appear to be relatively easy to deal with. We decided to go to small restaurants and small drug stores, many of which in those days also had coke bars. Fifteen stools were situated along a counter and our group entered the drug store and as many as could sat down at the coke bar while others had to sit at a table in another corner of the room.

After some delay the waitress came over to tell us that the management of the drug store didn't wish to serve black people, therefore we should leave. As planned, we did not argue with her, we simply remained in our seats. Finally she came over again and repeated her request for us to leave. We indicated our wish to speak to the manager. She returned to a room in the rear of the establishment and after fifteen minutes, came out again and began to fill the glasses with coke. Many of the group indicated later, that they really felt like cheering at that point because they thought we had won a great victory and that things would be different in the future. Unfortunately the situation did not quite turn out that way.

We drank our cokes, paid our bills and were prepared to leave when we heard strange noises and noticed what the waitress was doing. To our amazement, she was smashing our glasses on the floor of the drug store. We could hardly believe our eyes. She and the management believed that any glasses we had used would not be suitable for other customers in the future. Therefore the glasses we used must be destroyed.

We left the building and went outside on the sidewalk and stopped for an evaluation of our next step. We agreed to return to the restaurant and order another round of cokes. Again the glasses were smashed when we had finished drinking the cokes. We went out again, had a brief discussion and decided to return for a third time. By now some of the students were running out of money for cokes so we agreed to share the costs so that each of us would have enough to buy at least one more drink. By this time a group of people was standing around and observing the action. When we returned for a third time it was obvious that there was some hostility directed toward us. However, that did not stop us and we sat down at our seats and ordered our cokes!

By this time there was a considerable amount of glass on the floor and the waitress had gone to get a pan and broom to sweep up the mess. Our ordering another round of cokes interrupted this process. We were served, paid our bills, and our glasses were not smashed. It was obvious that the snack bar was running out of glasses and could not afford to smash the few that were left!

This first small victory was very encouraging to members of our group. Many of our people felt they would like to involve more of their friends in it. We encouraged the enlargement of the group because we realized that many young people would not be able to come to campaign meetings every Saturday morning. It was important to have twenty-five or thirty total members so that we could be assured of having at least fifteen or twenty for each of our campaigns. In addition, meetings were planned for mid-week evenings for information sharing, planning and selecting our next target.

It was amazing to see the courage and resourcefulness of these young people in their first campaign. I had expected that some would back out, particularly as they arrived upon the scene and found that initially we would not be served. However, they stuck to plans and did not break ranks. They persevered in spite of the possibility that they might be identified and subjected to verbal or physical abuse. Subsequently, they could more easily handle the tension building up in other campaigns against other restaurants. Most of them were aware that their parents would be shocked to find that they were engaging in this type of activity. Thus, it was even more surprising that a large majority of the young people who had participated in the initial campaign returned for the second. Five had even brought other friends who had not been present at our initial activity. We continued our testing every other Saturday for five or six months until the end of the school year terminated our project as most of the students were leaving school and returning home.

While there were common elements in each testing situation, there were also variations based on time, place and circumstances. For example, in restaurants our group would divide into two, three or four people at each table and scatter around the restaurant. We did not want to sit in the same place, which led to developing a tactic of not all going in at the same time. The interesting aspect of the program was that white students received much more hostility than black students. Name calling was more frequent as were other expressions of hostility. We were never subjected to physical attack but we had a tremendous amount of verbal abuse directed at our group. I was surprised at how well our group held together. There were some variations in each campaign activity but for the most part, a core group of about fifteen people attended and participated in every activity and became known as the "veterans of the wars". Many young people developed warm and lasting friendships with others in the group and with me which in a few instances lasted for several years.

In the meantime, our group received unwanted newspaper and other publicity. We were highly praised by many members of the black community but were equally condemned by many whites. Some of the students were asked why they joined that group of "communists" who were trying to upset the status quo. My activities were becoming known to the board of directors of Flanner House and to the executive director. On one occasion, he called me in and asked me for an explanation of what I was doing. I gladly gave him a description of the group and the degree of success it had enjoyed. I pointed out, for example, that there were probably four or five times as many places where blacks could eat in downtown Indianapolis than before we initiated our campaign.

It was very obvious that he was upset, I believe because some board members had put pressure on him to either force me to cease these activities or to fire me. He did not put it in quite those words but he made it clear that he was under some pressure.

A few weeks later I was called to the office of one of the top members of his board of directors. This man was a vice-president of one of the largest business establishments in the city. He invited me into his plush office, called his secretary to bring us a cup of coffee or tea and we sat down for a chat. Initially the chat was very friendly and I kept wondering when he was going to get to the point. Finally he did. He wanted to talk about the possibility of my damaging the reputation of Flanner House as a result of my activities in the community. I pointed out that I was doing volunteer work on Saturdays and this was not a part of my work at Flanner House. It should have no impact upon my relationship to the Flanner House community. He was not satisfied. What he really wanted to know was exactly what I was doing, what my motives were, and what I expected to accomplish? I responded to his questions but it was obvious that we would not reach any agreement. At the end of our lengthy session, he escorted me to the door, suggested that I think about the matter and then we would have another talk in the next two or three weeks. He had been friendly and cordial during more than an hour of discussion and obviously felt that he was providing helpful counsel to me in this situation.

Two or three weeks later, Mrs. West, a prominent white woman and chair of the community development committee, came into the office at Flanner House and suggested we get together for a chat. She invited me to her home for lunch, to which I readily agreed. Mrs. West lived in a very wealthy and exclusive part of the city in a home with expensive furnishings and grounds. She was a very gracious person and invited me for tea prior to lunch. I had told her of my activities earlier in the year. My assessment of her was that she was also a woman of liberal instincts and attitudes. She had supported me strongly when the director of the organization had been upset because of my invitation to the mayor.

She listened carefully and often nodded her head in agreement with what I was saying. On the other hand, she made it clear that she was aware that some members of the board were upset with my activities. As I was departing following our lunch and discussion she said, "Leave the matter to me and I'll see what I can do to get things straightened out." (Among staff only the executive director was permitted to attend board meetings). Apparently the matter was discussed by the entire board at a subsequent meeting. There were obviously some strong concerns expressed and some feeling that my activities were damaging the reputation of Flanner House. There was no evidence supporting this view since all evidence pointed to the opposite direction. Members of the black community were not concerned and strongly supported me. With one exception the staff members of Flanner House were strongly behind what I was doing, although very few were willing to come out and join in the campaigns. They were afraid to be seen as involved in the anti-racist activity in which I was engaged: however, they consistently encouraged me to continue the work. They were enjoying some of the benefits of a more open and accepting community.

My second meeting with the vice-president of a major corporation who was on the board occurred three weeks after the first. It appeared that he had some conversation with Mrs. West. Again, we had a lengthy and largely unproductive session. I did inform him, however, that our activities for the summer months were ceasing because the students were leaving school for their homes. I was also planning to spend additional time on building new community organizations in the local neighbourhood. I told him that our initial organization had been very successful and that it was time for me to determine if it was possible to organize additional community projects in nearby neighbourhoods. He seemed to be satisfied with that idea and made no further comment. I left his elaborate office and returned to my modest office at Flanner House. I was quite aware of the power of the white establishment members of the board, but had no intention of abandoning a campaign just getting under way. Neither did I feel that the board had any business attempting to control my outside activities.

The summer of 1947 was a very hectic one for me. In addition to my regular work at Flanner House, I also had another project in mind, namely to take my one-month vacation to prepare for my marriage in September. My activities at Flanner House and in the community had made me very well known as a public figure. I had established relationships with many local people and leaders of neighbourhood and community organizations. I was on good terms with the executive directors of the YMCA and the YWCA, the principal of the Crispus Attucks High School and members of the Indianapolis chapter of the National Association of Social Workers. I was becoming well known as an individual who was available for speaking at various events including local colleges and universities. I had also developed a very strong and enduring friendship with Mike Ransom, a young black lawyer who was just getting started in practice. Mike was to defend me on a number of occasions in subsequent months. My activities also brought me to the attention of the editor and publisher of the local black newspaper.

One reason for my rapid emergence as a leader in the black community stemmed from the fact that the existing black leadership was weak and ineffective. An example of this failure was that the local chapter of the National Association for the Advancement of Colored People (NAACP) had disbanded as a result of internal bickering and arguments. The general public had shown that it was quite willing to let the organization die without protest. In the absence of effective leadership in the black community, Blackburn had stepped into the vacuum. There were other aspiring leaders but none seemed to be able to develop effective contacts with the downtown power structure and to extract concessions on behalf of the black community.

This was an embarrassing situation for me since I had no interest whatsoever in becoming a so called "black leader". Secondly I had no intention of remaining in Indianapolis for any considerable length of time. I wanted to build the foundation of my career there and then move on to another city. A more sensitive factor, of course, was my relationship to Cleo Blackburn. I knew very well that he enjoyed his position of leadership in the community and would be quite upset if he felt that I was threatening that position. I couldn't work very long under the control of a man who would be continually looking over my shoulder to see if I was doing something to undermine his status. In addition, I was determined to continue my volunteer work in the area of civil and human rights.

Except for one or two incidents, the summer went very quietly and uneventfully. The first exception was that I had decided to test a restaurant on my own and went into a restaurant on the border of the black community and asked for service. I was told by the waitress that they did not serve blacks. I demanded to see the manager who finally came out and repeated what the waitress had said. I answered that we would become involved in a waiting game because I would sit there until they decided to serve me. Within a few minutes the manager announced that the restaurant was closing for the day. There were only two or three other people in the restaurant at that time. We were all asked to leave, which we did. It was only about 4:00 in the afternoon and I had the feeling that the manager was using this as a ploy. I was almost certain that he would reopen the restaurant as soon as we were out of sight. I walked two or three blocks away and found a drug store which sold paperback novels and other reading materials. I bought a book and went back to the restaurant and found it open as I had expected. I sat down with my book and began reading. I didn't ask any questions or order anything but simply sat at a table and read. Other customers, all white, began to enter the restaurant.

The manager seemed to be getting more and more worried. He would come from his office at the back of the restaurant and look out to see what was happening, then go back into the kitchen or some other room at the rear of the restaurant. The waitress also would appear and then return to the rear. After about thirty minutes the waitress came over and asked for my order. She was ready to serve me! This type of situation could be quite a problem in the sense that one did not know what was being bought. One would place an order but could not be sure that the food or drink would be exactly what was ordered. There were stories from Chicago and other places of blacks whose order had been accepted only to find that the meat or vegetables were totally saturated with black pepper or a whole shaker of salt. At the same time, the owner would insist that the cost of the meal was ten to twenty dollars for a sandwich or a hamburger. I did not want to take a chance with rotten meat or vegetables. I ordered a salad which I examined very closely before eating it. It appeared to be okay and I ate a part of it.

However, I had not been hungry and my intention was simply to test the attitude and behaviour of the restaurant. That having been achieved I was quite happy to leave most of the salad on the plate and pay the regular price, as indicated on the menu. Prior to that encounter, I had alerted my lawyer, Mike Ransom, who was available in case of need. Mike was one of the few blacks in Indianapolis who openly supported the activities in which we were engaged. For the most part, the financial and moral support I received was given behind closed doors. Many individuals offered money in support of the cause although they clearly indicated that any contribution they made must remain anonymous. Their contributions did help, however, in providing necessary funds which enabled some students to enter restaurants and test their willingness or reluctance to serve blacks and interracial groups.

It would be a mistake to believe, however, that these donors were unmotivated and unconcerned. They were not ready to get out into the street and stand on soap boxes or to make their anger public. Black rage had not reached the level where it was expressed in an open and candid manner. Disillusion, cynicism, apathy and fear characterized the behaviour and attitudes of many members of the black community. These attitudes and behaviours were not limited to Indianapolis and could be found in abundance in most cities, whether in the North or South. The difference was that Indianapolis did not have access to a set of countervailing attitudes and practices. In other cities one could always find a minority of the black leadership who spoke out very strongly regarding their distaste of Jim Crow segregation laws. I heard speeches of this type from university presidents, professional faculty members at the university and individuals in other settings. I have noted my admiration for the courage of Mr. Harper, the principal of my high school in Atlanta. Even in Indianapolis the black branch of the YMCA sponsored a series of meetings where outside speakers frequently strongly criticized the evils of segregation and discrimination. The local black newspapers also carried articles criticizing the city management and the policies of the state of Indiana. Little was ever done, however, in implementing the ideas and suggestions deriving from these forums so the power structure had no reason to fear the possibility of significant change. The history of the black community in Indianapolis provided ample evidence that little or no change was likely to occur in the near future.

My difficulties with the board of directors of Flanner House, however, provided some evidence that attitudes might be changing. I had learned that those who oppressed and exploited others usually found ways to attack or destroy anyone who challenged their ability to manipulate and control. I felt certain that the more extreme methods utilized in the Deep South, such as lynchings, killings and beatings, would not be employed in Indianapolis. But I was aware that my vulnerability as a staff member of Flanner House would prevent open support from the black community. I had to contend with the hostility of the Indianapolis power establishment which was well represented on the board of directors of Flanner House. It was also well represented on the board of directors of the United Way, the funding agency which provided most of the financial support for the various programs operated by Flanner House. I was aware, but not intimidated by these considerations.

The summer was rapidly passing and I met with the staff to plan programs for the fall. On the surface, it appeared that everything had blown over and that the situation was back to normal. I had a very strong feeling, however, that this was not to be the case. The situation would be reopened in the future for at least two reasons. The first was that I would continue my work with the students in testing restaurants and other facilities serving the public. The second was that I was getting married to a white woman. In terms of personal orientation, I am a very private person and did not discuss my fears and concerns about what was happening in the community. I simply kept these matters to myself and made preparations for what I thought would be appropriate.

The one individual I did talk to was Mike Ransom. As a lawyer, his services might be needed in the event that the police stepped in and tried to restrict our activities. Mike offered his services without a fee. Depending on the circumstances, this offer could be a tremendous contribution. Many of the students would not have funds to pay the considerable sums of money required to hire a lawyer. I had often wondered what we would do in the event of a mass arrest and the importance of having a lawyer representing the students and me could not be denied. Mike's offer was of major importance because it meant that we could continue our actions without excessive concerns about what would happen in case of an arrest. We were aware that an arrest would be illegal since we were careful to not break any law. Nevertheless, an arrest or a series of arrests could be extremely inconvenient!

The Fall Program

The fall program at Flanner House began in early September, shortly after the opening of the public schools. Registration in the nursery school, the adult and all other programs was done in the previous year. The director and staff were very pleased. Through our initiative and the cooperation of the AFSC we had also established a weekend work camp program at Flanner House based on the model established by the Service Committee. We worked in cooperation with the local health and social welfare officials who were in constant contact with members of disadvantaged groups. It was necessary to have a staff person from Flanner House to act as a liaison person responsible for contacts with the local staff of the Service Committee. I was selected because I had previous experience with weekend work camps.

A young, newly-married white couple, the Petherbridges, were appointed by the Service Committee as their representative, with direct responsibility for the operation of weekend work camps. They were also responsible for contacting various colleges, universities and high schools in their efforts to recruit work campers. The AFSC staff was very successful in this endeavour and with one or two exceptions, each of the seven or eight work camps conducted over that school year were filled to capacity.

I had three basic programs in operation in the fall of 1947. Foremost among them was the necessity for continuing my community development work at Flanner House. It was very important to me to see black people begin to get a feeling that they could exert some degree of control over their lives. They could protest against injustices and try to make positive changes in their own personal and community lives and in the lives of their neighbours. Organizing to bring increased social change was important, both at the professional and personal level.

The initiation and development of the work camps provided a second orientation and possibility for a significant contribution. I was able to work with, study, and help young people learn about the nature, structure and goals of their society from a very practical point of view. This involved working with and supporting underprivileged people as they struggled to survive in a highly exploitive and oppressive situation.

My third orientation during the early fall was the reestablishment of our interracial testing group. Many members had returned from vacation and were ready to revive this program. We agreed that many of the establishments which we had tested in the previous school year would require retesting. The need for monitoring was one of the lessons we had learned. Often when a restaurant or other public facility agreed to serve blacks or racially mixed groups, it was only done for the purpose of getting us out of the place, with the hope that we would never return. We had learned the importance of urging town people to also use those facilities. A pattern of restaurants serving blacks had to be established and this could not be done by university students alone. It was not solely for the benefit of students that a test had been conducted: the purpose was to desegregate facilities in the downtown area for the use of black people in general.

During the late summer of 1946, I began to date two local young women, one of whom worked in a social welfare agency. These dates, from my point of view, were friendly and pleasant but nothing intense or romantic. I accepted their invitation to escort them to dances, parties and occasionally to a play or a movie. We had much in common and became unusually good friends. However, they were not my only friends and on occasion, I went out with other young women. Thus, when I announced my engagement in the summer of 1947, I was quite surprised to learn that these two young women were not very pleased with the news. I suppose they had felt that our friendliness meant we were becoming romantically involved which might eventually lead to marriage. That was never my intention and I suspect that their disappointment and unhappiness derived from the fact that they felt I had been "leading them on". I can see why they may have felt that way as I had not divulged the fact that I had kept in constant contact with Phyllis, a young woman whom I had met at the Flanner House work camp in the summer of 1943.

Phyllis and I had kept in contact through letters and occasional visits while she was a student at nearby Antioch College in Yellow Springs, Ohio, a small town within easy travel distance from Indianapolis. I only announced my engagement two months prior to the date of the marriage. For me, that was not an unusual occurrence. I had always been a very private individual, who, for the most part, kept thoughts, attitudes and intentions to myself.

In the early fall, I decided to take some of my vacation time to prepare for my marriage, to find a place for us to live and to spend some time with my wife to be. We found an apartment, located in a two-story house only two blocks from the street separating the black from the white neighbourhoods.

We were married by a very prominent minister in one of the larger churches in New York City. Reverend John Haynes Holmes was an outstanding spokesperson for the peace movement and other social justice issues. Both my wife and I were very honoured to have our marriage ceremony performed by such an outstanding individual and leader in the New York community. One of my best friends, Dick Stenhouse, a colleague at Big Flats, served as my best man. We returned to Indianapolis in mid-September just as the new fall program was getting underway at Flanner House.

We enjoyed an idyllic marriage during our stay in Indianapolis and for many years thereafter. We had a great number of things in common, including our love of music. Phyllis had played the oboe in the orchestra at Antioch College and could also play the piano. We often played duets in the evening after work. Even though "mixed" marriages were not very well accepted at that time we were not aware of any difficulties. I mention "not aware" because I am sure that many people in the community, both black and white, did not approve of mixed marriages. Even some members of the local Friends Meeting were not happy with the fact that I had married a white woman. We were told informally that the local Friends Church would not welcome a request that we be married in their facility. On the surface everything was fine and I continued my various activities in the community, my professional activities and my duties with the work camps. Phyllis found a job and began working shortly after we returned to Indianapolis. Everything looked rosy but that appearance was a bit misleading: a few storm clouds were on the horizon!

A New Crisis

I did not know whether or not my marriage would have any impact upon my future relationship to Flanner House. I was quite aware that the press was playing up the issue of black and white relationships. I had no way of knowing whether that issue was being discussed by members of our board of directors. After all, the staff did not attend board meetings. It was probably about a month later that I was informed, along with the staff, that a special meeting of the board would be called to discuss staffing at Flanner House. That was a shock to all of us, since we had no idea that the question of staffing was under consideration.

On the night of that meeting a number of us stayed after work in the event that board members wanted to ask questions about any aspect of the program. We sat and chatted in the staff room, some distance away from the board meeting room. There was some attempt at humour but it was apparent that the staff was quite concerned about the possible impact of this special meeting. Presumably, on instructions from the board of directors, the executive director had left town for some undisclosed location. Therefore he was not present to defend his own staff if necessary.

Finally, the meeting of the board ended and staff members began to drift toward the board room. We were in plain sight of members of the board but nothing was said to us. Board members quickly left the building, leaving nothing for us to do but to follow suit. Two days later I received a telephone call from Mrs. West who told me that it was her responsibility to inform me that my services were being terminated. She wanted me to know that she was not expressing her own point of view but that some people had concerns about my activities in the community. I told her, as I had done previously, that my activities on weekends should not be the business of Flanner House which, in my view, should be concerned with whether or not I was doing the job I was employed to do. She stated that there was no question about the quality of my work. When I pressed her, she finally admitted that the reason why board members were unhappy was my activities involving testing restaurants and other public facilities as well as the fact that I had married a white woman. The date of my termination would be the middle of March, 1948, accompanied by two months severance pay.

I immediately informed the remainder of the staff of the decision of the board. As one could easily guess, staff members were shocked. Programs were interrupted or put on the back burner while staff members gathered in small groups to discuss the situation. Curiously, very little action or protest occurred regarding the action of the board. I think most of the staff had expected it. What really got them upset was that the executive director was not present at the time the staff was being discussed. He had been pushed aside and the board itself had taken on his administrative responsibility as executive director.

A fairly interesting perspective emerged when news of my firing hit the public arena. The white members of the board made a strong attempt to defend their position. The few black members remained silent. On the other hand, my support in the black community was almost unanimous: many people called to offer whatever help they could. It was suggested that I should call on Senator Brokenburg, the one black state senator in the Indiana legislature. While I had little faith in the senator or his willingness to participate I decided to go and see him alone. I did this and received the kind of response which I expected. The senator felt that there was nothing he could do, although he was sympathetic. He was demonstrating that he did not dare challenge the power establishment of the city.

The two white members of the staff became quite alarmed at the possible negative impact the controversy might have on their jobs. I was advised by these individuals that I should not speak to the press but try to let the matter die down quietly. This I was not willing to do and insisted that I would present my side of the story publicly. When I was finally contacted by the press, I gave them a full and comprehensive story. Cleo Blackburn and members of the board refused to comment when contacted by the press or by the concerned public.

My professional association, the Indianapolis chapter of the National Association of Social Workers (NASW) also showed interest in becoming involved. An investigating committee was appointed who met with the board of directors, the executive director, and subsequently with me. This attempt was fruitless and the committee reported that having talked to all sides they could not see how the organization could do anything useful. They felt that the board of directors was adamant and so was I. I repeatedly made the point that I had a perfect right to use my own spare time in my own way and that Flanner House had no right to dictate what I did outside the job. I further made the point that there was no concern in the community about what I was doing. As mentioned earlier most members of the community strongly supported me. It was only powerful white representatives of the establishment who were upset about my marriage and how I was using my time as a citizen in the local community. I learned how powerless the black community and the professional organization were when they attempted to deal with the power elite.

The matter had come to a stand-off and I began to think about finding other employment outside of Indianapolis. Shortly afterwards, I was approached by a group of four men who asked if I would be willing to take on a job for them. They had thought about this before but had done nothing further because of my attachment to Flanner House. When they learned that I was no longer on the staff they felt it was appropriate to put their proposition before me. That proposition was, in view of the fact that the NAACP had become defunct many months earlier, would I be interested in taking on the responsibility for rebuilding the organization? That proposal seemed to me to be very challenging, although in all probability very temporary. The organization had practically no funds but some of the gentlemen felt that they could raise enough money to justify my coming on staff for a period of three or four months.

They were successful and I agreed to start working for the NAACP as executive director in April, 1948. I viewed this temporary position as an opportunity to have some time to find a permanent job elsewhere. I was quite aware that under the conditions it would be impossible for me to stay in Indianapolis in a voluntary agency supported by the United Way because the United Way in Indianapolis was controlled and dominated by the larger corporations and other members of the power elite.

This opportunity gave me the possibility for continuing my work with students in testing restaurants and other places of public accommodation. It also enabled me to continue my activities with the Service Committee's sponsored work camps. At the same time, I would have time to embark on a job-hunting operation.

The NAACP was and is a national organization founded in 1909 by black and white people concerned about the increasing segregation and discrimination directed against blacks in the United States. One of its major founders was the writer and intellectual, W.E.B. DuBois. It had grown steadily in effectiveness, membership and in standing within the various black communities. It published the magazine, *Crisis*, initiated by DuBois which had a considerable influence among black people throughout the country. The famous black writer and activist James Weldon Johnson was prominent among its founders and became its first executive director. The NAACP initiated a militant program of legal action against racism in all of its many forms. The goal was to obtain full participation of black people in the affairs of the United States and in their local communities. It strongly opposed segregation, discrimination and any other treatment which impinged on the progress of black people.

By the 1940s the NAACP had established more than 60 chapters and branches in cities throughout the United States. Its structure also included a number of state-wide organizations. Before its demise, the Indianapolis chapter had been a member of both the national organization and the Indiana state branch of the NAACP. The organization, however, was not universally accepted and many black leaders including some of the more prominent ones, felt that it was too moderate, because it focused primarily on legal means rather than organizing the community to demand its legitimate rights in a supposedly political democracy.

The National Negro Congress, a more militant organization, was founded in 1930 as a counterbalance to the legalistic approach of the NAACP. The Congress and a number of other organizations made a valiant attempt to mobilize masses of black people through their various local churches, clubs, labour unions, civic organizations and lodges. The Congress was initially headed by A. Philip Randolph, perhaps the most prominent black individual in the country at that time.

But by 1950, the Congress was falling apart because of internal disputes, leaving the NAACP and the National Urban League as the two major remaining national black organizations. This situation remained fairly constant until the 1950s when Martin Luther King emerged and established his Southern Christian Leadership Conference. Many of the school desegregation and other victories had been won by the NAACP, and others were to come later.

In late 1947, the need to rebuild the NAACP chapter in Indianapolis was obvious. It was very clear that there was need for a strong militant organization which could mobilize the concerns and interests of black people in support of necessary change. Although aware of criticism of its "moderate and legalistic" reputation, I felt that in view of the considerable period which had elapsed since the demise of the organization, the achievement of this task might be possible. Perhaps the passage of time would have healed "old wounds" and former members would see the value of returning and reestablishing the organization. That was to be my major challenge for the next four months.

After consulting with a number of people, including several community leaders, I identified five men and one woman who were interested in putting energy and time into rebuilding the local chapter. That was a good start, but, in my view, not enough. I held a few preliminary meetings with that small group, out of which came names of other people who could be invited to meetings. This process took three or four weeks and by that time we had a committee of about fifteen people who were pledged to bring the Indianapolis chapter back to life.

I began a two-fold campaign. First to reestablish the organization and, second, to raise the necessary funds for its continued operation. I had been correct in my guess that people were now ready to re-establish the organization. We began by holding public meetings in which local militants or out-of-town individuals were invited to address the group. The several volunteers recruited to work in the office were a major factor. Mike Ransom and Mrs. Jacobs, the wife of a local undertaker, became the unofficial leaders of the group during its early stages. A journalist, a few young black students and working people struggled to form a viable organization which was ready for action in less than six weeks after I arrived on the scene. I had not created the new organization, I had only been a facilitator. The real work was done by local people who had previously been active in the NAACP and who wanted to see it reestablished.

In the meantime, the young college students and I had continued our program of testing downtown restaurants and other facilities. We had established a group of black adults who could be used for tests in "high-class" restaurants that were too expensive for most students. Five of us, including four members of our board of directors, began planning for these tests. The first target chosen was the restaurant in Blocks, a highly regarded department store which included a large, sumptuous restaurant on one of the upper floors. The secretary of its board of directors and director of personnel was also a member of the board of directors of Flanner House. We dressed in our best clothes and embarked on the test. Our board member, Mrs. Jessie Jacobs, led the way into the restaurant. We were met by a beautifully dressed hostess, who looked at us with some curiosity and asked if we had reservations. We responded that we did not but saw many empty tables and chairs in the place. There should be no difficulty in serving us. Apparently she was not sure what to do, so she led us to the extreme rear of the restaurant and seated us at a table which was practically invisible from other parts of the room. She then called someone who brought out a screen and set it up so that we could not be seen by other customers. The meal was good and we enjoyed it thoroughly, but it was expensive and we were not very happy with the way we had been tricked into sitting in a part of the restaurant which was virtually invisible. We agreed that we would leave after the meal and return at a later date.

Three weeks later we returned and the same hostess approached us and asked for our reservations. We informed her that we did not have reservations but there were many empty tables which were not reserved. She turned to lead our group to the back of the restaurant. As we walked down the aisles we suddenly stopped and sat down. She did not notice this and continued walking. When she reached the back of the restaurant we had already seated ourselves at a table near the entrance. This manoeuvre had clearly defeated her plan to have us again sit behind a screen where we would not be seen. She came back and stopped as if she were going to speak, but said nothing and sharply turned away. We have no way of knowing to whom she spoke, but she came out and took our orders. We were served very promptly, enjoyed a good meal and felt very pleased with our achievement.

We had guessed rightly that a high-class restaurant would not dare create a commotion with respect to services to the general public, including blacks. That was an important lesson for us. We were aware of the problems which many black testers had encountered in Chicago and a few other cities. In several instances, young blacks had been physically assaulted by hoodlums and had been pushed off chairs and stools, burned on the face or neck with cigarettes and even brutally beaten. We were not forced to face this type of assault in Indianapolis; however, we recognized that assaults might occur.

Another problem was racial discrimination in theatres. Blacks were not permitted to attend the Capital Theatre. I wanted to see the movie, *Great Expectations*, a highly regarded British movie in the late 1940s. I was aware of the policies of the theatre regarding blacks but decided that I would personally challenge these policies. When I went to the theatre to buy a ticket, I was told that they did not admit blacks. I questioned this and asked to see the manager. Shortly thereafter, the manager came out and informed me that the ticket sales person was correct. After a short discussion, I told him that I would be going down to the court house the next day and filing a suit against the theatre. He suggested that I go right ahead. He didn't feel there was any problem in that respect and he was quite confident of his stand. My threat did not intimidate him in the least.

I had heard that the state of Indiana had a law forbidding discrimination in public places. I called Mike Ransom and asked him to check it out. Mike was aware of the law and gave me information regarding the specific section of the appropriate act. Armed with this information I went down the next morning to the office of the district attorney to file my complaint. He was very surprised and did not feel this form of behaviour was covered by the law. The district attorney then went through his law books, spent some time checking over various acts and finally found the appropriate section. He expressed astonishment. He then asked me what would I like him to do. I told him I intended to file a complaint and take the theatre manager to court.

It was the district attorney's job to prosecute the case. My job would be to serve as a witness, with or without a lawyer. The district attorney filled out the proper papers and gave them to me to sign. I then left his office and returned to my work. Within two or three weeks I was sent a notice informing me that a date for the court case had been set. Mike was interested in the case and agreed to accompany me.

Mike and I arrived on time and went into the courtroom, only to find the respondent was not present. His lawyer asked the judge if it would be possible to arrange a remand. Apparently the respondent's mother was seriously ill and he had to leave town for a temporary period. It seemed to me that the judge granted the remand with undue haste and we left the courtroom with the intention of returning within a week.

Again, the theatre manager did not appear. His lawyer again said that there was a very important reason why his client could not be present. Could the judge, he asked, grant a second remand. Although the judge seemed unwilling to do this without questioning why the respondent was not present, he nevertheless granted the remand. My lawyer and I discussed this matter and decided that we would go back to court a third time and see what happened but if a third remand was granted, we would be prepared to take further action. We had not decided exactly what that action would be but we would wait and see what would happen next. We had the right to challenge the request and to object to a third remand. Again on the third court date the lawyer for the respondent was in the court room but the respondent was not. My lawyer asked why the gentlemen kept asking for remands. He felt this was unfair, much time was lost coming back and forth to the courtroom. He suggested that perhaps this was deliberate, that the respondent was trying to wait us out hoping that at some point we would not appear and the case could be dismissed.

It was at that point that I spoke up reminding the court that I was not working in the morning, that I was always available and that no matter what date the court case was set, I would be there. If necessary I would be sitting on the steps to the court house every morning waiting for the court to open.

My lawyer and I could not be sure but we had a strong feeling that the defense lawyer and the judge were playing games with us. These remands, we felt, were deliberate and we were determined to not be caught in a trap so that the case could be thrown out of court and forgotten. The request for the remand was granted but not as quickly as before. We were certain that the next time we came to court the case would be heard.

Two weeks later, we again appeared in court. This time, both the lawyer and the theatre manager were available for the hearing. The judge listened to my charge and asked the manager to respond. He said that he would prefer an out-of-court settlement. The judge then turned to me and asked if I was agreeable to this arrangement. I said that my purpose in filing the complaint was that I wanted to see the film and I was not there to punish the manager. If the manager was willing to admit blacks to the theatre, I would be willing to drop the complaint. The judge turned to the respondent and asked if that would be satisfactory to him. On the basis of this discussion the judge ordered that an agreement be drawn up and signed indicating that blacks would be allowed to attend the theatre at any time it was open. That was agreeable to me and we both signed.

The agreement was reached in the morning and by noon I was on the phone calling various people suggesting they should go to the theatre and test whether it was actually open to them as the agreement stipulated. Unfortunately, I was not able to go until late afternoon. As a result of my telephone call at least six black people had attended the afternoon performance of the movie and were leaving the theatre when I arrived. They had been treated well and had no complaints. Although I was the initiator of the complaint, I was not the first black to gain access to the theatre. Three other blacks were ahead of me when I entered the line to purchase my ticket. We entered without incident and sat together. Those of us who were present at the end of the film decided to go to the nearest restaurant, have a cup of coffee and discuss our experiences. We felt very good about the experience. Our long-awaited victory would be highly regarded and appreciated by other members of the black community.

Fundraising

The second but equally important function of the reestablished chapter of the NAACP was fundraising. It was necessary because the organization had no office space, no facilities and, with the exception of myself, no staff. It was known that my position would be for only four months, after which the organization would be on its own again. Continuation as a viable organization would depend upon the ability to raise several thousand dollars. Fortunately for me and for the organization, a prominent local entrepreneur provided us with free office space for a limited period of time. That generosity made it possible for me to avoid having to use my own home as the office of the chapter.

The gods must have been smiling on the emergence of the chapter of the NAACP because within a few days of my accepting the position, a letter arrived informing us of a drama group which was on tour presenting a play entitled

Home of the Brave. The cast was interracial and the purpose of the group was, through drama, to raise the consciousness of the community around racial and social justice issues. The theme of the play was that of a young black soldier returning home from the wars in Europe. To his surprise he found that nothing had changed; however, in spite of obstacles, he developed a romantic relationship with a young white woman. Their struggle to overcome racism and bigotry and to find a resolution to their personal problem was the basic thrust of the story.

Our board of directors had a difficult time making a decision regarding the fundraising potential of this play. The cost for the play would be very high. For that reason, it required a great deal of thought before a decision could be made. A project of this scope had never been undertaken by the black community of Indianapolis. However, the decision to go ahead was finally made.

I was given the responsibility for recruiting board members and other volunteers who could help in producing this mammoth operation. My experience was limited, although I had been a member of the Little Theatre and had directed two plays at Tuskegee as well as directing three plays in Atlanta during the summers of 1941 and 1942. However, I did not have the experience of staging a production which required raising several thousand dollars in order to break even. It would require developing a public relations campaign, including ticket sales, handbills, ads in the daily newspaper, in the black press and in places patronized by blacks. We had already established contacts with the small community of liberal whites in Indianapolis. At least 1,500 to 2,000 tickets would have to be sold, in order for us to avoid a deficit.

We learned from our negotiations with the agent that the theatrical troupe would only be in the city for one day. We decided to go ahead with programs on Saturday afternoon and evening which helped to reduce expenses. The project was greatly aided by the services of four or five young volunteers who did much of the typing, telephoning, and other clerical and promotional work. Essis, a young white classmate of Phyllis at Antioch College was visiting the city and took charge of the office. Her work was invaluable. I worked day and night on that project. In fact, I had never worked so hard in my life!

The project was a tremendous artistic and theatrical success. The cast received standing ovations from an audience who had never before seen a romantic encounter between blacks and whites on the stage. It was good theatre and it was good race relations. In this sense we were quite pleased with what we had achieved. On the other hand, the financial picture was less encouraging. After all expenses were paid, we only earned a profit of three or four hundred dollars, far less than we had hoped, but I think all of us breathed a sigh of relief when the accounts were all added up and we found that we were not in the red! It had been a tremendous and exciting experience and one which I will never forget.

Two or three other smaller projects were attempted during my four month contract. We raised a small sum of money but not nearly enough to open an office or to hire permanent staff. We had agreed to use a room in the home of the president of the organization for office space, and to hire temporary staff as the need arose. In the midst of all this activity, I had made trips to Pittsburgh and to Chicago, seeking possibilities for employment. I had a good interview in Pittsburgh but did not think the opportunity would be satisfactory in view of my own personal expectation and requirements. The Chicago situation was different. The two agencies I talked to made it very clear that they would like to have me join their staff, but there were no immediate openings available. I was told that at the first opportunity I would be brought in again for a second interview. However, another offer came before either position opened up. I was invited to accept the position of Program Director at the Parkway Community House in Chicago three weeks prior to the termination of my contract with the Indianapolis NAACP.

One of the highlights of the experience with the Indianapolis chapter was the opportunity to attend and participate in the Annual General Meeting and Conference of the National Organization held in Kansas City in 1948. A group of four men and one woman drove the five hundred miles from Indianapolis for the event. Two aspects attracted my attention. First was the opportunity to meet many of the top officials of the organization, including Walter White, the long-time executive director, and Thurgood Marshall, the general counsel who is credited with winning many battles against racism in the Supreme Court of the United States and was later named as the first black justice of that court.

Second was the intense conflict within the organization regarding its fear of communism. As indicated earlier, it had been criticized by the National Negro Congress as overly moderate and not willing to engage in mass organizing and attacks on white supremacy. But the fear ran deeper. It was the fear of being "smeared by the rampant anti-communism" so widespread in the country at that time. Anyone exhibiting slightly "leftist" ideas was immediately branded as a communist. This struggle weakened the NAACP at a time when its role in the fight against racism was sorely needed. I observed this problem with apprehension because Mike Ransom and I were on the side of the more militant delegates. We left the conference with great concern regarding the future of the organization.

My mother and two brothers were living in Cincinnati during my stay in Indianapolis and since Cincinnati was only a hundred and twenty miles away, Phyllis and I drove down for visits fairly frequently. With the exception of Minnie, who lived in Berkeley, the family could get together fairly often for reunions. Phyllis enjoyed these activities as much as I did. I was pleased that she and my mother got along very well since I was aware that my mother had some doubts regarding my marriage to a white woman. When they met, however, they found that they liked each other. I think that within an hour my mother was satisfied that I had made a good choice.

Glenn never tired of talking about his attitudes and feelings regarding the treatment he had received in the U.S. Air Force. Frank, on the other hand was still reluctant to talk about his experiences. His positive experiences had little relationship to his actual participation in the Armed Forces. What he really enjoyed was that he had lived with a Dutch family during the period between the end of the war and his discharge in early 1946. That had been a good experience and was probably the first time he had been in a situation with whites in which he was treated without some degree of discrimination. The Dutch people had been liberated from the German occupation by the advancing American and Canadian armies. They were very pleased to have American soldiers visiting or boarding in their homes. Frank had an opportunity to develop a positive personal relationship with the Dutch family. The other factor which helped him to endure the war without undue damage was that he appeared to be less sensitive than Glenn to racism in the army.

Phyllis and I left Indianapolis at the end of August 1948. We had enjoyed the short time we spent there, even though we had mixed feelings about some aspects of it. Our feelings were mixed because I was disappointed, but not surprised, at the outcome of my work with Flanner House. However, we had great experiences working with our many friends and supporters.

We had become involved with the more liberal groups in the city including some churches, social service organizations, the YMCA and YWCA, the Quaker meetings, the Unitarian Church and some labour unions. Some groups were considered by many to be "left wing" and therefore not entirely respectable. However, it was these people who made life tolerable and happy for me. Their appreciation for my work was demonstrated by a large dinner for Phyllis and me shortly before we left for Chicago. It was nice to hear all of the accolades I received, although I was certain in my own mind that some were exaggerated and not fully deserved. My greatest disappointment was the necessity to leave my group of young students who were left to continue restaurant testing without my support. I hoped some other adult would come forward and pick up the challenge when I left the city. My experiences in Indianapolis were over and I was on my way to Chicago, another type of city, bigger, rougher, more violent and more exciting!

CHAPTER 10 *A Struggle Against Poverty, Alienation and Racism: Chicago*

Parkway Community House was a recreation and social centre that provided a strong community development program, including programs for adults, senior citizens, a little theatre and others. It was located in an all-black community and thus served an all-black clientele. I was informed by the director that my wife and I would live for the first few days in the community house itself. In the meantime we would be looking for accommodations elsewhere but not too far from the house so that in an emergency we could quickly return.

Driving down Lakeshore Blvd. one could view a very beautiful, attractive and dynamic city. Its skyline included panoramic views of Michigan Boulevard, water fountains in Grant Park and other attractive amenities. Massive skyscrapers provided the picture of a thriving, prosperous and dynamic metropolis. It was indeed a dynamic city which appeared to be a very pleasant and exciting place in which to live. On the other side of the boulevard was the vast expanse of Lake Michigan which provided a waterfront and a beach of fifteen to twenty miles. Thousands of people were sunning themselves on this warm August afternoon. That was, however, only one side of Chicago.

One had to go a few blocks west of Michigan Ave., the city's main north-south street, to find the teeming slums, tenements and other dilapidated houses in which many immigrants lived. The "boom town" had also attracted migrants from all over the United States and particularly from the southern states. This influx of migrants and immigrants had overwhelmed the housing market. The result was that people were forced to double up and even triple up in inadequate spaces. Shortly after arriving in Chicago, I learned that many families were living two or more in a room. In other situations, one family slept during the day and another family during the night so that they could use the same beds. Many former mansions had been subdivided into "kitchenettes", with a family living in one room which included a hotplate. Often four or five families lived on one floor with one bathroom to serve the entire group. This was the other side of Chicago, the one of which the city officials rarely, if ever, spoke.

There were major differences, however, in experiences and lives of European immigrants and black migrants from various parts of the South. European immigrants had some breathing space. They had a choice. Once they were able to get a decent job and some money, they could move out of the ghetto and find a home in a better part of the city. The situation was totally different for the black migrants. In some respects the level of segregation in Chicago was much greater than in some parts of the South, certainly than in the rural areas where blacks and whites often lived in the same general community. They may have been a quarter of a mile apart but they were not subjected to strict residential segregation. In Chicago the demarcation between whites and blacks was clear to all. Normally a street served as a dividing line between the black and white communities and with few exceptions this unofficial boundary was generally observed by inhabitants of both communities.

Parkway Community House was located squarely in the centre of the black community. In the late 1940s and early 1950s, the boundaries of the black community began at 21st or 22nd Street on the north, to about 67th Street on the south. My wife and I eventually found an apartment at 63rd and Woodlawn Ave, an area not far from the University of Chicago. Black people had only recently been permitted to move into that neighbourhood.

According to historians, a young black man was the founder and first permanent settler in what is now Chicago. Jean Pointe Baptiste DuSable was a black trader who built a cabin on the south side of the Chicago River around the year 1790. However, historical records do not inform us whether or not he was able to establish a community. According to available reports, the first black community in Chicago was established in the 1840s, mainly by ex-slaves fleeing from the South. The population of the community increased very slowly, and established a few of the usual social institutions, among which was the African Methodist Episcopal (AME) Church, the first black church in Chicago.

The Chicago black community in 1948 was composed of a predominantly southern-born population. Most people in the institutions and on the streets spoke with a "southern drawl" and a stranger walking in the streets of the south side of Chicago would almost certainly have felt that he or she was in a southern city. This phenomenon was expressed most strongly in the religious services of the churches. The gospel singing, vocal responses and general behaviour during services were identical with the pattern of religious services in the South. The urban black ghetto of Chicago was as strongly circumscribed, contained and controlled as one would find in Atlanta, Birmingham or New Orleans. The major difference was that segregation and discrimination were not enshrined in law in the northern city but were enforced by custom, violence and fear.

The restrictive covenant was one example of the non-legal restriction on blacks moving into "white neighbourhoods". This was an agreement drawn up between a buyer and a seller in which the white purchaser pledged that he or she would not, in the future, sell the house to a black. These contracts were informally enforced in spite of the fact that there were state laws forbidding discrimination based upon race, creed or colour. As long as both parties kept the terms of the contract, there was no way blacks could buy or rent a house in a "white" neighbourhood. Several years later, as a result of a court case, restrictive covenants were declared null and void and therefore ineffective, but unofficially the practice continued. When I lived in Chicago black people, with few exceptions, were limited to 67th Street on the south.

It was within this context that I began my work at Parkway Community House. A few days after my arrival, I was informed that the Welfare Council of Metropolitan Chicago had completed a study of the agency which had begun several months earlier. The agency had been under investigation as a result of concerns of the United Community Fund. A staff member of the Welfare Council came to the agency to present his findings and I called a meeting of the staff to hear and comment on the report. The staff seemed to be calm but still resistant to some findings of the study. Horace Cayton had taken no part in these discussions. This was surprising since, as the executive director, he was primarily responsible for the overall direction and fiscal management of the agency.

Three weeks after I arrived, the president of the board of directors called and said he would like to have a chat with me. I was advised also that the executive director would not be present. The president, a prominent Baptist minister, arrived at the appointed time. We met at the entrance and he said that he would like to have a talk with me alone in the office. I could not imagine what was going on until we sat down in the office of the executive director. The president immediately said, "I want you to take over the leadership of the agency on a temporary basis." The board of directors had authorized him to fire the executive director and to approach me regarding my willingness to act as executive director until a permanent person could be found. I remember feeling that, either they had a great deal of confidence in me or they were caught in a situation where they had no other alternative. After all, I had not even met the members of the board of directors and was caught in the challenge of having to operate the organization for an unforeseeable period of time, a test which I did not particularly relish. Dealing with the minute details of administrative work had never been one of my major strengths or interests. Fortunately the agency had a good business manager who could handle that aspect of the agency operation.

I did not find the job difficult and was well accepted by all members of the staff. Nevertheless, I was very pleased when two or three months later, I was told that the board had hired a new executive director, a native of Chicago and a woman who had been a dean of women at Hampton Institute, a black college in the state of Virginia. The staff and I were never told the reasons for the departure of Horace Cayton. I had enjoyed my limited contact with him and the possibility of learning from his knowledge and experience.

The new director, Mrs. Faith Jefferson Jones, was the daughter of a very old and influential family in the Chicago black community. She was held in very high esteem by the community and by members of the board of directors. I felt that they were fortunate to attract her to the position. Her appointment also reflected the fact that she had many influential friends in the city.

Parkway Community House changed considerably after her arrival. Streams of well-off people were constantly coming and going. Many of these visitors were black, but many were white. A part of this "coming and going" was because Faith Jones had friends in both communities. Many of the very wealthy white people could provide needed financial support to the institution. The two of us worked very well together with no conflicts in our relationship, even though our backgrounds were quite different.

One of the programs which Horace Cayton had successfully initiated was a monthly forum which focused on the many problems of the black community. It brought together many influential blacks from a wide variety of backgrounds. The general public was also invited to participate. Cayton, himself, was a very charismatic figure and his leadership of these forums gave them great prestige and status. The result was that the forums were far more significant in attracting public attention and awareness than were the regular community house programs.

Other programs included a black theatrical group which presented plays related to black interests and concerns. The name "SkyLoft Theatre" was chosen because the group met and held its rehearsals in the loft of the building. Cayton had also brought in other cultural activities, including art exhibits, dance groups and a class in creative writing which met weekly and attracted a wide variety of people interested in developing skills in drama, modern dance, short story writing, novels and poetry. Although I never learned why Cayton was fired, it is quite likely it was because of this heavy emphasis on "high culture", which appealed to the upper classes of black society, but achieved little impact on solving the massive problems of the black community.

The basic program of the organization, however, was more "down to earth" and was attempting to meet the basic needs of the people living in an overcrowded and poverty-stricken neighbourhood. Our programs for adolescents included Friday night dances held in a large "multi-purpose" room, also used for community meetings held by outside groups, and for programs sponsored by the community house. Teenage dances were the most popular event in the entire neighbourhood and the large room was always filled to capacity.

The young adult discussion groups were also very popular. Young men and women attended these forums which focused on their particular interests and needs. A committee of young adults was formed to plan and select resources. On one occasion, the planning group decided they would like to sponsor a discussion regarding crime in the local community and invited an assistant district attorney as their speaker. During the course of his address, he mentioned that he could go out of the building and return within twenty minutes with any drug that anybody wanted. The group was horrified. They could not understand why a law enforcement officer could not arrest a person who was selling drugs on the street. He told the group that it was not his job to conduct arrests. The police had to arrest and to charge individuals committing crimes which he could then prosecute. This discussion was very useful in providing information and insight which young people needed as they tried to become informed on some very important problems in the local community. It was on that occasion that young adults and I learned that organized crime exists only where there is tacit collusion between criminals and law enforcement officers. The collaboration and collusion usually includes police, court employees and prosecuting officers.

Our staff came from varied backgrounds and many members, both black and white, had acquired degrees or diplomas in nursery school education, social work, group work, recreational leadership and in adult education. In addition to me, three other social workers were heavily involved in dealing with many of the serious social problems brought to the agency by community members. These included wife battering, child abuse, alcoholism, drug problems and poverty. Many individuals were unable to make ends meet on what they earned or what they were given through welfare payments. As a result the staff found it necessary to develop a wide variety of supportive contacts in the general community which included individuals and organizations which provided services, such as helping people to find affordable homes, homes for senior citizens, nursing homes and information regarding social services. Health needs were referred to other public and private agencies.

Crime was rampant in the neighbourhood. It was fairly common to indicate jokingly that anybody who lived in that community was a criminal who simply had not been caught! In fact some of the children related that their parents had told them to go out and steal whatever they could: hubcaps, apples, oranges, or other small grocery items. The only warning was that the kids should make sure that they did not get caught!

There was one occasion when some teenagers stole a valuable item from the community house itself. We had held a dance that evening, and had gone home at approximately 11:30 p.m. When we returned on Monday morning, we found that a very expensive record player which had been given to us had disappeared. That Monday evening when the teenagers arrived, I told them that there would be no more dances because someone had stolen our record player and we could not afford to buy another one. Three of the boys left the building, telling me they would be back shortly. They returned within half an hour with the suggestion that if no questions were asked and nobody made an attempt to discover who had stolen the record player, they would make certain that it would be returned.

The teenagers were true to their word. The next morning we found the record player outside the back door of the community house. We were learning that many children and adolescents could police themselves when they could clearly see the connection between their behaviour and a positive and constructive result.

The Children's Camp

The Community House had never had a children's camp of its own. Although some settlement houses located in white communities operated their own camps, they accepted only white children. Parkway operated a day camp program which included only black children. On one occasion Emerson House, one of the white centres, invited our staff to join in a discussion of the possibility of a joint camp experience. The director of Emerson House, Bill Buchner, was well known in the settlement movement as a creative and innovative thinker who had made an outstanding reputation for fairness, honesty and non-discriminatory attitudes. He gave the project his full support. We readily joined in the planning of the project. To our knowledge this would be the first time that a joint interracial camping program was organized in Chicago or, as far as we knew, anywhere else in the United States! The program was launched in the summer of 1950 and continued through the summer of 1952. Jenny, the program director of Emerson House and I, as program director of Parkway, were assigned to serve as co-directors of the proposed interracial children's camp.

Both Emerson House and Parkway, as most similar agencies, were located in low-income and deprived neighbourhoods. The children from both agencies were very poor, and many of them had little clothing, inadequate meals and generally little family support. Going to camp would be advantageous as many, perhaps for the first time, would get decent food, live in the country and be supervised by trained staff who were not involved in various aspects of criminal behaviour. Our program was designed to achieve these goals as well as interracial awareness, cooperation and positive relationships. With all of the discussion and goodwill among liberal-minded people, very few adults, black or white, had ever experienced that kind of positive contact on a day-to-day basis. Jenny and I felt it was necessary to run an orientation program to acquaint the two staffs with situations they might face in their contacts with the children, and focus on staff relationships with each other. Both staffs felt that this experience was of key importance. If the staff could work closely together without tension, then it would be easier for the children to relate to each other in a positive way. The children would be assigned to cabins of eight, with four black and four white campers and a counsellor in each cabin.

Our first orientation program was held at Parkway Community House with members of the two staffs who would serve as counsellors at the camp. Discussions and role playing were utilized as a part of the orientation. It was interesting to observe how easily the two staffs related to each other, particularly during the square dance party. This was the first time that most had ever had close physical contact with people from another racial group. The two groups enjoyed themselves and began to look forward to the summer camp.

The second orientation program was held at Emerson House where their staff were the hosts and we were the guests. Again the orientation program went off very well and I began to feel that perhaps we had been overly cautious regarding the possibility of racial tensions among staff members. From my observations during the two orientation sessions, there would be no difficulty in the working relationship of the two staffs.

A significant aspect of taking children to camp, particularly underprivileged and deprived children, was to observe how they behave in the presence of adequate food, clothing, shelter and caring adults. Unless a staff person wanted to take money, watches and other personal belongings to the administrative building every morning before leaving, they would have no alternative but to leave personal belongings in the cottage. Some of us had concerns about that because we knew a few of the children had records of stealing, even from their own parents. However, during the three years in which programs were in operation and in which there were approximately eighty children each session, we had only one incident of theft.

The theft was brought up before the group to inform the children of what had occurred. The eight members of the cottage group got together and decided that they would find out who had stolen the money and return it to the owner. Within less than two days the money was found and returned. The amazing part of this story is that none of us expected this to happen. Knowing the backgrounds of these children and their desperate need, we felt that the money was totally lost and had reached the point where the staff was discussing how to repay the counsellor. The return of the small amount of money obviated that plan and we were very pleased with the outcome.

Following each of the four camping periods the program director of Emerson House and I met to discuss what had actually happened in terms of relationships, behaviour and possible changes in attitude. We came to the conclusion that the experience had been positive for everyone involved. We also surveyed the attitudes of parents and of the children. Parents of both groups gave a very positive reaction to the experiences of their children. The only problem was that parents felt the camping period was too short. Two weeks, in their view, was not enough. They would like to have had their children spend the entire summer at the camps.

Another interesting aspect of camp life with children was the informality. Jenny and I, as co-directors, instructed the children and staff to call us by our first names. Some children found it a bit difficult as they had been conditioned to call adults by their last names prefaced by either Miss, Mrs., or Mr. It required a few days before most children were able to change old behaviour patterns comfortably. However, the change did occur and by the second week each child was calling adults by their first names. The interesting aspect of this experience was that when they returned home and resumed participation in the regular program of the Community House, they again resorted to calling us by our last names. In the old setting we were again Mr., Miss or Mrs. This told us something about the influence and impact of the environment on behaviour. In the more formalized structure of the Community House Program, children responded to the familiar setting by returning to familiar patterns of behaviour. It is apparent, then, that one of the most important things we could do in rearing children was to provide them with a positive, constructive and caring environment, one which avoided formal and rigid structure but rather was concerned to meet their basic human needs.

When I look back on my five years as program director at Parkway, it was my relationship with children that struck me as most important and which gave me the greatest satisfaction. That is not to say that I did not enjoy my work in other areas including supervision of the staff, even though I always remembered the caution of Frankie V. Adams about "snooper-vision". I also enjoyed my contacts with the senior citizens, the nursery school teachers, the recreational workers and the social workers. However, I do not remember the adults as well as I do the children, both in the settlement house itself and at the camp.

Relationships

Phyllis and I had been married since September 1947. It was now eleven months later and we were expecting our first child. Norman was born in October, 1948 at the University of Chicago Children's Hospital. He was named after Norman Thomas, one of my most admired men and a long time leader of the Socialist party of the United States. It was impossible for any socialist to be elected president in the States, but he was an outstanding man and the first politician I would ever have voted for.

We were probably the most finicky parents in the world. We were so careful that we would not even let him play in his playpen without making certain that everything was sterilized, aside from the playpen itself! He was a very active, healthy boy and only on one occasion did we become upset with what appeared to be a serious illness. He contacted a fever of about a hundred and three degrees Fahrenheit when he was about six months old. We rushed him to a doctor as quickly as possible but when we arrived at the office, the doctor found nothing wrong. The fever had gone completely. After that experience we were a little more relaxed. We were of course, very proud and very happy to have him as part of our family. I think we probably spoiled him, at least to some degree. In other respects we were probably only a pair of typical parents relating to their firstborn in a very normal manner.

Strangely, we were not so concerned with Gregory Darnell, our second child who was born a few years later in February, 1953. We treated him quite differently: his bottles and toys could be washed in ordinary tap water. Gregory grew up to be as healthy and happy a boy as Norman had been. By that time, we had learned that young babies need care but are much tougher than we had originally thought.

By the time our two boys were born, we had joined the Hyde Park Cooperative grocery and department store located on the south side of Chicago. The Co-op, as it was called, was making an attempt to encourage a spirit of cooperation among its members instead of the ruthless competition so characteristic of the market place. This concept strongly appealed to Phyllis and me. Unlike a capitalist organization, in which the number of shares an individual owns determines the number of votes allocated to that individual at annual business meetings, each member of the co-op had one vote regardless of the number of shares owned. The idea of placing value on an individual, instead of on their financial status, seemed to be a much more democratic process of participation and decision-making than the usual capitalist enterprise.

A year later we moved from our first apartment to a more spacious apartment on Drexel Ave. near the campus of the University of Chicago. Two or three black families lived on our block. St. Clair Drake, a black professor of sociology at Roosevelt College, was one of this group. Drake co-authored *Black Metropolis*, a very important book describing the history and development of the black community in Chicago yet a publication which aroused considerable controversy and confusion. Many blacks were not very pleased with the picture painted by Drake and Cayton of the early days of blacks in the city. Many were angry and upset at their analysis of the current condition of blacks in the city. People could not dismiss the contents of the book, but many argued that these facts should not have been published! The two men vigorously defended the results of their research and won great respect among those who admired honesty and candour. We were pleased to have Drake and his wife as two of our best friends during our stay in Chicago.

The Drakes and our family joined the Hyde Park Co-op cooperative child care project based on some of the basic concepts underlying the philosophy and principles of the cooperative movement. These principles suggest that people should not only work cooperatively for their own benefit, but also to develop other cooperative structures for the benefit of members and of society as a whole. The child care project was one of those structures and involved setting up a "labour bank" in which people did not deposit money but deposited time which was recorded when an individual or family babysat for other members who were also members of the "bank". Over time a family might babysit for four or five other families, thus depositing perhaps twelve or fifteen hours in the "bank". This family, if in need of a babysitter, could then draw upon the hours deposited in the bank. It was a transaction similar to depositing and withdrawing money from a regular bank, but was owned and controlled by its members.

In addition to its economic feature the Hyde Park Co-op was also an educational, social and cultural arrangement. Among its several educational and social committees were those concerned with child care, employment, political issues, community development, education and recreational programs for its members. Phyllis and I became deeply involved in activities of the cooperative and its many subcommittees. My special interest focused on the co-op educational program based on the concept of cooperative education and living. Their major thrusts were twofold: an understanding of the various aspects of the community in which one lived and the special role of the economic system in that community; and second helping members understand and appreciate the social and cultural values of cooperation as opposed to the usual struggle for economic and social power and status.

Many of our unique and valuable experiences while living in Chicago were results of participation in subcommittees of the Co-op, which owned and operated the Circle Pines Camp, a family camp located in Michigan and less than a hundred miles from the city. The camp included a number of permanent buildings, plus space for tents and for trailers. Except for the high-level educational activities, as much as possible all activities included both parents and children. Circle Pines also included the usual camp activities as well as gardening. Its chief recreational activity, however, was the evening folk dance program.

My most important function with the Hyde Park Co-op came when I was elected to the Board of Directors shortly after arriving in Chicago. It is doubtful that I could have learned half as much from attending college or university courses in management studies. This learning was done through a combination of practical experience as a member of a board of directors and through the special educational programs conducted for members of the board. For me this was a very informative and valuable experience as I had no previous knowledge of the "inner workings" of business establishments.

Walker Sandback, the manager of the Co-op, and his wife Mary became, with the Drakes and the Selmanoffs, our highly valued friends during our stay in Chicago. I had known Walker at Big Flats, the Civilian Public Service camp in which we were participants. Following the war Walker was employed by the Hyde Park Co-op as general manager. Walker and Mary were outstanding people, full of energy, enthusiasm and initiative. Weekends at their summer cottage on Lake Michigan were among our most enjoyable experiences. We continued this friendship long after we left Chicago and were living in Columbus, Ohio and later in Windsor, Ontario.

Another involvement was with the Hyde Park/Kenwood Community Council, which served the needs of another community in transition located immediately to the north of Hyde Park. Members of the cooperative and other progressive community groups, including the Friends Meeting, had come together to form the community council devoted to community development and improving the lives of people living in those two geographical areas. Among the most important concerns of the council was the inadequate housing for families. Historically, Hyde Park and Kenwood had been areas of considerable affluence but as time passed the more affluent people moved further into suburbia. Poor people were able to move into these neighbourhoods as the houses became older, less desirable and cheaper. Kenwood was the first to receive new residents that included a wide variety of immigrants from European countries and a small but increasing influx of blacks from the southern states.

The process had only made a small beginning when we moved to Chicago. At that time Hyde Park was almost entirely white with the exception of a few black or racially mixed families. Many of the old mansions had been subdivided into small apartments. Phyllis, the two children and I, lived in one of these apartments. The division of large single-family homes into apartment buildings resulted in a rapid increase in the population of the two communities, and more particularly in the Kenwood community. This problem was the focus of the activities of the Hyde Park/Kenwood Community Council. Our friend, St. Clair Drake, was one of the founders of the Council.

Bitter struggles and increasing hostility had characterized the early days of black movement into both areas. The white population of the twenties and thirties had stubbornly fought to keep blacks out of what were considered "white" areas. When we arrived in Chicago, the struggle to keep blacks out had weakened, largely because the whites were moving out, and a few blacks could afford to buy or rent the small apartments. In addition, an increasing number of liberal-minded whites had joined the struggle for "open housing", that is housing without racial restrictions. Although the movement of blacks into the two areas was slow and halting, we had no difficulty in finding and renting the apartment in Hyde Park. With the exception of St. Clair Drake, the leadership of the Hyde Park/Kenwood community council was all white. Many of these people were also involved in the Co-op, the Friends Meeting, the University of Chicago, and other progressive groups.

The Hyde Park community included a wide variety of educational, social, cultural, civic, business, and other institutions. The University of Chicago was located near the southern boundary of Hyde Park. The complexity and scope of problems in Chicago, and particularly in the black area on the south side, made it urgent that workers in that community should be as well informed as possible about the structure and practice of community development and political organization. The Council was organized to meet that need.

In addition to the Council and the Co-op, a number of other organizations existed in the neighbourhood and were concerned with similar problems. Phyllis and I became active participants in the social justice concerns of the Friends Meeting which from its beginning had been concerned with the need for adequate housing, educational opportunities, positive social relationships, the conditions of the poor and cooperative living arrangements. The 57th Street Friends Meeting became an active member of the Council and played a prominent role. Julie Abrahamson, a member of the society, became the executive director of the Council and many social justice activities of the society were conducted in cooperation with the Council. It was through membership in the Friends Meeting that we became members of the Hyde Park/Kenwood Community Council.

As in Indianapolis, I had also become heavily involved in weekend work camps sponsored by the Chicago branch offices of the local American Friends Service Community (AFSC). Since I had experience in this area, the Service Committee was pleased to have me take over the leadership of several of its weekend work camp programs.

These camps followed a similar model to those in Philadelphia and in Indianapolis. My evaluation of the experience and result of the camps was three-fold. First I had a great sense of satisfaction that students were actually becoming acquainted with the city and its many problems. Second, they were learning about themselves and their own values and goals, and third they were learning about the complexities of the vast economic, social and political system under which they lived. This was a frustrating task in many respects but also a valuable experience.

I was obtaining first hand experiences of these problems in my various associations, the Friends Meeting, the Hyde Park/Kenwood Community Council, the Co-op, and Parkway Community House but I needed more knowledge and understanding. I had read a very stimulating book, *Reveille for Radicals* by Saul Alinsky, a pioneer in community development. It was written as a description and analysis of his work on a south-west area of the city. He had helped to organize a Polish neighbourhood to fight against the lack of ordinary civic services in the community. Alinsky succeeded in creating a very strong community organization, which had developed considerable political and even some economic power. His achievements in Chicago had brought Alinsky to the attention of many other deprived communities across the United States. One of his most widely known projects was a successful community organizational project in the city of Rochester, New York. He had also helped the residents of Woodlawn, an area south of Hyde Park, develop a moderately strong organization which fought a long struggle against slum landlords. Its attack on a powerful political and economic lobby was only moderately successful.

Alinsky's theories of citizen participation, community organization and development were very appealing to me. He was a militant who thrived on doing battle with the so-called "establishment", a term referring to a power structure which exists in any local community or at any level of government. Alinsky, however, was no great friend of social workers and felt that they were too concerned with professionalism, accommodating their employers and oppressors and therefore unwilling or unable to tackle the sources of the problems they were attempting to resolve. Social workers, in his view, were vulnerable to the varied powers in the community which created the social problems in the first place.

Earlier I had studied the work of social settlements such as Toynbee Hall in London, the Henry Street Settlement in New York City, and Chicago Commons and Hull House in Chicago. Their work, among the poor and deprived, had been of very great value during early waves of immigration and migration. Two outstanding leaders had been largely responsible for this development in Chicago. Graham Taylor, a community activist, founded Chicago Commons, a settlement house located near the downtown area of the city. The second person, Jane Addams, a pioneer in social reform, founded and was still active at Hull House, located in the south central area of the city. These two reformers had fought for the rights of immigrants and other poor people for decent housing, employment, health care, English language training, city services, garbage collection and other needs of people living in deprived neighbourhoods. They lobbied, pressured, threatened and persuaded politicians until some needs were met. They recognized, however, that even if these needs were met, they could not change the basic nature of a society which created and maintained these conditions.

European immigrants and black migrants from the South were brought to Chicago by employers in a successful effort to create a cheap labour pool paying workers minimum wages to work in often difficult and unsafe conditions. A cheap and compliant labour force was deemed necessary for meeting the needs of an expanding industrial society. A major purpose of settlement houses (community centres) was to support and provide leadership in the struggle against exploitation of powerless newcomers by unscrupulous employers in an oppressive environment.

In 1948 a total of thirty-five settlements and neighbourhood houses had been established in Chicago of which Parkway Community House was one. This large number, possibly the largest in the country, reflected the widespread poverty and deprivation still existing in many powerless neighbourhoods. The need for closer cooperation and ability to work together among the settlements and neighbourhood centres led to the formation of an umbrella organization, the Chicago Federation of Settlements and Neighbourhood Centres which was the local branch of the larger National Federation of Settlements and Neighbourhood Centres with headquarters in New York City.

I became deeply involved in the activities of the Federation and sat on the board of directors of the Chicago Federation. I was involved in a number of attempts to bring pressure on local governments to improve the quality of housing in poor neighbourhoods. Since all settlements were located in poor and largely immigrant neighbourhoods, we faced many similar problems. Thus a federation was an ideal mechanism for sharing experiences and learning new skills for meeting similar problems. It was in the midst of this complexity that I felt my previous studies and experiences had not adequately prepared me.

Two years after arriving in Chicago and beginning my employment at Parkway, I decided to investigate the possibility of taking appropriate courses at the University of Chicago. I was keenly aware of the reputation of the University of Chicago School of Social Welfare Administration but was quite surprised when I encountered difficulty in attempts to register for a course in community organization. I told the registrar that I was not exactly a newcomer, having already completed a master of social work degree program. I simply wanted to get the course in order to increase my understanding of the field of community organization and development in a large and complex urban area.

Following a fairly lengthy discussion, the registrar finally agreed to permit me to register in the one course in community organization offered by the school. Part of my difficulty may have related to the fact that the university felt itself among the few elitist organizations in the general field of social work administration and practice. It is possible that the registrar and others at the school felt that the Atlanta University School, being an all-black, Southern institution was, in some respects, inferior. Of course, nothing of that nature was said during my interview with the registrar but once I was enroled and began to meet students, I quickly picked up this sense of elitism. More important was the feeling that community organization and group work were not genuine social work. One could not escape the conclusion that the social worker trained at the Chicago School was strongly oriented toward the practise of Freudian psychoanalysis. The founders of the school had been strongly influenced by this approach to psychology and psychotherapy. This heavy emphasis did not include concerns with poverty, deprivation, inequality and the need for basic social change. In short the Chicago School was concerned with the neurotic problems of educated middle-class Americans.

I enroled in the community organization courses which was taught by one of the pioneers in the field of social welfare organization. The ironic aspect of this was that the course itself was neither good, stimulating nor exciting. Several students began to lose interest and dropped out shortly after its initiation.

Having already studied community development, I found very little new that I could learn from this course. Even more depressing was the fact that I could find nothing else in the university catalogue which would be useful. Following completion of the course I decided to make no further attempt to register for courses offered by the Chicago School.

Many of the reform activities of settlement houses and neighbourhood centres were severely limited since their early days and many had become little more than adult education and recreational centres. Before my arrival, the Community House had made some limited progress in this direction. A valiant attempt was made at Parkway to carry on the old tradition. Social work, perhaps even more than medicine or law, attracted a considerable number of bright young people with a high degree of social consciousness and a strong determination to become effective in advocating social change. Most came from varying levels of the middle class. While few could be labelled as radicals, the fact is that most did not like the society in which we lived and wanted to be effective change agents. These ideals were in conformity with those of the early founders of social work practice in both England and in the United States.

An examination of the board of directors, however, clearly revealed the limitations of Parkway as a leader in the social reform movement. The membership was almost identical with that of Flanner House in Indianapolis. Most were wealthy white business men, or the wives of wealthy white men. It did not take very long to discover who controlled the major direction and policies of Parkway. However, we were fortunate to find three wealthy white women who sympathized with the objectives of staff and made every effort to help us carry out a reform movement in the local community. In many respects they protected us from intervention by other members of the board by their close relationship and by not revealing their personal friendships with some members of staff. Many of our efforts would have been quickly terminated in the absence of these supporters.

I was not ready to abandon my attempts to gain additional post master's education at the university and began to examine the possibilities in other departments. I came to the conclusion that adult education gave the widest scope for further knowledge and insights. I decided to enrol on a part-time basis in that university program since I could not afford to quit my job and enrol in a full-time program. Although I had occasional morning meetings, most were relatively free and I arranged for morning classes, which included counselling, group psychotherapy and group dynamics. I felt that these courses might have some applicability in my work. At least I would increase my knowledge of education of adults and the problems of motivating others to explore and hopefully to improve their individual and collective lives.

I studied under three very eminent men who were quite different in orientation and in approach to life and education. Bruno Bettelheim, a neo-Freudian psychoanalyst born in Germany, had spent some time in a concentration camp but had eventually escaped to North America and become very well known through the publication of his first English language book, *Love is Not Enough*. I learned to appreciate much of the theory and practice of psychoanalysis under Bettelheim and I found much of this material extremely fascinating, but also much which I could not accept. For example, his concept of childhood as a period of omnipotence or all-powerfulness was an idea that grew out of the psychoanalytic theory that children consciously control parents by crying. When the child cries, parents rush to him or her and attempt to respond to demands for food or comfort and generally to meet the child's needs. My interpretation of the same act was that it was equally reasonable to theorize that the child cried out of a sense of helplessness and frustration. I also had some difficulty with his attitude toward women. Nevertheless, Bettelheim was an extremely interesting man, with great insight and knowledge regarding our common human condition. However, he had his faults. First, he was not a warm and friendly man. He appeared to obtain great joy in poking fun at psychology students and at the women in his classes. Even with his great insights, he appeared oblivious to the needs and aspirations of his students and his classes always reflected a degree of tension. In short, Bettelheim was one tough man! He died at the age of eighty-six, during the course of this writing.

No two men could have been more dissimilar than Bruno Bettelheim and Carl Rogers, the founder and developer of "client-centred counselling". This method, developed under his leadership at Ohio State and the University of Chicago, became a central focus of the counselling and psychology program of the latter institution. The term "non-directive" counselling was often used to describe this philosophy and approach. I found the readings and lectures of Carl Rogers and his disciples extremely intriguing and often challenging. However, I recognized that this method and philosophy of counselling was much more appropriate to highly verbal middle class intellectuals than to ordinary non-college-educated people.

One of the most fascinating teachers with whom I've worked was Professor Herbert Thelan. He was a founder of the institution for the study of group behaviour at Bethel, Maine. The Institute, under the guidance of Kurt Lewin, a

German trained social psychologist, was also interested in training students in understanding group process, leadership, structures and group functions. The class of about twenty students was organized on two levels. First, a small group of three or four students engaged in intense interaction, and second, the entire class studied its own pattern of interaction and leadership on a larger group level.

More specifically, our purpose was to study how we actually functioned as members of a group. This focus was to provide insight into the dynamics of group organization, climate, morale and ability to function in an effective manner. These attributes of group behaviour were observed and evaluated by the class. This experience, I thought, was useful in the work in which I was engaged because it was very important to understand as much as possible of the interaction of groups at the family, small group and the larger community level.

One of my young classmates became interested in utilizing my knowledge to help her understand the "dynamics" of the Chicago black community. Louise asked if I would take her to black nightclubs and other social events. I told her that I would have to think the matter over before deciding on the appropriate club or other social organization to which I felt comfortable in taking her. I had little knowledge of local nightclubs, although there were several in the city. I selected a club near where I worked on South Parkway and one which I thought would be suitable for a young, middle class white woman. At the same time I wondered if what she wanted was to "go slumming" and to experience "forbidden fruit". I selected a club frequented largely by middle class young black people but when we arrived, she immediately expressed her disappointment. What she had wanted to see was "black culture". She had read and heard a number of myths about the hypothetical energy, drive, lust, sexuality and charm of black men. She was looking for a very exciting evening in which she could be pursued by men who would be interested in her, primarily because of her colour.

Even though I had some premonition of her goal, I decided to accompany her. Her disappointment was fairly obvious so at my suggestion we left the club fairly early and decided to take a stroll down South Parkway, the street on which the community centre was located. She wanted to "get a feel" of the city and the black community. To her this meant the poor, uneducated, lower class blacks whom she had not met at the university. Thus she wanted to stop at every group of people we walked past or enter every social club or activity along the busy street. I decided to remain with her for an hour or so. By then, I felt it was time to bring this incident to a close. Her disappointment was at the lack of "genuine" black culture but I decided that the experience was a failure and we should bring it to a halt and go home. However, I had to await her decision since I could not leave her alone in a slum area of the city. Her decision to leave the area and return home was a welcomed one. I had already made that decision for myself. That was the end of my budding friendship with this young woman and we rarely spoke to each other again, even in class, after that episode.

Chicago 1940–1948

The world had changed dramatically since I was at the AFSC Chicago work camp in 1940. A devastating world war had been fought in which forty to fifty million people are estimated to have died. The American armed forces were totally segregated and few blacks were permitted to engage in combat. Many of those who returned expected to find a changed racial situation. After all, they were told that they were fighting to defend democracy and freedom. They returned only to find that what they had been told was a lie and not to be realized. They did not find democracy and freedom in the United States and certainly not in Chicago. One could hope that the returned soldiers would have instituted an increasing militancy in the black community, and especially among the young blacks, but this phenomenon did not materialize for several years.

It is important to remember, however, that serving in the armed forces does not necessarily instil militancy. Rather its major focus is on obedience without question. The armed forces is not the place to seek progressive and militant social attitudes and behaviour. The well delineated black ghetto of Chicago still existed, although its boundaries may have expanded slightly. Some expansion of the black social, economic and political structures had occurred, but with little practical result.

The black middle class had increased slightly but the vast majority of blacks still lived in poverty-stricken, depressed, and crime-ridden ghettos. The casual observer walking down the streets of any black community in Chicago could be excused for believing that nothing had changed. This observer would in some respects have been correct, in other respects, mistaken. Segregation, discrimination, powerlessness and hopelessness were as deep-seated as in 1940. While the older European immigrant population had made significant strides in economic and political terms, black migrants from the Deep South had not.

However, there had been some changes in the political structure of the black community and its relationship to the increasing numbers of Filipinos, Mexicans, and Puerto Ricans who quickly joined the competition for jobs and housing. Germans, Polish, Finnish, Russians, Ukrainians and Italians had moved to suburbia and other surrounding communities as a result of improved social, economic and political conditions. The old pattern of immigration was repeating itself.

One of the most significant changes between 1940 and 1948 was the expansion of black participation in the political process. There were more black city councillors and bureaucrats with relatively high positions in the public service. Increasing numbers were involved in the electoral process but this participation did not make much difference in their level of influence in the city. The black politicians simply joined the old Democratic party machine which had dominated the city of Chicago over more than three generations. Many blacks found it more profitable to join and participate in the activities of the machine than to fight it. From my perspective, the level of crime and corruption had not decreased to any measurable degree as a result of the participation of black politicians.

I became quite conversant with the activities of the police department, the city council and other civic agencies when I sat as a member of the board of directors of the Chicago chapter of the American Civil Liberties Union (ACLU) having been elected a member of that board because of my work with the AFSC and the ACLU in Philadelphia and in Indianapolis. The executive director of the Chicago Civil Liberties Union was a man whom I had known during my CPS experience. He suggested that the president approach me with an invitation to join the board of the Chicago chapter. I agreed to accept the appointment. Case after case of police brutality was brought to our attention but aside from filing complaints, there was nothing we could do. It was simply the word of the police against that of the complainant. The prosecutors and judges always accepted the word of the police officer, even when many witnesses testified against him.

On one occasion, a member of our board of directors, a lawyer, witnessed the police beating a man on the street. Our board member remonstrated with the officer, asking him to cease beating this unfortunate individual. The officer then turned and arrested him, charging him with interfering with a police officer in the performance of his duties! On another occasion, a member of our board who was a lawyer told the group that he had been involved in a situation in which he was forced to act illegally. The lawyer, a wealthy man, had bought a large warehouse building located on a very busy street, with an alley at the rear of the building. He was finally able to rent the building to a tenant who wanted to use the back alley for loading and unloading trucks. The new owner needed to build a platform which would require a permit from the city. He applied to City Hall for a permit but received no response. After a few weeks he applied a second time, and still did not receive a response. He was asked by another board member whether or not he had made an "under-the-table" payment to the city council member of that ward. Our board member said he had not, he was an honest man and did not believe in paying bribes or any other underhanded activity. The second lawyer informed him that he would probably never receive a permit unless he actually did the "usual thing".

At a subsequent board meeting, the lawyer/owner of the building informed us that he had capitulated and had sent several hundred dollars in a plain unmarked envelope to the appropriate city official. Within a week he had received his permit. The honest lawyer learned that he had to "play the game" if he wished to succeed in the business/political world of Chicago!

Reference was made earlier to the ideological battle that occurred in Chicago during the latter part of the 19th and the early 20th century. These struggles involved whether blacks should take a militant approach demanding civil rights and other measures to improve their status in the community or whether they should focus on establishing their own community institutions and structures necessary for the operation of a ghettoized community. It appeared in 1948 that this ideological struggle was over since the black community had settled for the latter approach. However, an isolated all-black community could not possibly provide enough jobs for even a small fraction of its members with the result that most members of the black community still found it necessary to leave their community and to travel downtown for employment. The "Don't trade where you can't work" campaigns were important but of minimal significance as employment strategies. The booming economy during the war years, based on the manufacture of war materials was now over. Blacks were, again, facing difficult economic times. This was the situation black soldiers found when they returned from the Second World War.

The Early 1950s

A growing fear of the Soviet Union was beginning to take hold of the American mind. This paranoia was stimulated by the activities of Senator Joe McCarthy of Wisconsin. By 1950, the fear of the Soviet Union had led to the establishment of a "House UnAmerican Activities Committee" by the U.S. Congress. The assumed function of this, and of a similar committee sponsored by the United States Senate, was to root out communism in the country and in the government of the Unites States itself. Senator McCarthy stood on the floor of the U.S. Senate, on several occasions, and announced that he had a list of between fifty and a hundred and fifty names of employees of the State Department and other government agencies who were members of the Communist Party. Although his "list of names" was never proved, the fact that he had made such incredible charges created havoc and ruined the reputations of many innocent people at various levels of American society. Hundreds of writers, artists, university professors, entertainers, politicians and even Hollywood movie stars, screen writers and directors lost their jobs as a result of the increasing paranoia. The great black baritone, Paul Robeson, was unable to hire halls in which to hold concerts. The last time I heard Robeson sing was in Chicago, where his concert was held in an outdoor public park. His left wing and progressive views had aroused the ire of the Senator who through his sensational charges, had made it impossible for any owner of a hall to rent to him or to Pete Seeger and many others for concerts.

At least a half dozen of my friends and acquaintances found themselves out of jobs, not because they were communists but simply because they refused to answer questions inspired by Joe McCarthy and his cohorts. The usual question was: "Have you ever been, are you now, or will you ever become a communist?" Men and women of principle, who believed in freedom of speech as guaranteed in the Constitution, refused to answer the question or to cooperate in any other way with McCarthy or the House UnAmerican Activities Committee: this refusal often led to their dismissal from their jobs or to other forms of harassment.

The strange and destructive career of Senator Joe McCarthy was terminated in 1953 when he was exposed as a charlatan and a crook, and finally he left the Senate in disgrace. The senator was not alone. There were others, among whom was president-to-be Richard Nixon who at that time was a congressman from California.

The campaigns of the House and Senate UnAmerican Activities Committees created a depressing effect upon American political and social life. Many victims of McCarthyism were never able to return to their former professions, businesses and other careers. They were branded for life even though they were innocent. I was fortunate in not being on the senator's phoney list but I was determined that had I been called to testify, I would have refused to cooperate in what I considered a disgusting betrayal of human rights and freedoms.

Although strongly concerned about what was happening during the McCarthy era, I had no direct contact with the senator. It was not necessary to experience direct contact: it was only necessary to live in the United States to feel the pressure of his cynical campaign against anyone who was slightly progressive or "left". However, I, like millions of others, found myself indirectly affected by his chilling methods. On one occasion at a meeting of the National Federation of Settlements and Neighbourhood Centres, I raised the question of our concern regarding the poor housing of people living in the slums of our major cities. I suggested a resolution calling for the construction of 100,000 new public houses to be built annually for the next five years. The matter was referred to the resolution committee, which agreed with me and recommended that the resolution be passed.

To my surprise, one of the leading figures in the organization jumped to his feet and argued that the resolution was out of order and could not be approved until the next annual general meeting. The debate on that issue clearly brought out the fact that, since the cold war had started, and McCarthyism was in its ascendancy, we should do nothing that gave the impression that we were criticizing the housing policies of the government. In spite of my arguments and those of others, my resolution was delayed for another year, when the entire matter was dropped.

The real issue was that even liberal or reform minded members of the Federation were afraid that my mild resolution would get them into difficulties with the senator and that they would be suspected of "left wing" ideas by the government. The federal government would be only too pleased at the opportunity to silence our criticisms of its housing policies. The senator won that round. Several of my friends came to console me regarding the defeat of my resolution and to express their admiration for my courage. I did not feel that my act was a courageous one, it was simply in line with what the organization was supposedly about, that is, the support of the interests of underprivileged individuals and families left out of the benefits of the "American Dream". I was determined that this climate not prevent me from continuing my work in poverty, race relations and community development.

I had earlier joined and worked with the Fellowship of Reconciliation (FOR) while still involved in the Civilian Public Service program. Among its offshoots was a new organization, the Congress On Racial Equality (CORE).

A local chapter of CORE had been established shortly after my arrival in Chicago. It was as a member of CORE that I became involved in restaurant "sit-ins" in Chicago, a program somewhat similar to those in Indianapolis but also quite different. First, the Chicago situation was much tougher than that in Indianapolis. Many participants in Chicago sit-ins were physically assaulted. Many were burned, kicked, struck and otherwise harassed. CORE, as a non-violent organization, had trained its participants to not respond to physical attacks by violent counter attacks. Participants were required to respond in a way which emphasized an attempt to understand and restrain the attacker from further violence.

The eight or ten sit-ins in which I was involved always ended peacefully, although negative and hostile attitudes were often expressed. The reason for this generally peaceful atmosphere may be related to what we had learned in Indianapolis: the best downtown restaurants can not afford to have a ruckus occurring on their premises. A disturbance would frighten away other customers. As I recall only two or three downtown restaurants successfully resisted our efforts at integration. In these instances, repeated visits and sit-ins did not succeed in changing the policies of management. The police were often called but they could take no action since we were not behaving in a disruptive manner. My colleagues and I always remained peaceful in spite of varying degrees of provocation. As usual the police made it clear that their sympathies were with the law breaking owners or managers.

I had never really been tested in my commitment to non-violence under pressure and threat of violence. In some respects I would have welcomed the opportunity to be tested by some kind of violent assault, in order to find out for myself exactly how I would have responded. It is quite possible that a positive commitment to non-violent resistance might have broken down under the pressure of a very strong violent attack. Of course, I was glad that I never had to suffer that kind of attack but in one respect I was sorry that the opportunity never came.

My only encounter with the law in Chicago, in spite of its reputation as a tough lawless city, was when I was the complainant. I had just moved to an apartment on 61st St., immediately south of the University of Chicago campus. The neighbourhood was of mixed racial backgrounds and in a state of transition. As whites moved out, blacks were moving in. It was almost a certainty that the neighbourhood would become all-black within a few years.

A white barber was operating a barber shop three or four doors from my apartment and on one occasion, I entered his shop and asked for a haircut. He replied that he could not cut the hair of blacks, it was too difficult. That was certainly a novel excuse for not serving me, even if I had so-called "curly hair", which I did not have. I have mentioned my mixed heritage which is manifested by my brown colour and non-negroid hair. He wanted to direct me to a black barber who, he said, could cut my hair. After a few minutes of this discussion, I said that perhaps he wanted me to file a complaint against him on the basis of discrimination against me because of race and colour. He felt that was O.K. and said "Go right ahead", apparently thinking that I would not follow up on the incident. I went home and immediately telephoned the court building to determine where I should go to file the complaint. I had no difficulty in filing the complaint and a court hearing was set for two weeks later.

The experience of Indianapolis regarding theatre discrimination was not repeated in this case. The judge listened to my complaint then asked the barber to respond. He admitted that he had refused to cut my hair but again said that it was too difficult and he did not know how to cut the hair of a black man. It happened that the judge was a black man and had no interest in hearing that sort of excuse. He turned to me and said that it was a valid complaint and what did I want done. I said I wanted a haircut. The judge turned to the barber and said that he had violated a section of the law of the state of Illinois, and could be fined or jailed, but if he agreed to cut my hair, that might be the best way to settle the case. The barber stated that he understood and would indeed cut my hair. The judge signed an order that the barber must honour his pledge or face serious consequences. The barber indicated his acceptance, and we left the court building just before noon. I returned home, had lunch and immediately went to the barber shop. He greeted me with a smile, cut my hair quickly and then asked if I wanted a shave. I looked up and saw that he was holding a long sharp razor in his hand. I had visions of an "accidental" slip of the blade resulting in my throat being cut. I immediately gave him a resounding "No thanks", jumped from the chair, paid him and left the shop. I had won my point and felt no great need to return to that shop again during my stay in Chicago. However, as usual, I advised every black man I knew to go to the barbershop for future haircuts. Many did follow up and were served.

SANE

My final organizational activity in Chicago was under the auspices of The Committee for a Sane Nuclear Policy (SANE), a New York-based organization whose founder and first president, Dr. Homer Jack, was a minister in one of the local Unitarian churches. Homer was a very energetic man who spent much of his time and energy travelling around the country organizing chapters in various cities. I became a member of the organizing committee of SANE in Chicago. Basically the purpose of SANE was to warn Americans of the dangers of nuclear warfare and how the nuclear arms race could eventually lead to the catastrophic destruction of life on the planet.

Robert Pickus, a FOR activist, became chair of the Chicago group, and under his leadership SANE became a major force in discussions of the arms race during the 1950s and early 1960s. Many union leaders, civic clubs, professional groups and entrepreneurs who were not interested in participating in a campaign operated by a mainstream religious group found themselves at home in SANE. As a volunteer member of the board of directors, I was involved in organizing workshops, seminars and conferences designed to promote the objectives of the organization. We often invited high profile speakers and leaders of labour unions as well as individuals from the business community, to participate in our meetings and workshops. Sidney Lens, a prominent labour union leader, became one of our most effective workers and participants. He wrote two books on the question of nuclear warfare and its implications for human survival. Somehow I managed, in the midst of many other activities, to play a significant role in the Chicago chapter of SANE. I was primarily concerned with contacting and recruiting potential speakers, leaders of workshops and publicizing coming events. My training in sociology, social work and adult education was of immense value in this task.

SANE played an important role in the overall struggle against nuclear war and mutual destruction. The times, however, were not favourable for an organization which had two strikes against it, the first being the implications and significance of the McCarthy period. The second problem was the clear intention of both superpowers, the United States and the Soviet Union, to continue the arms race regardless of public opinion. There were major obstacles. In spite of arms reduction negotiations, the arms race was continuing at an ever increasing rate. Of course, both superpowers blamed each other for the state of affairs.

The Chicago organization was not able to maintain its momentum because the power and influence of the military/industrial complex, as it was labelled by President Eisenhower, was simply too strong for a small, voluntary organization to overcome. The Pentagon with its vast amounts of money, and supported by the arms industry, was able to exert maximum influence over the media and other forms of public information. SANE was still alive and well when I left Chicago. However, it was apparent that it would be difficult to survive much longer and its demise was almost inevitable. That was a tragedy.

I had, by the summer of 1953, been in Chicago for five years and had thoroughly enjoyed the very challenging activities in which I had been involved. My contacts and activities with AFSC, FOR, ACLU, CORE and other organizations had been very stimulating. However, my problems were not those organizations and activities but rather with Parkway Community House. It was apparent that Parkway would be going through severe financial problems largely because the types of programs and involvements which I was trying to develop at Parkway simply would not generate adequate funds for its operational needs. Our middle class board of directors, all of whom were white with the exception of two or three powerless blacks, were not enthusiastic about programs leading to greater economic and political independence of blacks. The focus and thrust of these activities were not attractive to our funders. Board members were much more happy to support and raise funds for recreational programs, the nursery school for single parent families and programs for senior citizens. While I had developed positive relationships with individual members of the board, I had no illusions as to how they would react if they were fully aware of what I was trying to do.

For that wealthy group of white liberals, improved race relations did not include supporting changes in the political, social and economic structure of the black ghetto. There was nothing unusual about this attitude which was typical of individuals who felt kindly toward the black population and wanted to provide supportive social and recreational services. I often wondered what would happen if a black family moved into the neighbourhoods in which some board members lived. I suspected that they would have been shocked. Moreover, it was possible that some members of the board were aware that my wife was white but it was never mentioned, at least in my presence. I had the distinct impression that members of the board did not want to discuss my marital or family relationships. I think that by mutual consent the board and I operated on the basis of a "conspiracy of silence". The staff and most of our volunteers were quite aware of my marriage situation. Phyllis and I attended staff and volunteer parties, workshops and receptions together and she often visited the agency during working hours. There was never any attempt to conceal our relationship.

My unease at Parkway was soon relieved. At an annual conference for social workers, I happened to notice a flyer inviting applications for a position in Columbus, Ohio. The position was as supervisor of group work services at the State Juvenile Diagnostic Centre which was associated with the Columbus State Hospital, a mental hospital located in the west side of the city. A short, stocky individual noticed that I was reading the sign and came over to speak to me. He was a psychologist and wanted to know if I was interested. We had a chat and as a result he encouraged me to apply for the position. He was the chief psychologist at the Diagnostic Centre and had been sent to the social work conference to recruit two new staff people. Two or three weeks following our return to Chicago, I received a letter from the director of the agency informing me that on the recommendation of his staff psychologist, I was offered the position. I accepted the offer and began to make preparations for leaving Chicago.

It would be necessary to move furniture, family, car, clothing etc. from an apartment in Chicago to a house in Columbus. I rented a trailer for the task. Moving the furniture from the fourth floor and loading it onto the trailer was a bigger job than I had expected and it was only with the help of friends, neighbours and students that I was able to accomplish this by noon on the day of our move. The trip took seven or eight hours, much more than I had expected because the car was pulling a heavily loaded trailer. Friends in Columbus had helped Phyllis locate an apartment. She and the children had travelled by train to Columbus three days earlier for time to settle into our rented house.

In the meantime, they had lived with friends in Columbus, some of whom had been with me in CPS. We were met on my arrival by a number of friends who had gathered to help us unload the trailer and get established in our new home located near the eastern boarder of the Columbus black community. The owners of the house occupied the first and we rented the second floor. We knew that we would miss the vitality and challenge of Chicago, but were ready for the change.

I was interested in restablishing more frequent contacts with my mother and brothers who were living in Cincinnati. She had remarried and had moved to Cincinnati while I was still attending Tuskegee Institute. She had missed the opportunity to attend my two graduation exercises, first at Tuskegee and two years later at Atlanta University. Our communications at the time, however, made it clear that she was proud of the achievements of her eldest son.

Frank and Glenn, following their discharge from the army and air force, had also located in the suburban area of Greater Cincinnati with their families. By that time, Glenn and his wife Gerry (Geraldine) had two sons, Gerald and Michael and a daughter, Evelyn. My other siblings, Minnie and Marvin, were living in California and unable to travel the enormous distance for family visits. On one occasion however, Marvin did make the trip from California. He and a few others drove from Los Angeles to Cincinnati, picked up my mother and drove to Chicago. We met his new wife on that occasion. These get-togethers were always occasions of great satisfaction since we had seen each other only infrequently for many years.

The family had made a constructive adaptation to life in Chicago. Phyllis had obtained a position shortly after our arrival, and Norman had been enroled in day care shortly after his second birthday. Gregory, although less than a year old, was rapidly growing up and in his own way, carving out his place in the family. Our friends, the Selmanoffs, Sandbacks, Drakes and others in the Friends Meeting were valuable and solid supporters as we became welcomed activists in the social, religious, recreational and educational aspects of life in the city. Leaving these valued relationships would not be easy. But we had not suffered the more blatant forms of discrimination so prevalent in the South, or in Indianapolis. The one aspect we were sure of was that Columbus would, in significant ways, be quite different. Only time could provide the precise nature of these differences. My only real regret on leaving Chicago was that I had not become as closely identified with the black community as I would have liked. Even my volunteer work in peace, civil rights and race relations was, with few exceptions, with virtually all white organizations. Although I had been a staff member of the Indianapolis Chapter of the NAACP, I had found it difficult to become involved in the apparently closed ranks of the Chicago chapter. Consequently, my contacts with the Chicago black community were largely restricted to the Parkway Community House volunteers, staff and clientele.

Chicago was a community in which I faced a real dilemma. On the one hand, I had wanted to play a meaningful role in confronting some of the many problems faced by the black community. On the other hand, I had little interest in joining the many black churches, social, political, recreational and civic clubs on the south side. My interests in social justice issues involvement was in sharp contrast to the Indianapolis experience, a matter in which I experienced some regret. Columbus, however, would be another story. I expected it to be less hectic, blatantly racist, and more tolerant of differences. It was a smaller city with presumably smaller problems. I expected those problems to be different, but equally as complex and challenging.

CHAPTER 11 *Conservatism and Breaking Barriers: Columbus*

My mother and stepfather had lived in Cincinnati for several years. I had visited them on several occasions and had some knowledge of conditions in Ohio. However, never having been in Columbus, I looked forward to a new, challenging experience. Two of my ex-CPS friends, Marvin Van Wormer and Richard Stow, worked in Columbus and I had heard that there was a thriving Friends Meeting which conducted a number of projects in which I could easily become involved. I viewed the move as potentially very productive and constructive. It also provided me with an opportunity to work in an entirely different setting and structure. I would be a civil servant working under the State of Ohio Department of Mental Health and Correction.

Columbus, in the 1950s, was the third largest city in Ohio, following Cleveland and Cincinnati. A major educational institution, the Ohio State University did not appear to elicit the hostility by townspeople found in many other cities in the U.S. One could almost feel that the Ohio State University was Columbus and Columbus was the Ohio State University. However, it was not the excellence of the university which elicited such great admiration on the part of townspeople but the prowess and winning record of the football team. The Ohio State football team appeared to be the most important institution in the entire community if not in the state as a whole. It was a member of the "Big Ten", a league which included ten of the largest state and private universities in the mid-west. A game between the University of Michigan and Ohio State always filled the stadium, which had a capacity of more than eighty-five thousand fans. It was expected that every student of the university would attend football games at home and even follow the teams to games in other states.

The pattern of segregation and exclusion in Columbus was very similar to that in southern cities except that the black population was very small in size and was unwilling to accept racial discrimination without a struggle. A small group, led by Frank Shearer, a young black lawyer and Mrs. Connie Nickols, a tough "fair-skinned" black woman, organized the Vanguard League against restaurant and theatre discrimination in the city. Barbee Durham, the executive secretary of the Columbus NAACP, was also a prominent member of the League. They and their black and white supporters picketed theatres and restaurants which refused to serve blacks. After a lengthy struggle, the League was successful in forcing those businesses to change discriminatory practices. Unfortunately the history of the League was relatively brief. Its success in achieving its limited goals, plus some internal difficulties led to its termination by the end of the 1940s. For many blacks, the successes and failures of the organization were only a faint memory when I arrived in Columbus in 1953.

Many schools remained segregated and most blacks lived in the all-black ghetto which severely limited employment opportunities. Members of the black ghetto, as in many other cities, had developed their own social, economic and political structures. The majority of blacks attended black churches, black service clubs, and black political institutions. Their children attended segregated schools. As elsewhere, segregated schools reflected the fact that they were located in segregated neighbourhoods. However, for reasons which I will discuss later, my neighbourhood was not all-black and therefore my son Norman was not forced to attend a segregated school. Had that been so, there would have been considerable difficulty between the Columbus Board of Education and myself!

I began my work at the Juvenile Diagnostic Center within a week of my arrival in Columbus. The Center was located on ground adjacent to the campus of the Columbus State Hospital, a mental hospital which served the central region of the state. The Center had a capacity of one hundred and twenty five children. Approximately two thirds were boys between the ages of eight and fifteen and one third were girls between the ages of twelve and fifteen. The ratio of black to white children appeared to be fairly reflective of the population of the state, approximately 80 percent white and 20 percent black. The total professional staff included a dozen or more special education teachers, seven or eight social workers, several psychologists, and four or five psychiatrists who were usually residents who spent four months at the institution obtaining experience in working with emotionally disturbed children.

My title, initially, was "Director of Group Services" which included Recreational Activities. In addition, I had responsibilities for the supervision of the cottage programs. The twelve to fifteen children in each cottage were supervised by "cottage parents" who acted as parent substitutes to the boys or girls. In total, there were about seventy cottage staff, recreational leaders and cottage supervisors for whom I was responsible as supervisor. A "diagnostic or clinical team", composed of cottage parents and professional staff, was assigned to each cottage but cottage parents also had some responsibility to their teams. This responsibility to two structures, the team and to me as the overall supervisor was the source of much confusion. My duties also included hiring new cottage and recreational staff when vacancies occurred.

My first day on the job was a period of orientation and getting to know the staff operating the psychology, social work, psychiatric and education departments and the supervisors of the girls and the boys cottages.

In spite of the generally humane attitude of the director and a few of the members of the administrative council, the institution operated much as the old-fashioned training schools. The cottages were strictly sex segregated except when children were permitted to attend chapel services on Sunday mornings. As one could imagine, chapel was one of the most popular activities on the campus, not because the boys and girls were interested in religion but because chapel attendance gave them an opportunity to associate with members of the opposite sex!

I was told upon accepting the position that I would be free to make whatever changes I felt necessary to make the school a more attractive and professional setting which could attract additional professional staff. I was encouraged to make the Center a place in which the children would enjoy a more comfortable and constructive life experience. I accepted that challenge at face value, but questioned the emphasis on security, that is keeping the children locked in the buildings or inside the grounds of the institution: I thought this was extreme and unnecessary.

An initial attempt had been made by the administration to prevent runaways by constructing a ten-foot chain fence around the grounds. Some children still climbed over the fence and ran away. Secondly, why keep the children totally separated by gender in all except religious activities? This practice was considered a serious problem by many professional and non-professional staff. However, they had no answer to my question except the fear that the older children might become engaged in "unacceptable behaviour" which referred to romantic or sexual behaviour.

The first indication that I wanted to change much of the program emphasis resulted in a degree of confusion and anxiety. There was some open hostility on the part of some cottage parents and also some members of the professional staff. I was not surprised at the attitude and behaviour of the cottage parents and other non-professionals but I was surprised at the attitudes of some psychologists, teachers, psychiatrists and other professional staff members. It seemed that they should have reflected a more humane and positive attitude toward children in their care. I stated in a staff meeting my intention to introduce a limited program of co-ed activities in both the boys' and girls' cottages. On occasion the boys would visit the girls' cottages for card games, table tennis and other activities and on other occasions the girls would visit the boys' cottages for similar activities. In addition, on weekends I intended to initiate dances for selected children in our games room.

My second bombshell was that I was going to introduce volunteers into the program. The cottage parents would not have the time to supervise their cottages and at the same time supervise co-ed activities in another building.

Outside volunteers would include people who could teach a variety of social skills, including crafts, dramatics, grooming for the girls' and other social skills.

The major objection to this step was that the institutionalized children were tough and much too difficult to be handled by volunteers. I found this attitude almost humorous. I had only recently arrived from Chicago and had been working with children in a settlement setting who were far tougher and more street wise than anyone we ever saw at the Center. However, the cottage parents were not fully aware of this experience and were threatened regarding the possibility of volunteers losing control of the children. Many, having never worked with volunteers, felt that they would only complicate matters and make their own work much more difficult. In order to allay their fears, I first insisted that every volunteer be accompanied by a cottage parent whenever they left their cottage to go to another building for a specific activity. Fears regarding social dancing and close contact between boys and girls were alleviated to a large extent by the introduction of square dancing and other group activities. In each of these, volunteers were on scene, accompanied by a cottage parent from each of the various cottages. Much to the surprise of the cottage parents and even the professional staff, the children reacted to these activities with great enthusiasm and there were no serious problems. The enjoyment of the children was obvious to the volunteers, cottage parents and members of the staff who often attended the events. Occasionally, some of the professionals would return to the institution in the evenings to participate with the children in square dances and other party activities.

It took some time, however, before the cottage staff and some professionals could completely accept the volunteers as individuals with specific skills. It took almost five months before volunteers were permitted to work alone with children. Gradually the cottage staff began to accept the volunteers and permitted them to take children to activities outside the cottage without accompaniment. That was a major step forward.

By the end of my second year, most of the new program had been completely accepted. By then, it was possible to introduce social dancing into the activity programs. I made a visit to the Arthur Murray School of Dancing in downtown Columbus and conferred with the director. I was assured by him that he could get at least three women who would volunteer to come out and work with our boys. It would not, at least initially, be necessary for the girls to have teachers. There was, however, a tremendous amount of insecurity among the boys. They were scared to be found lacking in social dance skills and it was necessary to teach them. After they had achieved a degree of confidence we could then bring the boys and girls together.

Initially, the boys danced only with their teachers or with other staff who visited the classes from time to time. This behaviour was quite humorous. Within less than three months of weekly practice sessions we felt that it was time to bring the boys and the girls together for the first time. We had been extremely lucky in having two well-trained female teachers work with our older boys. The volunteers were aware of the fears and anxieties of the boys and adapted their teaching methods to this age group. Again, the experiment was a total success and both cottage parents and other staff were very pleased with the outcome. From that point on we could hold social and square dances on a weekly basis.

I had personally led many of these activities and helped the volunteer teachers teach the boys the dances. I also taught the girls some of the steps and "called" the square dances, skills I had learned in the Civilian Public Service project and at Quaker work camps. By then I felt that the time had come to withdraw and to leave these activities to the direction and supervision of our recreation leaders.

Two recreational leaders, one for boys and one for girls were employed on staff. With the success of the co-ed program I turned my attention to other activities. I was particularly interested in introducing a new form of counselling and therapy into the program. This group program was labelled as "group counselling" or "group therapy". In order to reduce anxiety and confusion regarding the new groups, I decided initially to organize only two groups of six to eight girls which met once a week. The purpose of these groups was to supplement the individual counselling programs by psychologists and psychiatrists. My groups focused on the development of social skills. Participants were chosen by cottage parents and other staff. Later I expanded this program by organizing a group of boys who also met once a week. Within two or three months I occasionally brought the two groups together for joint meetings. These groups, similar to adult counselling groups, began to provide their own therapeutic or counselling experience. They slowly learned to share their experiences with others and benefitted from the experiences of other members rather than solely from me. I found that children would take criticism from other members of their group much more readily than they would from me. The process was much more difficult than simply learning social skills. This was the nature of group therapy.

In less than two years, the whole recreational, social and cultural climate of the institution had changed dramatically. The relationships between various members of the staff had improved. The professional staff found it easier to perform their work and cottage parents found fewer problems in the cottages. My experiences with the experimental patients at the Philadelphia State Hospital had helped a great deal in designing programs for the benefit of the children at the Center. Even more important was the fact that the staff, once they saw the success of these programs, joined in and supported them with enthusiasm! Of course I had not accomplished these changes alone. Staff had become more enthusiastic as they became aware of the possibilities. By the time I left the Center, it would have been difficult for these programs to be cancelled by a new administration. This success, however, did not solve all of our problems. Children occasionally still ran away, although at a reduced rate. But the change in the atmosphere was significant and welcomed.

In-Service Training

In the meantime, I had suggested in a meeting of the administrative council that we broaden the in-service educational programs for our staff. In the past, we had occasionally brought in an individual who gave a lecture to the professional or cottage staff but this practice was not very helpful because these events were so infrequent, perhaps once or twice a year. I felt that the total staff needed in-service training and suggested to the superintendent that I would be pleased to take on this responsibility in addition to my other duties. He gladly accepted and appointed me as director of in-service training for the institution. Dr. Ross, a psychiatrist, was an unusual man in that he was "down to earth" with none of the arrogance often seen in the relationship of psychiatrists to nurses, social workers and other non-medical staff. He understood the difficulty of our work and was always supportive.

I had already begun setting up training programs to help the staff deal more effectively with children, particularly those who were hard to handle and resistant to authority. We had been engaged in role-playing, group discussions and interactions between cottage parents from different cottages which had been moderately successful, but there were still problems. To some extent, these problems related to the occasionally strained relationship between the professional staff, cottage parents and recreational leaders. There was some concern by the professional staff that cottage staff were beginning to learn too much about child behaviour and would therefore be more likely to try to intervene in the therapeutic programs for the children. Their attitude was that the cottage staff should not discuss problems with children but should simply be custodians and see that the children were available for professional intervention as required. This concept, in my view, was based on the false assumption that only professionals could provide a constructive role model for children. My contact with the cottage parents, recreation leaders, teachers and other workers convinced me that they often had considerable impact upon the attitudes and behaviours of the children. The example of the staff often played a very important role in the development of a diagnostic picture of the child's attitudes and behaviour in a variety of situations outside counselling sessions. Obviously there were some differences in emphasis. Nevertheless, all staff had a role to play in the overall diagnostic and counselling relationship with the child.

An interesting aspect of the racial atmosphere of the Center was that both children and staff appeared to have little interest in racial attitudes. Although I was the only non-white member of the senior administrative staff, all other staff positions were totally integrated. Since I was in charge of cottage and recreational staff, I was responsible for hiring the major proportion of the total staff, a responsibility which helped me to make changes.

Even more significant, from my point of view, was the lack of racial consciousness by most of the children, and especially the white children. Black kids, the victims of hostility, were much more aware of their position and thus more cautious in initial interactions with the white boys and girls. The white girls had no such inhibitions. They eagerly sought out blacks as "special friends". While motives are not always open and clear, it seemed that some white cottage parents were somewhat sceptical regarding this behaviour. It did not appear that these attitudes could be openly expressed in the overall atmosphere of the Center and the result was that these staff members kept their feelings largely to themselves, and I could only speculate as to how they actually felt.

I called the in-service committee together including representatives from all sectors of the staff. I was very careful to make no attempt to dominate the committee since my role, as I saw it, was basically two-fold: first to bring the staff together to examine the problems they faced in their respective areas of interests and concern, and second, to identify and collect materials which could be brought forward for their perusal and adoption for future programs.

The initial meetings of this committee went very well. Most people spoke openly of their own problems and interests. Cottage parents wanted to know more about how to control children, particularly those who were difficult to handle. Psychologists wanted to know more about the methods of motivating children, developing relationships between parents and children and dealing with the psychological development of the child. Through these discussions, all groups represented in the planning committee came to recognize that they had common problems including how to understand, diagnose and help children to cope with their own societies and environments.

Psychiatrists assigned to the Center for their internship were varied in their approach to working with children. Many of them utilized a purely psychoanalytic approach: others used a more non-directive approach and others, a variety of approaches between these two extremes. Having been trained as doctors, these psychiatrists were accustomed to conducting diagnostic studies and prescribing treatment. Once the treatment had been prescribed, it was usually considered up to the patient to get the necessary drugs and to follow the doctor's orders. This approach was not an effective method of operation in an institution of our type. It was necessary to understand basic psychological functioning and the social and economic background of the child. It was at that point that I came to understand and appreciate the remarks by Sigmund Freud more than fifty years earlier that doctors were the least appropriate candidates for training in psychoanalysis!

Community Activities

Life, however, is not entirely a matter of work, professional or otherwise. Since arriving, Phyllis and I had been active participants in the various programs of the Columbus Friends Meeting. Through that group I found opportunities for work in race relations and peace. My activities carried over from what I had done previously in Indianapolis and in Chicago. The Columbus Friends Meeting was unique in that most of its members were engaged in a wide variety of activities of different sorts, both professional and religious. The fact that they were functioning in a very conservative atmosphere did not prevent them from involvement in activities which would certainly not be labelled as "conservative".

Their opposition to military service and militarism in general was deep and profound. Their concern regarding issues of social inequality, poor housing and unemployment was equally deeply felt. Consequently, I was well aware that if I needed help with a problem in the community, it would be available.

This need arose less than a year after I arrived in Columbus and was related to the problem of housing. Very rarely indeed did a black family make the attempt to move away from this defined area and into a white community. Even if the family had wished to do so, it would have been unable to accomplish this goal. It would have been blocked at two different levels. First, the family would not have been shown houses outside of the black ghetto by real estate agencies, and second, it would not have been able to obtain mortgages from banks or trust companies, even if it had found an owner who was willing to sell to blacks. As in Chicago, this was not a barrier created by law, but by agreements by the major players in the real estate business.

A Housing Experience

By the end of the summer of 1954, Phyllis and I had decided that we would like to buy a house for our family. The problem was not that we were living in poor housing; actually we had quite an adequate apartment on the second floor of a private home. The problem was that we did not want our children to attend the segregated neighbourhood schools and unfortunately, as customary, the school districts were based on residential segregation. We decided that we would like to buy a house in another neighbourhood, one in which the boys could attend non-segregated schools. Norman was already school-aged, and Gregory would reach that stage in a few years. We put the word out among our friends and colleagues that we were looking for a house and asked for any support and suggestions they could make. Shortly thereafter we were informed of a vacancy on Indianola Avenue, an area about five or six blocks from the University Campus. The house seemed to us to be in a good neighbourhood and we were very interested in the possibility of a purchase. However, it became clear that the house was in a "white" neighbourhood and the chances of a positive solution to that problem seemed very remote indeed. The house was only a few blocks from the meeting house of the Society of Friends.

We raised the matter in the Friends Meeting and were successful in getting suggestions from members of that group. One of those members, Stan Robinson, a lawyer, was interested in our situation. Louise and Stan Robinson were among two of the many prominent members of the Society who were frequently involved in "social justice" issues with particular interest in the question of racial inequality and discrimination. Stan had also been involved in counselling and defending conscientious objectors and others who opposed military service. His defence of these people had made him a reputation as an individual who could be trusted to provide adequate defence for those who were in difficulty because of their unconventional beliefs or behaviour. Because of these activities, he had become known as one of the most militant and progressive lawyers in the city.

Although highly regarded by many people in the community, he was not highly regarded by the more conventional people in the affluent business community.

Stan had been looking for a test case in which he could act on behalf of a black family desiring to move into an all-white community. Phyllis and I were ready for the experience. Stan agreed to support us and briefly outlined the procedures we would have to follow. As a white lawyer he would have to do most of the work so we agreed to be guided by his counsel. Both parties were keenly aware of the possible difficulties which might arise. We were aware of the situation in Chicago, and Stan was cognisant of the dangers in which we might be involved. He informed us that while there were no legal problems involved, certainly there might be community opposition. Many members of the institutional structure of society, including bankers, mortgage holders and real estate agents, would be reluctant to show homes or to sell a house to a black in an all-white neighbourhood. This had been the pattern in the past and there was no evidence that any significant change had occurred in these attitudes during recent months or years.

Stan contacted some friends who were involved in the real estate and/or in the mortgage business who were ready to make loans available to us if the need arose. Over several weeks his negotiations succeeded in making all necessary arrangements for the purchase of the house. Phyllis and I had played no part in these negotiations: it would have been insane for us to make the attempt!

I assigned my "power of attorney" to Stan so that he could act on my behalf. Otherwise I would have been required to sign in person. At that point Stan felt that it was necessary for all plans to be kept secret and we were not able to visit the house. Had we done so, it was possible some of the neighbours might have guessed what was going on and created an uproar in the community. On one occasion Stan felt that Phyllis violated this confidence because she felt that it was important for me to stop by and view the house so we could make adequate preparations for decorations and other activities involved in the moving process. Stan had handled everything very quietly and there was no suspicion whatsoever of anything different from what appeared on the surface. Nevertheless, after hearing of Phyllis' indiscretion, he felt that it was absolutely necessary that we act with all possible speed and move into the house the next day.

Because of the possible reaction, Stan had arranged to have two or three policemen watch the house from a discrete distance to avoid any suspicion of what was happening. It had never occurred to me that such a laborious and complex arrangement would be necessary to assure our protection.

The move went without incident and although a few people stood around and watched what was happening, no negative remarks or comments were heard. In the absence of awareness of the arrangement made by Stan Robinson, we were still a bit surprised at how easy it was to move into the house. Several members of the Friends joined in support of our move. The presence of our friends, who were white, may have been a step in preventing any outbreak of hostile behaviour. In any event the move occurred without incident and we found ourselves quite pleased with our new home and surroundings.

The ease of moving into our new house, however, may have given us a false sense of security. The reverberations began within the next few days. Interestingly, we were welcomed by the family on the south side of our new home but were greeted with hostility by the family on the other side of the house. That hostility was reflected in their behaviour, attitude and activities. While the gentleman in that house refused to speak to us, he continuously placed pictures of blacks in servile positions, particularly those from Quaker Oats Boxes, in the window adjacent to our house so that we could not avoid seeing them. In addition, he obtained block letters which he arranged in such a way as to present negative and inflammatory messages. We ignored this behaviour and continued living in the house in as friendly a manner as possible. Whenever we met him on the street or saw him at his house we always spoke to him but never received a response. This behaviour continued for almost two years.

The house in which we had moved was very old and required a good deal of redecoration. We removed the old stained wallpaper and completely redecorated the living and the dining rooms. We were amazed at how difficult it was because there were six to eight layers of wallpaper on the walls. Fortunately, a number of our friends came to help with the work so we had a series of "work bees" or work parties which enabled us to become well acquainted with many members of the Friends Meeting. We began to feel very much at home, even though we had only been in the neighbourhood less than two weeks.

My first contact with the opposition came on a Saturday afternoon. I was on a ladder taking wallpaper off the ceiling of the living room when I suddenly heard a knock at the front door. I got down off the ladder and went to the door and met two men who were standing there waiting to be invited in. I invited them in and asked them to have a seat. I then asked the nature of their business. The two men were from the real estate agency which had sold the house to me through my wife and Stan Robinson. They wanted me to sell the house back to them and told me that I would not be happy in the neighbourhood. It would be much better for me and my family if I sold the house and then moved into another house which they would be willing to provide in another neighbourhood. I told them that with the exception of one person (whom I did not identify), I was quite satisfied and happy with the neighbourhood. Apparently my attitude surprised them and they reflected a bit of anger, insisting that I might run into violence of some kind and they would not be responsible. I responded that that was quite fine with me. I had bought the house and was the owner and they had no further responsibility. They began to talk about the profit I could make if I was willing to sell the house. They never suggested a specific sum but did suggest that if I were willing to sell the house a substantial profit would be forthcoming. Finally, after half an hour of discussion, I reminded the two men that I had no intention of moving or selling the house and that they were wasting their time attempting to change my decision. That decision was final. I then suggested that I would like to get back to my work and would be very pleased if they would leave. I was sure that they had other important business. They left, but not in the very best of moods.

The repercussions of the move did not cease with the visit of the two real estate men. Within two or three days, Stan Robinson was also summoned to the offices of some of the bankers, real estate agents and mortgage people who were involved. He was sharply questioned about his role in the affair and it was suggested that he had committed fraud since he had not revealed that I was not white, and that what he had done could lead to his disbarment as a lawyer. In the meantime, a bank with which his father and he had done business for many years informed him that they would no longer accept his deposits and that he could close out his account. Obviously these boys were playing "hard ball". However, Stan was not intimidated. He knew what he was doing and firmly stood his ground. He told them that if they wanted to file charges of any kind against him, they were free to go right ahead. He had conducted the negotiations in a legal manner, had met all requirements of the law and therefore they had no grounds for legal action. He had them over a barrel, leaving them with no alternative but to drop the struggle.

Although we were not aware of his reputation at the time, I later learned that Stan had contacted Thurgood Marshall, then Director and Counsel of the NAACP Legal Defense and Education Fund Inc., a subsidiary of the national association. Marshall had made a reputation as a formidable fighter against the legal and non-legal patterns which maintained segregation and discrimination against blacks in the North and South. He was later appointed as the first black Justice of the Supreme Court of the United States. I had met and had the opportunity to discuss issues of segregation and black/white relationships with Marshall at a national conference of the NAACP during my brief stay in Indianapolis. His energy, intellect and commitment to the cause of eliminating injustices in society were impressive. I felt that I was in the presence of an unusual if not a truly great man.

Marshall quickly responded to a letter from Stan informing him of the situation as it developed in Columbus. His response, in part, was as follows:

> I have gone over your letter carefully and for the life of me I cannot see anything which you have done which would merit even an investigation by the Bar Association. It is obvious that this takes the form of intimidation against future action on your part and the part of other lawyers who actually believe that our Constitution means what it says; and the Supreme Court of the United States meant what it said in the restrictive covenant cases. If the Bar Association does decide to take action against you I would be more than happy to help in any way possible.

Stan came out of the struggle unharmed and undeterred. He lost some business but gained other clients. For every client he lost, he gained at least one and sometimes two or three more. With his support our family had gone through an ordeal and had come out victorious. Nevertheless, our Quaker friends took no chances. For two or three more weeks they returned every day to our house to keep watch. They often came in shifts and often one or two of them would remain at our house until 10:30 or 11:00 in the evening. No further incidents occurred.

We had achieved our goal of buying our own house and had not been forced out because of violence in the community. Stan did not project the picture of a charismatic, hard hitting and aggressive lawyer so often portrayed in the movies and on television. Rather, he was quiet, unassuming, and even slightly reticent in manner and approach to problems. But in his own way he was totally dedicated to the cause of justice and fairness. He was quite aware of the potential dangers he might have faced when he accepted our case. But he was not deterred by that possible threat. I remember his response when he was accused of fraud because he had not informed them that I was a black man. His response was typical: "You didn't ask me!"

We bought the house for two major reasons. First, we wanted to own our own house, rather than live as tenants in a segregated ghetto. Second, we wanted to live in a neighbourhood in which our children could receive a good education. Both of those goals achieved, our next responsibility was to check the school out to see how it operated in practice. Phyllis had some experience working with the YWCA and also in education. We were in a fairly good position to make valid judgement regarding the quality of education in the public school in which our son, Norman, would be enroled.

We were pleasantly surprised with the atmosphere of the school and found the staff to be warm, friendly, and accepting of our son as were the other students. None of the difficulties we had experienced in buying a house appeared among the public school students. We were also surprised at our reception in the neighbourhood. The few people who had objected to our move seemed to accept us after we had settled in.

In general, we had found the experience very positive. This was particularly interesting because Columbus was, in general, a very conservative city. I missed the rough and tumble aspects of life in a city like Chicago where we lived in the midst of chaos, poverty, crime and corruption. Chicago, even with its numerous problems, was an exciting city: Columbus most certainly was not. However we had many good friends in Columbus and this made up for a lack of dynamism and excitement.

One of the attractions in coming to Columbus was that I had previously met a few members of the Friends' Meeting. I have a special feeling for those occasions in which we were treated to a homelike atmosphere and a home-cooked meal! They loved classical music, and I listened to many records of the great masters of the past, such as Beethoven, Bach, Brahms, Chopin, Tchaikovsky, Mozart and others, for the first time at their homes. In many respects I found the Columbus Meeting less formal and more outgoing than the Chicago Meeting and they contributed greatly to my pleasure and satisfaction in living in Columbus. Stan and Louise Robinson were a part of that friendly and stimulating experience.

Another significant event in my life was that I again returned to school. I enroled in the Ohio State University to take specific courses on a part-time basis since my work at the Center was scheduled in the afternoon and early evenings, leaving my mornings free. It was quite possible for me to take two or three courses at a time. I began a series of post-masters courses in the fall of 1954.

By my second year at the Center, I had began to accept field practice students from Ohio State University. This function included supervision of students from the department of education and the school of social work. Although supervision of students was not a paid position, the university provided free tuition for agency supervisors of its students during their field practice. Thus I was able to obtain four academic years of part-time education without having to pay tuition fees which was a mutually satisfactory arrangement and one which I welcomed because of my continuing interest in learning. The university benefitted from my providing supervision for its students and I benefitted from the fact that I did not have to pay tuition, while the Center benefitted from the contributions of students in field placement.

I faced the same problem at Ohio State that I previously faced some years earlier at Tuskegee Institute, that is the university's preoccupation and demand that its students follow its prescribed course of study. The students had the opportunity to choose a discipline, but once having enroled in that particular program, they were expected to meet certain required courses. However, I had my own goals in mind and these goals would not be met by programs of any one discipline. I therefore sought to enrol in a department in which I could take a wide variety of subjects. The program in adult education appeared to be the only place in the university in which I could obtain the flexibility I was seeking. Aside from adult education, my major focus was social psychology and the sociology of deviant behaviour which involved some studies in criminology, a field that could be useful in my work at the Center. In one sense social psychology was an interest I had developed as a result of observations of changing behaviour of individuals at football games, rallies, religious services and other large group gatherings. Otherwise quiet and withdrawn individuals could under the influence of the crowd, "let their hair down" and behave in a totally uncharacteristic manner.

After I had completed fifteen or twenty courses at Ohio State at the post-master level, Dr. Henderson, my advisor, suggested that I organize my courses so that they would lead toward a degree. I told him that I was not really working toward a degree but was concerned with what I could learn that would be useful to me in my present work and in my future professional life. He stated that under the rubric of adult education, I could, with a few exceptions, take almost any course I wanted without having to meet various departmental or discipline prerequisites. With his encouragement, I began to look at my completed courses in terms of a structure that would include previously mentioned courses in Chicago.

Again, I was studying on a part-time basis while working full time. This was obviously a handicap; however, I made up for the handicaps by the intensity of my study and my ability to relate my studies to what I doing in my professional work. I was able to test theories against actual practice. Although Ohio State University was generally not rated as a "top-notch" academic university, it did have a number of very good faculty members in certain departments. I deliberately sought out those men and women. The result was that I had some of the top people in their chosen fields as my professors. I learned a great deal from these outstanding men and women.

The final year of that Ph.D program was hectic. While I could attend classes on a part-time basis for most of the program, it was required that the final year be full-time. That meant that I must take at least five courses, in addition to writing a thesis. Both Phyllis and I were aware that it would be very difficult, if not impossible, for me to carry this heavy load and at the same time meet my responsibilities to the family. After much thought we agreed that I would go to school full time while she and the children visited her parents who were living on a co-operative farm in rural Georgia. "Koinenea", a Greek word for love and brotherhood, was operated by Clarence Jordan, a Baptist minister who had set up the farm in an attempt to change the pattern of racial segregation existing in that part of the South. He insisted on blacks and whites living, eating and working together in an extremely segregated and hostile area. We were not quite sure of what would happen during that summer. In fact, had we really known of the actual danger we would probably not have agreed that the two children and Phyllis would spend the summer in that environment. Their experiences on the farm were dramatic and hair raising.

The farmhouse in which the participants lived was about a hundred yards from the highway. It also operated a fruit stand immediately adjacent to the highway where many of the inhabitants sold fruit grown on the farm. At night, hoodlums would often drive by and take shots at the farmhouse and the fruit stand. On one occasion, the fruit stand was totally destroyed. Fortunately no one was hurt. But it is understandable that many people living at the farmhouse were upset and frightened by this shocking experience, however, none of the participants left the farm and everyone vowed to "stick it out".

The experiences of Phyllis, Norman and Gregory were very exciting but also very stressful. Nothing else could be expected by an interracial group living and working on a farm in rural southern Georgia. The idea of blacks and whites living and working together was anathema to the southern mind which demanded absolute segregation of the races except in conditions of black inferiority. The founders of Koinenea Farm did not believe in the inferiority of any one race. Everyone, as far as they were concerned, was equal and deserved equal treatment.

The experience as a whole, however, was very worthwhile and necessary. It proved that blacks and whites could live and work together without conflicts in the midst of tremendous hostility and antagonism. Clarence Jordan was a man of strong convictions and a determination to do what he felt was right. He was one of the few white men who challenged the "southern way of life" and refused to back down. He represented the best in an otherwise inhuman system. In some respects it was an experiment I regretted missing. I'm sure that had I been there I would have had to go through the same severe stress that others endured. In spite of threats and actual violence, Koinenea Farm existed and continued its work for several years after Phyllis and the boys returned to Columbus.

I made good use of those summer months. I studied very hard, completed the four qualifying exams of four hours each, and spent hours in the library gathering much of the material for my doctoral thesis. I had already completed a research project, conducted by the use of a questionnaire and administered to a sample of adult students. The fall of 1957 was used to write the thesis which was completed in November. I was ready for the winter convocation to be held on March 20, 1958. It was a cold windy day, but we were happy that the long ordeal was successfully completed. A candidate of Indian origin and I were the only non-whites to walk across that platform and receive doctoral diplomas. I was now a Doctor of Philosophy with "all the rights and privileges and honours appertaining thereto"!

Although I had many reservations with respect to the overall atmosphere of Ohio State University, including the overemphasis on football, my career at the school had been a positive one. My main advisor, Dr. Henderson, was an extremely intelligent and caring individual. He was one of the most helpful professors I have ever encountered during my educational journey. Viewing the large number of apparently unrelated courses I was taking, he advised me to concentrate my studies in the field of adult education — the one option which permitted me to take advantage of the flexibility of that program.

Community Involvement

The black population in Columbus had developed similar social, economic and political structures to Chicago. Both had organized a chapter of the NAACP, the Urban League, black churches and other social and cultural organizations. Both black communities had problems with boards of education, segregated housing and employment. The major difference between the two cities was the intensity of conflict. In general, the conflict level in Chicago was much higher than in Columbus. Blacks in Columbus were much more apathetic and less likely to challenge the power structure of the community or to engage in confrontation.

It was fortunate that I found a lawyer in Columbus who supported us in buying our house. Stan Robinson was an unusual lawyer possessing a degree of militancy and willingness to confront the power structures. The necessary structures were in place in the two cities. The problem however, was while these structures existed in both communities, they were neither dynamic, energetic, nor orientated toward the achievement of social change. Barbee Durham was one of the few exceptions. He was an employee of the Ohio State University and therefore in a sensitive position. However, this did not prevent his involvement in some very important programs in the local community. Barbee had no fear of the local power structure, including that of his own university. I learned of his work and was invited to become involved in the NAACP shortly after my arrival in Columbus. The NAACP was, on the surface, a one-man operation, and Barbee was more than pleased to have others join and support him in the struggles in which he was so deeply involved. Shortly after joining the organization I accepted the position of chair of the education committee because the primary focus of the NAACP at that time was a struggle with the Columbus Board of Education. Columbus schools, like Columbus residential areas, were almost totally segregated. Generally, black kids coming out of black communities went to black schools. White children living in white communities went to white schools.

Norman was one of these few exceptions when he attended the public school in our neighbourhood. I am still amazed at the variety of rationalizations used by many school board officials, including trustees, to justify segregation in school systems in the United States. Here were highly qualified teachers, principals and other administrators, many of whom were graduates of the Ohio State University School of Education, who insisted that black and white children could not learn together in a classroom. In their view, there were certain genetic differences that made it impossible for these students to engage in joint learning activities. This concept of black inferiority was so deeply embedded in their total outlook that they saw nothing wrong with the public expressions of these attitudes.

I had heard these same expressions by public school staff and administrators in both Indianapolis and Chicago. On one occasion the Indianapolis chapter was granted an opportunity to meet with the school board to bring forward our concerns. We met in the local school cafeteria. Following a lengthy discussion in which the president of the board of education and school officials argued against the possibility of blacks and whites going to school together, I happened to look out the window and saw what was happening on the playground. A group of black and white kids were playing happily together on the playground. There appeared to be no concern whatsoever about the question of colour. I suggested that we go to the window and observe the children at play. There was astonishment on the faces of the school officials. What they were seeing was in direct contradiction to what they had been saying at the table. To my surprise when we returned to our seats, the same argument continued. There was no indication that these people had recognised the obvious contradiction between verbalizations, attitudes and direct experience. It was unbelievable! But it demonstrated the difficulty of convincing people that deeply held attitudes may be faulty or wrong. That experience taught me a lesson I never forgot.

Columbus boasted that it had one of the best public school systems in the United States. We found however that Dr. Fawcett, superintendent of schools, was as rigid and authoritarian as were his subordinates. A few concessions were reluctantly granted over a period of time, but it could not be said that a smashing victory had been won with the Columbus Board of Education. What was won was a few adjustments in school boundaries so that a few blacks could attend predominately white schools.

This evidence of rigidity by highly educated people made very clear the difficulty our education committee was to encounter. In spite of our best efforts, substantial changes in this system did not occur until almost twenty years later during the civil rights revolution of the 1960s and 70s.

I met Dr. Fawcett a few years later in another capacity. By this time he was president of Ohio State University. The NAACP had received a complaint from a black female student at the university. Her complaint was that she and a white girl wanted to room together in one of the university residence halls. They were refused permission by the dean of women. Our committee first tried to talk with the dean of women and got nowhere. We then decided it was time to go directly to the president of the university and lay the complaint before him. It was on that occasion that we ran into our old adversary, Dr. Fawcett, who did not deny the validity of our complaints. He simply denied any responsibility. He insisted that this was not a part of his job. The matter was entirely in the hands of the dean of women and she made decisions with respect to the residence halls. We were quite aware of the powers of the dean of women. We were also aware that the president was the chief executive officer of the university and could overrule the dean of women anytime he chose to do so.

This incident reminded me of my feeling towards Dr. Fawcett when I marched across the platform to receive my doctoral degree at my graduation from Ohio State. I still had a keen memory of our previous encounter with him as superintendent of the Columbus public schools and was thinking, as I marched across the platform, would it not be quite a surprise to him if I poked him in the ribs with my forefinger (non-violently, of course) as he shook my hand and handed the certificate to me. At least a bit of excitement might have been generated rather than the boredom of sitting and listening to very forgettable speeches by some dull and obscure business executives!

The unacknowledged factor in this situation was that Ohio State University administration was very conservative. In addition to a conservative administration, it also had a very conservative board of governors. United States Senator John Bricker, a right wing republican, was one of the most powerful men in the city and in the state. He had a tremendous amount of influence, not only in the community, but also in the university. Senator Bricker would not have liked to see the university permit blacks and whites to live together. The president was simply operating within the limitations imposed on him by a right wing senator and his colleagues on the board of governors. It was only after a considerable fight, over a period of time, that we were able to obtain a change in their decision. In the end the two young students were permitted to room together without regard to the bigoted attitudes of the university administration.

Unfortunately, this was a limited victory. There was little or no evidence of any overall policy change at the time I left the university and Columbus. It is clear, however, that our struggle helped to lay the ground work for more significant changes which occurred in subsequent years. Given the conservatism of the city and of the university, even small changes might be considered significant and very much worthwhile.

One factor I have discovered in my various travels, both before and after Columbus, is that even in the most conservative community, one can find a small group of liberal-minded people. Having been a member of the board of directors of the ACLU in Chicago, I immediately joined the local organization and quickly became a member of its board of directors. Therefore, I had very little interruption in my experiences with the Friends and the ACLU. However, the two cities were different and the problems faced by the ACLU in each city were also different. The major struggles of the ACLU in Chicago had been against various levels of crime and corruption in government. The ACLU fought to protect individuals against the excesses of government-operated political machines and manipulation by political "bosses". There were no obvious or high profile political machines operating in Columbus, although there were some allegations of widespread police mistreatment of the black population. Basically the focus of the Columbus ACLU was to increase the impact of citizen participation on government policies. It was concerned about the rigidity and insensitivity of governmental bureaucrats in the provision of government services such as welfare. It was also concerned about the lack of input of citizens in the development of governmental policies. The ACLU placed its emphasis upon expanding the participation of citizens in the development of a more democratic society. These were ongoing considerations and not subject to immediate and significant change, at least in the short run. However, the ACLU chapter and several other organizations became heavily engaged in the struggle against capital punishment during my stay in Columbus.

At that time the criminal justice system of the state of Ohio occasionally condemned convicted murderers to death. The ACLU strongly opposed this practice and in the 1950s launched a major campaign to abolish capital punishment in the state. This campaign involved coordinating and working closely with a number of other organizations including churches, labour unions, civic clubs and other sympathetic organizations. The campaign strategy used speeches, demonstrations, marches, the production of brochures, seminars, workshops and other public relations activities which aroused wide public interest.

The opposition was also intense and highly motivated. A considerable number of people, including judges, lawyers and police chiefs, joined the battle to maintain capital punishment in the state. Nevertheless our ACLU chapter felt that we had done a good job and that we had a chance of winning that battle. The matter would be going before the state legislature. We intensified our lobbying of members of the legislature and were confident on the date of the vote. As expected the results were very close: however, we lost the struggle in the legislature by only two or three votes. While extremely close, a loss is a loss and capital punishment remained as a feature of the criminal justice system in the state of Ohio. The arguments utilized to justify retaining capital punishment were very interesting. It was argued that the state would be victimized by rampant and unrestricted violence, murder and chaos. The fact that the adjoining state of Michigan had abolished capital punishment but had a lower murder rate than Ohio had little or no impact. We were disappointed but insisted that results would be different the next time.

A major event in the city was the visit of Martin Luther King in the summer of 1957. He was invited by a group of black and white churches to address a large gathering. Dr. King had made his reputation based on his leadership of the 1955 Montgomery bus boycott. He was not an imposing figure, perhaps only five feet seven or eight inches in height but he lived up to his charismatic reputation. His dramatic speech emphasized the importance of black people winning equality and freedom. That speech made a very strong impression on the hundreds of people in the audience. Although in my view not up to the level of his famous "I have a dream" address delivered during the "March on Washington" in 1963, it was nevertheless a tremendous call for blacks and whites to work together to achieve a greater degree of democracy and freedom in U.S. society. Those of us in the audience were deeply impressed by his commitment, his words and his reputation as a fearless leader of a movement based on the goal of improving the lot of black people in the United States.

Following his address a reception was held in which many in the audience could meet, shake hands and enjoy a brief chat with him. As famous as he was at that time, however, I could not bring myself to force my way through the crowd to shake his hand. I stood on the outside of the crowd and listened to him speak informally to people as they engaged in brief conversations. I heard him speak on television, radio, and in documentary films since the Columbus address and have read his writings, including his "Letter from a Birmingham Jail". I have never forgotten that first encounter with this man of commitment to non-violent struggle. Dr. King was truly a great man whose death, at the hands of an assassin in 1968, was a monumental tragedy for the entire country.

Departure and a New Challenge

I was thoroughly satisfied with the changes I had initiated at the Juvenile Diagnostic Center. I felt that they had made life much easier and more comfortable for both the staff and the children. On one hand, I was never quite happy with the continuing emphasis on security. I felt that it would have been much better for us and for the children, if there had been more freedom available to them. That was the negative side of my experiences. On the other hand, I thoroughly enjoyed my work with voluntary organizations: the Service Committee, weekend work camps, world affairs camps, ACLU, the campaign against capital punishment, NAACP education committee and other similar activities and events. Hearing Martin Luther King in Columbus was one of the highlights of that experience.

Nevertheless, I felt that the time had come for me to leave. In 1959 a new superintendent had been appointed to head the institution. Shortly after he arrived, it became quite clear that he and I were on different wavelengths. Apparently the other superintendent was removed because of the state's concern about the small number of children who were still running away. In addition, the new superintendent did not agree with our informal operation — for example, our diagnostic teams chaired by any member of the professional staff assigned to the team and elected by team members. He felt that only a psychiatrist should chair and direct the teams. In the view of many of us this was a move back to older methods when it was assumed that if a doctor or a psychiatrist was on a team, he or she would automatically be the chairperson. The pattern of electing a member of the professional staff to serve as chair of the teams had been established before I arrived on the scene. I thoroughly agreed with that concept and felt that this had been a step in the right direction.

The attitude and behaviour of the new superintendent and the changes he wanted to make at the institution, convinced me that the time had come for me to move on. In addition, I had already decided that I did not want my children growing up anywhere in the racist atmosphere of the United States. By that time, my third child, Renée, had been born. My wife had always wanted a girl. I remember Phyllis on my first visit to the maternity room, gleefully saying "Now I have my girl". That welcome event occurred on November 3, 1958. All of us, including the two boys, were overjoyed to have this new addition to our family. This event occurred before the modern average of 1.7 children per family!

I was very certain that I would not return to the South and my experiences in the North — Philadelphia, Chicago, Indianapolis and Columbus — had convinced me that while somewhat improved, the racial situation was not significantly better than in the southern states. I had been thinking of the possibility of moving to some other country. However, it was difficult to arrive at a decision as to where we would go. The only place nearby was Canada and I had very little knowledge of that country. It just happened one day that while reading an article in the journal of the National Association of Social Workers, I noticed an advertisement requesting applications for the position of Executive Director of the Windsor Group Therapy Project in Windsor, Ontario. This was very intriguing as I had not thought seriously of going to Canada although the idea had been briefly considered. This seemed to be the opportunity I was seeking. Phyllis and I discussed it at some length. She was not enthusiastic, but did not reject the idea of moving to Canada. We finally agreed that I should send in an application for the position. A week or so later I received a telegram, inviting me to come to Windsor for an interview.

I was not quite sure of the reception I would receive in Windsor since it was just across the river from the city of Detroit, one of the worst racial problem areas in the United States. As a result, I had some concerns about the racial situation in Windsor. Nevertheless, I decided to travel to Windsor and to explore the possibilities of working there. The name of the organization, the Group Therapy Project, was intriguing and had a different connotation than the work in which I was presently involved and I was also curious about the possibility of working in Canada, a bilingual country. Given the circumstances occurring in Columbus at the Center and having already made a decision that it was time to go, I decided to take the chance.

I informed the organization that I would come for the interview and received their consent. The interview went extremely well and I was offered the position of executive director with the expectation that I would report for work at the earliest possible date. It was a mutually satisfactory move — apparently the new superintendent at the Center was pleased to hear that I was leaving and I was more than happy to present my resignation.

PART THREE

Canada, The True North Strong and Free

CHAPTER 12 *Crossing the River and a New Challenge (Windsor)*

The family and I arrived in Windsor in mid October, 1959, in the middle of a depression. I had visited the city previously and had arranged to purchase a house on Randolph Street, only a few blocks from the campus of the University of Windsor. It was a nice two-storey, three-bedroom brick house. It also had a front porch, a feature very common to Windsor homes at that time. Although we had moved into a new country, we were only one and a half blocks from the Detroit River, the border between the two countries. We often walked out into our front yard and looked across the river for a good view of Detroit. The tankers carrying products through the Great Lakes sailed within easy viewing distance. Fishing on the Detroit River attracted many people, including considerable numbers of Americans during the summer months.

The city of Detroit tends to overshadow Windsor. My first trip to Windsor was by bus when I went for the interview. From Detroit I took the local bus which travelled underneath the Detroit River through a tunnel. Upon arrival on the Windsor side of the river, I left the terminal and walked on Ouelette Ave., the main downtown street of Windsor. I looked around and was surprised to see gleaming high-rise office buildings just a few blocks down the street. My first thought was that I had no idea that Windsor was so large. It was not so "large"; what I was observing was the city of Detroit across the river which at that point was considerably lower than the street and could not be seen from where I was standing. It was only later that I saw the river when I walked down the street for a better view of Detroit on the other side!

Although very different, Windsor and Detroit enjoyed extremely good relations. For example, the two cities held joint birthday celebrations, Windsor on July first and Detroit on July fourth. Otherwise, the two cities were different in almost every respect. The population of Detroit was approximately two million while that of Windsor was approximately 220,000. Detroit had a huge black population, while that of Windsor was less than ten thousand. Windsor was a quiet, friendly, and law abiding city, while Detroit was near or at the top of per capita crime rates in the United States. Shortly after I left Windsor in 1965, Detroit experienced one of the worst racial riots in the country. The number of deaths and level of destruction of property was unprecedented. Much of the bitterness from that destruction remained for several years. But Detroit also had its attractions, among them its less expensive clothing and other items. For example, I, along with many residents of Windsor, crossed the river to Detroit to buy gas which was less than two thirds the cost in Windsor, even taking into account the difference between the imperial gallon in Windsor and the American gallon in Detroit. Buying in Detroit and smuggling items across the border to Windsor was perhaps the most popular game played by almost every Windsor resident.

Windsor in 1959 was an "automobile city". Ford, Chrysler and General Motors were the "big three", all of whom had plants employing thousands of workers in the city. The other large employer, the Hiram Walker Company was a distillery which produced a wide variety of alcoholic beverages. Windsor was also known as a "working man's town". A great number of the people and particularly clerical workers, travelled across the river to work in downtown Detroit. Assumption University, now the University of Windsor, was also one of the larger employers. However, the university made little impression on the overall life of the city and there was little conflict between "town and gown". In fact, the overall characteristic was a city of ordinary working class citizens.

Most middle class business and professional people lived in three small communities: Riverside, Walkerville and the area near the University of Windsor. During my stay in Windsor, I did not discover a single area which I would consider as "upper class" or "rich". It appeared that the well paid automobile workers and the middle class professionals were similar in social status and certainly in levels of income. There was no wide and unbridgeable gap between the two groups. To a very large extent, this relatively high degree of economic equality was because Windsor was a highly unionized town. The United Auto Workers of America (UAW) was one of the strongest pressure groups in the city and surrounding areas. Its considerable membership and status in the community enabled the UAW (now the Canadian Auto Workers) to exert great pressure on the political process.

Windsor included people from many different ethnic backgrounds, including a small number of blacks, with Ukrainians and Italians among the largest of these groups. Their numbers and importance to the community enabled them to exert considerable pressure on public policy. They were prominent in the business, economic, cultural and political arenas of the city. The black population, although relatively small, played a fairly significant role in the community. Among its prominent members were a black dentist, a city councillor, a black lawyer, the city solicitor, and a number of highly respected police officers. Dr. Kenneth Rock was one of the prominent members of the medical community.

The prominence of these men, however, should not give the impression that blacks were well accepted throughout Windsor society. The black population as a whole occupied a low position in the social, political and economic structure of the city. For example, during my stay in Windsor from 1959 to 1965, not a single black was employed as a mechanic or supervisor or any other highly skilled worker in any of the automobile plants. The great majority of blacks were relegated to non-skilled and low-paid work. With few exceptions, blacks were also excluded from participation in the decision-making process of the community, nor were they often found in the mainstream churches, social clubs or civic organizations. As a result of exclusion the small black population had established its own organizational structures.

Windsor Group Therapy Project

The Windsor Group Therapy Project used a psychological approach to solve individual problems. The program was based upon an analysis of the behavioural problems of school children referred by their individual schools and boards of education. The organization was founded because of a concern about the number of children who were exhibiting behavioural problems in classrooms. These children had been tentatively diagnosed as "emotionally disturbed". One of the jokes going around at that time was that children are considered "emotionally disturbed" when they disturb their parents and teachers!

The Windsor Mayfair Club had taken interest in these "problem children" and had decided to organize a program which, hopefully, would provide help in reducing these problems. Both school boards, public and separate, were very pleased to have this facility available so they could refer treatment for children whose behaviours were creating difficulties within the school system. Children referred to the Group Therapy Project (henceforth, "The Project") ranged between eight and thirteen years of age. Initially, only boys were included in the program.

The outgoing director was Bill Crawford when I arrived on the scene. Although highly influenced by the teaching of Fritz Redel, Crawford had also employed other therapeutic models in his practice. He recognised that "acting out" boys of eight to twelve were unlikely candidates for a highly verbal therapy model and selected the Slavson Model which focused upon the interaction of boys engaged in physical activity, a model labelled as "activity group therapy" and involved the boys working with wood, clay, paint and plasticine. It also included participation in games and other outdoor activities. The interaction of boys among themselves and with the leader, provided the materials for a diagnostic and treatment modality.

I initially agreed to continue the diagnostic and treatment methods employed by Crawford. Based on my experience, however, I recognized some limitations in that program and shortly decided to make changes. One change involved increasing the participation of parents. The importance of this approach was recognized but, in my view, had not been given sufficient emphasis by Crawford. It is not always easy to involve parents in treatment programs for their children. In general, parents wanted the treatment facility to deal directly with the child, not with themselves. Parents generally, and men in particular, do not recognize that the development of behavioural problems in children is related to the overall pattern of interaction within the family itself. Crawford had only a limited amount of success in obtaining the participation of a small group of mothers, and this for only one morning per week.

Upon arrival, I found three boys' groups were already organized, but there were practically no fathers in the one parental group. I decided to make a strenuous effort to change this participation since there should be, I felt, a specific parents' group for each group of boys. The groups would meet either in morning or in evening sessions. My goal, however, was far more ambitious. I wanted to have one hundred percent attendance of both parents in all parent groups. I also wanted to organize one or two girls' groups but after some initial exploration, I recognized that the time had not arrived to involve girls as well as boys in the program.

I had not anticipated how difficult it would be to get men to come out to group meetings. Even scheduling parents' meetings in the evenings could not attract some fathers. I had recognized that mothers were generally more likely to participate since they were usually more sensitive than men to the problems of their children. I felt, however, that some men would have concern about children in difficulty and would be willing to participate in a program designed to improve their understanding of child behaviour and attitudes. Some success was achieved in attracting fathers but not nearly as much as I had hoped. The participation of fathers was never more than fifty percent. The participation of mothers was much higher, ranging from a low of fifty percent to as high as one hundred percent.

I quickly concluded that we would not focus parent group discussion on the analysis of internal dynamics. My study in group dynamics at the University of Chicago had convinced me that the best approach to parent education would be through group examination of their own interrelationships, that is, through observation, feedback and analysis of their own behaviour in the group. Insight into the development of their attitudes and behaviours might be helpful at a later stage of group development. The groups should focus upon the "here and now". Although from time to time an individual wanted to go back and re-examine some aspect of the past, the focus of these parent groups would emphasize descriptions and analysis of present attitudes and behaviours.

Three groups of eight to ten members were organized and were becoming known in the general community. As a result several other parents were anxious to become a part, or at least to visit parent group meetings. One or two other individuals might visit and participate in discussions when invited by the group. I made it a practice to leave it to the group to decide whether they were willing to have other individuals sit in. It was their meeting and they had the responsibility for making the decision. We did, however, limit the number of visitors to a maximum of two per meeting. More would have interfered with the atmosphere of the group.

A number of models of group leadership existed and were promoted by different writers and practitioners. They varied from highly authoritarian models as used primarily in the old psychoanalytic approach or, at the other extreme, the almost totally leaderless group. In the latter approach the leader often played a very passive role leaving it to each group to decide for itself what type of leadership role would more effectively meet its therapeutic needs. The facilitator's role may be considered as between these two extremes and, in my view, was more appropriate for most parent groups. The facilitation role was the one in which I was most comfortable and more in tune with my own thinking and attitudes.

Various roles, however, were played out in the parent groups, particularly among the males. Often men who were obviously very capable looked to me as if I were some kind of god. I recall several of these men sitting back quietly, saying almost nothing and listening to any remark I made. After fifteen or twenty minutes these men would often repeat word for word what I said and then ask the question, "Isn't that right, Dr. Head?" What else could I say? I had just spoken the same words a few minutes earlier!

Women members of our group often played more varied roles which ranged from hostility to seductiveness. I had no difficulty with the hostile behaviour and was quite prepared to deal with it in a constructive and positive manner, often through jokes which relieved the tension and permitted the group to continue on its search for answers to its questions.

Most participants had limited education and, for the most part, the women were full-time homemakers or had part-time work. Most men were engaged in unskilled, low-paying or semi-skilled occupations. I did not expect very much of them, at least in the initial stages. I expected it would take several months before they could openly discuss their problems within the group. However, to my surprise, this sharing of experiences began to occur in the first two or three weeks for some participants. Some parents required a longer period, but positive and supportive interactions within the groups proceeded much more rapidly than I had expected.

I was finding that, in Windsor as in Columbus, I was rejecting most of what I had learned. Many of the boys and girls I was seeing at the Project were handicapped by serious emotional problems but in most instances, their parents were experiencing similar problems. Emotional reactions by parents to problems were, to some extent, transmitted to their children. The most important work I could do at that point was to help the parents deal with their own problems so that they could become more adequate parents. I began to view group and other therapies as merely substitutes for inadequate and inappropriate family and social attitudes and backgrounds. I wanted to move to a more practical approach toward planning and change.

The Maryvale Group

I felt from the beginning the need to have girls involved in the WGTP program and was informed by teachers and principals in the public and separate school systems that a number of girls were suffering severe behavioural problems. However, our financial situation was such that we were not able to enlarge our staff to take two or three girls' groups. Girls from the Maryvale School, a Catholic training school for girls suffering from emotional disturbances and problems in the home and community, helped to solve this problem. Maryvale was an "open institution" and did not have locked doors and was not surrounded by high fences. The girls could have easily run away from the school had they wished to do so. Apparently very few took the opportunity.

The girls, varying in age between eight and sixteen years, were served by social workers, teachers and psychologists and were under the guidance of nuns.

I was asked by Jim McIsaacs, the administrator and a social worker, if I would take on eight or nine of these girls in a therapy group. The girls would be chosen from among a group who were considered highly disturbed but who had some possibilities for attitudinal and behaviour improvement. I agreed to accept his challenge and the time was set for a weekly program. The girls selected for my group varied from twelve to sixteen years of age. The social and personal problems they demonstrated were very similar to those I had seen at the Juvenile Diagnostic Center in Columbus. Difficulties in interpersonal relationships included problems with their peers, teachers, social workers and administrators. "Acting-out" problems were only one symptom of their difficulties. They tended to "turn inward" which included self-inflicted injuries and other symptoms of deep-seated emotional problems. Members of the institutional staff were unable to understand or handle these incidents. It appeared as though the nuns were looking to me as their saviour and expected me to perform miracles in my relationship with these girls. This, of course, was impossible. At best, one can hope for gradual improvement and hopefully that some progress would occur in their behaviour and attitudes. Perhaps they would learn to cope effectively with their emotional problems.

I succeeded in establishing a positive working relationship with those girls, most of whom could express themselves in a highly articulate manner. The program was focused at two levels: first, a level of increasingly effective verbalization and second, an activity group orientation. As with the boys, all enjoyed a fairly high level of craft work and role playing. This improvement in our relationship, however, did not occur without some difficulty. Several of the girls were highly suspicious of me and any other male. I had to win their trust and this was not always easy. There were times when non-specific hostility was very much on the surface and I could feel that the girls wanted to express it. Much to their surprise I encouraged them to bring it out into the open. They "brought it out" with a vengeance! Their attack on the adult world was astonishing in its hostility, complexity and scope. Some girls expressed rage at every living adult, male or female. By the end of the second session, however, I began to sense changes in the attitudes of some girls. They began to tone down their harsh criticism and suggest that some adults in their lives had treated them decently and humanely. Within four or five weeks this group was engaged in a serious examination of the problems of everyday life, which included their relationship to the staff members. I heard complaints about teachers, the nuns, the male administrator (a good friend of mine), the groundskeeper, the cook and almost everyone else in the institution. I was the outsider who was expected to sympathize with them and to take their side against the staff. It took about two months before they were able to get the venom and rage out of their system, then they became more positive, looking at and examining their own relationships to the institutional staff and to each other.

Interspersed with these verbalization sessions were activities outside the institution. The school owned a station wagon which, with some squeezing together, could hold eight or nine girls plus myself as the driver. Unlike at the Diagnostic Center in Columbus, there was no concern about the security of the girls in regard to the possibility of their running away. It was assumed that I would drive the girls to our destination for participation in whatever activity I had selected. At the end of that activity, it was also assumed they would return to the station wagon and we would drive back to the institution. That is precisely what always happened. We did not have a single runaway during the two years I worked with them. Most of the girls were orphans: only a small number of them actually had a home to which they could return.

I thoroughly enjoyed working with these girls. In many respects I preferred that group to the three groups of boys with whom I was working at the same time. They were young, sensitive, intelligent and disturbed, but they were truly human. They had suffered greatly but were becoming increasingly open to new experiences and new relationships. I became a surrogate "father" figure with whom they could relate positively and openly. They looked forward to my weekly visits and I enjoyed the interaction. They had become "my girls". I am sure that some staff members had some difficulty with this relationship, but were not ready to express any overt opposition. That experience only lasted two years before I left Windsor and I was very sorry to leave them: however, many of the girls subsequently kept in touch with me for several years.

My work with the children at Maryvale School had not entirely come to an end. On one occasion the parents of one girl who was involved in considerable difficulty at the school called from their home, near Peterborough, and asked for a special appointment. Their daughter, Marion (not her real name), had been accused by the nuns of having attempted to push one of them down a stairway. Her behaviour in the school had reached the point where the nuns felt that it would be necessary to discharge her back to the home of her adoptive parents. I called the school and arranged with the nuns for an appointment with Marion before her parents were to arrive in the city. This would be the first meeting with her alone.

I waited for perhaps fifteen minutes for Marion to arrive. Suddenly she flung open the door and walked into the room. Rather than looking at me, she went straight to the windows and began to stare apparently at something or someone outside. She was a tall sixteen year old who had not been one of the more vocal girls in the school. I did not speak first, but waited for her to initiate a conversation. It took at least fifteen additional minutes before this occurred.

Finally she turned around and faced me. Her first words were, "What do you want to talk to me about?" I explained that I had been called out for a talk with her by the sisters because they felt that it was important for us to work through her feelings towards them and, more specifically, why she was so hostile toward them. I recall her standing there smiling at me as I related the reasons why I was there. She readily admitted what she had done and made no attempt to deny the incident since she was only sorry, she said, that she had not pushed the nun so that she would fall all the way down the stairs. In the group she had always been warm, accepting and easy to get along with. Now, however, she was clearly on guard and was initially cautious, suspicious, reticent and unwilling to cooperate.

After some time Marion began to "warm up" and to express her hostile feelings that she was an adopted daughter, she hated the school, she hated the staff and everyone she knew. I finally asked her if she also hated me. She looked at me in a curious way and said, "Well, perhaps not." This had opened the door to a flood-gate of anger and hostility. From this point on, my initial role was to listen to Marion express her feelings of anger and frustration.

I continued this relationship with Marion at both the individual and group level, during the entire period I was in Windsor and beyond. Her parents insisted on bringing her from Peterborough to Toronto, once I began working in that city. The relationship between Marion and her parents had not improved. She informed me that they drove from Peterborough to Toronto, a distance of seventy miles, without speaking one word. She was discharged from Maryvale but continued to come to Toronto, either alone or with her parents, over a period of eighteen months following her discharge.

I saw Marion after she had enroled at the University of Windsor and was married to another student but the marriage soon ended in divorce. She left Windsor after her graduation and moved to Toronto. I grew rather curious and, to some extent, fond of this unfortunate girl. Obviously, she was in great pain. She felt that she had to express this anger in some way and the best way to take it out was on people whom she knew liked her. On occasion she would try to bait me into becoming angry at her but I knew exactly what she was trying to do and simply refused to fall into the trap. Marion was trying to provoke hostility and rejection on my part which would have given her a reason for saying "Nobody loves me. I hate everybody." However, I gradually lost contact with Marion after her graduation. On occasion I would get telephone calls from her, usually from different locations. Following her graduation she had taken a number of jobs, all of which were of short duration. Finally she stopped phoning and the contact was terminated. I still wonder what eventually happened to this very troubled young woman.

Student Training

I had some contact with faculty members at the schools of social work at the University of Michigan in Ann Arbor and at Wayne State University in Detroit. Faculty members had visited the centre and were impressed with the work we were doing. They felt that the Project would be a good place in which to establish a field work training program for students in their master of social work degree (M.S.W.) program. The Project had always been understaffed to some extent. Therefore, the introduction of field work students would add to our staff complement. Having previously supervised field work students, I was quite aware of the responsibility which that project would entail. However, I accepted this responsibility because I always enjoyed working with young people, and particularly those who were in universities. I accepted one student from each of the two schools, a young man from the University of Michigan and a young woman from Wayne State University. Students spent approximately half of their time in academic studies and the other half in an agency assigned by the school supervisor in agreement with the agency director.

The supervision of students was not a very difficult process: however, it did require considerable time. A part of this time was given to the direct supervision of students in their activities as staff members of the agency. Another very important aspect of the supervisory process was the requirement that the field supervisor work in close harmony with the university supervisor. In this sense I became one of the part-time staff of the two universities. I found the supervisory seminars conducted by the faculty of schools of social work very stimulating and often exciting. In many respects they took us back to school while, at the same time, they were learning from our practical experiences in the field. I met some of the leading authorities and writers in the field of group work and community development during these seminars.

My position as executive director of the Project had brought me into contact with many of the leading citizens in Windsor and across the border in the United States. I was increasingly recognized as an expert in the field of child development and mental health. One result of this was that I was constantly invited to speak at academic and public gatherings and also was in considerable demand by local school boards for panel discussions, conferences and other education activities. These meetings were in addition to the two or three evenings per week I spent working with my own groups. Although I enjoyed this, it soon became apparent that this heavy work load was causing adverse effects on my relationship to my children and wife. Fortunately, the availability of the students from the two schools made it possible to change this situation. Initially, the students accompanied me and observed as I led groups. Gradually I began to withdraw from the groups and permitted the students to assume the leadership role which was one aspect of their training in the agency. My job was to provide guidance to students as they received that experience.

I had enjoyed the work with children and their parents at the Group Therapy Project. I had become acquainted with many of the leading individuals in education, social welfare, and health and with many of the politicians in the city during my three years with the Project. I had become well-known in the general community as a result of my professional work and through my voluntary activities in the larger community. However another challenge was brought to my attention when Clare Vinnells, the executive director of the United Community Services of Greater Windsor, asked if I would be interested in joining his agency in the vacant position of director of social planning. He emphasized that almost everyone was pleased to have me in my present position, but that I could make a much greater contribution to the larger community in the social planning position, which would provide the opportunity to utilize my knowledge and experience in the larger social welfare and health field of the total community. As my initial interest lay in race relations, human rights and social change, perhaps the time had come when I should move to the wider field of community and social planning.

Upon leaving the Project, I was given a very nice gift and a warm send-off by the board of directors of the Project and was told jokingly that I could leave on one condition; I would have to help the board find another executive director to succeed me. I gladly agreed to attempt to fulfil that condition. I had worked with a young woman at the Diagnostic Centre whom I felt would be ideal as a new executive director. Dale Swaisgood was just graduating from the McGill University School of Social Work and had achieved considerable recognition as a child care worker before returning to school for further training. I contacted her, and to my great relief, she was willing to accept the position.

Social Planning

In Windsor the fundraising organization for most social and welfare services was the United Community Services, now called the United Way. I was theoretically under the direction of the director of United Community Services but in practice we operated very much on an equal basis since our responsibilities were distinctly different. This arrangement could have resulted in some difficulty as we were both under the same roof and operated under the same board of directors. Potential conflicts between planning and fundraising were addressed by a separate committee.

The position had been vacant for several months when I arrived as the new director of social planning. It became my responsibility to repair any damage which had been done and to reconstruct the agency so as to regain public confidence. Thanks to the constructive cooperation of my board of directors, members of my social planning committee, and the general community, I achieved this goal within a relatively short time. My reputation as a leader in social welfare and in the community as a whole was of great value in the process of recovering public confidence. We were able to recruit several new members who agreed to serve on the Social Planning Committee. The Reverend Bill Lawson, a prominent local Presbyterian clergyman, was elected chair of the Committee and members included prominent businessmen, journalists, academics, social workers, directors of social welfare agencies and citizens. The major function of the social planning committee was to describe and analyze community needs, to monitor and evaluate community services programs and to recommend changes in existing programs or the creation of new programs to meet unmet community needs.

The achievement of these goals required close cooperation and collaboration between the social planning committee and local service organizations. It was obvious to me that the possibilities for actual planning or modification of local community services could not be accomplished in the absence of close collaboration and agreement. Agency directors were unlikely to cooperate in any attempt to modify programs of vital interest to their members. Without that cooperation any attempt at planning for the future would run into road blocks and would be unsuccessful.

I was largely successful in achieving this initial goal because my method was to meet with agency directors and ask for advice on community needs. I avoided any attack on present ineffectiveness and indicated my understanding of problems. After all, I had just left an agency with financial problems. The result was that the Social Planning Committee was able to achieve a number of very significant successes during my tenure as director.

One of my methods for achieving this goal came through the existence of a group of men and women from the social welfare sector, who had been meeting together for some time prior to my arrival in Windsor. It was through this group that I managed to make contact with leaders of the various social welfare and public health organizations in the city.

My success as a social planner had brought a considerable degree of acclaim in the general community. This reputation was built in part on the achievements made at the Group Therapy Project. Success in planning was not based on any special expertise but on my ability to develop positive relationships with the various men and women who headed community social welfare and public health agencies. The increase in my reputation did not derive from social planning endeavours, but from concrete achievements in meeting specific community needs.

It was common knowledge that aside from the monthly meeting of community service directors, little was known of the precise nature of those services. A mechanism was needed to address this need. I floated the idea of establishing a community forum in discussions with several agency directors and received enthusiastic support. I then took the matter to the social planning committee, and again received strong support. Reverend Lawson, chair of the committee, was more than helpful. He wrote and signed the initial letters of invitation to the forum. Since this was the first time a project of this nature had been attempted in Windsor, we were uncertain of the number of people to expect. Our fears were unjustified. The basement hall of a local Anglican church was overflowing. The meeting started with lunch prepared by a church women's organization, followed by an in-depth presentation by two staff members of the Children's Aid Society and ended with a discussion from the floor.

The forum was a tremendous success. It was followed by demands that it be continued on a monthly basis. Reverend Lawson, my secretary, Mrs. Black and I had performed the major part of the work. In the future, the work would require a broader structure of support. The social planning committee agreed that a forum committee with membership drawn from several agencies would be organized for this purpose. This step was taken and the forum grew steadily in popularity and support in the wider community. It had been in operation for more than two years when I left Windsor, and according to subsequent reports, continued for several years thereafter.

The planning committee also took the initiative in establishing a volunteer bureau and a community information service during my tenure with the United Community Services. The community information service, operating from my office and staffed by my secretary, began slowly but demands for its services had, in a few months, increased beyond our capacity to cope. It became necessary to recruit and train a corps of volunteers to meet the increasing demands for information with respect to community service needs.

Previously efforts to meet a specific community need revealed other unrecognized needs. Recognition of the need for information led to a recognition of the need for more community health and welfare services. It also became clear that Mrs. Black and I could not possibly add on these responsibilities while maintaining other tasks as social planners. We were trying to recruit volunteers to handle many of the needs of community and health agencies. That problem was still under discussion when I left the city. Prominent people and boards of directors of voluntary fundraising agencies usually expect that social planning will reduce the need for additional funding. Instead, unrecognized needs are uncovered and the requirement for additional funds arises. Raising funds for concrete services, however, is easier than for planning. The community forum, community information service and the volunteer bureau provided direct services to many individuals and families. They became an asset rather than a liability in fundraising and this helped increase the level of funding for all voluntary agencies.

Community Involvement

Being so close to Detroit and the State of Michigan, I could become active in both communities. The whole family could attend the Friends Meeting in Detroit or we could drive to Ann Arbor for a smaller but more active meeting. We also attended and participated in the Unitarian Church in Windsor — where we first met Howard McCurdy and his family. At that time, Howard was a fairly recent graduate with a doctoral degree in biology from Michigan State University, and a relatively new member of the Biology Department of the University of Windsor. Howard was the leader of the Guardian Club, the only race relations or human rights organization in the city. I had not been in the city more than a few weeks when Howard persuaded me to join the Guardian Club. One of my first activities as a member was to become engaged in "testing" various public facilities alleged to discriminate against blacks. Among our first targets were swimming pools and golf courses. Having been involved in "testing" in Indianapolis and Chicago, I was thoroughly familiar with the process and the dangers.

Windsor, however, was quite different from U.S. cities in which segregation was virtually total. Windsor was not altogether segregated, nor was it completely integrated. For example, I joined and played tennis at the Jackson Park Tennis Club without incident during the entire time I was in the city. On the other hand, other blacks and I were not permitted to play golf at either public or private golf clubs. Theatres had been opened but most nightclubs did not admit blacks. As a result I agreed to accompany another black male to test one of the better golf clubs in the city, a club which was partly subsidized by the city and thus by all taxpayers, including blacks. On arrival my partner and I were told that we could not play golf unless we were members of the club. When we asked how we could become members, the manager stated that we would have to be recommended by a present member. I asked to see the membership list because I had become well known in the city and was sure that the list included one or more members of the Kiwanis Club or some other white individual who would recommend us. That didn't work. He told me that the list was confidential. At that point both of us said that we were not going to leave. It was obvious that the manager didn't want a verbal confrontation on the premises but we were prepared to remain until we were permitted to play. The manager finally agreed to permit us to play for free if we agreed to never return. We did not agree, but he said "Go ahead, but don't come back." We did not reply but left the building and walked out to the course. My partner was an experienced golfer while I did not even know how to hold a golf club! With a bit of instruction, I took my first swing and completely missed the ball. By the second or third swing, I hit what appeared to be a great drive down the course, only to see the ball curve off to one side and into a group of trees. It must have taken me ten or twelve swings before I could get that ball back on the course. My partner was doing fine but we only played four holes; by that time I think my partner was aware that he was not going to get any competition from me. We had made our point and decided to go home. We had played on the segregated golf course and had not agreed to never return. We felt perfectly free to return at our convenience. That was my first and only experience on a golf course.

"Testing" that golf course was only one of many others, including restaurants, night clubs and resort facilities, but the golf club experience still stands out in my mind as unique. This is probably because I had no real interest in playing golf. "Testing" public facilities in the United States had a practical nature. I wanted to see the movie, eat in the restaurant or move to a non-segregated neighbourhood. But Howard McCurdy was a persuasive man, and the Guardian Club needed volunteers. I had no intention of letting the members down.

A few years later, and after I had left Windsor, Howard McCurdy was elected to the Windsor City Council and among other duties he was assigned to represent the city on the board of directors of that golf course. Bigots sometimes face unpredictable circumstances which, because of their stupidity, can be both ironic and highly amusing.

Through contacts with the Ann Arbor Meeting of the Society of Friends. I found myself directing weekend work camps in the Detroit area. The location was a segregated slum area on the northern outskirts of Detroit. I will not go into the details of that work camp: its pattern of operation was similar to those in which I had been engaged in other cities. My most striking memory of the many work camps in which I was involved was during the Cuban Missile Crisis of 1963. The crisis reached a peak on a Saturday morning following the arrival of the campers on a Friday evening. The radio news gave the impression that the outbreak of nuclear war between the U.S. and the Soviet Union was imminent and many campers were crying and wanting to go home to die with their families. One boy had brought his records which he played continuously. Whether symbolically or not, he played one record, "Hit the Road Jack and Don't Come Back No More!" continuously and until reports came that U.S. President John Kennedy and the Russian leader had reached a compromise and that the crisis was over. But the world had been on the brink of a nuclear war which would have resulted in unparalleled destruction and perhaps even the end of civilization, simply because the Russians were planning to install nuclear weapons in Cuba. This was precisely the same step that the U.S. was doing in many other countries near the borders of the Soviet Union. Hypocrisy knows no bounds.

One surprising aspect of life in Windsor was that it was there that I had my first experience with anti-French attitudes. From my perspective, that attitude was more shocking than racial prejudice and discrimination. After all, I was quite acquainted with racial discrimination — it was simply a part of the American "way of life". But I had never come into contact with bigoted attitudes by one white group against another. The occasion was the hearing of the committee initiated by then Prime Minister, Lester Pearson. This "Bi and Bi" (or bilingualism and biculturalism) commission held hearings at the University of Windsor. Anti-French attitudes were vocalized while many French-speaking people were in the audience. In the early 1960s, there was a substantial French-speaking population in Windsor and in surrounding areas. In addition, there were large numbers of Ukrainians, Italians, and other non-Anglo Saxons in the area. I had no idea why the venom of the local population was directed against the French. That was the first time I had heard such bitter words since leaving the American South. But prejudice and discrimination are irrational attitudes and behaviours which cannot be evaluated from a logical or reasonable point of view. It was also during that period that I read *White Niggers of America*, a title referring to the plight of the French-speaking population in Canada. I had no difficulty in giving my complete sympathy and support to the minority French population.

While I enjoyed my stay in Windsor, I still find it difficult to comprehend the nature of that city. On the one hand, it was a mild, easy-going city with very little racial conflict. Even with its strong union character, it appeared as though labour conflict was infrequent and generally "low-key". Windsor was largely lacking in the extreme poverty and the vast gap in income levels so often found in cities in the U.S. On the surface, Windsor gave the impression that it was a city of moderate people who accepted and appreciated each other but the "Bi and Bi" hearings at least partially exploded that image. Underneath the accepting and egalitarian atmosphere, there were areas of bitter hatred so characteristic of my experiences in the South. For the most part, those attitudes were kept under control and rarely appeared in the public arena but when they did, they could be vicious as revealed by attitudes toward the French population.

I had made the decision, even prior to arriving in Canada, that at the earliest possible date I would become a Canadian citizen. I had to visit a federally appointed citizenship court judge three months before my actual swearing in as a citizen. Having been in Canada for nearly five years, I was fairly familiar with the political, social and economic structure of the province of Ontario and of the country as a whole. I expected to be asked questions in those areas and I had "boned up" on the names of the provincial and territorial capitals, the names of former prime ministers and other basic Canadian facts. The judge and I never got around to those questions, instead we spent more than an hour in discussions of our personal interests in life, including our families, hobbies and other interests. Finally at the end of the interview, he said that based on our discussion, he would like to have me make a few remarks at the swearing-in ceremony. Normally he carried out this duty himself, but he thought that it would be good to have me talk about the benefits of Canada to other citizenship applicants. I agreed to that suggestion and found myself looking forward to the opportunity to address other applicants in the Canadian citizenship court room.

It was at that point that I had my first legal difficulty since arriving in Canada. There were two problems for me. In the first place, I had no intention of placing my hand on a bible and swearing allegiance to the queen of England. Somehow among preparations for taking the necessary oath, it had not occurred to me that I would be asked to swear allegiance to the queen. Even more distasteful to me was that I was expected to say, in effect, that I was a "subject" of the queen. I considered myself to be an independent self-directed man and was not "subject" of anyone and certainly not the queen. I made my feelings known to the friendly citizenship court judge and was given permission to simply affirm my allegiance to Canada as a country. The compromise was acceptable to me and I affirmed the oath of citizenship and became a citizen in February, 1965. What I remember most about that occasion was that for the first time, I actually saw a Mountie dressed in a red coat!

Nevertheless I had experienced that city as no other in which I had or would likely ever live or work. There was a "down to earth" atmosphere and a degree of equality which I had never previously experienced. Although blacks were not represented in the high-paying industrial jobs available to white workers, a result of limited membership in the United Automobile Workers Union, a few blacks still managed to achieve a degree of prominence in civic and social affairs. Dr. Ken Rock, my family doctor and Dr. Perry, my dentist, were both black men. Dr. Perry was also a long-time member of city council. Phyllis and

I did not join and participate in the most important black organization in the community, that is, the black church. Neither of us was interested in the religious activities of the black community. We continued as members of the wider cultural and liberal-minded society. There was no Friends Meeting in Windsor but we became active in the Ann Arbor Friends Meeting and quite often attended the Unitarian Congregation of Windsor. The relatively high levels of social equality and acceptance of most citizens of Windsor made it possible for us to meet and associate with residents of all levels, including politicians, professionals, business men, skilled craftsmen, public employees and members of a variety of religious organizations. Membership in the Kiwanis Club was of great value in that achievement. It was my impression, though, that members of various racial groups tended to remain in their own organizations.

While in Windsor I was invited to join several of the so-called high prestige organizations, including a part-time faculty position at the University of Windsor, the board of directors of the Windsor Museum of Art and the monthly meetings of agency directors in the broad field of health and social welfare. I still have very fond memories of my many friends and colleagues, who included Joyce Meanwell, Patricia Whiteside and others. Particularly close and cooperative relations were developed with the executive directors of the two family service organizations, Jim McIsaacs, administrator of the Maryvale School, and the sisters who worked with the residents of that institution. Anti-French attitudes apart, the city demonstrated the possibilities of human beings living in a city not characterized by rigid class and social lines.

Meanwhile on the homefront my youngest daughter Cynthia Lorraine was born in 1963. She became our first and only Canadian-born child. We were surprised when Gregory became upset. He had one brother and apparently he wanted another. However, he quickly got over his disappointment and the two became good friends. Cynthia, like the other three, was a strong and healthy baby, and rapidly grew up into an independent young girl. She was the only 'banker' in the family, that is, she saved her money while the others spent theirs as rapidly as they received their allowances. We could always borrow from Cynthia when the family ran short of funds!

My stay in Windsor was drawing to a close. Windsor was the first place after leaving the South in which I did not feel a sense of exclusion. I was keenly aware that many blacks were relegated to menial employment in low-paying jobs, but some segments of the black community were active and I quickly found a place in their struggle against racism, Canadian style! I had no dissatisfaction with my work but it was of great concern to me that my relationship with Phyllis had developed seemingly insurmountable problems. In spite of my training, my professional experience and relative success in helping others find solutions to their personal problems, I seemed unable to resolve the tensions in my own marriage. I determined that I would try a period on my own. As new challenges were lying ahead as in earlier situations, I was looking forward to those new opportunities and experiences in Toronto.

CHAPTER 13 *Toronto: The First Decade 1965–75*

The new assignment in Toronto was not a great or unusual challenge. I had visited the city and had met with the staff of the Social Planning Council of Metropolitan Toronto to become acquainted with some of their activities, programs and goals. I had also met some of the key players in the various social welfare organizations. My initial impression was that it would be much easier to work in Toronto than in the highly charged metropolis of Chicago. I looked upon the assignment with anticipation. I had been pleasantly surprised with the behaviour of the staff during my previous visit. They were bright, alert, intelligent and determined to do a credible job in the area of social planning. My experience in Windsor, however, had taught me that effective social planning is difficult to achieve since it involves the cooperative working relationship of a number of community health, welfare and educational organizations. The words "coordination" and "cooperation" are usually viewed as good things in which every organization should be happy to become involved. In practice, this involvement and cooperation is rarely attainable because most organizations wish to maintain their own autonomy and very few wish to risk that autonomy by coordinating their services with others. When I arrived in Toronto in March of 1965, there were at least four different organizations providing the same services to people with disabilities. None of them wished to have their services coordinated with those of the other three organizations in the same field. They were protecting their own turf. To achieve this goal would require a tremendous effort and real cooperation on the part of all concerned. I had no illusions that this goal would be easily attained.

In 1965 Metropolitan Toronto was composed of 13 municipalities which two years later would be streamlined into six municipalities, the City of Toronto and the boroughs of North York, Scarborough, Etobicoke, York and East York, then over the next few years the first four of these boroughs would each become cities in their own right, leaving East York as the only borough in Canada. The city of Toronto was the largest of these municipalities but other areas were growing very rapidly. The population of Metropolitan Toronto was highly diversified with thousands of people migrating to the city each year from various parts of the world. Changes in the Canadian Immigration Act of 1967 removed many barriers which had effectively kept most non-whites out of the country. A new set of non-racist criteria was established for the admission of potential immigrants into Canada. The result was a massive increase in non-white population in Canada. The majority settled in the Metropolitan Toronto Area. This and other social, economic and political developments provided the context in which I began work in the Metropolitan Toronto community.

After arriving at the Council and meeting with the staff, I felt that my most urgent task was to find a place to live. I decided to stay at the local YMCA hostel since I had left my family in Windsor and could manage temporarily in a men's hostel. As a result of its pleasant atmosphere and many facilities for sports and other activities, I remained in the hostel for several months, longer than expected. It was decided that the family would join me when the school year was completed.

The Council operated under the general direction of an executive director and a fairly large board of directors composed primarily of upper middle class men and women who had an interest in meeting the most pressing community needs. It included entrepreneurs, professionals, educators, labour union leaders, university professors and others. Programs were operated on two different levels: one focused on the needs for professional services in the areas of family and child welfare, health, immigration policy and housing. The second focused on community development work in the various municipalities of Metropolitan Toronto. My job, as director of planning and research, was, in cooperation with the project committee, to supervise the staff in each of these program areas.

Shortly after arrival, I found there was some disagreement among various members of the staff and that one of my most important tasks would be to try to mobilize this disparate group into a smoothly functioning, professional team. The position, director of planning and research, which I was now occupying had been vacant for more than a year and there had been very little policy direction for the professional staff. Individual professionals were doing as they saw fit with little coordination or sharing of experiences.

The executive director, Doug McConney, was engaged in his many tasks of fundraising, public relations and liaisons with other community agencies. With few exceptions, the entire staff had looked forward to my coming and gave me a very warm welcome. On the other hand, a few staff members had become accustomed to operating without supervision or accountability and demonstrated some resentment at the prospect of a supervisor "looking over" their work. I was not surprised at this attitude since previous experience in other cities had shown that supervisors of professional staff are usually viewed with some suspicion until they prove that their function is to support rather than to spy on the staff. Although members of the Council team, they preferred to play their cards "close to their chest" and not permit other staff and members of the board of the directors to become aware of their many activities. Fortunately, this group was very small and had little influence on the overall attitude and behaviour of other members. Nevertheless, the problem could not be ignored, and one of my most important functions was to discuss the various operations with each staff member, either individually or in regular staff meetings. My function was primarily to listen to complaints, to offer suggestions on specific problems and, in general, to play the complex role of supervisor, facilitator and counsellor.

Unlike responsibilities in Chicago, Columbus and Windsor, I was responsible for supervising the activities of an entirely white staff. Aside from one secretary, I was the only black on the staff but the former occupants of that position, Dan Hill and John Gandy, had also been blacks. I was following two illustrious predecessors, who had made considerable contributions to the field of social planning and had gone on to other important positions in the university or in government services.

A dramatic episode occurred in my relationship to the board of directors of the Council shortly after my arrival in Toronto. Leon Kumove, the housing consultant, had after a long delay completed his "Preliminary Study of the Social Implication of High Density Living Conditions" in early 1966. Leon was one of the two staff members who appeared reluctant to share his "work in progress" with me. The result was that even following several requests, I was never able to view or comment on the project. I could not meet my responsibilities for overall supervision of the project and his final report although it was my responsibility for deciding when the work was ready for presentation to the board of directors prior to publication and distribution to the public.

Research and other professionals were also partly responsible to project committees for the general direction of their work. This generally was a desirable opportunity for community input but it also had its limitations in that staff could play community attitudes against staff responsibilities. Doug McConney called a meeting for the three of us to work out a suitable arrangement, but the result was nil. Leon was relying on his committee chairperson for support in this matter. Again nothing happened following a second discussion. The result was that Doug finally decided that the report would be presented to the board without my assuming responsibility for its quality and contents.

The report was mailed out to board members prior to the actual meeting. As usual, some members had read the report, others had not. All seemed to be going well until one member began a lengthy attack on the report. He attacked its methodology, sampling procedures, contents and finally its recommendations. I had reservations concerning the study, but the attack was entirely unfair since the housing consultant had no opportunity to defend his work. I expected the executive director to spring to the defence of his staff member, but there was total silence around the table. It appeared as if everyone was stunned and did not want to take issue with the esteemed and acknowledged expert on housing issues in Metropolitan Toronto. The board meeting was terminated a few minutes later, and the matter was discreetly dropped. I was quite upset at the behaviour of our highly qualified board member but under the rules of that time, staff (with the exception of the executive director and myself) were not expected to attend board meetings unless one of their reports was under consideration.

My second reason for anger was that neither the executive director nor I felt that we could respond to the attack without violating existing protocol. The pattern of non-participation by staff, except as indicated above, was well established and rigidly followed. However, the tension in the room was palpable and members of the board were happy to get out of that situation as quickly as possible. I had wanted an opportunity to speak to a few members before they hurried out but there was no opportunity since the meeting was officially closed. Eventually the incident did result in some limited changes in the ability of staff to speak in defence of work they and their committees had completed. My responsibility to review work prior to presentation to the board was reaffirmed and made effective but I could not forget that attack on a member of the staff by a prominent member of the board of directors. I vowed that, in the event of another incident of that nature, I would indeed support the staff against unjustified board attacks on the quality of staff work. In this situation, however, the quality of the report was not up to my standards and it would have been difficult to strongly support it. Fortunately that problem did not recur during my tenure at the Council.

A number of other important research studies were conducted during my tenure at the Council. Among these were The Don District Study, the first large-scale area study in Metro Toronto. "Families in High Rise Apartments" also broke new ground on social planning research. Other studies focused on agencies serving immigrants. "Guide to Family Budgets", another important research project at the council, involved developing the criteria for determining the cost of living, for families in Metropolitan Toronto. Many of the research methods and findings of those studies were adopted by Statistics Canada in the development of its publication relating to the cost of living.

Relationships with the United Way

One of the most important functions of a social planning organization is to develop positive relationships with a variety of community organizations and groups. The United Way, as a major fund raising organization for voluntary agencies in the community, was one of the most important of these community agencies. My relationship with other agencies in the health, welfare and education fields was generally extremely positive and constructive. On the other hand, I had some difficulties in my relationship with the United Way.

I felt that the director of the United Way was overbearing, aggressive and demanding because quite often he summoned Doug McConney to his office for a meeting and on a number of occasions I was invited to go along to these meetings. His "summons" to Doug usually meant that he had something he wanted to complain about. He was not altogether happy with the way the Council operated and it became quite clear that he felt that it should operate under his control and direction. Demands were made to change the Council's values, goals and methods of operation to make them more in conformity with those of the

United Way. His major objection to our work was that he felt we were too concerned with human values. He said that our most important task was to support the efforts of the United Way to raise adequate funds in support of the many United Way member agencies. We agreed with this view in part but insisted that our function was different. It was not to raise funds, but through good planning to ensure that funds were being spent in the most effective manner. Mr. Yerger could never completely agree with this assessment. Difficulties in our relationship with The United Way arose when it became quite clear that it was I who disagreed most strongly with his views. Doug and I were in total agreement but he was somewhat reluctant to voice his views. I had made no attempt to convert John Yerger to my views; I had simply resisted his attempts to convert me to his!

There have been very few people in my life whom I have neither liked nor respected, but John Yerger was one of them. It became clear that our relationship would be a turbulent one because I saw John Yerger as an arrogant man who wished to control not only the Council but also the other member agencies of The United Way, a desire based on the fact that The United Way was the primary source of most funds for member agencies. The responsibility of the Council for the quality of services provided to people in need was paramount. Those two objectives did not always coincide.

Their role as leaders of the corporate community makes it difficult for United Way board members to understand the need for "maximum citizen participation" and involvement in decision making in programs designed for their benefit. On one occasion, a member of the Council's board of directors and also of the board of The United Way explained his view as follows: "They don't need to be consulted, we know what is best for them." Nevertheless, we on the Council staff had to work with these board members, most of whom were men of influence and power.

During the time I was with the Council, the organization was under the distinct impression that the United Way upper echelons, if at all possible, would like to eliminate the Council which was seen by them as an irritant, whose major purpose was to upset the status quo, which would antagonize its corporate leadership and thus reduce their fundraising capacities. We never had the opportunity to meet with the United Way Board and thus could not test these perceptions. These men actually believed in their right to control since they were products of an earlier era and had not recognized the changes occurring in society.

It is easy to understand why business executives felt that way. After all, these were the 1960s, a period in which there was a tremendous amount of social and political upheaval. The civil rights movement in the United States was moving at a tremendous pace. Institutions and organizations were under constant attack by students and others demanding participation in the planning and control of them. The spirit which motivated the efforts in the United States spilled over into Canada. Educational institutions, social agencies, health organizations and corporations were not exempted from this challenge. The cry for citizen participation in mainstream organizations was insistent and continuous and was not to be satisfied until at least some changes in organizational structures and programs were made. In spite of its generally liberal and progressive stance, however, the Council did not escape demands for increased participation by the disabled, women's groups and the underprivileged.

As a result, the 1969 Annual General Meeting (AGM) was disrupted by "militants" demanding certain changes in the constitution and operation of the Council. The Council leadership was accused of being elitist, uncaring and ignorant of the needs of ordinary people whom it was supposedly designed to serve. The chairperson of the meeting, a prominent lawyer, was finally forced to admit that the election procedure did, in fact, eliminate poor or underprivileged people from election to the board of directors. For the first time in its history, the AGM of the board of directors and membership was terminated with the understanding that another meeting would be held in the near future.

The hostile attitudes towards the Council and other organizations reflected in that meeting provoked considerable discussion within the council staff and by members of outside groups. Some weeks later, another AGM was held in which calm prevailed. Some new members were elected to the board of directors, although not in the numbers which protestors had expected. As a result of complaints, one elected member of the board gave up his seat so that a single parent welfare mother could be nominated and elected to that position. Unfortunately, she was the only welfare mother elected among the new members and participated in only one meeting of the board subsequent to that AGM. She said that she was unable to attend meetings simply because she could not afford the fees for babysitters and, in addition, she could not afford to dress in a suitable manner for such occasions. She then offered her resignation thereby ending what might have been a substantial change in the thinking and programs of the Council.

I had previously been approached and asked to support the activities of the protesting group. However, as a member of the staff, I did not feel that it was appropriate for me to be publicly associated with the protesting groups. Although I sympathized with their goals, if not with their methods of operation, I have always preferred calm and what I call reasonable discussion rather than denunciations, charges of bad faith and reckless rhetoric. Nevertheless, I recognized that the goals of this group were similar to my own and so I made an attempt to offer whatever support I could to attain their goals, but with the proviso that I would not be a part of what I considered to be unrealistic and unreasonable actions. It seemed to me that I should be ready to resign from the Council staff if I accepted the request for a public protest against policies and programs in which I had been directly involved.

My background was not that of a bureaucrat sitting inside an office behind a desk, rather it was one of community activism. It was not very long after my arrival that I became involved in this process in Metro Toronto. I did not make a conscious decision, but events led me into the community. This movement, however, was done carefully and with the full support of the appropriate staff. A community development staff worker was assigned to each of the six municipalities in Metropolitan Toronto and these were supported by experts in various fields of activity. Both community development workers and those with expertise in a given area of service were involved in working with local community groups. I found myself being frequently invited to attend meetings of their groups. I never questioned why I was invited to meetings which were already in operation and apparently doing fairly well. However, I suspect that it was because the staff involved felt that my presence would bring additional support to his or her position on a given issue. In time, visitation to these community groups led to my being invited to attend larger conferences, workshops and other community meetings.

Political Involvement

I am clearly a political man but one who has never been an active member of a political party. I have occasionally supported parties in the United States and Canada, and it was interesting that I was invited to speak to policy conventions of the three major Canadian parties in the 1970s. The first was when Bob Stanfield was leader of the Progressive Conservative Party. Gordon Fairweather, the newly appointed director of the Canadian Human Rights Commission and I shared the platform, having been invited by the Youth Committee of the party.

I cannot remember the exact topic of our discussion but my colleague and I were on the same general wavelength. The group of approximately 200 young conservatives asked a few questions regarding my comments but their major target was Gordon Fairweather, probably because he was one of them. His speech, like mine, was about human rights, decidedly not conservative. I supported his position on a number of occasions but Gordon handled himself extremely well and needed little help from me.

My meeting with a policy group of the Liberal Party of Canada was quite different. A plane load of Liberals and I flew out to Harrison Hot Springs in picturesque British Columbia to a policy convention whose keynote speaker was the new prime minister, Pierre Trudeau. Depending on how one views the situation, I had the good, or bad luck to speak on a panel immediately following the highly unusual, at least in my experience, address by Trudeau. There were only a few reactions to my comments at the meeting but I was cornered and questioned by several delegates following the formal session. I was well prepared and had no difficulty responding to questions and comments, most of which were not at all hostile.

The three days of policy discussions were often heated and intense and I was struck by the wide variety of views expressed by several delegates. Obviously the Liberal Party was as divided on major social issues as were the conservatives, but I enjoyed meeting and discussing issues with some of the top officials of the party.

My meeting with a group of New Democrats was less formally structured and was held in one of the colleges of the University of Toronto. The controversy regarding the "Waffle", a group which was making a concerted attempt to push the party further to the left, was in full swing. I spoke to this group of regular NDP members and to their more militant opponents, both of whom I felt were making an attempt to enlist my support for their cause. Jim Laxer, a subsequent contender for the leadership of the party, Mel Watkins, an economist at the University of Toronto, and other party leaders gave a mixed reception to my remarks which were focused largely on social justice issues. None of the participants attacked my views, but there were many differences in attitudes and approaches to achieving social, economic and political change. I could approve of many of the changes sought by the "Waffle" group but had considerable difficulty with their methods, i.e., organizing an opposition party within the New Democratic Party. They wanted the support and backing of the party while, at the same time, making a determined attempt to force changes which, in all likelihood, would have driven many of its loyal supporters from the party, for example, their position on the nationalization of industry. Stephen Lewis, then leader of the Ontario NDP, was one of the leaders who finally demanded their disbandment. But before giving up its struggle to reform the party, the Waffle had raised some extremely important issues which were in need of vigorous debate. In that sense the Waffle made an important contribution to the discussion of vital public issues.

Although I gained a considerable reputation as a social critic, two of my speeches resulted in considerable public concern and muted criticism. One speech was delivered in Hamilton, Ontario at a meeting of police constables and senior officers. I criticized two aspects of police operation and structure. First, I asked why it was necessary for the police to be organized on a military basis. I pointed out that, as far as the public could see, the police department in any given city was a para-military organization. The "cops" and "robbers" concept was out of date in the highly complex societies of today. The need for police with specialized training to deal with increasing "white collar" crime was obvious. Why then the need for drill and other forms of military training? Secondly, I was concerned that a police officer was not allowed to speak on any public issue, unless he or she had prior permission from a senior official. I could not understand why an individual once he or she was a member of the force, lost the right to free speech. I pointed out that the bottom level of police officers worked directly with people on the streets and in communities. They had a much clearer idea of the problems they faced than their senior officers. I suggested that the time had arrived to reexamine the British concept of the officer being the servant of the state but having no voice in the decisions which affected his or her life as a citizen in the community.

The next day, the *Globe and Mail*, self appointed as "Canada's national newspaper", ran an article covering some of the points in my speech. The council, and my office particularly, were flooded with telephone calls from those who agreed with what I had said and those who did not. Some callers expressed the view that rigid discipline was necessary and if the police were given some right to free speech, it would undermine the whole system of law enforcement. A few police officers called to indicate their agreement with my views, but made it very clear that they did not want to be identified, a clear reflection of the fear felt by the lower echelons of the force. Although some of my opponents felt that I was trying to undermine the effectiveness of the police, other callers felt that my suggestion would lead to increased sensitivity and greater effectiveness on the part of the police.

I was repeatedly reminded that the British tradition of law enforcement required neutrality. Public servants should not be allowed to speak their mind on matters of public importance. While obviously there are and should be some limits to freedom of speech, these limits should be based on reasonable and accepted definitions of the concept of "clear and present danger". A reasonable understanding of the importance of this very vital right is an essential requirement of a "free and democratic society".

A second and more humorous area of controversy grew out of the speech I made to the North York Family Service Association in one of its annual general meetings. The focus of that discussion was the problems of adolescents in modern society. I pointed out that the cultural mores and practices in the South Pacific island of Samoa were quite different from the normal pattern of behaviour expected in North America. I cited the fact that Margaret Mead, an anthropologist, had studied the sexual behaviour of adolescents in that island. Among other items, she had found a great deal of sexual freedom was permitted to adolescents. Later in the address, I cited findings of recent research related to the sexual behaviour of adolescents in Canadian and North American society. I had placed my remarks in the context of changing marital and sexual mores that had developed in different cultures and at different times throughout human history.

The next day one newspaper carried the headline that I had advocated that teenagers in North America should behave similarly to those in Samoa, an example which indicates the damage that can be done when material from one context is added to material from another and the suggestion is made that both are linked. The article did not arouse an outcry, but I was the subject of a great deal of teasing because of my presumed advocacy of teenage sexual promiscuity!

It was in that address that I made my first public statement of my views on the equality of women. I pointed out that it was difficult to understand why women passively accepted their stereotypical portrayals in the mass media. I noted that women were rarely seen in prestigious occupations or in situations in which they had some degree of authority. Most portrayals of women in mass media advertising or in drama, placed them in a secondary and inferior position. I wondered why so many women went into nursing rather than into medicine as doctors and particularly as specialists in certain areas of medicine. I noted that while the men could be ordinary in appearance, women in the mass media had to always be young and beautiful. I suggested that my host, the North York Family Service Association, should begin to look at services to women in terms of helping them to project themselves as fully functioning and intelligent human beings. This suggestion was in direct contrast to services provided by most social service agencies, most of which were focused on helping women to cope with serious community and individual problems. That part of my address was never mentioned in the daily press, probably because it did not focus on female sexuality!

Youth Corps and John Howard Griffin

I had a telephone call in the early spring of 1967 from a man who identified himself as a Catholic priest. I was puzzled but invited him to stop by my office at the council. He was a tall, serious appearing man who wasted no time. He was director of Youth Corps, a Catholic youth group and wanted me to meet and speak to his group regarding social problems in the downtown area of the city. Members of Youth Corps, he informed me, were young, middle-class kids who were getting their first view of life in Toronto's poverty ghetto. His group was serving meals to homeless men at the Good Shepherd Refuge Centre on Queen St. East. The young people were shocked at what they had seen and experienced.

My agreement to meet with his youth group was the beginning of a lengthy relationship with Father Tom McKillop (better known as Father Tom) and his high-spirited Youth Corps. Although I was not a Catholic I was intrigued with what Father Tom was doing with this group. It became common knowledge that many priests were not overly pleased with the success of his work. He was attracting scores of youth when many parish priests were unable to interest their own young people. I had never met a man who had such success in attracting and inspiring young people and it was certainly not because of overwhelming oratory, it was a simple, complete faith and attachment to basic Christianity and a love of young people. They adored him in turn and so did their parents.

Meeting with and trying to help young people understand the nature of a socio/economic system which provided great wealth to some while others lived in desperate poverty was not easy. These were committed young Christians who could clearly see through the rationalizations and justifications of those who supported a system which was and is, clearly not based on Christian principles of love, mutual support, charity and cooperation. It was painful to observe their reactions to knowledge of the reality of modern society in which they were growing into adolescence and young adulthood.

Family camps at the Sisters of the Good Shepherd retreat centre near the small village of Sharon, Ontario provided the setting of another aspect of the work of Youth Corps. I agreed to participate in a family camp but was surprised to find that I was committing myself to five early morning sessions thirty five miles north of Toronto, which meant getting up at approximately six a.m. and meeting with two to three hundred men, women and children, most of whom had arrived the previous evening and had camped out overnight. They were in a festive mood, singing, stamping their feet and generally having a great time.

I was totally surprised when I was introduced by one of the young people. I had been involved in dozens of public speeches over a period of twenty-five or more years, but I had never seen or heard the enthusiasm or the warm welcome I received when I ended my speech to thunderous applause and then had to remain on the lectern for almost an hour of questions and comments, many of which were from priests and sisters. I remained and enjoyed a simple lunch with several members of the group.

Although there were mornings in which I reluctantly arose, got dressed and headed off to Sharon, the enthusiastic welcome I received upon arrival always revived my flagging spirits and enabled me to meet their requirements. I always enjoyed the lusty singing which reminded me of the old revival meetings I knew so well in the rural South. A favourite song was "Let Justice Roll like a Mighty River", usually led by Paula, and two young men with their guitars. That was a noisy group, but enthusiastic and friendly.

I did not keep count, but continued fairly frequent visits to Sharon. One interesting aspect of those visits and involvements was that there were always two or three black families in the larger group and I never saw a single instance of racial prejudice or discrimination during the seventeen year period.

It was at Sharon that I first met John Howard Griffin, the author of *Black Like Me*, the story of a white man who shaved his head, dyed his skin and travelled through the South as a black man. Although southern-born, Griffin had spoken and written against prejudice and oppression of blacks for several years. He recognized that he could not speak with authority until he concealed his identity and was viewed by blacks and whites alike as a black man. The evidence is uncertain but many feel that his experiment eventually led to skin cancer and death. Griffin was a totally dedicated man who lived what he preached. The success of his book had made him a very important man and in constant demand as a speaker on radio and television, and as a writer of newspaper and magazine articles. Although increasingly disabled by illness, he made every attempt to communicate his message. He was a man of extraordinary strength and commitment. The last time I met him at Sharon, Griffin was restricted to a wheelchair. His indomitable spirit remained until his death in the mid-1980s. Race relations and human rights lost a valiant champion with the death of this man of courage. The country needs many more men or women of his courage, insights, sensitivity and commitment to justice.

It has always been interesting to note how strongly the Toronto business elite supports The United Way. Obviously there was some motivation for this strong interest and support. My work with the Council often brought me into contact with many of these people. On occasion, I had mentioned my curiosity regarding their motives in spending so much time working freely on behalf of United Way campaigns. Many of these men and women were given leaves of absence from their jobs and spent long hours in planning and implementing the annual United Way fundraising campaign for voluntary health and welfare services in Metropolitan Toronto. My inquiries revealed that most of these women and men were interested in the United Way because they wanted to limit the role of government in modern societies. If voluntary agencies could do the job, there would be no need for the expansion of government services which would require additional taxation, a result which they strongly opposed.

Town Talk

Other exciting events were in store for me, outside of Toronto. I have no idea why my name was selected but two years after my arrival in the city I received an invitation to participate in "Town Talk", a highly unusual event in community participation. Lois Wilson, a relatively newly-ordained minister of the United Church of Canada, friends and colleagues had arrived at the conclusion that their community (Fort William and Thunder Bay) needed a community-wide discussion of its many unaddressed problems. The idea of engaging the entire community in wide ranging discussion of alcoholism, child abuse, broken families, delinquency, inadequate housing for the poor and other problems was virtually unprecedented in Canada. The ad hoc planning committee with limited funds, decided to persuade local organizations and agencies to hold their annual general or other meetings during the week long Town Talk sessions. I was invited to be the keynote speaker at the AGM of the newly formed Lakehead Social Planning Council and, on the following day, to speak to three sociology classes at Lakehead University. Several other activities were held concurrently in different parts of the community.

The planning council had limited funds so organizations paid the expenses of their invited guests. It appeared that although an active committee was established and was functioning effectively, the Rev. Lois Wilson was the guiding spirit behind the week long activity. Although physically small, she was a charismatic and dynamic figure who instilled confidence in others. Lois Wilson was the catalyst which made Town Talk a tremendous success.

Returning to Toronto following that inspiring event, I immediately thought of the possibility of holding a similar event in the Metropolitan area. My consideration of those possibilities soon convinced me that the Town Talk model would not be appropriate for the huge Metropolitan Toronto community. It would be difficult indeed to mobilize the hundreds of social, health and adult education agencies to cooperate on a single-week-long program. It seemed, however, that with the appropriate leadership the Town Talk model could be effective in smaller and perhaps less competitive communities. Apparently that leadership was not available, and as far as I am aware, no other city has accepted that challenge.

According to some of her friends and acquaintances, Lois Wilson was initially concerned with family, friends and the congregation of her local church. Town Talk opened her eyes to that larger world of community, regional, provincial, national and international issues and problems. It initiated a process which for Lois Wilson led to national and international prominence. She has never turned back!

Although recognizing that the Town Talk model was probably inappropriate to Metro Toronto, I was intrigued with the idea. It was at the back of my mind when I suggested an all day staff conference to examine Council methods, philosophy and goals. Two months later I wrote a paper which led to a major controversy in the Council.

In fact the most significant and controversial contribution to thinking in the social welfare field in Metropolitan Toronto grew out of the paper which was presented in the spring of 1969 to a staff seminar. By this time, Doug McConney had resigned and moved to Vancouver. Some of us on the staff, including Glenn Drover, had suggested that the time had come for the Council to take a new look at its programs and operations. It was agreed that a workshop of staff members only should be held to discuss its future. At that time, John Frei, the new executive director, had arrived on the scene and had taken up his duties. John had come to the Council from Montreal where he was director of a similar agency. His reputation was that of an innovative and creative thinker and we welcomed him with great expectations.

His appointment, however, was discouraging to most members of the staff. A few had drawn up a petition, signed by practically all members of the staff, asking that the board of directors appoint me as the new executive director. John Frei was sought out, encouraged to apply for the position and appointed. I was aware that the petition on my behalf was, at best, a symbolic act. On the basis of the reputation I had made in the community, there was no way the board of directors would appoint me as executive director of the council. I was not particularly interested in the job and am not certain that I would have accepted it. However, I did not want to disappoint the staff and had the job been offered, I would have had to make a difficult decision. Fortunately that was not necessary.

The staff seminar was held at Cedar Glen, a camp near Bolton, Ontario, within a few weeks after the arrival of John Frei. My paper entitled "Some New Directions for the Social Planning Council of Metropolitan Toronto" was distributed, read and discussed by the staff. During this all-day discussion, however, it became quite clear that John Frei was concerned regarding its contents. His concerns never came out directly, but were expressed by the manner and tone in which he asked questions and demanded clarification on certain points. My paper had, among other items, suggested that the council should play a more active role in the general community, focussing primarily on the problems of the poor, the disabled and the dispossessed. I suggested that we should help organize poor people and minority groups so that they could play a more effective role in the solution of their own problems. I felt that it was not acceptable for decisions regarding the poor to be made entirely by doctors, lawyers, business people and other professionals and rejected the concept that because these people had "made it", they were more capable of making decisions on behalf of the poor than the poor themselves. The board of directors was all-white and middle-class. Our volunteer program committees were also from that group. We were a group of middle class volunteers and professionals planning services for others but a truly democratic society, in my view, depended upon the full participation of all citizens.

A discussion took place following the presentation of my paper, in which almost all staff members participated fully. Although there were some concerns expressed as to how my ideas could be activated, there was general agreement that they were the direction which we should take. The staff appeared to be ready for some new ideas in social planning. The consensus at the end of that seminar was that it had been a huge success.

That all-day session at Bolton was held on a Saturday and was restricted entirely to members of the Council staff. There had been no board members present. Nevertheless, on Monday morning, I was summoned to the office of John Frei and to my surprise, he expressed great concern about the contents of the seminar and of my paper. Apparently he had been telephoned by John Yerger of the United Way complaining about my paper and the subsequent discussion. Someone had leaked the paper to the United Way, in spite of the fact that the seminar had been considered confidential and restricted to staff members. I was subjected to the accusation that many of my thoughts were similar to communism. John was afraid that the United Way, being very upset, might instigate reprisals at the council because of my remarks. I had no difficulty refuting his charges but insisted that the views of other staff be heard.

I had learned that one of our staff had taped the entire proceedings and demanded that this staff member be brought to the office and asked to play back his tape. This was done and it became very clear that I had not been advocating "communism" in my paper, nor had the staff been advocating "communism" or any other "ism" in their discussions. John calmed down and admitted that perhaps he had overreacted. The most surprising aspect of his remarks, however, was that he agreed with members of his board, that the professional and business community knew best what was good for underprivileged groups in society. The issue of participation by the deprived was to arise again and again. It was at that point that the thought came to my mind that I should begin preparing to leave the Council.

Three years earlier I had been promoted from my position of director of planning and research to associate executive director. This meant that the two of us would work in close cooperation. But it was obvious that we were not going to get along well, our positions were too far apart. Several staff members sensed what was going on and came to ask advice regarding what I thought they should do. John had expressed his attitude but had not taken any concrete steps to implement those ideas. It was not my intention to support a mass resignation of staff members because of the position of the new executive director. My best advice was that they should take a "wait and see" position until his intentions became clear. I felt that it was important for the agency to continue and to become even more effective rather than be destroyed. I did not point out that I was beginning to think of resigning from the organization. I felt that the staff was a group of highly qualified and committed individuals who in their own way were making a real contribution to the community. This contribution was still needed and unless things became worse there was no need for a precipitous resignation by most members of the staff. The heavy work load of the staff left little time for any considerable discussion of the matter in subsequent weeks. The matter appeared to have died down.

Poor People's Conference

The movement of the poor, however, continued on an increasingly intensive scale. I helped to organize and became a member of a poor people's organization committed to holding an historic national conference to discuss issues of importance to them. Led by "The Just Society", a term which had been popularized by Prime Minister Pierre Trudeau, that group had requested and received funding from the federal government. A newcomer to the city, Howard Buckbinder, an American activist, was employed by the committee to coordinate its activities in preparation for the conference. The committee was mostly composed of poor people, and members intended to plan a conference which would develop a strong action plan and to pass recommendations in opposition to present social welfare practices of the federal, provincial and municipal governments. They wanted the government to hire poor people as staff workers in its various social welfare programs and they felt that poor people should be given the same pay as professionals. Many members of the planning committee felt that the poor had a better understanding of their problems than did professional staffs or administrators.

After many hours of sometimes acrimonious debate, the final plans for the conference were agreed upon. Howard Buckbinder had played a very important role in helping the committee reach some agreement on compromising the divergent views of the poor and the professional members of the committee. I was in somewhat of a quandary as a member of the committee. While I agreed with the general aims of the poor members, I was certain that their tactics would be counter-productive and made a feeble effort to raise this question but was quickly shot down! I was certain for example that in the absence of political or financial power, governments at all levels would simply ignore their recommendations. A first endeavour should be to mobilize poor people for political action, become active in political parties and getting out the vote. Politicians recognize that in general poor people do not vote in large numbers, exert minimal political influence and thus can be ignored.

The grant from the Federal Department of National Health and Welfare provided $50,000 in support of the weekend conference. People were brought from across the country from as far as Newfoundland on the east and Vancouver and Victoria on the west coast. The first, and thus far only, National Anti-Poverty Conference in Canada, with 300 delegates, was held in Toronto in 1969. Major problems requiring action included inadequate income, poor housing and a lack of affordable day care. Having been on the Planning Committee, I was expected to make some contribution through either chairing meetings or offering suggestions to discussion groups. My interest, however, was not so much in participation as in learning. I wanted to listen carefully to what was being said by poor people themselves. There was no question that the people who came to that conference were angry. They felt keenly about the way they were treated by the welfare system and were determined to force governments to make constructive changes. From my perspective, their anger and discontent made it very difficult for them to think rationally. There was no possibility that many of their demands would be met. The government was not likely to hire a large number of poor people of limited educational and work backgrounds to provide services to poor people, neither was it likely to pay them the same salaries paid to well-qualified and experienced social workers. Poor people were not aware of what had occurred in the U.S. during the "War on Poverty" when a few of the poor were employed in agencies serving that group. Once they were on the payroll, the newly employed poor people began to identify with the professionals, thus in effect, losing their status as poor people and their ability to appreciate and advocate on behalf of the poor. However, it appeared that being together and sharing their experiences was a very important and significant aspect of the total weekend. Many participants shared a conference experience for the first time. Although the plight of the poor was not significantly changed as a result of the conference, it appeared that at least the government listened.

The proceedings of the conference received considerable publicity in the print and electronic media and this coverage aroused discussion among the public. One government reaction was to set up the National Council of Welfare, a new advisory organization in the department of National Health and Welfare (now Health and Welfare Canada). This new federal government appointed organization was composed of poor and middle-class professional people. I was among the ten middle-class professionals selected to serve on the twenty-one person committee. Members representing both groups were chosen from across the country. The first meeting of the committee, held in Ottawa, was an experience I shall never forget.

The middle-class professional members of the new National Council of Welfare were immediately attacked by some members of the poor contingent. From my perspective we handled the attacks in a very rational manner by simply listening and making no attempt to counter the charges made against us. My Quaker philosophy was of immense value as we went through some difficult sessions. Over a period of several meetings, the negative attitude of poor members began to subside and more constructive dialogue became possible.

It had been planned that anti-poverty conferences would be organized in each of the ten provinces and the Yukon and Northwest Territories. This expectation was not fully realized. I participated in the founding of the Ontario Anti-Poverty Conference and remained a member of the executive committee of that group for several years. It remained in operation until it was disbanded in the mid 70s. We were successful, however, in enlisting the efforts of a number of outside groups, including labour unions, churches, social agencies and poor people themselves but the stubborn inaction of governments after repeated efforts to push them into effective action, gradually wore down those individuals and groups supporting poor people's organizations in Ontario, as in other parts of the country. By 1974, the Ontario Anti-Poverty group was virtually defunct. Poor people are the victims of a tremendous amount of physical and emotional pressure. Sheer survival is an ever present problem in the minds of many who cannot afford to take time to think about the future, including organizing themselves into strong, compact groups capable of a sustained struggle. Unfortunately, it appears that this task must, at least to some degree, be shared with liberal minded people including professionals. This utilization of middle class professionals, however, is a potential trap. The anti-poverty movement demonstrated that many professionals, with the best of intentions, usually end up in control and the champions of the poor often become their masters. Professionals and other middle-class people are more likely to have the time and energy to give to a sustained struggle but liberal minded people should always remember the words of the "War on Poverty in the United States": the goal was the "maximum participation of the poor in all activities existing on their behalf."

The Council's and other studies simply documented what was already well known. The important concern at the Council was that studies could provide solid and well documented information which hopefully could have considerable impact on the housing decisions made by the municipal, provincial and the federal governments. The conclusions of these studies and reports were virtually unanimous. People with limited income very rarely could afford to live in Metro Toronto. The various levels of governments were unable to decide on building new public or assisted housing. Thus the politicians at all levels of government simply ignored their pleas and those of middle-class supporters who attempted to help them. "The walls of indifference..." as one critic claimed, "...were somewhat like a marshmallow". "One could drive their fist into that wall up to the elbow and nothing happens."

I have mentioned that working at the Council gave me an opportunity to meet and share experiences with a wide variety of individuals and groups, and on occasion, with staff members of provincial and federal agencies. My closest outside contacts were with staff members of three offices of the local city planning board who were responsible for developing rational and appropriate planning of the physical environment. The City of Toronto, through the impact of interested and committed citizens, had made an effort to involve local citizens in the planning process, particularly in the poorer and more disadvantaged areas.

These developments occurred during the turbulent sixties in which new approaches were advanced and old approaches and methods under continuous attack. The struggle to reduce the power of the land development industry over planning decisions was gaining ground but the planning process in Toronto and other cities was not the result of thoughtful decisions, but rather the outcome of the decisions based on opportunities for the maximization of profit. Their goals and those of the Council were in direct conflict since the Council favoured increased citizen groups. I visited and asked the staff of a local neighbourhood office if they were satisfied with the results of their planning efforts. They were not. It was agreed that social and physical planners would be pleased if forty to fifty percent of developed planning exercises were implemented by local municipal authorities. Since the Council's planning efforts did not always require the approval of municipal councils, the chances were that our batting average was considerably higher than theirs. Nevertheless, the social planning staff recognized the need for more research in community and small neighbourhood studies.

It was also at this period that I met John Sewell, Carl Jaffrey and June Rowlands, then actively involved in supporting the residents of the Trefann Court neighbourhood and who began their community and political careers while supporting poverty-stricken individuals and families struggling to obtain decent and adequate housing against the wishes of the powerful development industry.

The few available studies enabled me to interact with individual, family and community groups in their own settings. The opportunity to work cooperatively with other researchers was also of great interest to me. While I was the principal researcher and director of several projects, in practice I attempted to foster a spirit of cooperative teamwork.

Ideological attitudes, such as "it is the business of the private sector to provide housing for all", remained a serious barrier to necessary government intervention even when it became abundantly clear that the private sector could not (or would not) build housing for poor people. Someone had to assume at least minimal responsibility for meeting the needs of the indigent and vulnerable. I continued my involvement in the struggle although fully aware of the odds against success.

President Johnson declared a "war on poverty" un the U.S. in 1965 and our then prime minister, Lester Pearson declared a similar "war on poverty" in Canada. In neither case was poverty defeated. It was very clear that the war on poverty, or more accurately, the "skirmish against poverty" in Canada was lost: poverty had won!

Relationship

My regular schedule of activities in Toronto were extremely busy. The work at the council was taking a considerable amount of my time but I was still involved in many other activities including voluntary activity in mental health with the Toronto chapter of the Canadian Mental Health Association. However, not all was work. I had become a fairly good tennis player which was one of the best ways to relieve pressure or concerns about work. I simply forgot about everything when I went onto the tennis court. Playing tennis was also a great social experience where I met a number of young and middle-aged tennis players who were great individuals in different ways. The informality, the camaraderie and the simple friendship were important aspects of the game. I met several young women at the tennis court with whom I became friends and some of whom I began to date. We practised for weeks in preparation for entrance into a mixed doubles tournament. One of the young women, Linda, and I won the tournament. That was my first victory in an official tennis tournament. I was not a highly competitive tennis player. I played for the fun of it so it was a novel experience for me to play in a tournament and to actually emerge victorious!

The most distinctive feature of my relationship with Linda was that she was a white South African. I derived great pleasure teasing her about her South African background and joking about her taking me home to meet her parents. We knew that this was impossible because in South Africa I would not have been permitted to visit their home or to live in her neighbourhood. I still have that cup, not only as a testament to my skill in tennis, but also as a souvenir of my friendship with Linda.

Another strong interest involved folk dancing which I had begun when I was in Civilian Public Service during the 1940s. It continued in the various places I lived since. As in tennis, I found many folk dancer friends to be very special — most were friendly, open, outgoing and anxious to help those who were not quite as proficient as they were in learning the steps. In both the tennis and folk dance communities, most of us never knew the last names of our friends. Years later, when I met folk dancers or tennis friends, I would hear, "Gosh I didn't know that you were Wilson Head, I only knew you as Wilson."

I often participated in conferences, workshops and seminars held across Canada. It was at one of these workshops that I met my future wife. I had been invited to speak at a conference of Unitarians, a liberal religious group who believe in free speech and the freedom to choose and practice one's own religious beliefs and practices. Although I had become a practising member of the Society of Friends in the 1940s, I still felt it was important, from time to time, to visit and participate in the religious observances of other groups and particularly the more liberal religious groups.

I had already been involved to some extent with Unitarians in Chicago, Columbus, and in Windsor and appreciated their freedom from dogma and their willingness to listen to all views. There was no pressure on anyone to join a Unitarian church. In fact, they rarely used the term church. They usually called themselves a "fellowship" or a "congregation". My wife-to-be was a member of a Unitarian congregation and she had participated in a religious education conference to which I was invited to speak. The conference was held at a camp near Bolton, Ontario, approximately twenty-five miles northwest of Toronto.

I received a warm reception following the speech and later a number of people gathered around for further conversation. I noticed a woman on the outside of the circle and thought she was quite attractive. However, she did not push forward to speak to me although she had been taking notes during my speech. Normally I do not expect people to take notes when I speak, but on that occasion there might have been one or two others who did. I had decided that I was going to call her and ask her for a date after returning to the city. I called her a few days later, and following several telephone conversations and "coffee" dates she invited me to her home for dinner. I accepted the invitation and began a relationship which eventually led to our marriage a few years later. Attending that conference and meeting Sandy was one of the most significant events of my life!

The NBCC

For some time there had been discussion in the black communities across Canada of the need for a national black organization. This need grew out of the many problems which blacks had faced in Toronto, Montreal, Halifax and other Canadian cities. Many other ethnic groups had established or were in the process of establishing national organizations for the purpose of protecting and preserving the language and cultures of their former countries. In 1971, Prime Minister Pierre Trudeau announced his "multicultural policy" suggesting, in part, that instead of the melting pot theory promoted by the U.S., Canada would become a multicultural mosaic. The government would take steps to support the efforts of ethnic groups to preserve their own culture and if necessary to expand the teaching of their languages. A heritage language program was subsequently announced so that children could be taught their family's language as well as English or French.

This announcement was considered a significant step forward in the attitude of governments toward the maintenance of ethnic culture in a bilingual society. With the exception of a national organization of people of native Indian background, there were no national organizations among non-white groups at that time. By 1969, many black individuals from across the country felt that the time had come to initiate a national black organization in Canada. The black population had been in Canada longer than other non-whites and yet were less organized.

A meeting was held in Toronto in 1969 for the express purpose of establishing this organization. Dr. Howard McCurdy, my friend from Windsor, was one of the leaders in this movement. A major effort was made to bring black people from across the country to serve on executive and other committees. An attempt had also been made to include every black organization which had even an indirect interest in the field of race relations and human rights. Several of the organizations were not specifically "race relation organizations" as such, but represented a wide variety of groups including churches, businesses, social clubs, civic organizations, labour unions and even a newspaper. However, the initial meeting was disrupted by the efforts of several black students to force the group to address their demands.

I sat in that audience with my friend Wilson Brooks, who subsequently was appointed the first black school principal in Toronto. We observed, with concern and distaste, events as they unfolded and as it became obvious that emotional reaction rather than rational debate was taking control of the meeting. My reaction to this behaviour was to remain detached and only minimally involved. However, my experience in this type of atmosphere was somewhat limited since I usually avoided meetings in which I knew there would be a great deal of name calling, shouting, arguing and little effort to reach a reasonable solution to the problem under consideration. My general tendency when these events do occur had been simply to get up and walk out. In this situation I remained in my seat and listened to the proceedings throughout that Saturday. I decided however, that I would not return the following day and later.

I learned that on Sunday the group had finally succeeded in establishing the foundations of a new national organization, the National Black Coalition of Canada (NBCC). Howard McCurdy became its first president. I was not interested in joining the new organization. I respected Howard McCurdy and wished him well but I didn't see a role for me in an organization which was so deeply involved in what I felt were self-destructive activities.

Atkinson College

In the meantime, I had been approached by Dr. Ted Mann, a professor of sociology at Atkinson College of York University to join his faculty as a tutor in a class of six hundred students. Atkinson College, the adult evening program of York University, made it possible for adult students to obtain a university education. Ted Mann headed a group of four instructors who gave primary attention to the entire class. The format for the classes was a lecture presented in the early part of the evenings, followed by tutorial groups, each of which contained twenty-five students. My function as tutorial leader was to guide a group of students in discussion of the material which had been presented by one of the four lecturers in the class.

I began work as a tutor in the fall of 1966. This new, part-time position occurred while I was still involved in full-time work with the Council. Two years later, I was asked to take over a small class of upper level sociology students, the Sociology of Deviant Behaviour, a field in which I had studied at Ohio State University. I had achieved a certain amount of teaching experience in work with university and graduate students from several schools of social work and schools of education and had also taught the first class in social work at the University of Windsor when I lived in that city. That class gradually expanded to the point where it later became the foundation of the School of Social Work at the University of Windsor.

In the meantime, some discussion regarding social work at Atkinson College had occurred between the Dean of the college, some professors and the director of the college counselling program. Three of these individuals, Ted Mann, George Eaton and Dorothy Campbell, took the leading role in those discussions. This group and the dean agreed that a social work program should be established at the college and that the new program should not initially stand on its own feet but should be a part of the Division of Professional Studies. The program was initially listed in the calendar as the Program in Social Welfare Administration. Having been a member of the part-time staff and known to Ted Mann, I was invited by George Eaton, the chair of that Division, to discuss the possibilities of my assuming responsibility for heading the new program. This would require my resignation from the Social Planning Council and accepting a full-time position at Atkinson College, York University.

However, there were factions on the faculty of Atkinson College who believed that the College should remain as an entirely liberal arts institution. Several members were concerned that Administrative Studies, not considered as an academic program, already existed and the establishment of a department of social welfare would mean that there would be two professional training programs on the campus. These attitudes were complicated by the fact that the university itself wanted to establish several other professional programs, for example, medicine, law, and engineering. However, the decision to initiate the establishment of a department of social welfare administration had been made by the Atkinson College Council, the governing body of the college. That decision, in the absence of compelling reason for a reversal, remained in force since apparently there was no intention by the dean or anyone else to oppose it. Therefore, I immediately planned to resign my position from the Social Planning Council and to accept the Atkinson College invitation. I agreed to begin my full-time employment at the college in September 1970.

I began preparation for leaving the Council. I had been a controversial figure and had achieved a fairly wide amount of publicity for some of the positions I had taken. In view of these and other considerations, I was ready to make the move. I looked forward to working with George Eaton, the West Indian-born chair of the Division of Professional Studies. I found him to be a very interesting man who was totally fearless. There were still occasions in which questions were raised about the appropriateness of a social welfare department in the college. Professor Eaton always mounted a very strong defence of the decision. Nevertheless I was warmly received at my initial meeting of the College Council. Many of the professors in that faculty were already known to me through past contacts. Initially, I was expected to be under the informal direction of Professor Eaton, but that arrangement never happened. My program, as a section of the Division of Professional Studies, had the status of a professional program within the college.

One memorable meeting of the College Council occurred when Professor Eaton was absent. A discussion arose regarding the appropriateness of having social welfare and administrative studies in the college. Some members of the staff still felt that the college should remain a small, highly liberal arts faculty. One professor of economics questioned the right of the two departments, social welfare and administrative studies, to be a part of the college even after it had been established and I was already organizing its programs. He suggested that perhaps the College Council should reverse its former decision and vote to eliminate those two programs.

Having just arrived on campus, I was stunned at his remarks. I had no idea that a few members of the faculty still held such negative attitudes towards the program. Apparently most other faculty members were also in a state of shock. They simply sat in silence. It was during this period that Professor Eaton walked into the room and heard what had happened. He immediately asked for the floor and delivered a stinging rebuke to his colleague for trying to destroy a program which had already been approved by the College Council and by the University. I recognized him as a strong supporter and one who did not condone any interference with programs in which he was concerned. It became quite clear that while some members of the council were willing to criticize the program in his absence, they were not prepared to stand up and attack it when he was present. The matter was quietly dropped and never again raised on the floor of the College Council.

I began my term as chair of the department virtually alone as the only faculty member hired for the first year of the program. In addition to teaching three classes, I also had the responsibility of developing the curriculum and administrative structure, selecting textbooks, interviewing prospective students and other aspects of an emerging department. I also had responsibility for publicizing the program in the general community and was quite surprised and pleased to find that a considerable number of students applied for admission even in the first year of the program. Enrolment was increasing more rapidly than expected and initial plans for a gradual expansion of staff and new courses would have to be sped up. By the end of the first term, it had become necessary to hire one additional professor on a part-time basis. I selected Eileen McIntyre, one of my former colleagues at SPC, to teach a course on family and child welfare. Eileen became my first colleague in the development of a Bachelor of Social Welfare Program (B.S.W.) at Atkinson College. Two years following its introduction, the program petitioned the college and a university committee to become an independent department and to change the degree to a Bachelor of Social Work, from a degree in Social Welfare. The petition was granted in 1972.

The rapid increase of students created severe growing pains. It required some time before funds were available to meet pressing needs. An initial task was to establish an advisory committee composed of leading professionals from the various social, health and welfare agencies in Metropolitan Toronto. The committee met over a period of three years and front line workers, supervisors and administrators provided extremely valuable knowledge and input in the evolving social welfare and later social work program at Atkinson College.

It was a fascinating experience to see mature students varying in age from twenty-one to as high as sixty-five, attending classes in the evening following their daily activities. They were older and more mature than the usual day students and many also had extensive work and family responsibilities.

Having so recently arrived on the campus as a full-time member of the faculty of Atkinson College, I was not prepared to become embroiled in a political struggle which was splitting the faculty into warring factions. The occasion was the introduction of the *War Measures Act* in October, 1970. Speeches, rallies and mass meetings were held on campus and attended by scores of students and faculty. The campus was divided but a large majority, probably 80 to 90 percent of the faculty supported the Prime Minister who acted, he thought, to prevent an armed insurrection led by the FLQ, a group agitating for an independent Quebec. A British diplomat and a Quebec cabinet minister had been kidnapped by the small terrorist group (the Quebec minister was later killed), and the country was frightened and demanding action. I was, at least to some extent, caught up in the stirring rhetoric of the events. Although it appeared that the entire campus supported the actions of Mr. Trudeau, I was not convinced.

I had maintained interest in events in the United States and was aware that President John Kennedy, his brother Bobby Kennedy, Martin Luther King and several civil rights workers had been assassinated and there was no cry for activating the military to suppress murderous activity by a relatively small group. As a civil libertarian, I could not join in support of what I considered an excessive reaction to an undeniably serious but limited threat to public order and safety. It was an unpopular move but I joined the small group of faculty and students opposing the overwhelming support for the *War Measures Act.*

As opportunities arose I tried to bring some balance into the debate and refused to join what I considered as the "rabble rousing" tactics on both sides of the issue. But we were told that we were ignoring the fact that the country was in danger and had to defend itself. We lost the battle for reason and careful consideration because the Prime Minister, it was said, had acted in the defence of the country and anyone who opposed his action was undermining the safety of the country. The true facts, however, began to emerge and within a relatively short time it became clear that the Prime Minister had been given biased advice and had overreacted, with the result that hundreds of innocent people, mostly in Quebec, were arrested and held illegally. The FLQ lost its credibility and gradually faded from the political scene. Those were harrowing days and I among others was pleased that our position was eventually vindicated.

I was approached early in my career in Toronto by the director of guidance for the North York Board of Education who was aware of some of the work I had done with boards of education and with other community groups. He was in need of an instructor of a course given by the board for its guidance counsellors. The course was entitled "Mental Health and Child Development" which operated two hours a day, five days a week and for a period of six weeks. The director of guidance felt that with my background, I could make a significant contribution to the education of guidance counsellors and through them to the mental health of children. I was still working full time for the Social Planning Council and teaching part-time at Atkinson College, York University. Taking on this assignment would be a significant addition to the work I was already doing. However, it seemed to be a challenging opportunity and I accepted the offer. I found on the morning of registration that two hundred and ten individuals were enroled in the course. I had no idea that the class would be so large. Many were already guidance counsellors working in the elementary and secondary schools of the city. Others intended to become guidance counsellors as soon as they could become qualified.

In preparation for that course I went back and reread some of the old classics including the works of Paul Goodman, Erik Erikson, Hannah Arendt, Rollo May, Karl Menninger and Erich Fromm which I had utilized when I was involved in in-service training programs at the Juvenile Diagnostic Center in Columbus. Although there were differences in the approach of these writers, there were also significant areas of agreement. From my perspective, it was important to draw from their writings ideas which would be useful to guidance counsellors working in the public and secondary schools of the city.

I focused my discussions in three general areas: physical, cognitive and emotional development. In my view child development could not be understood except in the context of the overall political, economical, social and cultural development of society. As usual in my teaching, I brought my own experiences into the picture because it was important to discuss my own experiences and developmental issues as a part of the material presented. I hoped that my behaviour would encourage prospective guidance counsellors to think about their own developmental problems and successes as children growing up in present day society.

Many of these people with several years experience as teachers were now behaving almost as if they were children themselves. They expected me to be the source of all knowledge which they could take down in their notebooks and perhaps give back to me at examination time. This was a summer course and presumably teachers had time for reading and other forms of study. I had restricted the required reading to just two books, Fromm and Erikson. However, on questioning students I found that very few of them had the slightest knowledge of the contents of those books. Only a small proportion of the class had done the required reading. I was sure that they would have much preferred being outside in the warm summer weather.

I was appalled when I began to think of the implications of having to evaluate examinations or assignments written by two hundred and ten students. Nevertheless, I thoroughly enjoyed the students of that class, many of whom I met in subsequent years. My only disappointment was that there was not a single black or other non-white in a class of 210 students!

I continued working in this program until 1974, when the pressure of full-time teaching and other activities simply became too heavy. Also I was beginning to resent the fact that teaching summer courses at Atkinson College left me with little time for tennis and other summer activities. It had been a challenging experience except for marking those 210 papers!

The CCLA

Shortly after arriving in Metro Toronto I met Sidney Linden, a young lawyer who at the time was a part-time executive director of The Canadian Civil Liberties Association (CCLA). Mr. Linden asked if I would be willing to sit on the board of directors of the Association. The organization was in its formative stages and could not afford to employ full-time staff. I agreed to sit on his board and worked with Mr. Linden for a few months before he decided to leave. I had the advantage of having been active in the Chicago and Columbus chapter of the ACLU (American Civil Liberties Union). Following his resignation, the board was successful in securing the services of its general counsel, Alan

Borovoy, whom I had met when I lived in Windsor. He visited Windsor on a number of occasions in connection with complaints of human rights violations. I quickly agreed when asked to continue my membership on the board of directors and within a short period, I was elected as one of the vice presidents of the organization. The CCLA, under the able leadership of Borovoy, has made a considerable contribution to the welfare of Canadian society through its attack on injustices in a variety of areas. It has focused primarily, but not exclusively, on government wrongdoing with attacks on various government departments and agencies, including the RCMP and local police. It has protested infringement of the rights of women, native people, handicapped individuals and those of the gay and lesbian communities. A major highlight of the work of the CCLA during the 70s was its campaign against illegal behaviour by the RCMP which involved burning a barn, illegal wire tapping and breaking into and seizing records of a private voluntary organization. These were acts which elicited strong opposition and the CCLA was at the forefront of the struggle.

As a member of its board of directors and as a vice-president, I found myself listening to many legal issues of which I had little or no real knowledge. The CCLA was not an organization involving the widespread participation of its membership in its many and varied activities. That lack, in my opinion, was a major weakness. It means that one person and a few junior staff with a small group of lawyers are responsible for most of the activities of the organization. My basic frustration was that even as a member of the board of directors, not being a lawyer, I was not privy to much of the discussion of legal matters. However, because I believed in the cause of civil liberties and human rights, I maintained my membership on the board and as vice-president from 1968 to 1984.

I left the board and the vice-presidency with some regret, however, in 1984, when I received an invitation to join the faculty of the School of Social Work at the University of Victoria as a visiting professor for a one-year term. Sandy and I discussed the matter and agreed that it would be a good change for the two of us. The decision to go to Victoria raised the question of my continuing relationship with the CCLA and several organizations. This was no problem in my relationship with the Urban Reliance and other organizations. With respect to the CCLA I simply could have asked for a leave of absence or left the city without informing them of my absence, or I could have said I will be away for a year but I will continue on the board when I return. Some very prominent and important people sat on that board for many years yet to my knowledge never attended a single meeting. I could have done precisely the same thing. I felt there was little need of discussing this matter with anyone except the general counsel. I spoke to Borovoy about my intention and left the matter to him as to whether or not I should resign, take a leave of absence or simply disappear. I was not surprised when within two or three weeks I received a letter from him thanking me for my services on the board and as a vice-president of the

CCLA. I took that as a clear signal that Alan did not want me to remain on the board.

Alan and I had a number of basic disagreements on some important issues regarding the program and operation of the organization. One difference was the question of whether the organization should accept project grants from the federal or any other government source. Alan took a very hard line, saying in effect that if we accepted funds from the federal government, we would be compromised and lose our ability to attack what we considered as unjust laws or unjust behaviour by that same government. I took the position that many other organizations, including the Urban Alliance, the National Black Coalition of Canada, and various international aid and other organizations in which I was a member, accepted project funding from the federal and provincial governments. None of these organizations had found it impossible to criticize government when they felt that criticism was due.

My other reason for dissatisfaction was more basic. While I agreed with what the organization was doing in relationship to the problems of the lesbian and gay community, issues relating to women's rights, native peoples, and the violation of basic rights by the RCMP, I was becoming increasingly dissatisfied that practically no attention was paid to the serious discrimination against blacks and other non-whites in Metropolitan Toronto and in Canada as a whole. This lack of interest was one of the reasons why a group of us felt the need to initiate an organization to protect the rights of non-whites in Metropolitan Toronto. Our general counsel expressed some objection to the formation of this organization on the basis that there was no need for a new organization of this type. In his view, the CCLA could handle problems related to the unjust treatment of blacks and other non-whites. Fortunately, this was one of the few times the executive committee disagreed with his position. One member of the executive committee, Terry Meagher, a labour union official, and I were founding members of the Urban Alliance on Race Relations.

In addition, the board of directors of the CCLA was "lily white", except me and one other black member, Bromley Armstrong, and I had never seen him at a meeting during my entire sixteen years on the board. He was, however, a high profile social activist in the struggle against racial discrimination in the Toronto community. It was probably for that reason that the name of Bromley remained on the letter head of the organization during my tenure. A young Chinese physician, Dr. Joseph Wong, was added to the board of directors shortly before I left for Victoria.

Looking back from this perspective, I left the CCLA board with mixed feelings. I appreciated the tremendous amount of work that it was doing, largely through the efforts of Alan Borovoy, but I felt that the organization was not very democratic either in structure or in its functions. It was probably less democratic than any other major organization to which I had ever belonged. Its successes and failures were due primarily to the efforts of its general counsel whose work I strongly admired. However, in my opinion, his views of the world and of the lack of civil rights of non-white minority groups were limited primarily by his overemphasis on legal approaches to selected social, economic and political problems. However, none of us is perfect: each of us have some limits in our view of the world based primarily on our background, history and experience.

A few years ago Alan received the Order of Canada and I will never forget his amusing remark when we met following the publication of that news. His response in typical Borovoy form was, "I can't understand, what did I do wrong?" This was a reflection of his total commitment for the cause of the civil rights of the Canadian people.

Professional Associations

I was involved in a number of community activities which included serving on the boards of directors of the local chapter of The Canadian Mental Health Association, the Ontario and Canadian Association of Social Workers and several other community organizations. However, most of my work had been focused on the central problem of attempting to change the direction of the social service and health fields, both at the government and voluntary levels. I had also become a member of the Social Action Committee of the Metro Toronto Chapter of the Ontario Association of Professional Social Workers and had become aware that social work, like most professions, was essentially conservative and reluctant to press for substantial changes in the status quo. The attitude of some members bothered me. As an activist and a person concerned with social justice issues, I wanted to see my profession become similarly concerned.

It would not be correct to say that the profession was not concerned with some aspects of the treatment of clients by society. That concern however, was expressed in a very proper and professional manner. I had felt that serving on the social action committee would give me an opportunity, at least to some extent, to shake up the profession. Perhaps it could be encouraged to take a more forceful role on behalf of its clients. Secondly, it might become more effective in working cooperatively with poor people in the advocacy of their cause. Three or four of us, including Eileen McIntyre, Jean Shek and others felt that membership on the social action committee might have some impact upon the general direction of the professional association. To our dismay, our efforts achieved very little. I gained the distinct impression that it was more difficult to change the major thrust of a professional organization than to change the direction of a community group. I reduced my role in the professional association dramatically as I became more interested in the broad field of multiculturalism and human rights.

CHAPTER 14

Toronto: Polite Racism and Marshmallow Politics (The Second Decade), 1975–85

I entered social work from an interest in the contribution I could make to change the status of blacks and other minority groups in North American society. Many people had been damaged through inability to participate effectively in society and were in need of help in their efforts to cope more adequately with the pressing problems in daily living. I was attracted because of its potential for social change which would require the mobilization of individuals and groups in the struggle against conditions which impoverished them. This was very much in line with the original thinking and practice of the early social work pioneers who were strongly concerned with the lack of civic services, including poor garbage collection, poor sanitation, child labour, inadequate housing, health and other ills created by the ravages of the industrial revolution of the 19th century.

The structure and function of self-governing groups, including the professions of law and medicine, did not inspire confidence since they appeared to be based primarily on notions of self interest. A strong emphasis on the public interest should, in my view, distinguish social work from other "helping professions". Unfortunately, however, many of those who attempt to change the treatment of the weak prefer to maintain good relationships with powerful and influential institutional structures. Therein lies the real dilemma of professional social workers. Consequently, social work has retreated from its original role as a champion of the weak, vulnerable and powerless sectors of society which, in many respects, means an abandonment of an enlightened tradition.

The major human rights issue in Toronto in the 1970s was not the practice of social work but rather whether or not certain individuals would be permitted to live in safety and security in this society. It was a period characterized by "Paki bashing" where young white hoodlums felt free to roam the streets attacking anyone whom they considered a Pakistani. Perhaps the most dramatic incident of this type occurred on a subway platform when a slightly built man of Indian origin was pushed off a subway platform by a group of young hoodlums and both of his legs were broken. Fortunately he was pulled off the tracks and lifted back on the platform before the arrival of the next train. This and other incidents were tarnishing the image of Toronto as a tolerant, accepting and non-racist society. While most Torontonians reacted with horror and anger, they were not prepared to do anything concrete or substantial about the incidents.

A small number of concerned Torontonians came together to discuss what could be done to improve the climate for minorities in Toronto.

I became aware of the lack of research in race relations issues in Canada. Aside from personal experiences, there was no real knowledge of the scope, nature, and intensity of racism in Metro Toronto with the exception of a very few studies of the experiences of black children in the public school systems. I drew up a proposal for a study of the perceptions and experiences of blacks in Metro Toronto and submitted it to the Secretary of State and to the Ontario Human Rights Commission for funding.

My proposal was accepted and funding was provided by the federal Department of the Secretary of State. I employed Jeri Lee, a young university graduate and a folk dance colleague, as a research assistant. She was a very effective worker and extremely helpful in meeting the responsibilities of that position. The study was finally published in the spring of 1975, entitled "The Black Presence in the Canadian Mosaic".

The call for a meeting was sent to a small group selected by Marvin Novick and Anella Parker, two staff members of the Social Planning Council. The initial group included Ben Kayfetz, Al Herskwitch, Terry Meagher, Sam Fox, Rabbi Gunther Plaut, Leon Weinstein and myself. The initial meeting was held at the Primrose Club on St. Clair Avenue West and was hosted by Leon Weinstein, the then president of Loblaws Grocer Incorporated. The group was in total agreement that it was necessary to organize a structure in which citizens from the community could express their concerns in a concrete and useful manner. It was also recognized that this small group was not representative and that there was a need to expand the initial committee by recruiting additional people from other communities and other backgrounds. Several other individuals agreed to join the committee; among whom were A. Dharmalingam, Rev. Bob Cuyler, Prof. Frances Henry, Geoff Brown and several others. Several additional meetings were held that spring and early summer, most of which were held at the Holy Blossom Temple and hosted by Rabbi Plaut.

Most plans for establishing the new organization were completed by June of 1975. It was agreed that mid-July was an appropriate time for it to be officially launched. A major difficulty was the selection of a name for the new organization. A variety of names were suggested, but no general agreement was reached. Finally Marvin Novik suggested the "Urban Alliance on Race Relations" (UARR), although it was a misnomer. There was no intention of forming an alliance of a variety of other existing groups and the Urban Alliance was to be a group composed of individuals elected on the basis of their individual interest and concerns about race relations issues. They would represent and speak only for themselves.

A major feature of the new organization was that it was designed to be interracial in character, unlike other similar organizations. It would not be "ethno-specific", a focus which required making specific and determined efforts to recruit members from groups who had not been accustomed to working in an interracial or multicultural context. The Urban Alliance has continued that policy and practice.

The Urban Alliance was officially launched with a press conference in a downtown hotel. Members of the press asked many questions about the organization and its projected programs. The meeting was chaired by Sam Fox and myself. We were somewhat surprised at the large attendance by members of the media. We were again surprised the next day when a local newspaper published an editorial attacking the new organization which clearly indicated that, in its view, the Urban Alliance would do more to harm race relations in Toronto than to improve them! However, it did not represent the view of the general public in Toronto. Most publicity was positive and supportive. A small but steady stream of individuals came forward to offer their volunteer support to the purpose and goals of the new Urban Alliance on Race Relations. Sam Fox, a labour union leader, and I were elected co-chairs of the founding group. Subsequently, after the organization was officially launched, we were elected as co-chairmen for the next calendar year.

The general purpose of the Urban Alliance on Race Relations was to try to create a stable and harmonious society in Metropolitan Toronto. There were a number of specific concerns, including scrutinizing the activities of the police, the education of the general public and a concern with the portrayal of non-whites in the mass media. It was agreed that the Alliance would operate on the basis of two general strategies: one, a reaction to racist incidents (attacks and other incidents related to the negative racial climate in Toronto) and second, a proactive stance which would begin a program of educating the public and attempt to create a climate in which harmonious racial relations would become a characteristic of the city and hopefully reduce the occurrence of future incidents. It was immediately recognized that this program would not be of short duration. Racism in Canada was a complex phenomenon which would require a well designed program under highly skilled and committed leadership. The organization was fortunate in that it possessed many individuals with these qualities.

The multiracial problems of the community were recognized since the founders were aware that there could be no easy and magical solutions. Nevertheless it was felt necessary that the UARR move rapidly in the development of its program activities. Therefore it planned to give priority to the most urgent issues, and particularly those which had received a great deal of media attention including relationships between the black community and the police, the educational system and the media.

The founding members were committed, but busy, people so a first step was to locate an office and employ staff. The solution to the first problem was easy: the Social Planning Council offered limited office space until more adequate space could be found. The second problem was the necessity to raise funds to employ a small number of staff. The organization was successful in securing financial support from a number of business organizations, notably Xerox, IBM, Shell Oil, Royal Bank and Bell Canada. Financial support was also provided by a number of labour unions, religious organizations, our own members and private individuals. Government funding sources included the City of Toronto, Metropolitan Toronto, and special project funding from the Ontario and Federal governments. The search for funds was more successful than we had anticipated and within a few weeks of its launching, the Alliance had met its initial challenges. However, there were sceptics and critics. For example, one prominent black lawyer speaking from his experience with black organizations, said that "the organization will be dead in less than one year!"

The Urban Alliance, like any organization concerned with social change, attracted a number of people of dubious interests and concerns. A few individuals were simply curious and wanted to know what was going on. Others wanted to attach themselves to an organization which might have some prestige and status in the community. In addition, there were a few individuals with whom there were specific concerns. My experience in the United States had taught me to be aware of the possibilities of infiltration by law enforcement or other hostile groups. It was important as a matter of self-defence for the organization to be very careful about whom it placed in leadership positions. In Canada, as in the United States, there was a general concern among certain groups that progressively oriented groups should be kept under continuous observation. These groups are usually suspected of subversion because they want to change many of the basic institutional structures of society. (We were happy to plead guilty to that charge). That was precisely the raison d'être of the Urban Alliance. Needless to say government and voluntary institutions do not appreciate the efforts of other organizations to exert pressure to make significant changes in their mode of operation.

Over the years research studies have contributed greatly to the knowledge of racism in Canadian society and to the development of strategies for reducing, if not eliminating, it. Racism in Canada was found to be widespread and pervasive. However, Canadian racism was not as open, blatant or visible as in the United States, and with few exceptions was hidden, subtle and denied. In Canada, for example, one would never hear the words, "We don't rent to niggers" or "We don't hire niggers". When a black or South Asian applied for a job the usual response was "I'm sorry, had you come yesterday we would have been glad to hire you." Or in the rental of apartment buildings, the statement usually was,

"I'm sorry but the apartment has just been rented. Had you come a few hours earlier, you could have had it."

I had personally encountered one incidence of this type during my early days in Metro Toronto. I had just arrived and was looking for an apartment to rent for myself since I had left my family in Windsor. I went to a single-family house to rent a basement apartment which was advertised in one of the local newspapers. I telephoned inquiring whether the vacancy still existed and was assured by a landlady that it was indeed vacant. She would be glad to have me take a look at it. I was two or three blocks from the building. I drove down to the house, parked my car and knocked on the door. The lady with whom I had spoken came to the door and looked at me with obvious surprise. She immediately launched into a discussion of how sorry she was that the apartment was already rented. I pointed out that I had spoken to her no more than three minutes earlier and she had said that the apartment was vacant. She insisted that the apartment had been rented and that she was sorry that it was not available. I walked back to my car and sat there for a few minutes thinking about the incident.

I decided to return to the house and confront the lady a second time. When I knocked on the door, the daughter of the lady appeared. I said that I wanted to speak to her mother but was not sure she would want to remain and listen to what I had to say. The girl went back into the house and summoned her mother who returned to the door where it was suggested we go over the scenario again. I repeated that I had called her from a telephone booth a few blocks away and I had been informed that the apartment was available. I wondered how it could have been rented within a space of three minutes. She said that it had. I then asked her if she was telling me that a person had arrived, was shown the apartment, had made a deposit and left within that short period of time. She assured me, yes, this was the way it had happened. I said, "Lady, you know you're lying, your daughter standing there behind you knows that you are lying and I know you are lying. I should go to the Ontario Human Rights Commission and file a complaint".

The lady became quite upset at that point. She insisted that she had nothing against me, that she "loved black folks" and that she would be more than happy to rent the apartment to me had it been vacant. It was obvious that she was very upset at the possibility of an official investigation of her discriminatory practices. As I turned to walk away, she lapsed into a combination of English and a foreign language which I did not recognize and was not sure whether she was trying to call me back or whether I was being "cursed out". I was angry on returning to my car but I realized that I would not wish to live in that basement apartment in any event. I found a much more satisfactory place in a location more convenient to my work.

My experience in the Toronto sales market was very different. When I decided to buy a house I had no difficulty finding real estate agents willing to show houses to me in any section of the city. I looked at houses in North York, Scarborough, East York and downtown Toronto. It was obvious that there was little or no real discrimination in the sale of houses to a non-white individual in Metro Toronto. The real discrimination, however, was in rental housing, a fact which was amply demonstrated in a study conducted by a team I led when at the Social Planning Council. Subsequent studies by other organizations had also demonstrated that discrimination in rental housing based on race and colour was widespread and deep rooted in Metropolitan Toronto.

The public school system was under constant attack by black parents who had complained for many years about the "streaming" of black children. The term referred to the practice of schools dividing their children on the basis of assumed academic ability which usually occurred at grade 9. The majority of black children were assigned not to the academic but rather to the vocational streams, which led to "dead end" occupational opportunities. It was denied that problems regarding black or other non-white children existed in the schools. A meeting was called by the UARR and directors of education and trustees of boards of education were invited to attend. All except the director of one board attended. All of these gentlemen — they were all men — were unanimous in their denials of a racial problem in their schools. This situation differed from the one I had experienced in Indianapolis in which we had seen children playing in the school yard while at the same time, school officials were insisting that it was impossible for black and white students to learn together in the same school. "Black children", those educators had insisted, "must go to separate schools." Our Metro Toronto officials insisted that black and other non-white children in the schools were treated equally in all respects.

This meeting was a first in a series which the UARR held at various boards of education in the Metropolitan Toronto area. Many boards, however, began to work on developing multiculturalism and race relations policies. With one exception, these policies met most of the requirements for a non-racist education program for children of various racial backgrounds. In practice, however, the situation was quite different because school boards, for a variety of reasons, were reluctant to move to implement these policies. Admittedly these policies had been adopted under some pressure from the UARR and a few black parent groups. I found these experiences tiring and frustrating since school board officials appeared to be congenial but totally ignorant of what was occurring in their schools. Or perhaps they were merely trying to deceive us? In the final analysis we succeeded in forcing the adoption of fairly adequate policies. Implementation is always another story.

Policing

From the beginning of its existence, the Urban Alliance was concerned about the treatment of non-whites, particularly blacks and Asians, by the Metropolitan Toronto police force. Many complaints were received of alleged harassment, name calling, verbal abuse and physical assaults. Those allegations were always denied by the police force, including its top officials. By early 1976, it became obvious that some public forum was needed to bring these matters to the attention of the public. The Urban Alliance and the Social Planning

Council decided that it was time to act. A major conference was organized on race relations and the police and held at one of the downtown hotels. Several hundred people, including police officials, attended and listened to speeches by a number of experts in the field of criminology and police activity. The keynote speaker, Dr. Daniel Hill, a black man and a former chair of the Ontario Human Rights Commission, focused on the need for better communication and cooperation between the police and ordinary citizens. He reminded the audience of the words of Sir Robert Peel, to the effect that, in reality the citizens are the police and the police are the citizens. He called on the group to implement that concept in Metro Toronto. The concept of cooperation between police and citizens required fairly substantial changes in the practice of the police forces of Metro Toronto, the province and across the country. Among these changes Dan Hill suggested that more officers be taken out of cruisers and placed on the streets so that they could develop positive contacts with the general public. The public would then have a better understanding of the police and the police would have a better understanding of the multiracial and multicultural community which they were sworn to serve. The conference, in my judgement, was an outstanding success!

Shortly after the conference, members of the Urban Alliance and the Social Planning Council met with the chair of the board of commissioners of the Metropolitan Toronto police force who was urged to support the establishment of a committee which included the Urban Alliance, the Social Planning Council and the Metro Toronto police. This meeting led to the establishment of a liaison committee on race relations and policing initially involving the three organizations. The first meeting of the three groups as a unit began a process which has continued until this writing. It has not always been easy and there have been many serious problems. It was very difficult for members of the police force to sit down and discuss community concerns in an objective manner. Members of the community were subsequently invited to sit on the committee. A major problem arose immediately after the establishment of this new and expanded committee. The police refused active involvement in any discussion of complaints of alleged mistreatment against one of their members. Second, members of the community who had allegedly experienced mistreatment or had heard about these allegations found it very difficult to accept this restriction. One of the most important aspects that attracted them to the committee was that they had complaints which they wanted to air. The refusal of the police to listen and respond to complaints in a co-operative manner was a major factor in a rapid turnover in committee membership. Without going into details it is fair to say that the success of this endeavour was mixed. Nevertheless the committee broadened its community representation to include a number of people from various government agencies, including the offices of the federal and provincial Solicitor General staffs. Although it would not be correct to say that the committee has reduced the number of complaints, nevertheless the expanded committee continues to function and to provide a forum in which members of the community could express their concerns around policing in Metro Toronto. Four pilot committees were established in different sections of the Metro area to hopefully enable better communications.

I sat on the executive of the committee from its founding in 1977 until 1984 when I resigned. My role, as I saw it, as a representative of the black community and of the Urban Alliance, was to raise questions regarding police activity as viewed by members of the so called "visible minority" communities, a role not always appreciated by members of the police force. This experience was difficult since I was not accustomed to dealing with people who could not speak their minds because of rules and regulations. Police officers were only allowed to speak in a committee meeting with the approval of a superior officer. On some occasions no superior officer was available and the officer was required to remain silent!

I resigned from that committee in 1984 partly because I was leaving the city to accept a position at the University of Victoria but the most important reason was that I had come to the conclusion that the committee, under its structure and administrative controls, could not create significant change in the behaviour and attitudes of the police force. Studies had been done, reports written and recommendations had been made but very little significant change had occurred. Minor changes, however, were made in some policies, including changes in height and weight restrictions, the recruitment of more women and non-whites and in placing more police on the streets rather than in cruisers. However, allegations of mistreatment by the police continued unabated.

I have mentioned the difficulty and frustrations I experienced serving on the Liaison Committee on Race Relations and Policing. However, there were at least a few satisfactions in that otherwise difficult and ultimately futile process, the most satisfying of which was the positive relationship I established with one man, a Sergeant Ed Pearson, the leader of the Police Ethnic Squad. He was not merely an outstanding police officer: he was a superb human being, open minded, outgoing, honest and fearless. I have listened in astonishment as he sharply criticized some idiotic behaviour or expression of a senior officer. I asked him how he managed to get away with that unprecedented behaviour. His answer was always that he could say what he pleased because he was not involved in the struggle for promotions and status. That lack of ambition enabled him to become a free man, an attitude with which I could identify since I had experienced similar feelings when I refused to be drafted into the United States armed forces. I will never forget Sgt. Ed Pearson, now retired from the Metro Toronto Police Force.

The Media
The importance of the media as a socializing force in modern society was clearly recognized by the founders of the Urban Alliance. One of its most important projects was to establish relationships with the various parts of the print and electronic media. Our perception of the problems with the media in Canada was somewhat different from what I experienced in the United States.

Although blacks were more frequently portrayed in the American than in the Canadian media, that portrayal was usually based on a negative stereotypical model. They were usually portrayed as lazy, shuffling, stupid and incompetent. In Canada, blacks and other non-whites were very rarely seen at all in the media.

The Urban Alliance held many meetings with publishers, directors and managers of the various organs of the mass media, and several of us also met and discussed our concerns with members of the advertising industry. It was always interesting, for example, that when we met with the advertising industry, they always said they did not control who appeared in ads. The ads, they said, were controlled and dictated by the advertiser, that is the owners of the business who were advertising their services of merchandise. On the other hand, when the big stores such as the Bay, Eatons, Simpsons and other businesses were approached they turned the situation around by stating that they did not chose the models used in advertising. These models were chosen, they said, by the advertising agencies. An attempt was made to trap us in a "catch-22" situation; no one was responsible and therefore no one was to blame.

Nevertheless, as a result of our continuous pressure, some small changes were made. We were instrumental in initiating the hiring of Hamlin Grange, the first black reporter at the Toronto Star, one of the three major newspapers in the city. Our influence with the radio and television stations led to the employment of a number of racial minority reporters and producers. A small beginning was made, but clearly not enough to satisfy us. Members of the committee recognized the "marshmallow" characteristics of Canadian decision-making and that it would require consistent pressure over long periods of time to obtain significant change in the recruitment and utilization of non-whites in print and electronic journalism.

Although no longer teaching summer classes, I continued my activities in mental health and I had become an active member of the Metro Toronto chapter of the Canadian Mental Health Association and served on its board of directors for three years including involvement in the provincial section of the Association. I spent some time as a volunteer in a "socialization" program which was intended to help ex-psychiatric patients become reestablished in the general community.

It was also during this period that I became acquainted with the works of R.D. Laing, an English psychiatrist who argued that what we now call "mental illness" is simply a matter of social maladaptation, or the lack of ability to adjust to the values, customs, ethics and conventional behaviour of modern society. Unacceptable behaviour in one situation might be acceptable in another society or at another time in history. Laing is reported to have argued that in the society of that day, approximately fifty percent of the population should be in insane asylums. They should be cared for by the other fifty percent. Within two or three years, he suggested the two groups should "change places". This view, however heretical, drew attention to social and cultural factors in the development of "mental illness". Although not entirely convinced, I have great sympathy for Laing. There is evidence that different cultures do produce different levels of stress which result in different types of behavioural reactions. I identify with those who emphasized the importance of culture and social factors in the development of behaviour whether "normal", "criminal" or "mentally disturbed". The works of Karl Menninger and many others supported this view.

My experiences influenced my thinking in a similar direction. I am not a geneticist or a medical researcher, but I have had fairly extensive contacts with "disturbed" people. The social/cultural context seemed to make sense to me as an explanation for most of what I had observed. I recognized that the facts were not all in and that much more needed to be learned. We could do very little indeed for genetic factors, but society, if it so desired, could be shaped in a manner which would reduce the possibilities of generating "mental illness". Thus far, our society had demonstrated little or no interest in taking the necessary first steps in that direction.

Habitat

My interest in cooperative attitudes, behaviour and practice began in my early life but did not take concrete form until I chose a cooperative enterprise (credit union) as the subject of my master's thesis in social work. The reader will also remember my involvement in the Hyde Park Co-op in Chicago. I have been and remain a strong supporter of cooperation and of co-op activity. The news in the mid-1970s that Canada and the city of Vancouver were to host Habitat, an international conference on the utilization of local materials in the construction of housing by people of third world countries was especially intriguing. The conference was to be a week-long event.

I had, for several years, not seen my sister Minnie who was living in Berkeley, California. Participating in the conference would permit me to visit her and to fly to Vancouver following that visit. It was unfortunate that Sandy, whom I had only recently married was still working for the Scarborough Board of Education and could not spend a week away from her job. Minnie was living in the "hippie" section of Berkeley, a situation not to her liking. The behaviour of the hippies, several of whom lived next door, was highly unconventional and she was having a difficult time living in close proximity to a group of noisy young men and women. Nevertheless, I had a great time visiting the many attractions of San Francisco and the University of California at Berkeley.

The Habitat conference provided an astonishing vision of the ingenuity of people from all parts of the world and what they could achieve when given the opportunity and freedom to work in their own interests. Many of these families had been forced from their lands, their homes destroyed, leaving them homeless and landless peasants. At Habitat they demonstrated what could be accomplished when people lived and worked in cooperating communities. Those projects were supplemented by a week-long series of lectures and demonstrations of work in progress. Barbara Ward, an English environmentalist and writer; Margaret Mead, an American anthropologist and author; Pierre Trudeau, then prime minister of Canada; and others discussed the need for developing and utilizing more appropriate technologies so that everyone could have access to land, adequate food, clothing and shelter. Poverty and deprivation could be ended when people could again reclaim the freedom to manage their own lives.

These were inspiring words but I had read enough of the histories of colonialism and imperialism to know that the masters had no intention of giving the land back to the people. I listened to speeches and participated in some of the numerous seminars, but I recognized that they were exercises in idealism. The ringing declarations regarding the rights of the people to decent housing, food and clothing would have no impact on the behaviour of the rich landowners who often with the support of local armed forces had seized the land years earlier. I have read or heard nothing to suggest that Habitat made any observable impression on the plight of the poor in either the developed countries or those still struggling and suffering deprivation in "third world" countries. Poverty, homelessness and starvation continued unchecked: plus ça change, plus c'est la même chose!

Lagos

Earlier, in 1976, I was invited to present a paper at the Second World Festival on Black and African Arts and Culture in Lagos, Nigeria. The National Black Coalition of Canada (NBCC) was asked by the federal government to represent Canada. The result was that a total of fifty-three Canadian blacks including artists, writers, dramatists and academics were selected to represent Canada in that major international event. Having never been in Africa, I quickly accepted the invitation for this opportunity. My assignment was to present a paper on the "Black Diaspora in North America", a subject that took me somewhat by surprise having always thought of the term "diaspora" as related only to Jewish people. It was surprising to find that many Africans considered those of us living in North America as in the "black diaspora".

The trip, at the outset, was somewhat problematic for me. My visa had not arrived from Ottawa on the day prior to our scheduled departure. The president of the NBCC was to fly to Ottawa that day and pick up the visas. Mine was the only visa which had not arrived by departure time and the president could not be located. Nevertheless, I decided to take the flight to New York with the hope that he would meet us there. He did not arrive in New York and without the required visa, I would not be able to enter Nigeria. By that time we were almost frantic in our search for him. It occurred to me that he might be looking for me outside the airport waiting room so I asked and was given permission to leave the room to search for the NBCC president. Again, he could not be found. The guard, remembering that he had permitted me to go outside, permitted me to return. Inadvertently, I was able to board the aircraft without a visa and flew to Lagos without the necessary document for admission to the country. Unless some arrangement could be worked out, it looked as though I might be forced to return to Toronto by the next flight.

It was at that point that an official of the Canadian Embassy came to the rescue. He heard of my predicament, contacted Nigerian officials and arranged for me to remain in the country until the NBCC president finally arrived. (He had taken a different flight from London, England and was delayed two days). In the meantime I was given a temporary visa until he finally arrived with my visa. I was then a legally admitted visitor to the country. That experience was an example of living on the edge!

The festival was a great success, although there were problems. Prior to the opening of the event, delegates had free time to become acquainted with some aspects of Nigerian life and culture. Among other things we learned what it is like to live under a military dictatorship. It is possible that the military may be disciplined, orderly and in control of its behaviour. However, that could not be said for the city of Lagos which was a veritable madhouse. There were no traffic lights, no speed limits and people drove any way they liked. The constant roar of traffic, honking horns etc. was an ever-present irritant. The traffic jams were horrendous and it was almost impossible for anyone to move in excess of five to ten miles per hour.

Two events struck me as unusually significant. A group of us walking near the edge of the city saw a dead woman lying on the side of one of the streets. People walked by, looked and ignored her. We learned later that she was ignored because she was from a different tribe. None of the Nigerians would touch her until a member of her own tribe arrived. It was a sobering sight for most members of the Canadian contingent who had never been aware that tribalism was so strong a force in modern Nigeria.

This was a nation which was increasing its revenues from its sale of oil to the outside world and the oil boom created great wealth for some Nigerians. I had never seen so many Mercedes Benzes as in Lagos but the vast majority of its people were extremely poor. The gap between the rich and poor in Nigeria seemed to be quite similar to that in modern capitalist societies throughout the world. The very rich and the very poor existed side by side, except, as usual, the rich had a section of the city of their own into which very few poor people ever penetrated.

The second shocking experience occurred when we prepared to march into the stadium during the final celebrations of the festival. Those of us who were academics had already presented our papers, the artists had exhibited their paintings and sculptures and the poets had read their poetry. It was now time for the event where each of the 53 delegates was to march into a huge stadium to present themselves in a manner similar to that at the Olympic Games. Our delegation, along with those of fifty-two other countries, had lined up outside the stadium prior to entrance. The crowd was getting larger and there was some pushing and shoving by people who wanted to get into the stadium before our entrance. Soldiers on horseback were present to maintain order but the soldiers, carrying whips, moved into the crowd and began to beat the local people! Many were fleeing in a desperate effort to avoid these beatings and some were almost trampled by the horses. What had been an orderly meeting suddenly turned into a violent confrontation between soldiers trying to maintain order and people trying to get inside the stadium. We watched this exercise with a sense of unbelievable horror. Finally, the soldiers cleared the area and we marched in order as outlined on the program. Once inside, we marched around the stadium to the tune of the Canadian national anthem while the crowd cheered. Fifty-two other delegations performed similar rites as each presented its national flag, sang national songs and performed various dances during its march around the stadium. It was an attractive and inspiring event to view and cheer the delegations of 53 nations as they marched, many dressed in their colourful native costumes. It was a great show: however, I could not forget the image of those soldiers on horseback, beating inoffensive, unarmed civilians who were merely trying to exercise their right to enter the stadium.

Our delegation would have liked to travel throughout the country while we were in Nigeria but that was impossible. A soldier, with a rifle or sub-machine gun, rode at the front of every bus into town and back again to our encampment. The military government obviously was taking no chances of any harm occurring to us while we were its guests. I joined many other delegations in complaining about what we considered an overemphasis on security, but to no avail. For some of us the most important aspect of the experience was the opportunity to meet and discuss various social and cultural matters with people from all over Africa and other parts of the world. It was a great learning experience and one which I will not forget.

I have mentioned attending the 1969 meeting in which the NBCC was founded. However, it was not until 1976 that I actually became involved in the activities of the organization. By that time the organization was practically dead. It had managed to survive a number of internal crises, but arguments and bickering had driven most of its members out. Consequently, when I was approached in 1976 and asked to join and help the organization survive, I was very reluctant to do so. However, Roy States, the executive secretary, was persistent. Even though the organization was virtually dead and could not support his efforts, he was trying to carry on alone. The time had come, he felt, to try to reestablish the organization so that it could play the important role for which it was initially created.

Within a few months of my return from Nigeria, the NBCC executive secretary successfully assembled a meeting of individuals whom he felt might have some interest in reviving the organization. That meeting was held in Toronto in the spring of 1977 and was attended by approximately twenty-five or thirty individuals from across the country. A strong interest in the establishment of a national black organization was expressed by all participants but there was debate as to whether it should be the old NBCC or an entirely new organization. A committee of six people was structured to investigate the attitudes of black people across the country on this question. I was asked to serve as the chair. It is possible that I was asked to accept the position because I had not been active in the organization and therefore not involved in the internal struggles which had led to its collapse.

I was aware that previous experiences had left a residue of anger and bitterness among many members and some former officials of the organization. There were charges of incompetence, fraud and misuse of funds allocated for certain specific projects. I had no interest in becoming involved in what I considered a messy affair.

Contrary to what I expected, the Toronto meeting was peaceful and harmonious. There was general agreement that an effort should be made to determine the attitudes of as many blacks across the country as possible. I was joined by six others who had demonstrated strong interest in doing what they could to achieve the goal of re-establishing a new NBCC or another national organization. There were no funds, and it was necessary for our committee to travel by car and to seek lodging from interested individuals in each local community. It was surprising and invigorating to observe and participate in meetings in several cities, and to contact others by telephone. Our report was completed and presented at a meeting held in Ottawa. The report recognized that many former members were not interested in a revival of the NBCC but the majority felt that another effort should be made. With a few objections, the report was accepted and approved. It was heartening to see many of the older veterans of race and human rights struggles in Canada among those present and enthusiastic about the future of the NBCC.

Following the Ottawa meeting, the committee was asked to continue its work with the new mandate of planning for the new founding meeting to be held in Halifax within the next few months. I continued as chair of the planning committee. The federal government had demonstrated interest in the possibility of a revival of the NBCC and had provided funding for the travel expenses of delegates to the founding conference.

Even with all of its problems, it was felt that it would be better for the community if the NBCC was re-established. This was a recommendation to go to a larger meeting held in Halifax in the spring of 1978. The founding conference finally agreed that in spite of some opposition, the NBCC would be re-established and that I would be asked to serve as its president. I had heard the arguments of both sides and had strong reservations regarding what had happened at the original establishment of the NBCC. I had lukewarm feelings about my continuing presence in the organization. I had done my duty by chairing the committee which reached the decision to reestablish the organization and was not sure that I wanted to continue my relationship with an organization which was so prone to disruptive (and often destructive) behaviour. However, I was nominated and unanimously elected as president; I felt that I had no other choice but to accept the position and attempt to lead the organization through the challenges and dangers which might be involved in that decision.

The Halifax meeting was generally positive, constructive and harmonious, with little or no antagonistic discussion. The general atmosphere was good and everyone apparently felt that we were on the right track to creating a strong and successful organization. Howard McCurdy, the founding president of the NBCC, was elected vice-president. In addition, individuals were elected from the five regions of the country to serve on the executive committee including Dorothy Thomas (Atlantic), Eric Mansfield (Quebec), Jean Gammage (Ontario), Ralph James (Prairies) and Delicia Crump (B.C.). This group was to meet at least four times a year.

It only required two meetings of the executive committee before some of the old attitudes began to rise to the surface. Some attitudes were related to locality. For example, differences of opinion existed between the West Indian and the Canadian and American-born black populations, and even between blacks from the different islands of the West Indies. It also appeared that an underground struggle for control was underway between blacks from Toronto and Montreal, a struggle of which I had not previously been aware. These differences had, in part, led to the previous destruction of the NBCC and if they remained, would lead to its destruction a second time. By the end of the first year and the first Annual General Meeting of the new organization, the beginning of the self-destruction process was already evident. Divisions were apparent even in the executive committee. It became very clear that the NBCC had embarked on a dangerous journey.

Inadvertently I had helped propel this movement toward destruction by my effort to develop a stronger and more effective NBCC. The organization was composed of a number of groups who had little or no direct interest in human rights or race relations. Many were social or recreational clubs. I decided perhaps the way to deal with this problem was to establish a structure somewhat similar to that of the National Association for the Advancement of Colored People (NAACP) in the United States. The proposal, in the eyes of its opponents, would have meant that social, cultural and sporting activity groups would no longer be full members but might have to accept associate membership status. I proposed to organize NBCC chapters in various sections of the country which would provide local services as chapters of the national organization, each with a certain amount of autonomy but operating under the requirements of the constitution of the NBCC. This proposal created a tremendous stir in the Quebec region. At that time, the Quebec region had eleven organizations operating under the auspices of the Negro Community Centre of Montreal which in essence, was only one organization but with eleven different programs each with voting powers in the NBCC. Each program claimed to be a separate organization and therefore eligible for full membership in the NBCC.

Our proposal made good sense to me. It had been tried, tested and had worked in the United States and other countries. But the Quebec delegation and a few other individuals made it very clear that they did not accept a proposal that would reduce the voting power of the Montreal group.

The organization survived in spite of these differences and surprisingly, achieved a degree of success. Support was received for various projects from the federal government and the operating budget was raised from private funding agencies, including churches, labour unions and private individuals. The 1979, 1980 and 1981 annual general meetings were successful, but not without stormy sessions. In the meantime we had established eight local chapters across the country, but these chapters, located in eight different cities, had only one vote each as compared with eleven votes in Montreal alone. The Quebec delegation fought to maintain this advantage.

The 1982 annual meeting was when the matter of chapters came to a head. The actual program of the day which had been planned by the executive committee including the Quebec region representative was immediately attacked. The Quebec (Montreal) group insisted upon an immediate election, feeling perhaps that it had the votes necessary to win. Again, regional and other considerations intervened in the discussion. By the end of the day, I knew that I would no longer remain as president of the organization. Before the actual elections began on Sunday morning, I announced that I would not be a candidate for reelection and that I had had enough. Following my announcement, each of the Ontario representatives who had planned to run for office, decided to withdraw. When the final vote was taken, the former Quebec representative had been elected president and a few people, mostly Quebecers, held all other offices. Ontario, the largest region, was not represented on the executive committee. This situation was obviously a recipe for disaster and that disaster occurred by the next annual meeting in 1983.

In spite of the often disruptive atmosphere of some meetings of the executive and even of the general meetings, some good work was done. Ralph James of Winnipeg began the process of drafting a new constitution. When Ralph James ran into difficulty, Howard McCurdy took on the responsibility and presented the organization with a "model constitution" which was quickly adopted, and clearly set out the goals, purposes, functions and structures of the organization. In addition we embarked on a fundraising campaign which netted nearly $30,000 in the first year, and more than $31,000 in the second. (Previously the organization had existed on the basis of grants from the federal government). Al Mercury, the first executive secretary of the new organization, and I were responsible for raising those funds through personal contacts in the Metro Toronto area, which in all likelihood would not be available to the new leadership in Montreal. That is precisely what happened. To my knowledge, no funds were ever again raised by the NBCC from private sources.

Although disappointed that it was not possible for me to continue for another year as president and to consolidate the process of renewal, it was clear that renewal could not occur and I had no interest in further participation in the organization. While not at all under the illusion that I was indispensable, I was certain that the organization had embarked upon its familiar pattern of self-destruction. I mentioned in an interview with Hamlin Grange, then a reporter with *Contrast Newspaper* and now a reporter with CBC television, that the organization would be lucky if it did not self-destruct within the next year.

The tragedy is that, as of this writing, the black communities of Canada have no national organization designed and capable of supporting their struggles for equality and non-discrimination in an age of neo-conservatism and government inaction.

Although I had retired from the presidency of the reactivated National Black Coalition, I still remained actively involved in the board of directors of the Urban Alliance. My involvement in race relations, human rights, peace and poverty issues had come to the attention of the president and the senate of my university. Early in 1982, shortly before the annual meeting of the NBCC in Ottawa, I was advised by Ian McDonald, the president of York University that I had been selected to receive an honourary degree. I found this highly unusual. In my experience it was very rare that a member of the staff of a university was selected for this distinction. However, I wrote a letter to the president thanking him and members of the board of governors for bestowing such an unusual honour on me.

The honorary degree of Doctor of Laws (LL.D) was bestowed on me at the spring convocation of Atkinson College on June 12, 1982. It was a gala occasion with my friends, relatives, wife and children present to witness the event. Many of my present and former students were also in the audience. It is a custom at York University for the honoree to deliver an address following the bestowal of the honour. I have been to many convocations and am well aware of the almost total uselessness of speeches so I decided to keep my speech short and to make only two or three major points, the most important of which was my concern about the importance of peace in the world. I pointed out that while I spoke, a mass march and demonstration was occurring in New York City. It was expected that more than a half million people were participating and had I not been there to receive the honour, I would have been in New York City. This remark was highly applauded. I pointed out the relationship which existed between poverty, inequality, war and human rights and noted the importance of defending human rights for everyone, even those with whom we disagree. I attacked the nation state for its reliance on war to get its way in human affairs and pointed out that the possibility of nuclear war had made war obsolete. The only way in which nuclear war could be fought was at the risk of annihilating the human species. No cause in human history, I suggested, could be so important as to justify that risk.

I received a very enthusiastic reception following the speech and again when the president, others and I marched off the stage and mingled with the crowd. I was very pleased to hear from some students that I had "made their day". I was also very pleased that my two sisters-in-law, Geraldine and Estelle, had travelled from Cincinnati to be present on the occasion. Having two doctoral degrees now reminded me of a statement made by my youngest daughter, Cynthia, when she was only four or five years of age. She had said, "Daddy, if you're a doctor, why can't you cure us when we are sick?" I said to her "Cynthia, there are doctors and doctors and doctors; I happen to be one of the last type."

Encounters with "the Right"

I suspect that my verbal attacks against police mistreatment against black youth was, to some extent, related to the fact that several months previously I had been physically assaulted in downtown Toronto. I was walking from the Ontario Human Rights Commission, located on University Avenue, to a meeting at the Urban Alliance on College Street. The two buildings were some distance apart, but because it was a bright sunny day I decided to walk. There was nothing unusual happening on the streets at the time. However, as I walked up the stairs into the building, I felt a hand on my shoulder and I started to turn around, thinking that perhaps it was a friend who was also attending the same meeting. Before completing my turn, I suddenly felt a blow on the side of my face. I had been attacked from behind. Two or three other blows followed and I found myself thinking, "This cannot be! I am under attack in downtown Toronto in broad daylight!" But I remained on my feet and was finally able to turn fully around and push the man away. I had never seen him before. We were standing on the edge of the stairway into the building. As I turned to push him, he also pushed me which resulted in my falling down the stairs and bruising my knee. I had suffered cuts under both eyes but I remained conscious and upright.

There is no question about the target of this attack. The building in which our office was located was also the venue of a small collegiate institute whose enrolment was primarily Chinese. There were probably fifteen or twenty of the young people standing around on the sidewalks and stairwell of the building. This man had pushed his way through that group of young people to attack me. Even today, several years later, I have no clear indication of why the attack occurred.

The young Chinese students were obviously frightened and remained apart from the incident. The assailant had not spoken and following the attack, pushed his way through the students and walked away. I went on up to the Urban Alliance office to call the police and then waited outside for their arrival. Twenty minutes later the police had not responded to my call. I went back into the building and again called the police. Thirty-five or forty minutes after the attack, a policeman arrived by streetcar! He had travelled by streetcar and bus quite some distance to arrive at the scene of the attack. There was no discernible reason why he had to travel from a considerable distance when the local police station was only four or five blocks away. The delay was simply inexcusable.

An ambulance finally came to take me to a hospital. I remember how frequently the ambulance attendants kept asking me "What day is it? Do you know what time it is? Do you know where you're going?", assuming that I was groggy and therefore not in full control of my senses. I was in full control, but I had a fairly bad bruise on my right knee. The two police officers who accompanied me to the hospital kept taking pictures of the bruised knee and I wondered why they felt it necessary to take many pictures of the knee before it was cleansed and bandaged. Apparently, it was because they wanted to use those pictures for evidence in case the assailant was captured.

Many of us at the Urban Alliance, however, were concerned about the attacks from another perspective. We felt that since I had made a number of verbal attacks on the way police had treated visible minorities perhaps they were out to "get me". Many people then (and even recently) have said that they believe the attack was carried out by an off-duty officer. That may be true, but neither they nor I can be certain. After the hospital staff bandaged my knee and washed the cuts on my face, I was released and returned to the building where I was questioned by two detectives and later taken to look at "mug shots" at police headquarters. I must have been shown two or three hundred pictures of alleged or former criminals. I could not recognize my assailant from any of the pictures.

There was no meeting at the Urban Alliance but everyone was sitting around waiting for me to return. There were hundreds of questions regarding precisely what had happened but I could only tell them what little I knew. I could not identify my assailant nor could I give any reason why I had been the target of an attack. The general feeling among board members was that his attack was the result, at least in part, of anger and resentment at my criticisms of the police and the press a few weeks earlier.

In Toronto alone, less than five or six percent of the population was black or native, yet I have been told by people who work in the prisons that up to forty to fifty percent of prisoners in Toronto jails are black or native and many of whom have a background of poverty. If that is true (and my own observations have borne out these allegations), then one has to either argue that black, native people and the poor are genetically more criminally inclined and more likely than others to commit crimes, be caught, convicted and jailed than the white population, or one has to look at the behaviour of the police themselves. We have to ask the question, "Are the police more likely to suspect, seek out and arrest people from these three groups than others?" My experience in the United States and in Canada suggests that the latter comes closer to the truth than the former. *The Donald Marshall* case in Nova Scotia is a perfect example of a widespread problem. However, in my situation we could only speculate.

Two or three weeks later, I received a letter from one of the police superintendents regretting that the attack had occurred and that the police had been so late in arriving on the scene. He pointed out that the attack had occurred around 3:30 in the afternoon, a time when shifts were changing and that this was at the time in which the traffic was very heavy. In my view, these assertions were merely excuses and not a satisfactory explanation, but they were the only ones that I ever received from the Metro Toronto Police Force.

I received, as one result of that attack, one of the kindest comments that I have ever received. That was a letter written to the editor of the *Newsletter* of the Ontario Association of Professional Social Workers. It is as follows:

It is a sad commentary on Toronto the Good when a man like Wilson Head must experience what appears to be a racially motivated attack. A passionate defender of human rights, Dr. Head has dedicated himself to mending that widening gap of misunderstanding and intolerance that threatens the very fabric of our society.

The pitiful assailant can take some comfort in knowing that, were his own rights threatened, the first to leap to his defense would be kind and gentle Wilson Head.

Vic Wille
Joe Couchi
Carman Perillo

My appreciation for the letter to the editor is indeed great. I have received many awards and honours in my life, but none touched me as much as those kind words from former York University students.

The attack became a matter of national and international attention and concern. Telephone calls were received from friends, including one from John Howard Griffen in the U.S., and from people I had never met but who were concerned that an incident of this kind could happen in broad daylight in Toronto. Howard McCurdy, vice president of the NBCC, immediately demanded that I be provided with a bodyguard to prevent further violence. I felt that it was perhaps an isolated incident and not likely to occur again but Howard was adamant. Within a day he had discussed the matter with the publisher of *Contrast* and arranged that a strong, healthy, young man should accompany me on all trips outside the building. This arrangement continued for two weeks when I told my bodyguard that I felt he was no longer needed. But for several months I was very alert to any possibility of a further incident. None occurred and I gradually returned to my usual relaxed pattern of life.

Perhaps the most unusual and almost unbelievable encounter of my life in Toronto was a brief session with Alex McQuirter, then the leader of the KKK in Toronto. I had been invited by a local radio station to debate racial issues with a leader of one of the local right wing groups. I immediately agreed since I had no concern regarding my ability to handle any member the right wing group might choose. I was not informed of the identity of the individual and was surprised when Alex McQuirter turned up with a big burly "bodyguard"! McQuirter was a tall, slender, fresh-faced young man about twenty-two years of age. He gave no indication that he was leader of a vicious anti-Jewish, anti-Catholic and anti-black organization. The KKK had, on a number of occasions, made attempts to establish a strong presence in Canada and had achieved a small degree of success several years previously, particularly in the western provinces. These successes had been short-lived and now the organization was attempting to establish a base in Toronto. Many of its members were simply retreads of other right wing groups, such as the Western Guard, The Nationalist Party and the John Birch Society.

I arrived first at the radio station and took a seat in the lobby. McQuirter arrived with his body guard a few minutes later but I had never seen a picture of him and did not recognize him initially. But the host came in, greeted us and introduced us to each other. We entered the studio and began the debate. I am sure the audience did not consider the debate an overwhelming success because he gave his pitch which I immediately challenged on the basis that he had not presented the real story and history of the KKK. I then gave the version which I considered a more accurate picture of its purposes, methods and goals. He was young, just out of high school, and I had the advantage of knowledge based on my experiences in the South of which he was totally unaware. I think, from a debating point of view, I clearly won the encounter. However, that does not mean that he was convinced in the slightest, which did not surprise me. I was experienced in debating and he was a relative newcomer in the field of race, religious and ethnic prejudice and hatred.

My real shock came when he approached me as we left the studio and said that he would like to have a word with me. Although surprised, I agreed. He suggested that I join with him in a campaign against the Jews! I came as close to being stunned as ever in my life. I asked if he was joking. He said that he was not, but he thought we blacks were Christians and could join in a campaign against Jews because they were "Christ killers" and against our religion. I finally recovered and told him to forget it and walked away. I left the studio in a state of disbelief. I could hardly believe that a leader of the KKK would make such a completely outrageous suggestion. The one thing that was completely obvious was that he had "blocked out" everything I had said during the debate!

His dour and heavily muscled bodyguard had not spoken but had simply glared at me as if he would like to get his hands around my throat. I did not stay around to give him that opportunity. A few months later, McQuirter was caught with illegal drugs in his car, charged and jailed. I have heard nothing of him since that time but I still wonder at his audacity and foolhardiness. He obviously was not an effective leader for the KKK or any other organized group.

The Canadian Ethno-Cultural Council

The Canadian Ethno-Cultural Council (CEC), originally the National Council of Ethno Cultural organizations, was indirectly a result of the multicultural policy of the federal government established by Prime Minister Trudeau in 1971. It stated that Canada was a multicultural society and that various ethnic groups had a right to maintain and protect their heritages. A multicultural department was established in the Department of the Secretary of State to support the efforts of the various ethnic groups. An Italian pharmacist, Dr. Leone, was the guiding force in establishing the new organization which included approximately thirty-five national ethnic organizations in its membership. I became a member because I was then president of the National Black Coalition of Canada. In addition to its European constituency, the Council included the presidents or representatives of Chinese, black, Japanese, and South Asian organizations.

Following several discussions of the situation in several Eastern European countries, I raised two questions. First, would the members also want the Council to publicly condemn the government of South Africa for its treatment of blacks in that country? Second, was not the council formed to support the efforts of ethno-cultural groups to secure their rights as Canadians in this country? I stated that, in my view, our attention should be focused on demanding that the government of Canada actually protect our rights and we should not get involved in the affairs of foreign countries, that is, unless we intended to treat all violations of human rights equally, whether by the governments of communist or non-communist countries of the world. I listed a few of those countries accused of human rights violations, including torture, killings and disappearances. The discussion of my questions was very brief and it was quickly decided that we would not become involved in the affairs of foreign governments unless we were prepared to be even handed in our concerns for violations of human rights.

One of the troubling aspects of the heavily European majority on the Council Board of Directors was the question of "appointments" to government boards and commissions. Most were actively seeking these appointments. There was no question that "ethnics" and non-white groups were under-represented on federal agencies, boards and commissions. At that time, as today, government boards and commissions were dominated by Anglo-Saxon males. I could not identify with and support this emphasis and the result was that the four non-whites formed our own informal caucus so that we could maintain what we considered the major raison d'être of the group. I became chair of a newly established Committee on Race Relations and Human Rights.

I cannot say that this committee was successful although it was strongly supported by Andrew Cardoza, executive director of the council. But resources were limited and its members were scattered around the country. In the absence of funds for travel and other expenses it was impossible for it to meet. We were left to infrequent telephone contacts, although we published our interests and concerns in the council newsletter.

I left the Council and the Committee when I left the presidency of the NBCC in 1982. The picture however, was not all negative. I met some outstanding men and women through participation on the council and I particularly remember and maintain infrequent contacts with Dr. Joseph Wong, Navin Pareth, George Imai, and Khalid Mouammar. I have very high regard for Jim Fleming, the Minister of Multiculturalism at the time. He was thoroughly committed to the cause of human rights and race relations. According to rumours, he was removed from his post because some ethnic groups objected to his strong emphasis on increasing funding for race relations groups. His successors certainly did not provide evidence of a similar interest in our struggle against racism in the government of Canada or in Canadian society as a whole. Neither were we sufficiently knowledgeable or aware of the political implication of his position, and therefore unable to press for his retention in his ministry. As a result, the struggle against racism lost a very good friend and supporter.

The Peace Movement

Although not always actively involved, I have never forgotten my attachment to the peace movement in which I was heavily involved in the United States. Much of this continued after I arrived in Canada. I continued to travel to the World Affairs Camps in Germantown, Ohio and to other places in the States for various meetings of peace groups. I also continued my activities with the AFSC, particularly in its work with young people in work camps and seminars. My Canadian participation was much less direct since Canada was not overtly a part of the Vietnam fiasco, although it was, as usual, indirectly involved by exporting weapons and supporting the Americans in other ways.

I was appalled by the brutalities and atrocities of the American Army in Vietnam, a small "third world" country existing almost entirely on support from other countries but was attacked on the grounds that the U.S. was defending democracy and fighting the "spread of communism". There was not and never had been democracy in Vietnam. As usual, a nation attacking another must lie to its own people regarding the reasons behind that aggression. The United States was no exception. I spoke against Canadian involvement, wrote letters to editors of newspapers, spoke at high schools and universities and talked to men and women on the street. However, nothing seemed to matter until the news of the increasing casualties began to come out into the open. It was at that point that indignation rose to the surface and forced the United States government to withdraw its troops from Vietnam. The American troops had been fought to a standstill by the Viet Cong and the North Vietnamese army. U.S. soldiers lost the war because the public no longer supported them. In my view, that development was a victory for the peace movement and an aroused public opinion.

I was quite aware of the work of the Christian Movement for Peace, the Canadian Friends Service Committee, Project Ploughshares and other peace groups. I supported many of these groups, and a small number of non-violent direct action groups in Toronto. However, I was looking for a more direct involvement to the struggle for peace and against nuclear armament. That opportunity came when I received a phone call from a member of the United Church of Canada, inviting me to attend a meeting in Mississauga at a Catholic retreat centre. The meeting was to consider the establishment of a Toronto chapter of the World Conference on Religion and Peace (WCRP). Never having heard of the organization, I was curious regarding its purposes and goals. I decided to attend the meeting and I heard the names of individuals whom I recognized from past experiences. One was Homer Jack, who at one time was pastor of a Unitarian church in suburban Chicago. He had also been the executive director of the Chicago Chapter of "SANE", the organization promoting a sane nuclear policy during the 1950s. I had been a member of that group when we lived in Chicago and looked forward to the opportunity to meet people who were on the leadership of SANE at that time.

Doug Roche, a conservative party M.P. from Edmonton, was one of the sponsors of this group. Roche was involved in WCRP activities in Japan, India and the United States. The World Conference seemed to be an opportunity to increase my direct involvement in the Canadian peace movement, a movement whose values and goals were similar to mine.

I particularly liked the fact that the group was composed of people from a variety of backgrounds and religious orientations: Muslims, Buddhists, Hindus, Sikhs, Christians and Jews were participating. In addition, the conference included several people from other minority religious traditions. The World Conference was interested in how religion could help to create a more peaceful world, but many of us were keenly aware that religion had often supported wars and military conquests. The Indian leader Gandhi had demonstrated to the world the power of non-violence and avoidance of war. He had brought down the British Empire and forced the end to British colonialism in India. However that is only one side of the picture. As soon as India was independent and free, it fought the first of several wars with Pakistan and these wars were not non-violent, they were fought with deadly weapons. The clash between Muslim and Hindu religious ideology was perhaps the most important factor in initiation and continuation of that and subsequent wars between the two countries. To my surprise, these facts were readily admitted by participants in the consultations.

It was during those discussions that I met Floyd Honey who had been an active member of the United Church of Canada, and, at one time, a member of the staff of the Canadian Council of Churches. Floyd and I accepted some of the responsibility for helping the new organization get off the ground and into operation. Reverend Bruce McLeod, a former moderator of the United Church of Canada, also played a very important role in the initial stages of the World Conference. It was through my participation in this organization that I became familiar with many of the leaders of the United and Anglican Churches of Canada.

It was agreed that a Toronto chapter of the Canadian section of the WCRP be established and I was elected chair. The head office for the national and Toronto chapter was housed in an ecumenical organization in Toronto and Floyd Honey became the part-time executive secretary of the Canadian section. As expected, the early meetings of WCRP were focused primarily, on getting to know and to understand one another. We were the recipients of information concerning religious practices through interaction with people who lived those religions on a daily basis. I felt a tremendous need to know more than could be learned through casual discussion and began to study the history and beliefs of Buddhism, Hinduism, Islam and the Sikh religions. Two facts stood out to me. I learned that many basic beliefs and philosophies of most religions are very similar. They adhere to certain basic cultural, social and religious values but there are also considerable differences. Only the Mennonites, Quakers and Brethren are considered in the Christian tradition as "Historic Peace Churches". It was perhaps for that reason that most of the early meetings of the WCRP avoided discussion on questions of religious beliefs and practices. Very little attention was initially given to attitudes on world war and peace. I raised this question in a meeting of the WCRP on two different occasions and I found, to my astonishment, that many of the minority religious groups felt that they were under attack and threatened with being "swallowed up" by the dominant Christian faith in North America. It had never occurred to me that Christians were considered as exploiters and oppressors. However, we had to face the fact that dominant values in western society are derived from western philosophy and religions. There is little recognition of the existence and validity of other religious faiths and traditions, a situation which obviously must change if we are to live in peace.

My situation, however, was also changing. I served as president of the Toronto chapter of WCRP from 1978 to 1984. I had held the position for six years and it was time to leave. Leaving Toronto to move to Victoria for a year at the University of Victoria made it necessary to give up my position as chair of the Toronto chapter during this absence.

In the meantime, Floyd Honey and I had discussed the possibility of bringing the various peace and disarmament groups of Toronto together into some kind of a federation or coalition. There was some objection from a few religious groups because of the nature of the peace movement in Toronto at that time. For example, the Toronto Peace Congress was considered by many potential members as a "communist front" organization. I was quite surprised to hear this and immediately I spoke to members of one of the church peace groups. It appeared that divisions had already emerged within the peace movement in Toronto and in other parts of Canada. The movement was divided along at least three different dimensions: religious, secular or non-religious and politically oriented organizations. In order to overcome the objection of some peace groups to working in association with others, we placed a stipulation in the bylaws of the proposed organization that political organizations would not be permitted to join the alliance or coalition, a move that seemed to allay some fears.

Floyd and I mailed invitations to the various organizations in the city to discuss the creation of some form of cooperation with the initial meetings held at the Bloor St. United Church in mid-town Toronto. I chaired the early meetings and Floyd acted as secretary. The result was that the various groups were successful in establishing the Toronto Disarmament Network (TDN). The label "network" was adopted because several groups were not ready for a more structured coalition or alliance. It was also considered more informal and less threatening to groups fearful of losing their autonomy and independence. Neither were some founding groups ready to include the word "peace" in the name. Disarmament was considered okay and was easily accepted by delegates to a founding meeting. That and many subsequent meetings of the WCRP and the Toronto Disarmament Network were continued at the Bloor Street United Church which graciously permitted us to use its premises without cost.

Initially, the Toronto Disarmament Network brought together only twenty-five or thirty organizations. Later the number increased to as many as eighty organizations, all of whom claimed adherence to the peace movement. The staging of mammoth parades and demonstrations became a hallmark of Toronto Disarmament Network activity in the public arena. Floyd, I and several others were disappointed with the final outcome of our negotiations but recognized that some groups were not ready to go public as "peace" groups.

Victoria

One evening when Sandy and I were sitting in our living room reading newspapers and magazines, I noticed an ad requesting applications for a one year contract as a visiting professor at the University of Victoria. I was intrigued and asked Sandy how would she like to live in B.C.? She felt that it would be a nice change from Ontario, but only for the one year. I responded to the ad and was immediately asked to come to Victoria for an interview. Not only was I interviewed by the faculty of the School of Social Work, but also by the student body! It appeared to me that staff and students were pleased with my responses to questions and my general openness and candour. They were good interviews and I felt certain that I had a good chance to be invited to accept the position. It was in early March and many of the flowers were already in bloom while we still had snow on the ground in Ontario. Victoria looked extremely attractive. I found the Director, John Cossom, the staff and the students very friendly and compatible. Following the interviews, I was driven back to the airport by John Cossom who gave me his informal opinion that I could have the position if I still wanted it. They moved quickly and I received and accepted the offer within a week following my return to Toronto.

The physical beauty of the place had attracted me more than the actual opportunity to teach students in Victoria. British Columbia is probably one of the most beautiful parts of the country and a trip through the Rocky Mountains and coastal regions of British Columbia is exciting and breathtaking. I had always reluctantly faced the rigors of the cold Ontario winter and had expected to find heavy rain in B.C. I was pleasantly surprised when I was told in Victoria that they received only thirty to thirty-five percent as much rain as Vancouver. The rain clouds, they said, passed over Victoria, struck the mountains behind Vancouver and dropped their rain on that city.

In fact, Victoria, was actually suffering from a drought when we flew out in August. My son Norman and his wife Jennifer drove our car out, arriving a few days later.

My relationship with the faculty and students of the School of Social Work at the University of Victoria (UVic) was warm and friendly. The Bachelor of Social Work program at the School was basically at the third and fourth years of an honours degree level within the Canadian university context. The orientation program, held at a camp some distance from Victoria, included both student groups. The interaction between faculty and students was very interesting because the faculty made every effort to make students feel comfortable and at home.

That was not difficult in this camp setting. Everyone was expected to participate in various activities of the camp, including washing dishes, preparing food, taking care of the campgrounds and arranging for transportation. There is something about eating together which breaks down many of the inhibitions and barriers to communications. The fourth year students were well known to the faculty, but the third year students were totally new. By the end of the two-day orientation program, the ice had been broken and a positive relationship between faculty and students had been established which continued through the incoming school year.

The degree of that warm and friendly relationship between faculty and students was a new experience for me, at least at the university level. There had always been a certain distance and some tension between faculty and students in the universities where I had attended or been on the faculty. Although there were exceptions, in general this distance was a very important matter for many faculty members who gave the impression that they enjoyed the attitude that they were more knowledgeable and consequently could occupy a superior social status. That feeling was not restricted to attitudes towards students. Some faculty members enjoyed the struggle to increase their status in the university context which was related to their professional status in the university. At UVic however, faculty/student workshops, seminars and parties held at the homes of faculty members helped to maintain that sense of camaraderie and mutual friendship and respect. I found this relationship quite pleasant and satisfying.

There were times. however, when I felt the process went too far, particularly in relationship to the participation of students in school government. For example, a series of meetings were held at the university shortly after the start of the school year. The new students were asked to make decisions regarding matters of which they had little or no knowledge. This looked very democratic, but the ability and knowledge of some students, particularly those entering the school for the first time, was much too limited for the task. Meetings ended inconclusively and without decisions having been made.

The early founders of the British and French colonies in the United States and Canada recognized the need for education if democracy was to work in an effective manner. They knew that information was essential if proper decision making could be arrived at in a democratic fashion. For this reason they established high schools, colleges and universities across the country. Democracy, however, as many philosophers have pointed out, creates a dilemma between the educated, knowledgable and influential person, who is often considered as "elitist" and ordinary people with limited background less than adequate. On the basis of democratic theory, both should have an equal voice and equal participation in the democratic process.

The need for a broadly based educational program for university professors was illustrated at UVic shortly prior to my arrival. I am unaware of how the event was initiated, but Noam Chomsky, an American professor and well-known critic of American foreign and domestic policy was invited as a speaker at a special event on campus. Noam presented his usual devastating analysis and criticism of American policy in Central and South America and in the Middle East. Apparently many UVic professors found it extremely difficult to accept criticism of American imperialism and took sharp issue with their guest. The campus was still "buzzing" when I arrived in August of that year. From the reports I heard, it was not possible for professors to criticise his statements on the basis of knowledge; the problem was that they felt he was "anti-American". I regret that I missed the opportunity to participate in that discussion because of general agreement with the basic thrust of Chomsky's position. However, I might have been tossed out of the auditorium even before I could begin my teaching responsibilities at the university. So much for academic freedom! Repercussions from the event were reminders of the McCarthy days in the 1950s.

The Distance Education Program (DE) was one of the unusual and attractive aspects of the curriculum at the School of Social Work in Victoria. Recognizing that not all students could afford to come into the city and live for two years in a university residence or in the community, the school had developed this program to meet the needs of students living in outlying small towns and rural areas. Flying to and meeting those students was the most exciting aspect of my work at UVic. Students in the Distance Education program were much older and more experienced than the regular students. Many of them had, without training, been practising social work for a number of years and were returning to school to get the necessary qualifications to maintain their jobs and possibly to obtain promotions.

Flying over those British Columbia mountains, however, was no picnic. On more than one occasion the plane flew in over Okanagan Lake and then appeared to head directly into a mountain. Suddenly it swerved off to the right and landed in a very safe and comfortable way. As a passenger, that was a frightening experience. The pilots were quite accustomed to it and were not the slightest bit concerned. To make the matter worse, a similar event occurred when the aircraft took off. On its return flight, again the aircraft flew over the lake and toward distant mountains. Before reaching them, however, it suddenly swerved and flew between two mountain peaks. Again that was a somewhat unsettling experience but not as bad as the first. I could easily understand where, in some parts of British Columbia, during the winter months, more flights were cancelled than were completed because of bad weather including heavy fog. The Pacific Western Airlines no longer exist, but I will never forget my flights on those small planes dodging between mountain peaks as I flew in and out of cities in the interior of British Columbia.

I taught three courses during the school year: Social Work in Multicultural Settings, Social Work and Human Rights, and Evaluation Research in Social Work. The first two were also open to the general public, although without credit. I was particularly interested in the reaction of students to my presence on the faculty since I was a black person in a school that had not enroled a single black student during that year. The issue of race and colour, however, seemed to be non-existent. My students were friendly and frequent visitors to my office for chats. I was a person from "back east" as they called it and the most insistent question was, "Which do you like best, out here or back east?" And secondly, "Which university is better, our university or your university back east". I had not anticipated these questions but it appears that I handled them well by making jokes such as, "Since I will be out here for at least a year, I had better say that I like the west and that I like the University of Victoria better." However these answers did not quite satisfy some students who insisted on a serious answer. I simply said that the two university programs were very different. There are times when "discretion is the better part of valour"!

Living in British Columbia was a very interesting experience. British Columbia was severely divided economically and politically. I was told when I arrived that I would enjoy the climate and the scenery but that the politics were completely polarized. One person said, "The people out here don't talk to each other, they shout at each other." Operation Solidarity, one of the most stimulating and challenging political events of the century, had occurred in British Columbia a few months before I arrived. The term "solidarity" was borrowed from the movement of the same name in Poland. The Solidarity Movement in British Columbia, stimulated by severe government cutbacks in education, health and social services, brought together a wide variety of people from many different organizations and backgrounds: labour union leaders, teachers, nurses, small business people, university professors and a wide range of other concerned people. The movement was a reaction against the policies of the premier of the province who had decided to cut back on government programs which supported the poor and underprivileged population of the province. He also announced a twenty-five percent cut in provincial civil servants. These draconian acts by the provincial government brought together the wide variety of groups who formed Solidarity.

Thousands of people took to the streets in various parts of the province. In Vancouver, almost a hundred thousand people marched in a huge demonstration and fifty thousand were estimated to have marched on the provincial capital in Victoria. The government did not back down from what many considered a cruel and heartless program. Apparently it was determined to ignore any movement of people joining together to fight its drastic action regardless of public opinion. The Solidarity Movement was one of the few times in the history of Canada in which labour union leaders, academics, high school teachers, nurses, social workers and others joined together in a massive protest against cutbacks in government policies and programs.

Shortly before my arrival in Victoria, some members of the movement had agreed to try to work out a resolution to the problem with the premier. A meeting was scheduled at his home in Kelowna and several leaders of the movement were to meet with him to determine what, if anything, could be resolved. When the meeting actually occurred, only one member of Solidarity, a labour union leader, was able to meet with the Premier. According to reports, the two sat on the front porch and worked out a deal which gave labour much of what it wanted. Other members of the coalition were not so fortunate and many felt that they had been betrayed by the union leader. They were dispirited and virtually paralysed concerning the possibility of future activity. Many efforts were made by some people to hold the coalition together and to keep the pressure on the government. However, these attempts failed and the teachers and a few groups gradually returned to work, while others felt defeated and the momentum was lost.

In spite of the social and political climate in British Columbia, Sandy and I made a number of very solid friendships. Many of these people had lived in Ontario and other places back east. At least two thirds of the members of the faculty of UVic School of Social Work were ex-Ontarians and many of them had moved to British Columbia to escape the harsh Ontario winters. As a southerner, I could sympathize with that.

Victoria and Vancouver were extremely nice places in which to live. People were, in general, more friendly and open than one would find in Ontario and especially in Toronto. The social atmosphere was more relaxed, slower and less stressful than in hectic Toronto. That pace was defined as almost too slow by one individual who had lived in Ontario. He suggested that more happens in Toronto in one week than in three months in Victoria. My experience suggests that he was probably accurate in that assessment. Another Ontario friend had clipped a headline from the Toronto Star which described Victoria as "the city whose pace has quickened to a stroll"!

In spite of the generally idyllic social and cultural atmosphere of the city, however, Victoria could not escape the influences of a divided society, that is one characterized by affluence, and on the other side of the coin, poverty and deprivation. The city, similar to virtually all North American cities, included affluent, middle class and poor areas. It also included youth crime and delinquency.

I was very much surprised when the Aryan Nation, a right wing U.S. extremist group, planned a public meeting in Victoria. The Aryan Nation was one of the many offshoots of the KKK, Western Guard, Nationalist Party and other similar groups which spring up from time to time in Canada as branches of American extremist groups. The KKK had made limited inroads in British Columbia, Alberta, Saskatchewan and in Ontario during the 1920s and 1930s but had not been able to expand largely because of its blatant anti-semitism and other "isms". It was not overtly active in B.C. for several years but had come to the conclusion that political unrest, high unemployment, and increasing Asian migration set the stage for a new attempt to become established in Western Canada.

This new attempt had the appearance of a religious organization and held its first meeting in a local church. Having been active in the Victoria Chapter of the Vancouver Island Human Rights Council, I was immediately informed of the planned gathering and joined other colleagues in organizing a protest to be held outside the church. Approximately 45 to 50 of our members arrived on the scene several minutes prior to the beginning of the meeting but were not permitted to enter. Two huge bodyguards blocked the doors and would only permit entrance to those who were identified as local sympathizers. One older woman in our group made an unsuccessful attempt to push between the two men and was struck in the face, her glasses knocked to the ground, and she was pushed from the doorway to the sidewalk. It had become clear that some Victorians supported the racist views of the speaker, a religious leader from a right wing and anti-semitic church in the western United States. The only way we could have entered the church was by an overwhelming attack on the two men and we were not prepared for initiating a violent attack which would have had unpredictable results.

Our group gradually drifted away and we had to recognize that other methods would have to be used to counteract an overt attempt to organize a racist organization in Victoria. Preparations were made to deal with similar meetings if and when scheduled but no further meetings were held during my tenure in Victoria. That stand-off had made an unforgettable impression on our inexperienced group. They had experienced their "baptism by fire".

I also received a shock in Toronto when Sandy and I returned for the Christmas break. During that week and a half, we were invited to the home of friends for dinner. Perhaps ten or twelve people were present and I knew most of them but one had been a special close colleague at the Urban Alliance. Kathy had been a volunteer on one of our committees and had been an extremely valuable worker until she returned to complete work on a graduate degree at the Ontario Institute for Studies in Education (OISE). She was accompanied by a black man, a person whom I did not know. I was under the impression that we had never met. This illusion was shattered, however, by his statement that he had been a member of the Metro Toronto Police Force and had been assigned to "keep an eye" on me. I had unknowingly been under surveillance for unknown reasons!

He told me of his assignment as an undercover officer. He had been assigned to cover me when I spoke at public meetings. He listened to my speeches, made notes and reported them to his superiors. He read materials which I had written and accumulated files of newspaper clippings reporting what I had said on previous occasions. Apparently the police department felt that I was a fairly dangerous person and must be kept under close surveillance. I had the feeling before leaving Toronto that my telephone was tapped but never had it checked out. The testimony of this man at that dinner convinced me that my telephone in fact had been tapped for at least three or four years, perhaps even longer. The thought also came to my mind that this story might be related to the attack which had occurred on me two or three years previously. I have since wondered how many ordinary citizens of the community are unknowingly being spied upon in this supposedly democratic and free society! Some years later, I heard that RCMP files on Canadian citizens contain more than 30,000 cases.

My contract at UVic was now over and we expected to return to Toronto in July 1985. We made a leisurely trip driving from Victoria to Toronto, stopping at several places along the way including nights with friends, relatives or former students at Kelowna, Calgary, Regina, Winnipeg, and Kenora. We often camped out at night in various provincial or national parks. We visited Lake Louise, Emerald Lake, the Banff National Park and other places of interest. It was a very pleasant trip although a part of it was during a drought accompanied by very hot weather.

We had enjoyed our friends and activities in Victoria. Sandy had become involved in several activities almost as quickly as she arrived on the scene. One of the most important was with the Victoria Board of Education. David Turner, one of my good friends and a colleague at UVic, was also a member of the Victoria Board of Education. He asked Sandy if she would be willing to undertake a research project in which he wanted to examine certain aspects of the counselling programs in the public schools. Sandy agreed and quickly embarked on that project which became a very important part of her activities in Victoria. She took part also in a research project involving the use of computers. She met the appropriate individuals at UVic and embarked on a program of developing public domain software for educators and students.

I had become involved in the Victoria Multicultural Council, the Vancouver Island Human Rights Coalition and the Victoria Peace Committee. Activities in these committees were very similar to my involvements in Toronto and I simply continued the same type of volunteer work in a new setting. I met many highly committed people in the Human Rights Coalition. Shortly after joining the organization, I was elected as chair of the education committee and one of my functions was to supervise the development of a study which focused on the teaching or lack of teaching of human rights in the Victoria public school system.

Sandy and I made ample use of the many social, educational and recreational facilities available in the Victoria area. It seems that almost everyone in Victoria made regular trips across the Strait of Georgia to Vancouver and we were no exception. I must have travelled across that strait a dozen times during the year I was in Victoria. Glenn Drover, my friend from the Social Planning Council, had moved to the University of British Columbia School of Social Work. It was possible for Sandy and me to visit him and his family on numerous occasions. I also participated in seminars or meetings of the faculty and students. Glenn and I reestablished a relationship which had been, at least to some extent, broken because of our several moves over the years.

Our two closest friends, however, were Jesse Dillard and Janna Ginsburg who were also a racially mixed couple, Jesse being black and Janna white. Both Jesse and I were born in the American South, he in South Carolina and I in Georgia. Jesse Dillard is a huge man, about six feet eight inches tall and over two hundred and sixty pounds, but probably one of the most gentle men I have ever met. We had previously worked together for two years in Toronto when I was president of the NBCC.

Relationship with the Dillards, Turners, Cossoms and others made it difficult to leave the West Coast. We had found that Victoria and Vancouver, like every other city in which I had lived, possessed many people of different backgrounds who were involved in a variety of social, economic and political activities in which we could feel at home. They were small "L" liberal-minded people who could be found in the local Society of Friends, Unitarian church, labour unions, teachers' organization and other similar groups. They are a minority in almost any society but the important fact is that they do exist and can be located, identified and become a part of one's social life experiences. We found this to be true in Victoria and appreciated that fact, knowing that in general, Victoria was a very conservative British-oriented city. We were told before we went to Victoria that we had to participate in at least one ritual: having tea at the Empress Hotel. We had lunch on one occasion at the Hotel, but missed having tea in the lobby.

Returning to Toronto meant returning to many of the old familiar activities and friends. Sandy returned to her employment as a coordinator of family studies for the Scarborough Board of Education. I returned to my many activities including teaching classes at York University, although on a part-time basis. I also resumed my position on the board of directors of the Urban Alliance. There had been some changes at the Toronto Disarmament Network. There was now a competing peace coalition in Toronto, known as "Act For Disarmament" (ACT). I was a founding member of the Toronto Disarmament Network and on my return to Toronto, I immediately inquired about relationships between the two groups and between the individual member organizations. I also inquired about the possible role which I could play now that I was back in Toronto.

I discovered that there was a great deal of internal controversy within both organizations and particularly in TDN. Many of my old friends who were among the founding members had dropped out because of dissatisfaction. The TDN had been initiated to provide information, opportunities for cooperation and coordination between a number of disparate groups but it was becoming a large, centralized bureaucratic organization and no longer as responsive to the needs of its member organizations. Of course, that is only one side of the controversy. Many groups, I was told, whose names still remained on the letterhead, had simply dropped out and were no longer active. I seized the opportunity to work with some of the disillusioned members in an attempt to bring them back into the organization. I felt they could then play a more active role in the control and direction of the organization. My efforts resulted in some limited success.

In the interests of obtaining a balanced view of the problem I also talked with leaders of ACT. The gulf between the two groups had widened during the year and there was little possibility of a merger. Others and I felt it was important to support the demonstrations, marches and other activities of both groups.

I had become convinced that the focus on armaments, and particularly nuclear disarmament, was not likely to get very far in a world still divided into two mutually hostile alliances built on the concept of mutually assured destruction (MAD). The arms race was moving ahead at full speed with the world spending nine hundred billion dollars annually on arms. The people and nations of the world were becoming less secure. Nothing could be more obvious, it seemed to me, than that peace would never be secure as long as there were vast differences in the standards of living between the third world and the rich western societies. It was known that the gap between the income levels and standard of living between the rich and poor nations was increasing. At the same time, within Canada and the United States the gap between rich and poor individuals was also increasing. We were heading toward a conflict in which the poor nations of the world would be engaged in constant guerrilla warfare in an attempt to break out of their poverty and powerlessness. That struggle would inevitably result in their being seen as threats by the rich nations. We have seen this phenomenon in many poor countries whose rich landowners control the country, usually on behalf of rich western nations and particularly the United States.

Shortly after arriving in Victoria, I had become increasingly aware that my eyesight was undergoing change. My eye doctor had previously told me that I had a cataract developing slowly in my left eye. This problem had not required surgery at that time but in Victoria, however, it became obvious that the problem was getting worse and an operation would be required shortly.

I checked with my doctor while in Toronto for the Christmas holidays and this diagnosis was confirmed. I was to undergo eye surgery immediately after my return to Toronto. I was lucky that the problem did not affect my ability to read which would have been a tragedy since I remained an avid reader. My distance vision, however, was increasingly affected, and it was necessary to give up driving. Sandy became the family chauffeur. Except for short rest periods, she drove most of the distance between Victoria and Toronto. She also drove me to the university each morning, but there were always two or three students ready to drive me to my home after evening classes.

I still had enough sight to move comfortably around the city by bus and subway and I made good use of these facilities. The result was, while somewhat handicapped, I did not find the situation onerous or a serious impediment in my work. In fact, it became a valuable learning experience as I made the adjustment to living with two handicaps — first, that of being black in racist North America, and second, the adjustment to a reduction in vision.

I underwent my third operation for detached retinas in August, 1985, shortly after returning to Toronto. By mid-September, I was again in the classroom at York University. Then I underwent cataract operations later in 1985 and in 1986, leaving my sight reduced further with each operation.

CHAPTER 15 *Changes and Challenges 1985–1991*

Within a month following my return I was back on the board of the Urban Alliance and attending meetings. One of the first things I noticed was that there had been a significant change in its climate since I had left the previous year. Although unaware of the reasons, I detected a degree of tension in the meetings of the board. Over the next few months I learned that part of this tension was due to events within the board itself. I gradually began to develop a picture of what had happened while I was away. (Actually, this tension had been building up even before I left for Victoria. I was not aware of the severity, however, until I returned). Without going into the ramifications, that tension was a reflection of differences of opinions and attitudes of some members of the board and the president at that time. Although not intentionally, I had opened a can of worms by my suggestion that the organization should engage in a self examination since it had been in operation for ten years (1975–1985). This idea was quickly picked up by members of the board and since it was my idea it was suggested that I should assume the responsibility of chair of that committee. I resisted and suggested, instead, that A. Dharmalingam, an original member of the board, should assume that responsibility. "Dharma" accepted and five other board members and I agreed to serve with him.

The first meeting of the committee was held at my home and we agreed that a questionnaire should be designed and mailed to as many present and former members as we could locate. I prepared the first draft. The evaluation committee began its work in late December and completed it in early April of 1986 when a public conference was held to examine and if necessary, suggest changes in the evaluation report which reflected generally positive attitudes and opinions of both members and non-members of the Urban Alliance.

Many respondents expressed agreement with the criticisms made by members and the general public. There was a feeling that these criticisms should receive close attention by the board of directors in its future plans. I was one of the people who felt that the time had come for a change in leadership. Having been the initial president of the organization in 1975, I was not willing to take on that responsibility myself. I shared the feeling that it was time for new leadership to emerge. However, when it came time to select the new president and other officers, those of us who felt the need for new leadership ran into difficulty. No one was ready to take on the job at that time, although two or three people indicated that they would be ready to do so a year or two later. It became fairly clear then that being officially retired, I would have to assume the responsibility simply because I was the only person with the necessary time available. Finally, and after considerable persuasion, I agreed to stand for the position for the second time.

When elected at the next board of directors meeting, I stressed that I was taking the job only on a temporary basis because I had a strong sense that the organization should be able to identify, cultivate and develop its own leadership without having to return to a former leader. I stated that I would be willing to accept the presidency for only one year and at the end of that time someone else should be prepared to step into the position. I also noted that the time had come for us to employ a staff coordinator. The Urban Alliance had not had a coordinator since its early days. Carol Tator had acted as both president and coordinator. I felt that this was asking too much for any volunteer and it would be necessary to raise funds to employ a coordinator, at least on a part-time basis.

We received partial funding from the United Way and from a foundation which allowed hiring a part-time coordinator. As a result of this development, my role as president was reduced and much less stressful.

By the next annual meeting (May 1987), I had to face the prospects of staying on for another year. The organization had enjoyed a good year because the former tension had disappeared and the board was again functioning at an adequate, if not superior, level. It had become fairly obvious by that time, however, that the number of prospects with available time to do the job was very limited. We had also lost Robert Adetuyi, our part-time coordinator who resigned to give full time to his interest in film making. I then made a deal with one of the potential presidents. I suggested to her that I would be willing to serve one additional year if she would guarantee that she would take over the job the next year if it was offered to her. She agreed and I made plans to remain as president, if re-elected, for another year. I informed the board at its next meeting that this would certainly be my final year. I again reminded members that it was the responsibility of the board to identify and cultivate its potential leadership. Any viable organization should be able to produce its own leadership corps at whatever level necessary. The board responded positively and that decision was carried out. Kamala Jean Gopie was elected president at the next annual meeting in May 1988.

I have always felt that leadership in voluntary organizations is very important. However, it is not a task which should remain too long in the hands of one individual. In my experience, I had seen principals of schools, pastors of churches, presidents of universities, leaders of political parties and others, who stayed in their jobs too long and had come to feel that the organization belonged to them and that no one else should have the opportunity for leadership.

I had applauded the decision at York University that department chair people would only serve a three-year term, and deans a five-year term, and they would not be eligible for a second consecutive term. The president of the university was also elected to serve a five-year term but with the possibility of a second five-year term under certain conditions. In voluntary organizations, I felt that five years is much too long. My personal view was that a two-year term is ideal with the possibility of one additional year under certain circumstances. Kamala Jean Gopie had already demonstrated the capacities and commitment necessary for carrying out the responsibilities of a strong president for the Urban Alliance.

The year 1991 marked the sixteenth anniversary of the Urban Alliance. A. Dharmalingam and I were the two founding members still active in the organization. I felt that it was time for me to make room for new members, new ideas and new energy. I announced that I would not be a candidate for re-election to the Board at the May 23, 1991 annual general meeting. There was some concern expressed by a few members of the board, but they were assured that I was not dropping out completely. I planned to continue working on a few program committees, and because of the absence of the immediate past president, I would remain in that position until she returned from a trip around the world. I had no intention of completely leaving the organization and am already committed to working on the justice and other ad hoc committees. The Urban Alliance elected its officers at the first meeting of the board following the AGM in May, 1991. It was at that meeting, held on June 26, 1991, that my resignation became official.

A Race Relations Network

I felt the need for a federation or coalition of multiracial organizations in the struggle against racial prejudice and discrimination in the province of Ontario. My thinking at that time was that a network or a coalition should be limited to multiracial organizations similar to the structure and functions of the Urban Alliance. A number of ethno-specific organizations already existed in the city and province, i.e., the Chinese Canadian National Council (CCNC), the National Association of Canadians with Origins in India (NACOI), the Japanese Canadian Association (JCA) and others. In addition, a few autonomous organizations in the province, based on the model of the Urban Alliance, already existed in 1986 and were located in Windsor, London, Ottawa and Sudbury. A small multiracial organization was also being formed in Kingston.

I wrote a letter to the presidents of these organizations suggesting that the time had arrived when the five of us might join together in a federation or a coalition based in Ontario. That idea was enthusiastically endorsed, first by the National Capital Alliance in Ottawa, and later, by the London, Windsor and Sudbury groups. A meeting of these groups and the Urban Alliance was scheduled to be held in London, Ontario in the summer of 1987 which began the process of developing what is now the Federation of Race Relations Organizations (Ontario).

The new organization faced a number of important difficulties including a lack of funds to pay the transportation and other costs of delegates to attend meetings. Also it was recognized that some organizations had specific program objectives relevant to problems in their own local community and not necessarily to those of another city. But there was a number of areas of common concern. For example, all organizations were concerned about the treatment of non-whites by some members of the police, the lack of employment of non-whites in the mass media, and the lack of effective employment equity in the province. The Federation could launch joint campaigns in an effort to initiate necessary changes on a province-wide basis.

Those of us who launched the Federation felt that this organization might be the first step in the development of a national organization. This long-term goal is limited by the fact that only a few multiracial organizations exist in Canada. Outside of Ontario, we are aware of only three similar organizations in Vancouver, Calgary and Montreal. Canada has not had the experience of multiracial organizations working together over a period of time. Usually multiracial organizations come together around a crisis such as an attack on a Jewish synagogue or a police shooting of a black youth. These crisis-generated organizations tend to die out after short periods of activity and the Toronto experience clearly illustrates this assertion. The immediate prospect of a viable national multiracial organization was remote. In the meantime, the local chapters of the Federation were dedicated to build the Ontario organization into a strong instrument in the struggle against racial prejudice and discrimination in Ontario.

The Donald Marshall Prosecutions

In the fall of 1987, I was asked if I would take on a new organizational task. Several members of the UARR had, over the years, expressed concern regarding the treatment of blacks and native people by the criminal justice system. This issue had been discussed on many occasions but we had never been able to discover an entrance into the criminal justice system. The Donald Marshall Inquiry in Nova Scotia gave me that opportunity. I accepted the challenge and began my work on the Donald Marshall Prosecution in the late fall. The Royal Commission was composed of three judges with the mandate of investigating the circumstances surrounding the imprisonment of Donald Marshall, a young native man, for murder. Marshall had spent eleven years in jail before an investigation found that he had been wrongfully imprisoned. The circumstances surrounding this case became the focus of the Royal Commission's investigation. Bobby Seales, the murder victim, was a seventeen year old black youth. The black communities and the Micmac Indians of Nova Scotia wanted representation before the Royal Commission and John Briggs, the research director of the Commission, asked me to prepare a proposal for a study focussing on the perceptions and adverse experiences of the black population of Nova Scotia. Studies were to address the social, economic and political environment, including the criminal justice system, as they impacted on the two non-white communities of Nova Scotia.

On my first trip to Nova Scotia I ran into some opposition regarding the nature and scope of the study. The Black United Front (BUF), a provincial black organization, wanted a study which they hoped would condemn the behaviour of the police and the Crown Attorneys in the prosecution and imprisonment of Donald Marshall. Second, that organization also wanted to have the name of the victim cleared of any wrongdoing. There had been some suggestion that Marshall and Seales were involved in an attempted robbery and both the Micmac and the black populations were concerned that law enforcement officers had concocted false evidence in an attempt to justify their role in the imprisonment of Marshall.

In part, I rejected the argument that my task was to deal initially with these suspicions. If I was to conduct the study, it would be as objective as possible. I would not be caught in a trap of conducting a study designed to prove that someone was guilty of malfeasance. That function was the responsibility of the Royal Commission who had no difficulty in accepting that approach to my study. The Black United Front also finally agreed, but only with reluctance. I was authorized, in cooperation with John Briggs, to recruit and employ local staff to conduct the local field work and immediately began work on developing the instruments to be utilized in conducting the study. One instrument, a questionnaire, involved approximately thirty-five questions on perceptions and experiences in the daily lives of blacks in the province of Nova Scotia and the criminal justice system.

A study of the factors underlying the Donald Marshall case would not be valid without also studying the context in which the event had occurred. Initially the members of the Commission expressed some opposition to this approach. These men, all lawyers, were not accustomed to a sociological approach to the understanding of human behaviour. However, I stuck to my position and made it very clear that it was the only basis on which I would be willing to conduct the study. Members of the Royal Commission finally agreed and gave me permission to zero in on the factors I considered important including a study of the degree of discrimination, if any, against blacks in housing, public services, education, employment and the criminal justice system of Nova Scotia. The criminal justice system, from my perspective, was only one part of a pattern of systematic prejudice and discrimination against blacks throughout the province. My study included attention to the interrelationships of these various factors which in the final event led to the wrongful conviction of Donald Marshall. Ms. Rhonda Crawford, a young criminology student at St. Mary's University was employed to assist in recruiting and training staff for conducting interviews in Halifax/Dartmouth and each of eight local communities.

The study, like most studies in the social sciences, did not tell us a great deal that we did not already suspect. What it did was to demonstrate through objective research that discrimination not only was present in Nova Scotia but was pervasive and adversely affected almost every aspect of the life of blacks in the province. Of particular interest was the often cordial relations existing between blacks and whites on a personal level. Yet, that relationship was not found on the institutional level, i.e., employment, education, housing, police treatment of blacks and native people. The cross tabulation of these and other variables provided the basis for the findings of the study.

The conduct of the Study of Discrimination Against Blacks gave me the opportunity to obtain considerable information and insight into life in Nova Scotia in both specific and general terms. I found that most complaints against the criminal justice system were not directed against the police. Instead the largest number and the most bitter complaints by blacks were directed at the courts, including the attitude and behaviour of crown attorneys, defence lawyers, clerks and judges. Another surprising finding was that black people in small towns and rural areas expressed a more positive attitude toward the police than did people in the metropolitan Halifax/Dartmouth area. Often in small towns, white and black populations were acquainted with each other and co-existed on a friendly basis. In these situations many blacks who were picked up by the police, were often returned home rather than charged. It was not the police and courts who provided the punishment but rather the parents.

The study of the records of police charges of a specific crime clearly suggested that blacks and whites were subjected to different treatment. Blacks were more likely to be treated harshly than whites. None of this was surprising to us. Previous studies in other parts of the world, particularly in Britain and the United States, had arrived at similar conclusions. However, to our knowledge, this was the first time in Canada that a study of the operations of the criminal justice system had been conducted. Other studies of the experiences of native people, the behaviour of crown attorneys and of the police became a part of the background of the Royal Commission Report on the Donald Marshall prosecution.

Members of the Commission held a series of hearings in which, over a period of several months, more than a hundred officials and ordinary citizens testified. That report was officially released in January 1990. It quickly aroused a tremendous degree of public discussion and concern throughout the country. It will, in all probability, continue to make a major impact on the thinking and perhaps even the practices of the criminal justice system, not only in Nova Scotia but throughout Canada. Professor Don Clairmount, a sociologist at Dalhousie University, became a valuable asset in the conduct of the study. One aspect, the investigation of sentencing practices, was a special concern to him and he designed and supervised that entire section of the study.

My overall supervision of the study was conducted through regular visits and telephone contacts with Rhonda Crawford. I flew to Halifax for conferences seventeen times during a nine-month period in 1988 and 1989.

Following my research work with the Royal Commission on the Donald Marshall Prosecution, I was ready for a more active role in the prison reform movement. In addition to its many other significant findings, the Royal Commission had clearly directed its criticism to the province of Nova Scotia but there were similar problems in other provinces. I had made several attempts during the latter part of that study to interest Nova Scotia blacks in recognizing the importance of a strong advocacy organization. Having been aware of the poor state of organization in the Nova Scotia black community, I felt that little or nothing would happen in the absence of pressure from a strong and determined group. I was also aware that two older organizations, the Black United Front and the Nova Scotia Human Rights Commission, were not in a position to assume this aggressive stance and was certain that the black community was losing an opportunity to assume an effective role in changing the exploitative and unjust conditions under which they had lived for more than two hundred years. That opportunity would probably not occur again for another decade or more. The impact of that project was not totally lost. The injustice done to Donald Marshall, and a similar case involving a young native woman in Manitoba, had aroused tremendous public attention to the many limitations of the system, including blatant racism. In Ontario, the Attorney General expressed interest in a similar, but more limited, study of the performance of crown attorneys and of the courts generally.

I was pleasantly surprised to learn a few months later that some movement had been made with respect to the development of an interprovincial black organization, including Nova Scotia and New Brunswick. It is to be hoped that this organization would confront the many problems encountered by blacks in their day-to-day lives as citizens of the Maritime provinces. But it was also concerned with the problems encountered by both black and native young people involved in the criminal justice system of Ontario. Some evidence of this situation in Ontario is based on observations made by my son Norman and others, who, with a small group of Quakers, spent considerable time visiting and working with prisoners in two of the local detention centres. They found a disproportionate number of blacks and natives in both centres. The characteristics of the detainees were similar.

Several studies have shown that a disproportionate number of inhabitants of correctional institutions are young, poor, black or native, and of limited educational backgrounds. It seems strange that officers and staffs of these institutions have not, as yet, drawn what appear to me to be obvious conclusions. That is, that individuals from these groups are more likely to be arrested by the police, detained in detention centres, tried and convicted of the same offences that others of different racial or socio-economic characteristics. Other observations in Toronto indicate that the large majority of inmates of federal and provincial institutions are from similar circumstances. The conclusion could easily be drawn that the criminal justice system exists to punish those who are classified as members of these disadvantaged groups.

Return to Tuskegee

I have spoken earlier of my career and experiences at Tuskegee Institute. My 1990 visit to the campus, the second in 50 years, was one of the two highlights of my recent experiences. Returning to Tuskegee was more than an opportunity to visit old friends and acquaintances and even to celebrate the 50th anniversary of my graduation. It was both, but there was another dimension: it was an opportunity to go back in time and to re-examine one of the formative experiences of my life, and to learn how I would react to a new and changed atmosphere. I have already mentioned my love/hate relationship to Tuskegee. I made the trip with anticipation and a degree of anxiety. Although I was only in residence at Tuskegee for three years, it had played a major role in my social and intellectual development. It was a vital part of me, largely because of the opportunities first, to leave home and second, to test out my emerging philosophical maturity.

My struggles against military training, the early morning drills and the requirement that students must wear semi-military uniforms were, in retrospect, rebellions against what I considered as unnecessary restrictions having little or nothing to do with the educational responsibilities of the institution. Both concerns were, at least to some extent, addressed. As mentioned earlier, the campus was dramatically changed and much to my surprise I was unable to locate the old familiar landmarks, the dining hall, residence halls, and classroom buildings, which in some respects was quite unsettling. This was not the old familiar Tuskegee, frequently known as "Skegee" by students. In addition the name of the institution had been changed to Tuskegee University which was greeted with muted disapproval by some graduates.

Aside from my old classmates, I hardly knew any of the present staff, most of whom had been retired many years ago. I was quite aware that many changes would have occurred over a period of a half century, but it was the massive scale of the changes which astonished me. Many activities were planned which helped to reorient the returning graduates and to help us feel at home, an important part of the 50th anniversary of the class of 1940 and the usual Founders Day celebrations held each spring. It was good to return for the celebration and I was surprised that it was possible for so many members of our class to attend. An unexpected joy was the presence of the former Deborah Cannon, my field work supervisor. She was invited to return and present the Founders Day address to the student body and many distinguished visitors on a warm Sunday morning in March, 1990.

My class of 1940, aware that she was to be on campus, invited her to attend and participate in a Saturday noon brunch. As expected she had changed to some extent but she had not lost her youthful enthusiasm and energy which had made her one of the most popular professors on campus. I detected that enthusiasm while among a crowd of 50 or 60 graduates in the relatively small dining room of a local church. I immediately recognized Deborah's voice and made my way through the crowd and tapped her on the shoulder. I said, "I am one of your former students." She paused for a moment and stated with emphasis, "Yes, I know you. You are Wilson Head." We gave each other a bear-like hug, and moving away from others, began an animated discussion of our recent careers and family life. Our conversation ended when she had to join her group for the meal. Although she is married and with a different surname I will always remember her as Deborah Cannon, a woman who loved and was loved by her students.

Other items, such as the political conditions of blacks in Mason County, the county in which the town of Tuskegee and the university were located, had also changed, largely but not exclusively as a result of the work of Tuskegee University faculty, staff and students during the 1950s and 60s. Only one or two blacks were allowed to vote during my tenure at the Institute. Although blacks outnumbered whites by a ratio of six to one in the county, the white population kept a strangle-hold on economic and political power. Dr. Gomillion, one of my sociology professors, was instrumental in organizing a local black group, the Tuskegee Civic Association, which made the first step in an attempt to mobilize blacks for achieving a series of limited goals but initially steered away from an effort to gain the vote and political power.

A decision of the U.S. Supreme Court later removed the long-established barriers to black participation in the political process and the influence of black participation was quickly felt as increasing numbers were elected to local municipal and county offices. Unfortunately written records and information from local people indicated that students and faculty of Tuskegee University played only a minor role in this significant development. That information was a disappointment to me because I was familiar with the significant roles of black students in the civil rights movement.

Nevertheless it appeared that the class of 1940 was enjoying the camaraderie, fellowship and well-being of former classmates. There was the not unexpected news of deaths. We also learned of another unexpected issue early in the celebration. Dr. Payton, the current president of the university, delivered a stirring address to the visitors on the first morning of the celebration in which he referred to an unknown critic, at least unknown to us, who had severely attacked the university and his performance as president. Most visitors were quite puzzled since we had no idea of the issues under discussion, but it subsequently became known that the critic was a member of a local alumni chapter of the institution who held a personal grudge against the general direction of the educational process at Tuskegee. He also felt that the president was spending too much time seeking financial support from the corporate community. Being aware of the desperate plight of most black colleges and universities, many of us felt sympathy for the president. The incident was quickly passed over and the celebrations continued on an upbeat level. None of us should have been upset at the attack. Tuskegee, as with other black institutions, was perennially short of funds and it was generally accepted that fundraising was one of the most important functions of a president.

I left Tuskegee with mixed feelings. I felt that many progressive changes had been made, such as the elimination of compulsory military training and compulsory attendance at Chapel, and a reduction in the authoritarian atmosphere. The old School of Mechanical Industries was gone and new schools of engineering and veterinary medicine were established. My friend and classmate

Bob Judkins had officially retired but was still teaching at the school of veterinary medicine. The institution had grown, lost much of the sense of community and the students were clearly not interested in attempts to introduce a variety of cultural programs. Outstanding speakers, musical groups, the famous Tuskegee Choir and Band, and other events attracted extremely small numbers of students. Tuskegee students appeared to be following a trend of many others elsewhere, "I simply want to get my degree and get out of this place". I was disappointed with this trend but recognized that it was one aspect of a lack of interest in other than the commercial aspects of the educational enterprise in North American societies.

Rio de Janeiro

Early in the spring of 1990, I was invited by a staff member of the Canadian Council of Churches to attend a consultation to discuss and help the churches develop approaches to the issue of racism in Canadian society. The consultation was co-sponsored by the World Council of Churches (WCC) located in Geneva, Switzerland. I attended and addressed a meeting of approximately 150 individuals from many different backgrounds and from many parts of the world. The group included church officials, activists, bishops of various religious organizations and ordinary citizens. I presented my remarks, enjoyed a lively discussion period following the address, and went home feeling that it had been an extremely stimulating evening. As is my usual custom, I quickly became involved in other issues and within a few months almost forgot the experience.

In August of 1990, I received a letter from the headquarters of the WCC inviting me to participate in a "Global Consultation on Blacks, Indigenous Peoples and the Churches in the Americas". The general theme of the consultation was "Ending the Pain, Beginning the Hope". The meeting was convened by the South American Commission of the WCC "Program to Combat Racism" and was held in Rio de Janeiro, Brazil. It was attended by more than 150 men and women from virtually every country in Central and South America, and a few others from North America and the Caribbean. It was held from September 22nd to 29th, at a Catholic retreat centre located in the mountains partly surrounding the city. Joanne St Lewis (a young black lawyer), and I were the only Canadian participants.

The major topic of the several days of workshops, speeches and panel discussions was the upcoming planned commemoration of the Columbus "Discovery of America" in 1492. Rather than commemorating the 500 years (1492–1992) of this "discovery", the black and indigenous people called attention to "500 years of slavery, genocide, exploitation and oppression". The cry for freedom and liberation, the invitation said, "has been at the centre or at the bottom of the struggle for land rights and racial justice". It was an inspiring call for justice which has been denied to blacks and Indigenous people in all parts of the Americas and the Caribbean.

I have attended and participated in perhaps too many conferences, workshops and seminars and, over the years, have become somewhat cynical regarding the importance of the proliferation of these gatherings which now dominate much of the social and cultural life of modern societies. Aside from the opportunity to meet and renew old acquaintances, I find them virtually useless as far as new ideas, intellectual stimulation or increased innovation and creativity are concerned.

These thoughts ran through my mind as I considered the prospects of travelling to Rio de Janeiro. The decision however, was not difficult to make. I quickly wrote my acceptance of the invitation to Geneva and began planning for the event. I had a strong feeling that this experience was to be no mere gathering of professional, business people or others of similar backgrounds, experiences, tastes and interests. It would not, as so many other gatherings, be merely a group looking for good food, drink and opportunities to break away from what is often a dull life. This, I felt, would be an adventure of the mind and a revitalization of the spirit. That was to be my first trip to South America and I was not disappointed.

The flight to Rio was long and tiring. It began shortly after 10:00 p.m. and continued, non-stop to Rio, arriving at 7:30 a.m. As usual in my travels, I make an effort to acquire at least some knowledge of the physical, social, economic and political conditions of the host community. We had agreed that Sandy would also take advantage of the opportunity to visit Brazil. She obtained several books from the local library and was better equipped than I for the trip. Being extremely busy, I had neglected to make these arrangements. I read some of the materials she had acquired, but otherwise, had to count on the presence of Brazilians who spoke English. I was fortunate in this respect. While the Portuguese language was the primary mode of expression, the consultations included a considerable number of English- and Spanish-speaking individuals. I cannot claim to be a "two-week expert" on the country but I did gain a considerable amount of information which helped me to understand the attitudes, cultural backgrounds and political characteristics of Brazil and of delegates from the Spanish speaking countries of South and Central America.

This was not the typical North American conference, with simultaneous translation in French and English, since English was distinctly a minority language in this consultation. Our interpreters spoke Portuguese, Spanish and English. Although Brazil was the host country, perhaps two thirds of the delegates were from Spanish-speaking countries, including Peru, Columbia, Uruguay, Paraguay, Argentina, Ecuador, Bolivia and the Central American countries. They were bright, energetic and committed to the work in which they were engaged, the support of the poor and oppressed people of their countries. In that sense, they may not have been examples of "ordinary people". They were ordinary people but also leaders of ordinary people.

Three characteristics impressed me upon arrival at the consultation centre. First, the generally small size of the men and women. Second, their open-armed friendliness. They approached others, including me, with open arms for a big hug and kisses on both cheeks. Being unfamiliar with this behaviour, I had to get used to it, but once that was accomplished, I wondered why we in North America are so cold and stand-offish. The third characteristic which impressed me was their passionate espousal of their causes. Their faith in their religious experiences was deep and strong. With this strength, they had little difficulty in facing personal danger and the threat of torture and death. I found myself wondering how in the midst of a materialistic world, they could, against all odds, maintain that faith. Their willingness to sacrifice and face danger in achieving social change and social justice stood in sharp contrast to North American, and I suspect European values. I could only admire these committed men and women.

The initial picture of the physical aspects of Rio de Janeiro was breathtaking. Much of its downtown area was the epitome of luxury, wealth and leisure. Its hotels and beaches, all officially "public" but used largely by tourists and wealthy businessmen, are famous throughout the world. But this picture is only one side of a more grim and depressing aspect of life in that city. It is easy to get the impression, as I did, that Rio, with its mild climate, attractive buildings and artistic sidewalks, would be the ideal place in which to live. However, we were warned to be on guard against thieves who have been known to "mug" tourists in full daylight in downtown Rio. We received our first taste of the validity of those warnings when, on the second day of our consultation, three of our delegates were robbed by thieves who had broken into their rooms at the conference centre. The slums, called 'favelas', which occupy the hillsides are, for the most part, barely habitable; many have no running water, little or no sanitation facilities, and are characterized by poverty and disease. Sao Paulo, the largest and most highly industrialized city in the country, was perhaps even worse than Rio. At least Rio possessed great natural beauty.

Sandy, whose flight was delayed by other commitments, arrived in Rio a few days after me, and had already made arrangements to visit several parts of the country by bus while I was engaged in the conference. She visited and observed a considerable part of southern Brazil, the more wealthy part of the country. Most indigenous people and the majority of the black population lived in the poorer north-east and west regions. While the minority groups in the South were also poor, at least they were not suffering from the killings, beatings and torture faced by many in the north-east and western regions.

I have mentioned my active membership and support of Amnesty International and my awareness of the hundreds of occasions in which men, women and even children are routinely abducted, tortured and killed by "death squads" in many South and Central American and other Third World countries from reading the monthly bulletin which provides details of human rights abuses in many countries. On occasion I have taken copies of the bulletin to my classes and asked students to read and critique the contents. Without exception, they have reacted with horror and question whether the reports are actually true. But I had never met individuals who were actual victims of such treatment. My reading of Amnesty bulletins had not prepared me to face the reality of this evidence of the inhumanity some people subject on others.

I had expected adventure and mental stimulation, and I found both in abundance. I am, as are many Central and South Americans, aware of the role played by the United States in supporting dictators and killers as a part of its intent to maintain control over the resources of those countries. The 1990 invasion of Panama was merely one addition to the long list of invasions and support of military coups against the governments of several other countries in that region. With that knowledge, I could easily understand and sympathize with the bitter anger in which many delegates referred to crimes in their countries. The "American boot", as one indigenous woman stated, "is never far from our necks and from the necks of anyone who attempts to support the struggle of the poor for land and independence!"

The poverty and deprivation of the South and Central Americas, however, did not originate with the greed of the United States, it began with the European conquest and enslavement of the indigenous peoples, and later of African slaves. The adverse effects of that colonization and enslavement still exist. The descendants of black slaves and the Amerindians (mixed black and indigenous peoples) were bright, passionate and bitter. They expressed their anguish and frustration but we and they knew there was little we could do about their condition. American economic and military power is simply overwhelming but perhaps we can help to arouse the peoples of the rich western countries to the massive injustices done to poor and vulnerable people by our own governments. We can do something, however small, to provide accurate information about the crimes committed by the American and Canadian governments, and hopefully the peoples of our countries will express their anger and outrage at these crimes. An aroused public is the most potent weapon at our disposal.

In spite of the grim messages we were hearing, I found myself thoroughly enchanted by the joyful singing and dances presented by these exploited people. While some men and women had been subjected to warnings or death threats, they nevertheless reflected a sense of inner freedom and peace. I remember very keenly talking with a young South American woman who could speak a little English. I asked her how, in the context of death threats, did she manage to carry on in such high spirits? She replied that she was certain that she was doing "God's will" in her efforts to organize the poor of her little village to struggle against oppression and exploitation. The land of the villagers was seized by a rich landlord, with the armed support of government soldiers. The villagers and she had been warned to stay away from their lands and any attempt to regain them would be severely dealt with. She continued her work with the feeling that someone had to stand up for "what was right", and she had no intention of giving up the struggle. We have read and heard much regarding the impact of "Liberation Theology". These people were living examples of a powerful idea whose "time had come." It is fair to say that this spirit of liberation is rarely found in the affluent populations of rich western nations. I could identify with this attitude since I had felt in a similar manner when I refused induction into the U.S. Army and faced imprisonment. Many delegates expressed similar attitudes.

I left the conference with the feeling that I had been in the presence of an unusual group of men and women, many of whom had risked their lives to support the struggle of the poor, and many would probably pay a heavy price for their determination and courage. I could only admire those qualities and regret that I did not have the opportunity to share more with them. It was a rare opportunity and I do not expect to enjoy its challenges again. But if the opportunity does arrive, I will gladly seize it!

The paradox of Rio and Toronto is that after two weeks in the "city of the rich elite", Rio de Janeiro, I returned to the city of the large but shrinking middle class, the city with 80,000 to 120,000 individuals who depend on "food banks" each week for survival. The poor are the dominant population group in Rio but it would be easy to exaggerate the differences between the two cities.

Another of my life experiences which, in some respects, reminded me of the events of Rio de Janeiro occurred shortly after my return. I had already become marginally engaged in supporting the struggles of the native peoples of Canada as a result of the Oka incident in which the native people had, for the first time in many generations, defied the RCMP, the Quebec provincial police and the Canadian military in defence of their treaty rights. In general the courts, in spite of clear evidence, had ruled against the land claims of the native peoples of Canada. Again, a weak and demoralized people had suffered cultural genocide, the increasing loss of their languages, poverty and exploitation and again the same old pattern of oppression by the strong of the weak was played out with little chance of redress.

The Oka incident, in which a small Quebec town was planning to seize lands which were still under claims of native ownership and where the project was going ahead without regard to the fact that the land in question had been occupied by natives for thousands of years, a matter quite similar to the present seizure of native lands in Brazil. The invitation to attend and participate in a major conference of natives and others living in northwestern Ontario was gladly accepted. The conference was held in late November, 1990 in Thunder Bay, Ontario.

Approximately 150 individuals, one-half of whom were native people from Thunder Bay, surrounding areas and more distant areas of the province participated. Many had travelled by car more than six hours to attend the proceedings. Several "elders" were present and provided some insight into native religious and cultural practices. Many of these men were impressive in their quiet bearings and dignified manners. I was particularly impressed by Phil Fountaine, a Manitoba native leader whose grasp and ability to articulate native issues were impressive and convincing. Much of his discussion focused on the implications of the Oka incident. The significant fact, however, was his view that Oka was not an isolated incident: native people have grown in maturity and confidence in their ability to manage their own affairs and a strong feeling was expressed, which I supported, that the Canadian Indian Act should be abolished and replaced by treaties between the Canadian and the various native nations. Aside from the death squads, the treatment of native people in Canada by the majority population was similar to that of native people in Brazil.

My participation and support appeared to have been well accepted. I was asked and agreed to supply many groups with appropriate materials collected from a variety of sources by the Urban Alliance, and when appropriate, to invite their organizations to join our umbrella group, the Federation of Race Relations Organizations in Ontario. The native people of north western Ontario are badly isolated by distance and hostility in the small communities of that area. The atmosphere and optimism of the participants suggests that real possibilities may now be available for mutual support in a common struggle for justice and freedom for all people of the province.

Unfortunately the possibilities for increased cooperation between northern and southern Ontario communities did not materialize. There were some similar goals, i.e., the demand for justice, fair treatment by the police and the courts and basic respect for the dignity of human beings, but the differences were too wide for effective collaboration. Protecting their ways of life and an end to government reluctance to settle land claims were top priorities for the native people. Ben Fiber, a board member of the Urban Alliance, made some contacts with the national leadership of the Assembly of First Nations. He drafted a brief submitted to the federal government on their behalf and kept in contact with them for several months. Many natives and non-natives have stated publicly that unless progress is made on settlement of land claims, it was likely that there would be more Okas during the summer of 1991 and afterwards. That possibility has not emerged.

As a non-native I could not participate actively in the affairs of the struggle of the native people of Canada in the absence of an invitation. But I closely followed events as they occurred and found myself facing a dilemma: while strongly supporting their struggle, as a believer in non-violence I could not support the tactic of the Mohawk Warriors in their armed standoff against the Quebec Provincial Police and the Canadian armed forces. On the other hand, the act of the Canadian government in calling the armed forces to possibly turn their weapons on poverty stricken natives struggling to assert their rights was a travesty of freedom and justice. The "footdragging" of the previous two hundred years by those with power continued. The appointment of a recently announced Royal Commission of inquiry into the conditions of native peoples in Canada may be a first step, but it may be merely another example of the usual delaying tactics of successive federal governments. The new confidence and militancy of various native organizations, including the Assembly of First Nations, may end government inactivity and force the resolution of hundreds of outstanding land claims and perhaps lead to a measure of self government, a necessary step in the long march of native peoples toward a sense of dignity and self respect.

The struggle of blacks, Chinese, South Asians, natives and other disadvantaged groups must be viewed as one. I hope to have the opportunity to work with native people in their part of the common struggle. I have repeatedly mentioned my concern regarding the social and cultural isolation of the various racial and ethnic groups from each other. A recent event (December 1991), provided grounds for hope that this behaviour may change. A conference entitled Agenda for People, sponsored by the Canadian Labour Congress, was held in Ottawa and attended by more than 600 delegates. It was an inspiring affair which brought together representatives from labour councils, environmental groups, the women's movement and a variety of community groups. Shirley Carr, the outgoing president of the Congress, led an imposing group of speakers including Bishop Remy de Roo of Victoria, B.C., Bob White, then-president of the Canadian Auto Workers, and several others.

Although not on the conference program I had the opportunity to express my views in three different workshops and I took full advantage of those opportunities, focussing largely on the difficulties in developing coalitions based on a wide variety of interest groups. Few, if any of these groups had ever worked together and it was obvious that the strong and well organized labour unions could dominate the new coalition. I also raised the question of the lack of participation by blacks and other non-whites in the upper echelons of the labour movement. It was obvious from the number of women present and holding executive positions that they are well on the road to equality in the organizational structure of the labour movement.

My particular interest was the workshop on native issues in which the featured speaker was Ovide Mercredi, the newly elected Grand Chief of the Assembly of First Nations. Although quiet spoken, Mercredi was a man who demanded attention and respect. Following his brief address, Mercredi was attacked regarding the treatment of native women by some chiefs on reservations. He sympathized with the position but noted that these were matters which the native people themselves had to solve. He stated with great emphasis that he "was not a dictator and would be working with his colleagues on this question". I had not intended to participate verbally in the workshop but following this interchange, felt that I had to state my views and I pointed out that we had been talking about self-government for native people and were now trying to impose our views on them. It was their decision and if we were serious we had to let them decide to what extent they would abide by our human rights codes and charters. I would hope that they would encompass the best of western concepts of human rights but suggested that in some respects their views were on a higher level than ours. For example, many native groups already have a social charter and don't require guidance from westerners whose heavy emphasis is not on collective but on the protection of individual rights. Unexpectedly I received a loud and sustained applause for my remarks. Later I had a brief chat with Mercredi. I assured him of my strong support for the cause of native people on whose land we were holding the meeting. Perhaps this initiative by the CLC may be the first step in a long-needed development.

It appeared almost impossible to concentrate on my writings. I continued to receive invitations to speak at a great many important conferences, seminars and workshops or to visit and speak to high school students concerning racial issues. In spite of my best intentions, I usually accept these invitations. A recent visit to a local high school, however, gave me quite a shock. Many of the young males were in an angry mood and demanded to know why I was speaking of the importance of remaining in school, graduating and preparing themselves for universities and professional schools. They insisted that the only way to get ahead was by taking guns and defending themselves. They rejected the philosophy and tactics of Martin Luther King and preferred those of Malcolm X, that is, armed struggle. I jokingly suggested that perhaps they should go out and begin buying AK-47 assault rifles. That "tongue in cheek" suggestion appeared to exert a "calming effect", but they were not finished. They insisted on continuing the discussion in the hallway following the meeting. Twelve to fifteen joined me for a "rap session" in which the discussion continued for approximately 15 minutes.

I recognized their rage, alienation and hopelessness and the need to express their frustrations. I was certain that these teenagers were not going to take up rifles immediately, but wondered what would happen within the next ten to twenty years if Canadians refused to listen and respond to their cries of pain. It is the task of many others and myself to exert sufficient pressure for change so that they will not feel the need for destructive and self-destructive behaviour.

One of the most enjoyable of my many visits to local high schools was an April 1991 visit to Oakwood Collegiate in midtown Toronto. This was not the usual pattern in which I met and spoke to a class or an assembly of black and white students. I am usually told, when invited, that the principal and staff want me to serve as a "role model" of a non-white who has "made it", meaning someone who might inspire black students to remain in school, graduate and go on for further post-secondary education. The goal on this occasion was different. The collegiate had been chosen to host a meeting of high achievement black students selected from all Toronto secondary schools. I was asked to be the "keynote speaker". In addition, entertainment, dancers and food were on the program. More than two hundred crowded into the small auditorium, including approximately thirty-five honourees, their parents and teachers accompanying with them. I praised the students for their hard work and high achievement and my remarks were warmly applauded. I remained on stage following my remarks because a part of my responsibility was to present the prizes to the winning students. Although aware that in general girls tend to achieve higher academic standards than boys, I was nevertheless surprised that two-thirds of the awards were won by girls who ranged from grades eight to twelve.

This was a joyous occasion for parents, teachers and students. I had the opportunity to participate in informal sessions with individual students and parents following the formal part of the program. It is unusual that opportunities are available for achieving black high school students to receive public recognition. I was pleased to share this experience with a splendid group of young people and their parents.

Aside from the very significant trip to Rio de Janeiro of September, 1990, I have rarely been as emotionally caught up in an event as the 1991 war in the Persian Gulf. I had joined with thousands of Canadians in a futile attempt to prevent that war. But it became increasingly clear that the stubbornness of Saddam Hussein and the need of American president George Bush to defeat and destroy Iraq were insurmountable barriers to a peaceful solution to the conflict. Without excusing the behaviour of Hussein in invading Kuwait, it was nevertheless a highly convenient justification for the destruction of Iraq. Although presumably justified by United Nations resolutions, it is interesting that the United States has consistently vetoed resolutions against its own action and the actions of its client states, for example, support of the Contras in their aggression against Nicaragua, the UN resolution demanding that Israel return the West Bank and the Gaza Strip to the Palestinians, the aggression against tiny Granada and Panama .... the list goes on and on. But there is nothing new regarding American aggression against Central and South American countries.

Many of us in the peace movement had worked hard to prevent that war and were extremely angry at our impotence and helplessness. Propaganda had done its job well and had prepared many people to support a war in defence of a continuing supply of cheap oil. The demonstrations and marches of hundreds of thousands of protestors around the world could not stop Mr. Bush from initiating a mass slaughter. The war ended with thousands and perhaps hundreds of thousands having been killed or wounded with no possibility for medical care. One estimate of children whose lives are at risk was in excess of 170,000 because of a lack of medicines, starvation and disease. If this is "the new world order", please leave me out of it. The slaughter in Iraq will soon be forgotten and life will go "almost uninterrupted". We cannot remain angry and disillusioned forever.

That incident, however, and the dogged determination of one man to punish an "enemy" cannot be left unchecked. The peace movement and humanity as a whole must find new ways to curb its madmen, not all of whom were Arabs. For the future of humanity we must, in my view, waste no time in addressing that challenge.

The frustrations of work in the area of social justice, including anti-racist activity, human rights, anti-poverty and peace are daunting and whatever success I have enjoyed is due to the efforts of the many men and women with whom I have worked. There have been many failures in spite of our best efforts, but the successes have been satisfying and have inspired us to greater efforts to remove the cancer of racism and injustice from society. It would be impossible to name the numerous men and women I have worked with but their contributions have been invaluable.

Over the years I have met some wonderful and committed individuals through involvement in the WCRP, including Jacques Langlais, Sister Leyla Raphael, Douglas Roche, Prof. Doris Dyck, Jamshed Mavawala, Rev. Bruce McCleod, Muin Muinuddin and many other people from the Jewish, Muslim, Buddhist, Hindu and native religious traditions. They have broadened my perspective and awareness on the many different religions and cultures of the world.

New and unexpected problems arise requiring attention and I am one of the few retirees with the time, commitment and energy in cooperation with others to push for solutions. My official responsibilities terminated prior to the end of 1991, but I have no doubt that I will remain in the "trenches" as long as needed. For example, I am well known in the community of Metro Toronto and across the country as a whole, which results in all too many invitations to address, consult, and support organizations involved in a wide variety of social justice issues. In spite of my best intentions I find it difficult to reject these invitations and have arrived at the conclusion that there will be no end to these aspects of the struggle as long as I am able to respond. That is the road I have chosen and I have no complaints.

The hard and consistent work done in anti-racism activities has probably achieved some limited results but old problems persist. The year 1992 saw the continuation of campaigns against police brutality and killings. Ironically it appears that Metro Toronto and Montreal are engaged in a race to determine which police force will kill more black youth. At the moment, Toronto police are ahead in the shooting of blacks by one. I am outraged and intend to make every effort to stop this genocide of young blacks. Police brutality is only one example of injustice. The educational systems, the lack of fair employment opportunities, poverty and oppression, discrimination and exclusion are still major areas requiring continued and sustained attention. The last decade of the 20th century must not be viewed as a period in which the struggle can be abandoned, but rather one in which persistent and intelligent attacks must be mounted. The difficulties and complexities of racism must not deter us, but serve as a catalyst for intensifying the struggle.

Changes

It requires little energy or special sensitivity to observe that major changes are occurring in Toronto as in other parts of the world. For the first time in history many Canadian police departments are making a major effort to recruit women and people of colour or "visible minorities". School boards in the Toronto area are struggling with the vast influx of newcomers, many of whom are from developing or "third world" countries. Pressure has been brought upon local school officials to employ more blacks and other non-white teachers and administrators to serve as role models for the increasing numbers of non-white students in the various school systems. The media, that so-called "leader" of social and cultural change, is slowly beginning to move toward the employment of more non-whites as reporters, researchers, and even as producers in the electronic media. An increased interest in the concept of "employment equity" is making its presence felt. For the first time the business community has become conscious that it has no alternative and must employ increasing numbers of non-white workers. The development of policies in these areas has been fairly rapid but the implementation of those policies has been much slower.

The increasing number of non-Anglo-Saxon immigrants has changed the complexion, the culture and the atmosphere of the former staid old Toronto "the dull". However, its problems remain since these immigrants arrive from "non-traditional" countries which, in all likelihood, will result in difficulties in adaptation, and increasing apprehensions of its Anglo-Saxon majority. Toronto faces the problem of whether it absorbs these newcomers in peace and harmony or whether its racism will come to the surface and create additional problems. Confusion and chaos are inevitable in the absence of knowledgeable and sensitive thought, planning and action. Meanwhile, life marches on and we become masters or victims of its processes. Nevertheless, many Torontonians can claim that population changes have been relatively harmonious. That situation may not be permanent.

In the meantime my family was also changing. My younger brother Glenn, with whom I had the closest relationship, died from a heart attack. He had become a chain smoker and his health had gone steadily downhill. He had also left his first wife and remarried. I felt that Glenn had never fully recovered from the psychological wounds and trauma suffered during the Second World War. His encounters with prejudice and discrimination in the U.S. Air Force left a deep and destructive impression on his general approach to life. He was an extremely bright and sensitive man and probably never fully revealed the extent of his anger and humiliation.

My mother, still living in Cincinnati, also died during this period. She was only two weeks short of her 85th birthday, had lived an active life, but was beginning to suffer from a variety of illnesses prior to her death. As noted in a previous chapter, her hard work and dedication to her family were of immense support to us as we moved into the larger world outside the family. Then, in 1988, my youngest brother Marvin also died at the age of 63 from a respiratory illness. He too, in my view, was a delayed casualty of the Second World War. His reactions to treatment received in the U.S. Navy were well concealed, but there is no question that he was a different man when he emerged from the military services. The remainder of our family, Minnie, Frank and I, appear to be "hanging in there"!

My own children, Norman, Gregory, Renee and Cynthia are apparently quite satisfied with their present lives. Norman is a high school teacher; Gregory, who completed grade 12 and dropped out of school, is satisfied with his former career as a rock musician and in the many other activities in which he is now engaged, including working in a day care centre. Both Renee and Cynthia have completed their university studies and are engaged in their chosen occupations, Renee as an entrepreneur, operating an apparel store in Guelph, Ontario and Cynthia as a worker in a shelter for battered women and children.

It was my philosophy that my children should be given the widest range of educational opportunities they felt was suitable and appropriate to their needs as they saw them. Except Cynthia who was born in Canada, the others could have retained their American citizenship but none chose to do so, a matter of pride to me. Norman has been an active member of the Society of Friends for most of his life and remains committed to a non-violent philosophy of life, as does Cynthia. Norman and Gregory enjoy playing touch football and baseball, both relatively non-violent sports. Renee and Norman are also better than average tennis players, a legacy of their former tennis playing father!

Sandy accepted an early retirement and, like her husband, is now busier than ever. From 1990 to 1992 she was the president of her Unitarian congregation. We are enjoying our active lives and have no regrets over the past. Both of us, and my former wife Phyllis, apparently are determined to live as fully as possible.

Although officially retired, I still maintain some contacts with institutions of "higher learning", including involvement in community college adult education, and a race relations committee of the North York Board of Education. Although pleased to be away from the responsibilities of full time teaching, I rather enjoy the opportunity to remain at least on the edge of the academic world. This involvement is a result of invitations from several professors and departments at the Ontarian Institute and at York University who occasionally asked me to sit on their oral examination committees, a requirement of masters and doctoral degree candidates for graduation. This work is not demanding and keeps me in touch with happenings in the academic community.

There is still too much work to be done for anyone to drop out of the struggle against injustice. It is necessary to recruit, orient and help activate many more young men and women who may become interested in issues of social justice. I often look back for a renewed view of the pioneers of the past since thanks to them some progress was made. The struggle is not over and discrimination is still rampant in spite of our dedicated efforts. Those of us who have become senior citizens must be prepared to pass on the torch. My goal was to help fledgling young organizations increase their strength and effectiveness.

Nineteen ninety-two was not one of my best years. I had received occasional treatment since 1979 for cancer. All seemed under control until mid-1992 when I began experiencing some pain. With the help of painkillers, the pain was brought under control. It quickly became clear that more effective treatment was required and I was admitted to hospital in late 1992 and subjected to massive administrations of radiation. By that time, however, the cancer cells had spread to other parts of the body. Cancer is a life-threatening disease and I am preparing myself for the worst. In the meantime I will depend on my relatives, friends and neighbours for psychological support which my doctors indicate is helpful in dealing with the potential rough spots. Thus far that support has been effective and extremely gratifying since I fully intend to continue the struggle against the deadly disease.

Throughout these memoirs I have stressed the need for persistent and continuous struggle if progress is to be made in eliminating or at least reducing racism in North American society. I have also cautioned that powerful forces are determined that progress not occur and that the powerful elites in North America are aware of the struggle and are determined to prevent progress, which, if successful, will result in a reduction of their power and influence. We have tended to view racism and other "isms" as unique phenomena which can be addressed in isolation from other aspects of social, economic and political power. Martin Luther King pointed out the relationship between racism, poverty and war, an insight which did not endear him to many blacks interested only in racism. I believe that King was correct in his assessment that the "isms" of modern society — militarism, racism, sexism, etc. are reflections of the dominant aspects of society as a whole. The racist aspect of the recent Gulf War clearly demonstrated the manipulation of public attitudes against Arabs, a pattern clearly seen in the definition of Arabs as the "enemy".

The struggle against racism must be broadened to include a focus on basic human rights for all oppressed groups. A mistake is made when we focus our attention on the problems of only one identifiable group. During the tense days of the revolutionary war when it appeared that the colonists might lose the struggle, Benjamin Franklin warned his fellow revolutionaries that "we must stand together for if we lose, we will hang separately!" The words of Franklin are as appropriate as they were in the 1770s. Conducting our struggle in isolation may mean that we continue to lose, a prospect we can ill afford.

Unlike Canada as a whole, Toronto contains a large non-white population, variously estimated at between 16 and 20 percent of the total. The interests of all minority groups can be best achieved by pooling resources and creating a powerful anti-racist organization which cannot be ignored. Otherwise groups continue their struggles alone, with limited access to power and influence. My dream is to facilitate increased cooperation of various racial or non-white groups who in spite of past efforts, still find it difficult to join in a common struggle against the complexities of racism in Canada.

Writing these memoirs has given me an unparalleled opportunity to look back over my life and to make these few observations. My generally quiet but determined personality has, over the years, changed only minimally. Although I have been labelled as a "radical", a "moderate", an "Uncle Tom" and other contradictory terms, these have had little effect on how I view my efforts and myself. The meaning of these terms changes with changes in the political, economical and social arrangements in society. Perhaps I am all of these. Many people, aware of my pacifism, would agree that my political, social, economic and cultural views are unconventional and I agree. The reader may have arrived at the conviction, and rightly so, that I am not a believer in the so-called "free market" system. I have not seen evidence that the modern market is "free" but that it is controlled, manipulated, and designed to support prevailing elite class systems in North American and Western European societies. How else can one explain the persistence of increasingly wide gaps between the incomes and wealth of the poor and members of corporate elites? I doubt that any well informed person believes that great wealth is based on "hard work", unless one means the "hard work" of others.

Politically those views place me within the current context of some form of socialism because I believe that individuals and groups can only live peacefully together in the presence of mutual support, a high level of equality, and respect for differences. This concept is a requirement of living in the increasingly multicultural, multiracial and multireligious reality characteristic of Canadian society during the last decade of the 20th century. By consistently propagandizing the virtues of "free enterprise" and castigating the "evils of socialism" and even worse, those of "communism", the prevailing ideology has made it virtually impossible for individuals to make choices based on an objective evaluation of reality. The clear evidence that the United States, that "citadel of unrestricted capitalism", was forced to develop a "welfare state" is unacknowledged and ignored because the facts do not fit the ideology. The media is, of course, the primary instrument of manipulation and control of the ideas, tastes, attitudes and behaviours of individuals in a mass society. The public school systems and the universities are not far behind. My preference is the social democratic systems based on the Swedish and other Scandinavian models, that is, a mixture of capitalism, socialism and cooperative social, political and economic activity. Thus far no better model of human development has emerged from the long struggle for human well being and equality.

I have not been interested in political leadership because I cannot see myself involved in the self promotion and aggrandizement so vitally necessary for success in present-day political campaigns, thus my extensive past and present participation in social movements rather than seeking political office. I am quite aware of the need for political leadership in a democratic society, but I have chosen to remain on the outside of partisan politics and to work for change from that perspective. Being aware of the foibles of human existence, I have not sought the ideal, but the desirable and the possible.

My commitment to non-violence is a result of a strong belief in the sacredness of and respect for human life and I have always known, even from childhood, that I would never kill a fellow human being. My initial attachment to the Quakers was through its courageous and non-partisan humanitarian work in the United States and abroad. I admired and still admire their philosophy, courage and practice.

I have always been a prolific reader and my ideas and insights have been influenced by many of the writers I have had the pleasure to read and whose thoughts attracted my interest. My thinking regarding the lack of "community" and the level of cynicism and alienation in North American society has been a source of considerable concern since my early college and university careers. C. Wright Mills, my favourite sociologist, and others were of great value as I pondered these issues. His stress on the social and psychological destructiveness of industrial society and the need to regain a sense of community mutual support and caring were extremely interesting. We need, in his words, to "rebuild the bonds which formerly held people together". A sense of social cohesion, he argued, is the most powerful defence against alienation, crime, apathy and mental illness. The lack of a caring society could explain the problems of poverty and racism. These and other fundamental questions are rarely raised and discussed, even in North American university settings. My experience at the University of Victoria is a case in point. The well documented comments of Noam Chomsky regarding aggressive American policies in the Third World were received with intense hostility and anger by many faculty members of that institution of higher education. This and similar experiences in other settings have convinced me that many, having accepted and internalized the results of miseducation, media manipulation and propaganda, don't want to hear the facts.

I have touched on some observations made during my long history in the United States and in Canada. One of my editors dryly remarked, "I know more about you than you know about yourself!" However, the observations made here are based on conclusions derived from my own experiences as interpreted through the lens of my background and history.

I have arrived at the conclusion that it is risky to trust government since probably all governments at some point lie to their own people, especially in wartime. The corporate sector, which includes the multi- or transnationals, is moving toward increasing concentration of power, in the name of improving competitiveness in the global market but never mentioning increasing exploitation of workers in Canada and in Third World countries.

In spite of its limitations, Canada still has good prospects of achieving its goals, but only if its multicultural, multiracial and multireligious societies turn from a destructive ideology of unrestricted dependence on the "free market" and learn to work together for the common welfare. It will not occur as a result of the present struggle of each for him or herself. I have some confidence that we will turn to a more humane philosophy, cooperative approach and behaviour before we plunge over the precipice.

I have a vivid memory of the picture of a little Indian boy sitting on the back and shoulders of a huge elephant. The elephant is much more powerful and could, if it chose, easily throw the boy off his back and crush the life from him but it has been indoctrinated to accept the boy as his master. The struggle for freedom and equality will not be won by those who accept and welcome the coronation of the economically and politically strong; it will be achieved, if at all, by those minorities and sympathetic members of the majority, who create a new vision of human relationships and insist on pursuing it against all odds. The struggle must not falter, but must be guided by a clear vision of a realistic future and must continue unabated until the goal of a non-racist, non-sexist and non-exploitative society is achieved.

The ex-slave Frederick Douglass insisted that freedom is only won when there is effective demand, words which clearly suggest that minority groups must move beyond begging the white power elites for freedom and equality. Effective demand requires the application or the threat to exert social, economic or political power. It would be foolish to expect the U.S. or any other imperialist country to relinquish domination in the absence of that pressure, either abroad or in its own borders. It is my firm belief that minority groups must achieve the power ability and determination to make demands which cannot be ignored.

EPILOGUE

Madame Rosalie Silberman Abella

It is difficult for anyone raised in an era unabashedly aggressive in its pursuit of rights, to appreciate the turmoil, frustration, confusion or anger caused by preventing the exercise of even the basic ones. Faced with an American constitution whose light was dimmed for blacks in the United States until 1954, and without a *Charter of Rights and Freedoms* to illuminate the possibilities, Wilson Head found himself at the beginning and often at the centre of struggles to reify the language of equality.

In countless ways over a lifetime, Wilson never seemed able comfortably to accept what made no sense to his egalitarian instincts. And being uncomfortable, he could never resist the chance to confront and stare down an injustice. Seemingly without fear, he challenged unfairness wherever he found it, thinking little of the personal risk and overwhelmingly of the public need. His principles, formed early and staunchly, remained intact whether as a student, employee, community organizer, social activist or professor, and whether in the American south, midwest, or in Canada.

His life was the story of a man pushing open the doors of tolerance ever wider, to that they eventually came to be wide enough that all who wanted could genuinely aspire to enter. Assisted by extraordinary courage, a disarming frankness, a patient integrity, and a peaceful confidence, he led the way over new terrain and made it familiar for those who followed. This was a visionary pioneer, who cared deeply about people and believed in their generosity. He refused to accept their insensitivity as anything more than a challenge.

His skill was dazzling and his impact was breathtaking. It is hard to imagine how he did it; it is harder to imagine how it will be done without him. Wilson Head was equality's child, grew up as its gentle, dutiful disciple, and became its gentle, tenacious mentor. Gentleness, tenacity duty — these are the tools of this remarkable advocate for social justice. His commitment, his ideas, his friendships — these are the legacies. How lucky we were to have known him.

Rosalie Silberman Abella
October 1994